THEIR WORDS ARE MUSIC

*The Great Theatre Lyricists
and Their Lyrics*

THEIR WORDS ARE MUSIC

The Great Theatre Lyricists and Their Lyrics

by Lehman Engel

CROWN PUBLISHERS, INC., NEW YORK

TO RICHARD RODGERS

who made music with two of our greatest lyricists
and has himself become the most distinguished
contributor to our musical theatre, this book
is respectfully dedicated

ACKNOWLEDGMENTS

The preparation of this book was made possible, first of all, by the cooperation of the many lyricists represented in it, and/or their estates. The author is especially grateful to Philip Wattenberg of Chappell & Co., Inc., for his patience, to Norma Grossman, and particularly to Robert Bishop and Robert Joseph in helping to develop the manuscript. The author also wishes to thank both the T. B. Harms Company and the Frank Music Corporation for permitting him to reproduce a number of their sheet music covers.

*Proper words in proper places make the true
definition of a style.*

JONATHAN SWIFT

Printed in the United States of America
Published simultaneously in Canada by General Publishing Company Limited

Library of Congress Cataloging in Publication Data

Main entry under title:

Their words are music

1. Songs, American—Texts. 2. Musical revue,
comedy, etc.—United States. I. Engel, Lehman,
1910-
ML54.6.T35   782.8'1'0922   75-25831
ISBN 0-517-51682-9

Contents

About three years ago Maurice Levine, head of the music department at New York's YMHA, called to solicit my advice. He was considering a program series for the following fall (1971–1972), during which he would present several leading lyricists in discussions of their works, their methods of writing, and their theories.

My immediate opinion was that such an idea could not interest or attract any sizable audience. This reaction in no way deterred Levine and he invited my participation as a master of ceremonies, inquisitor, and unglorified page-turner on the two projected occasions when he himself would not appear.

The series was announced and was sold out! One year later another set of programs was announced and each was performed twice to packed houses. Since that time, several lyricists, and Sammy Cahn in particular, have enjoyed considerable success with his kind of program. Years earlier Comden and Green also succeeded in an entertainment based on their own work.

Prior to this kind of activity, Oscar Hammerstein II, Ira Gershwin, and E. Y. Harburg published books of their selected lyrics. Noël Coward brought out an enormous tome of his. A book of Porter's lyrics appeared as well as selections by Hal David. Possibly there have been others that have escaped my notice.

In any case, interest in the lyric has grown considerably during the past several decades. I can take no credit for having originated a related idea, although the present volume contains a larger and wider sampling, and considerable analysis.

It is my hope that more writers will be moved to publish their complete works, which will provide pleasure to the theatre-minded public and models to the ever-growing number of interested students.

In working on this book I have found that many of the details that I have pointed out in certain lyrics never previously occurred in the conscious minds of their creators. I believe that this does not necessarily mean that what I have pointed out is untrue. It is more likely that such unconsciousness on the part of the creative imagination, after it has matured technically, points to a quite natural relationship between the artist and his work.

This book presents examples of early struggles, eventual accomplishments, and promises for a fruitful future. All of it, it should be borne in mind, was made for the stage, for singing actors and for audiences.

It is perhaps necessary that I explain that I have chosen some lyrics from songs that were never particularly popular. This was done because I felt that in these cases the lyric to be *read* was superior to the occasionally more successful one that was carried along by a wonderful tune.

Furthermore, some of the lyrics quoted here are different from their sheet music versions. Discrepancies of this sort are not uncommon, but the author has tried to use those versions written by the lyricist originally.

It is my intention to examine the evolution of lyric writing in the American musical theatre and to present samples of the most successful writers' achievements. It would be impossible to ignore the music in which these lyrics are embedded, but purely musical aspects are not to be considered. Attention to music in some degree, however, is essential, for in the best theatre songs, words and music complement each other, and in various different categories of songs one or the other (usually by design) assumes primary importance.

In most ballads the melodies, or tunes, take precedence over the lyrics, although the lyrics are of special significance in specifying the subject matter. When the tunes are truly memorable they can and very often do stand alone. They are frequently performed outside the theatre without words, and are recorded instrumentally, without voice, and even during the unfolding of the show they are employed wordlessly in overtures, entr'actes, in scoring under dialogue, and in many other incidental ways.

However, in spite of the independence of the music, the best ballads are indebted to the work of the lyricist. A good lyric, as distinguished from a poem, must "sing" well and be comprehensible to the listener. It must impose few if any difficulties for singers by supplying suitable vowel sounds for their peak high or low notes in the melody so that the performer is able, for example, to "open" his voice freely on an *ah* sound, as opposed to "squeez-ing" it with an *ee* sound. The succession of consonants must not create awkward and overhasty teeth-and-tongue sequences or unsingable sibilance. An example of one of Shakespeare's greatest sonnets will serve as an illustration:

When to the sessions of sweet silent thought . . .

Proper articulation of the first four words makes large demands on the teeth-and-tongue mechanism, for the consonants require rapid changes of oral position. And the poet's obviously intentional sibilance created by the four consecutive *s* sounds is hardly desirable for singing, especially since these effects would be elongated and heightened were they given note values. Of course, Shakespeare did not intend his sonnets as lyrics for music, and in this single line he created his own music, making any other superfluous.

The knowledgeable lyricist avoids hard consonants at the ends of phrases and especially at the end of a song when it is usually desirable for the singer to sustain the final note. I refer especially to final *d, t, b, f* sounds. Although the word's vowel sound is capable of being sustained indefinitely, the hard final consonant must inevitably conclude the phrase or song abruptly, and prolonging the vowel in spite of the hard consonant postpones definition of the word's meaning. For example, words like "brief," "neat," "red," "snob," and many others could not be immediately comprehended if the final consonant were delayed for several musical beats. "Brief" sustained would emerge for some time as "bree" and could presage "breeze," "breed," "breathe," "breech," or many other words. Words should be sung as closely as possible to the manner in which they are spoken. "Brief," sung or spoken correctly is indeed a short word that perhaps accidentally, suggests its meaning by its very sound.

The late Oscar Hammerstein II * pointed to his song "What's the Use of Wond'rin'" in *Carousel* as "severely handicapped" because the last line ("And all the rest is talk") ends on the hard *k* sound, making it impossible for the singer to sustain the final note.

Then there is the question of a specific meaning, which only words can impart. Music itself is abstract and incapable of conveying a specific thought. The meaning of a song is the contribution of the lyrics alone, however much this may be heightened by the feeling provided in the music. When lyrics and music are combined ideally each serves to emphasize the other, and together they may go on forever in deathless union.

"Blue heaven and you and I" (Harbach and Hammerstein II, 1926) is the line that introduces the refrain of the title song of *The Desert Song*. This song is a ballad. It is nearly impossible to hum Romberg's melody without remembering this lyric line and conversely, the line instantly recalls the tune, provided, of course, one has heard it before.

There is another consideration. These first six words, "Blue heaven and you and I" (five of them monosyllabic), characterize this ballad as a love song, while the attendant melody overlays the lyric declaration with its smooth

* *Lyrics* by Oscar Hammerstein II. New York: Simon and Schuster, 1949.

romantic tune. It is, of course, possible that the topic *might* have been "Death, take me away with thee." The words would "fit" the music and the music's mood would not really be violated. However, *this* contrived topic sentence would have led the listener's mind in another direction, although the song would still have been a ballad (the music characterizes it as a ballad), not a love song. Only the lyrics can give the song its distinctive meaning.

In comedy songs it is usual for the words to take precedence over the music and a song fails to qualify as a comedy song if the words do not make it so. Laughter is created by the words, the situations they set up, develop, and conclude. The music is seldom capable of standing alone ("Bewitched, Bothered and Bewildered" is a notable exception), since its prime purpose is to accompany and support the words, and it should in no way interfere with their meaning. Nevertheless, the song's musical construction can help predict the moment for the payoff, or joke, and can further supply a recovery period during which the audience can feel free enough to laugh without anxiety that it is going to miss the setup of the next explosive conceit.

In narrative-type songs one may expect the music to match in importance the storytelling words. "The Surrey with the Fringe on Top" is an excellent example of such a song.

It is my aim to trace the progress of lyric writing from some of our earliest musical theatre, through a number of significant changes, to the present time. These changes have been brought about by a number of different factors: the growing technical familiarity with employment of the materials and the gradual discovery of what did and did not work, changing times accompanied by changing styles, changing customs and moral points of view, and very often, as a result of the conscious efforts of creative writers to break away from the immediate past to establish something new.

In discussing and quoting representative lyrics by the leading writers at work in our most accomplished and talented era, roughly from 1925 to 1972, it is my intention to point out the qualities that made the writers' best work distinguished. Since they achieved so much that was and still is important, it would seem pointless and arrogant to select and comment on anything less than the best examples of their work.

It is regrettable that I am unable to quote more extensively, but economic considerations are limiting. Where I have failed to quote entire lyrics it is because some writers have refused permission for me to do so. And, in most cases, this position was taken because of their own intentions to publish their collected lyrics. Although I feel that my work would in no way impinge on complete collections, I bow to the authors' wishes.

one

BEGINNINGS AND PROBLEMS

The state of lyric writing in the late nineteenth and early twentieth centuries, when activity in this area was brisk, far more brisk than it is today, was fumbling, naturally lacked direction in the beginning, and seems to have followed false leads. Native American lyricists seem to have overlooked relevant models. It is my opinion that they were more influenced by poor English translations of Viennese operettas than by excellent English-language originals. The masterful lyrics of W. S. Gilbert had little effect on our new writers. Nor did English and American poets exert much influence.

It was as though the earlier lyricists had been misled in their choice of models by a mischievous Pied Piper, because later, in the thirties and forties, lyricists were putting *their* writing on a more creative track when, among other things, they became acutely aware of W. S. Gilbert. This awareness probably indicated a newer and more sophisticated point of view, rather than any actual conscious selection of Gilbert as a chief model.

In Max Wilk's anecdotal book of interviews with lyricists (chiefly), *They're Playing Our Song*, Ira Gershwin is quoted as saying: "Gilbert was the greatest, no question of that. If he were alive today, he'd be doing good musical-comedy songs, more, of course, in the modern fashion, rather than just versifying." And Lorenz Hart, on being questioned about his "steady attendance" at D'Oyly Carte performances, concurred with Wilk's father's saying that Hart was "taking a refresher course," and added: "Old man Gilbert was the greatest lyricist who ever turned a rhyme!"

One important factor that operated in the earlier period and that goes unrecognized too often is that creative people usually regard their immediate predecessors as old-fashioned. The lyricists of the 1900–1920 era undoubtedly shrugged off W. S. Gilbert because his spectacular successes in America had occurred between 1875 and 1889. But by 1930 and later, Gilbert had become fixed in history as a classical model. The passage of time had rescued him from obsolescence, and only then did he assume his rightful position as a viable model.

My contention that early American lyricists were chiefly influenced by poor translations must remain somewhat theoretical, but it is necessary that I attempt to substantiate it as far as possible with some examples.

Take a look at Lehár's *The Merry Widow*, heard here in 1907 with English lyrics by Adrian Ross. This is the ballad "Home."

If I could go with you
Beyond the distant blue
To some fair land unknown
Where we were all alone
No more would I demand
Than with you hand in hand
To wander through that magic land
That is the magic that fills the happy home.
The stormy world may be wild as ocean foam
We shall not care what the weary world may do
You're all my world, I'm the world to you.

Ah, that is all to live for truly:
Can happiness be found elsewhere?
Only the sun and sky above
Smiling on me and her I love!
Ah, when the world is all unruly
One refuge we can find from care,
It is the home,
It is our home and happiness is there, yes there.

Yet all the lovely dream
Is but a bubble's gleam.
A rainbow's magic ray
That breaks and fades away.
The home I thought so fair
We find not anywhere,
'Tis but a castle in the air
That is the vision of happiness at home.
But in the search for it vainly we may roam.
The world is cold that we have to wander through,
Though you're the world to me and I to you.
You're all my world, I'm the world to you.

In this song (truly representative of all the others in *The Merry Widow*) there is an abundance of cliché: "beyond the distant blue," "wild as ocean foam," "castle in the air," "weary world," "sky above"; and melodramatic extravagance: "when the world is all unruly"; frequent ambiguity as to meaning (does a "rainbow's magic ray" break? "The home I thought so fair/ We find not anywhere" (How can he have thought it fair if he has never found it? Also, what about "I" as a subject replaced by "we"?) "The stormy world may be wild as ocean foam" is followed by "We shall not care what the weary world may do." (Now which is it—"stormy" or "weary"? Physically, it cannot be both.) "The world is cold that we have to wander through" I *think* means The world we have to wander through is cold, but "through" is placed at the end of the line only because it must rhyme with the ensuing "you."

Word transposition was by no means uncommon in this earlier period. I have the feeling that it was thought to have been poetic. For whatever reason, the end result was confusing, and the departure from a more or less normal manner of speaking calls attention to its awkward employment for the purpose of rhyme.

This kind of carelessly translated lyric is far from unusual in this period. Two years after *The Merry Widow*, Oscar Straus's *The Chocolate Soldier* was presented here successfully and had English lyrics by Stanislaus Stange. I quote the trio "What Can We Do Without a Man." The italics indicate strong musical accentuation.

TRIO OF WOMEN
Fight*ing* for duty; sigh*ing* for *beauty*
Each soldier lad.
They sigh not *only;* we, too, are *lonely,*
Ah! *lonely* and sad.

Oh, how we miss them, long to kiss them,
Our soldiers brave and strong;
We would be *mating,* don't keep us *waiting* too long.
CHORUS OF SOLDIERS
We are searching for the foe,
High and low, high and low;
Searching for the foe in hiding,
Soon his fate we'll be deciding,
When we find him he shall die,
He shall die, surely die.
TRIO OF WOMEN
They have left. We are bereft.
Yes, they have gone. Ev'ry one.
Life is lonely, sad and lonely,
If you have not got a man;
Life is lonely, then deny it if you can!

Lonely women watch are keeping,
Hearts are sighing, eyes are weeping.
Just a year we have been waiting,
Much too long I don't mind stating.
For a kiss I'm nearly dying,
Oh, this waiting is most trying.
Would there were some mischief brewing,
But there's really nothing doing;
If we live too long alone,
We shall be but skin and bone.
Pity then our sorry plight,
Bad! Bad! Bad!
All our men are out of sight.
Sad! Sad! Sad!

We must do the best we can.
What can we do minus man?

We're unhappy,
Cross and snappy, without man.
Life is lonely, sad and lonely,
If you haven't got a man.
Life is lonely, sad and lonely,
Then deny it if you can.

Black-eyed soldier *on* me beaming,
White teeth *through* his mustache gleaming.
Ev'ry girl has lost her lover,
Not a man can we discover.
How I long for Cupid's prattle,
All our men have gone to battle.
Loneliness is most appalling,
Would I heard my lover calling;
If we live too long alone,
We shall be but skin and bone.
Pity then our sorry plight,
Bad! Bad! Bad!
All our men are out of sight.
Sad! Sad! Sad!

Note the awkwardness of "If you have not got a man"—hardly typical of speech, nor is it excusable as poetic. Examples of word transpositions are endless: "Lonely women watch are keeping"; "Black-eyed soldier on me beaming"; "White teeth through his mustache gleaming." The words themselves are stumblers and the very idea is repulsive.

In the following lines "just" is not only a pad word to fill out the meter, but it unintentionally adds an undesirable meaning: "only" a year:

For a kiss I'm nearly dying
Just a year we have been waiting

The couplet:

Would there were some mischief brewing,
But there's really nothing doing

indicates rather shockingly two diverse styles: the first line is echt-classical pretense while the second sounds offhand modern.

If we live too long alone,
We shall be but skin and bone.

We can easily surmise the lyricist's intention, but it is not stated clearly. Besides, the expression "skin and bone" is always used in the plural. The omission of the *s* here only points up the writer's desperate need to complete the rhyme.

To whom are these two lines addressed: "Pity then our sorry plight" and "Then deny it if you can."

These and similar lyrics must today be termed banal and cliché-ridden—the inescapable judgment of time. What we or the people of any later generation consider to be clichés are naturally to be found in nearly all the lyrics of our earlier past. Webster defines cliché as "a trite or stereotyped phrase or expression; also: the idea expressed by it." Time and frequent use have dulled these expressions. They also arouse in us a feeling of impatience and fatigue, of having been there again and again, and they make us regard their perpetrator as a lazy hack who was content to use any first thing that came to mind in place of digging harder to find something fresher and more interesting.*

Some words, now regarded as cliché, imparted the air of the period in which they were in general use. They were then "in" words: forsake, enfold, 'tis, hark, thrill, sigh, joy, lover, dream, sweet, spring, May, caress, moonbeams, springtime, romance, naughty, aching, distress, etc. All of them were romantic, although today they appear to be déjà vu.

It must also be remembered that in the middle of the nineteenth century and early in the twentieth, Austrian German wealth and culture flourished in New York, the new capital of musical theatre activity. The choral societies had German names (Deutscher Liederkranz, Männergesangverein, Mendelssohn Glee Club, etc.), the Philharmonic under Leopold Damrosch played a great deal of German music, the Manhattan Opera House and the Metropolitan operated largely with German artists, management, repertory, and conductors. Even French and Italian operas were sung in German. In the popular musical theatre Viennese operetta titillated upper-class taste while the poorer masses derived their pleasures from the shenanigans of Harrigan and Hart.

The long list of Harrigan and Hart shows began in 1879. Seventeen were produced by 1885 and Harrigan continued without Hart in twelve additional productions before 1900. Harrigan wrote the book and lyrics of them all, directed, produced, and starred in them. Dave Braham wrote all the music and was musical director. Contrary to popular belief, their audience was polyglot, not just Irish. Ned Harrigan was born and reared in New York. Dave Braham, born in England, migrated to New York in early manhood.

I should like to quote five of Harrigan's lyrics, selected at random from the enormous number available. Though most of them were New York Irish-oriented, there were Negro and Jewish dialect songs and even attempts at Chinese-American humor. The ballads were sentimental, the light songs bouncy and gay. These lyrics are not to be categorized as occupying any particular position in the evolution of American lyrics. They were unique and apart. In many respects they were like Topsy: they just grew. They flew in the face of their period's newfound pseudoelegance. Their words and phrases were seldom convoluted. They sang and danced good-naturedly. They smell of the New York of their time, as Frank Loesser's lyrics in *Guys and Dolls* smelled of his own New York. In a period in which theatre lyrics were full of pomposity, Harrigan's were wonderfully simple and folksy. Let the following five lyrics speak (or sing) for themselves.

"THE CASTAWAYS"
Mulligan's Silver Wedding (1881)

VERSE ONE
On the good ship Dolly Dorkins,
From London I set sail,
All bound for the Indian Ocean,

* I should like to make one thing clear as to my own point of view. Translators for many decades were considered hack operators. They were appallingly underpaid and were, therefore, able to give little time or serious consideration to their assignments. Aside from their obvious need to turn out hasty renderings, they in turn seem to have been unduly influenced by the grandiose verbiage of Handel and Purcell, lyrics written more than a century earlier.

Oh, hear my mournful tale;
The whole ship's crew, and Captain, too, the cook, a brown Malay;
In a hurricane of wind and rain,
Brave boys, we were cast away.

CHORUS
With a hay, hay, hay, and a ho, ho, ho!
I'll ne'er forget that day;
When the whole ship's crew, and the Captain, too,
Brave boys, we were cast away.

VERSE TWO
We'd a cask or two of water
Stowed in the old ship's boat;
A box of old sea biscuits,
By chance, we found afloat;
All tempest toss'd, with compass lost, we had no time to pray;
Our flag of distress, was a pants and vest,
Brave boys, we were cast away.

CHORUS

VERSE THREE
Afloat on the Indian Ocean,
Through fair and foul and calm,
I saw as the sun was rising,
An Island full of palm;
Ho, land! I cried, I never lied, says Captain, where away?
On our starboard bow, we're safe, lads, now,
Hip, hurrah, for the castaway!

CHORUS

VERSE FOUR
Says the Captain, do your duty,
All hands, when you're ashore,
The first man goes for booty,
I'll brain him with an oar;
We struck the beach, we heard a screech, 'twas Indian girls at play;
It drove away the blues, when they came out in canoes,
Hip, hurrah, for the castaway!

CHORUS

VERSE FIVE
An Indian Queen, of sweet sixteen,
Says we were drove from home,
A king of another Island
Sent us here to die alone;
One hundred wives, for all your lives, I give each sailor, gay;
Then each copper colored belle, sent up an Indian yell,
Hip, hurrah, for the castaway!

CHORUS

VERSE SIX
All sailors, bold, I have been told,
Who ship before the mast,
Will sail the ocean over,
To find that Isle at last;
But, bless your hearts, 'taint on the charts, all navigators say;
But I've done no harm, I've spun my yarn,
Hip, hurrah, for the castaway!

CHORUS REPEATED

"DON'T YOU MISS THE TRAIN"
Mulligan's Silver Wedding (1881)

VERSE ONE
I'm going down to Rahway, was the words I said to Nell,
My beau she was, but, now, alas,
I've bid my love farewell;
Be careful, dear, she sweetly said, then pressed her lips to mine;
Just one embrace, then I'd to race, the train left sharp at nine.

CHORUS 1
Don't you miss the train, love, don't you miss the train!
Of course I know that you must go, it fills my heart with pain;
Oh, don't you miss the train, love, don't you miss the train!
You cannot stay, so don't delay, or else you'll miss the train.

VERSE TWO
I started for the depot, but I missed the ferry boat,
I ran against a Negro man,
Who white-washed my new coat,
We had a lengthy argument, upon the right of way;
The whistle blew, I quickly flew, to me he then did say:

CHORUS 2
Hope you miss the train, sir, hope you miss the train!
There goes the bell, I'll warm you well when I see you again;
I hope you miss the train, sir, hope you miss the train!
You're too bran new, a man like you am sure to miss the train.

VERSE THREE
I rush'd into the depot, with one second left to spare,
Oh, I was filled with rage and fright,
No train or baggage there;
I seized the agent by the arm, said, ain't this very fine?
You've made an alteration, sir, she left ahead of time!

CHORUS 3
Now you've missed the train, sir, now you've missed the train!
Don't stay behind, you'll surely find, it goes against the grain;
Oh, now you've missed the train, sir, now you've missed the train!
At 8 A.M., stay here till then, you're sure to catch the train.

VERSE FOUR
I went back to my Nelly's home, and walked in very light,
I heard her whisper to someone,
"He won't be home tonight";
Oh, he's gone down to Rahway, or, the fool he's missed the train;
She was hugging a fat boarder while I'd gone to catch the train.

CHORUS 4
Don't you catch the train, boys, don't you catch the train!
From your love sweet, you'll catch deceit, 'twill fill your heart with pain;
Now don't you catch the train, boys, don't you catch the train!
Stick to her fast until the last, be sure to miss the train.

"AS LONG AS THE WORLD GOES ROUND"
Investigation (1884)

VERSE ONE
There once lived old Adam, and he courted Eve,
So slyly and coy like a dove; . . . . . .

He was the first suitor, we're taught to believe,
The accepted inventor of Love . . . .
He started the fashion of meeting his dear
In a garden where roses abound; . . . .
Oh, there will be lovers, don't you ever fear,
As long as the world goes round . . . .

CHORUS
Where strong-minded mothers,
Athletic brothers,
Cruel old fathers and uncles abound,
So sly undercover,
Oh, there will be lovers
As long as the world goes round . . . . . .

VERSE TWO
Where'er there's a maiden, with love in her heart,
A longing to meet her true mate, ...
Should they come together, oh, ne'er let them part;
They'll reunite sooner or late. . . . .
The King is old Nature, who makes his decree;
To follow his orders we're bound; . . . .
Oh, there will be lovers, so happy and free,
As long as the world goes round. . . . .

CHORUS

VERSE THREE
Where'er there's a soldier, that's noble and brave,
A longing to fight on the field, ...
He conquers with honor, but love is a knave;
It forces the hero to yield. . . . .
Oh, sly little Cupid, 'tis he leads the way,
Coquetishly tripping the ground; . . . .
Oh, there will be lovers, so merry and gay,
As long as the world goes round. . . . .

CHORUS REPEATED

"THE ALDERMANIC BOARD"
The Grip (1885)

VERSE ONE
Behold these statesmen bold,
Who never yet were sold,
We handle from one million up to ten;
The makers of your laws,
Each section and each clause,
The people's choice, the Board of Aldermen . . . .

CHORUS
As rulers of New York
We have a right to talk,
Supreme in district, precinct, or in ward;
From the Captain to a Cop
We bring them to a stop,
This ornamental Aldermanic Board.

VERSE TWO
Each foreign Potentate,
Who visits us in state,
Oh, let him be the Kaiser or a Lord,
We hurry them red-hot
On board the Herald Yacht,
This ostentatious Aldermanic Board . . . .

CHORUS

VERSE THREE
We look out for your votes,
Your lamp-posts and your goats,
In ev'ry district and in ev'ry ward;
Put up your apple-stands,
Engage your German Bands,
By order of this Aldermanic Board . . . .

CHORUS

VERSE FOUR
To stop all future strife
Just put us in for life,
Upon that point we members all accord;
We'll save the City's cash
When Banks they go to smash,
This intellectual Aldermanic Board . . . .

CHORUS REPEATED

"MULBERRY SPRINGS"
The O'Reagans (1886)

VERSE ONE
Let fashion assemble at Saratoga,
At Long Branch, or else at Newport . . . . .
Oh, I know a spot that's so awfully hot,
In alley way, hallway and court . . . .
The poor up aloof, on a tenement roof, so cheerfully, merrily
    sings, ...
We've every race in that tumble down place,
We're boarders at Mulberry Springs . . . . . .

CHORUS
It's Mulberry Springs, Spring, and Mulberry,
Neighborly people from Cork and Kerry,
Larry and Jimmy, Teddy and Jerry,
And boarders at Mulberry Spring . . . .
It's then you'll hear them cry
Rags, Bottles, rags, so loudly the pedlar he sings,
It's then you'll hear them cry,
Clock to mend, Fish,
Then *its* all day long,
Oh, they sing the same song,
For the boarders at Mulberry Spring . . . .

VERSE TWO
The music we have is an Italian band,
A fiddle, a harp and a flute . . . . .
There out in the gutter so nobly they stand,
And brush off the flies as they toot . . . . .
From window and door, there's a hundred or more, all listen as
    merry as kings . . . .
It's there in the heat, oh, we block up the street,
We boarders at Mulberry Springs . . . . . .

CHORUS

VERSE THREE
Our bedrooms are strong and they're airy, and fine,
We've organs and monkeys and apes . . . .
There's Turks and Chinese, and there's Dutch in a line,
All sleep out on their fire-escape . . . . .
The heat is intense, and the crowd is immense, all praying and
    whistling for wings . . . . .

To get up and fly to the clouds in the sky,
The boarders at Mulberry Springs . . . . .

CHORUS REPEATED

But Harrigan was a creative voice apart from the main line, the line that was to proceed from Viennese operetta to the new American musical.

In most of the other sixty-odd native pre-1900 shows, music and lyrics were decidedly secondary to production novelties and stars. Until the third decade of the twentieth century (1920), lyrics by the main line writers were not only cliché-ridden, but also stodgy, awkward, pretentious, stentorian, and grandiloquent. The following are some random quotes from Sousa's *El Capitan* (1898).

With cards and wine, our life's divine, and pleasures fall
    away.
Thieving, sleeving,
Each deceiving,
There's not a game that gamblers use, the innocents to
    rifle,
With which we do not trifle.

The little fife's defiance, (of confidence the science,)
Should give to all reliance, who waver in the field.

Your chest throw out in a marked degree,
Your arms extend to form a "V,"
Then bend your body, but not your knee,
To be a perfect soldier.

This last quotation seems to me to represent the period's taste for transposition of phrases: it was probably thought to have been poetic, because in the first two lines the meter would not have been disturbed at all had the writers *wanted* to say in a forthright declarative way:

Throw out your chest in a marked degree,
Extend your arms to form a "V."

Did they honestly feel that *their* version was somehow superior?

Near the end of Ned Harrigan's career George M. Cohan, another American lyricist (also composer, producer, and star performer), was born in 1878. It is strange that by 1901, Cohan, who had grown up in vaudeville, began to write and star in shows that seem to have been direct descendants of the Harrigan shows.

After several failures Cohan enjoyed his first big hit with *Little Johnny Jones* (1904), which contained two of his most famous songs, "Yankee Doodle Dandy" and "Give My Regards to Broadway," both of which follow.

Cohan's multifaceted career continued almost uninterruptedly until 1920, but did not end for another two decades. He died in 1942.

It is a curious fact that the following lyrics written very early in his career fully represent him and are perhaps better than anything else written later.

"YANKEE DOODLE DANDY"

VERSE ONE
I'm the kid that's all the candy,

I'm a Yankee Doodle Dandy,
I'm glad I am;
So's Uncle Sam.
I'm a real live Yankee Doodle,
Made my name and fame and boodle,
Just like Mister Doodle did by riding on a pony.
I love to listen to the Dixie strain,
I long to see the girl I left behind me;
And that ain't a josh,
She's a Yankee, by gosh!
Oh, say, can't you see
Anything about a Yankee that's a phoney?

REFRAIN
I'm a Yankee Doodle Dandy,
A Yankee Doodle do or die;
A real live nephew of my Uncle Sam's,
Born on the Fourth of July.
I've got a Yankee Doodle sweetheart,
She's my Yankee Doodle joy.
Yankee Doodle came to London, just to ride the ponies,
I am a Yankee Doodle boy.

VERSE TWO
Father's name was Hezikiah,
Mother's name was Ann Maria,
Yanks, through and through!
Red, White and Blue.
Father was so Yankee hearted,
When the Spanish war started,
He slipped on his uniform and hopped upon a pony.
My mother's mother was a Yankee, true,
My father's father was a Yankee, too;
And that's going some,
For the Yankee, by gum!
Oh, say, can you see
Anything about my pedigree that's a phoney?

REFRAIN REPEATED

"GIVE MY REGARDS TO BROADWAY"

VERSE ONE
Did you ever see two Yankees part upon a foreign shore,
When the good ship's just about to start for old New York once
    more?
With tear-dimmed eye, they say goodbye, they're friends,
    without a doubt;
When the man on the pier shouts, "Let them clear," as the ship
    strikes out.

REFRAIN
Give my regards to Broadway,
Remember me to Herald Square;
Tell all the gang at Forty-Second Street that I will soon be
    there.
Whisper of how I'm yearning to mingle with the old time
    throng;
Give my regards to old Broadway and say that I'll be there, e'er
    long.

VERSE TWO
Say hello to dear old Coney Isle, if there you chance to be,
When you're at the Waldorf, have a smile and charge it up to
    me.

Mention my name ev'ry place you go, as 'round the town you
    roam;
Wish you'd call on my gal, now remember, old pal, when you
    get back home.

REFRAIN

This was a period during which much of the budding native musical talent was educated abroad, and those with a bent toward popular musical theatre were addicted to Viennese operetta. Many of the other successful early and mid-twentieth-century composers also came to America from Europe and brought with them their thorough orientation in the Viennese model.

Reginald De Koven, an American educated abroad, had his first production, *The Begum*, here in 1887, followed by ten others prior to 1900. All of them had books and lyrics by the inexhaustible Harry B. Smith. Victor Herbert, Irish but educated in Vienna, was first produced three years earlier, with his *Prince Ananias* in 1894, and eight other shows were presented before 1900. Five of these had books and lyrics by Harry B. Smith, who is said to have provided books and lyrics for more than three hundred shows! John Philip Sousa also began his theatre career in 1894 with *Desirée* and was represented by four other shows before the turn of the century. The most successful of these was *El Capitan* (1898), which had lyrics by Tom Frost and Sousa himself. Within this same prior-to-1900 period, Gustave A. Kerker contributed nine shows, Julian Edwards six, and John Stromberg seven. Harry B. Smith was lyricist for one of Edwards's and one of Stromberg's.

The following is one of the several hundred Harry B. Smith lyrics. It is thoroughly representative of Smith and because of its association with Victor Herbert, it has been a classic for more than seventy-five years. It works today and is at the same time a revered period piece. Note in the first line the grandeur of the times in the use of "thee."

"GYPSY LOVE-SONG"
The Fortune Teller (1898)

VERSE I
The birds of the forest are calling for thee,
And the shades, and the glades are lonely;
Summer is there with her blossoms fair;
And you are absent only.
No bird that rests in the greenwood tree
But sighs to greet you and kiss you.
All the violets yearn, yearn for your safe return,
But most of all I miss you.

CHORUS
Slumber on, my little gypsy sweetheart;
Dream of the field and the grove,
Can you hear me, hear me in that dreamland
Where your fancies rove?
Slumber on, my little gypsy sweetheart,
Wild little woodland dove.
Can you hear the song that tells you
All my heart's true love.

VERSE II
The fawn that you tamed has a look in its eyes

That doth say we are too long parted;
Songs that are trolled by our comrades old
Are not now as they were lighthearted.
The wild rose fades in the leafy shades,
Its ghost will find you and haunt you;
All the friends say, "come, come to your woodland home,"
And most of all I want you.

Slumber on, etc.

The following example, from *Babes in Toyland* (1903), lyrics by Glen MacDonough, another Herbert collaborator, not by any means unique, will illustrate the quite general practice of transposition: "One kiss to capture tried"; "With cargo large of overshoes"; "You must near me stay"; "Soon will dawn the day"; "Since I a certain party saw."

Only two years later, Henry Blossom, still another Herbert lyricist, provided the words for *Mlle. Modiste*, a great success in 1905, starring the opera singer Fritzi Scheff. The great hit "If I Were on the Stage" turns into "Kiss Me Again" like a pumpkin into a coach. It is an entirely graceful narrative lyric, which provided the star with a sizable musical scene and gave her the opportunity to act and to show off her coloratura range, especially in the first four sections. Again, this song, seventy years old, is one of our theatre's great classics. It belongs to its period and yet has lived long beyond it.

"IF I WERE ON THE STAGE" ("KISS ME AGAIN")

(A) If I were asked to play the part,
Of simple maiden light of heart,
A village lass in country clothes,
As to and from her work she goes:
I'd sing a merry lilting strain,
And gaily dance to this refrain:

Tra, la, la, la, etc.

(A) If they should offer me some day,
A prima donna role to play,
A stately queen with powdered hair,
Her costly gowns and jewels rare;
I would not act the part amiss,
I'd sing a polonaise like this:

(B) "Ah, you will agree that happy I should be,
Ah! I'm queen of the land, Ah! Ah!
Ah! with lords and ladies great to kneel and kiss my hand;
A king upon the throne
To woo me for his own,
Ah! the fairest ever seen.
Ah! Ah! Ah! Ah! who would not be a queen!?"

(A) But best of all the parts I'd play,
If I could only have my way,
Would be a strong romantic role,
Emotional and full of soul.
And I believe for such a thing
A dreamy sensuous waltz I'd sing.

(C) Sweet summer breeze, whispering trees,

Stars shining softly above;
Roses in bloom, wafted perfume,
Sleepy birds dreaming of love.
Safe in your arms, far from alarms,
Daylight shall come but in vain.
Tenderly pressed close to your breast,
Kiss me!
Kiss me again.
Kiss me again,
Kiss me, kiss me again.

The first four stanzas follow the conventional AABA form. Yet the C section that climaxes the song is the one that posterity has remembered best.

While quoting Henry Blossom, I should like to point out a set of *sevenfold* rhymes he wrote in Victor Herbert's *The Red Mill* (1906). It makes much talked-about triple rhymes seem like child's play.

Mignonette
Soubrette
People's pet
Exclusive set
She has met
A baronet
Run himself in debt

Five years after *Mlle. Modiste*, Rida Johnson Young provided the words for another Herbert success, *Naughty Marietta*, written for two opera stars, Emma Trentini and Orville Harrold. One of that show's lasting successes was "I'm Falling in Love with Someone." Its period reaches us through contractions: the first line "ne'er" and "'Tis," which begins the second. Each of the two verses is as long as the chorus, which is in AA form. Each A is sixteen bars. This unusual verse length was quite common in Viennese operetta. Then there are words that echo 1910 to us: leap madly, unruly, a-whirl, scoff, flirtation, heartily.

"I'M FALLING IN LOVE WITH SOMEONE"

VERSE ONE

I've a very strange feeling I ne'er felt before,
'Tis a kind of a grind of depression;
My heart's acting strangely, it feels rather sore,
At least it gives me that impression.
My pulses leap madly without any cause,
Believe me, I'm telling you truly,
I'm gay without pause, then sad without cause,
My spirits are truly unruly.

REFRAIN

For I'm falling in love with some one, some one girl;
I'm falling in love with some one, head a-whirl;
Yes! I'm falling in love with some one, plain to see,
I'm sure I could love some one madly,
If some one would only love me!

VERSE TWO

Now, I don't mind confessing that I used to scoff
At this sort of a sport of flirtation;
I used to believe that I'd never be caught,
In this foolish but fond complication.
I'm losing all relish for things that were dear,
I'm looking for trouble and know it,

When some one is near, I'm feeling quite queer,
But I heartily hope I don't show it.

REFRAIN REPEATED

Still another Herbert lyricist, Robert B. Smith, furnished the words for *Sweethearts* in 1913. I quote some lines at random. To me, they sound earlier than those by Rida Johnson Young (1910) and Henry Blossom (1905).

If it comes not to your sighing

For love do I sigh

So for that hour
My heart will wait!

So Mother Goose one morning took
And shut them in a book.

Softly the Angelus to prayer now calls
With comfort in the knell.

And unto the darkness light impart
Unto my wond'ring heart!

In addition to whatever grandiloquence these transpositions were thought to have imparted, there was the matter of rhyme, which the practice of transposing greatly facilitated. The lyricist had the tacit right to say anything as awkwardly (poetically?) as he liked, so long as, in the process, he was then able to make his rhymes.

It may come as a surprise that after the word "love" one of the most frequently employed words was "gay." One possible reason for this is the fact that according to a rhyming dictionary it has more than 250 rhymes and assonances. A few "gay" examples covering the period from 1903 to 1933 (thirty years) follow:

From *Babes in Toyland* (1903):

So be gay Bopeep though astray your sheep.
Hail to Christmas, joyous Christmas, be gay the day draws
near.

From *The Red Mill* (1906):

Get gay vit me.

From *Naughty Marietta* (1910):

Mandolin's gay.
With castanets sounding so gay
I'm gay without pause/Then sad without cause.

From *Sweethearts* (1913): (five rhymes)

Gay—playing—swaying—betraying—day.

From *The Student Prince* (1924):

Let's all be gay boys.

From *The Vagabond King* (1926):

To spend a gay tomorrow.

From *Show Boat* (1927):

My role was gay
When the sports of gay Chicago.

From *The Cat and the Fiddle* (1931):

Your gay dreams
. . . gaily going by.
Take what she offers and be gay.
To her gay retreat.

From *Roberta* (1933):

. . . gaily laughed.
With carols gay.

Some lyricists employed archaic or archaic-sounding words in order to create a feeling of the long-ago past, or a churchly mood. We associate these words with the King James version of the Bible, begun in 1604, although they are generally intended to relate to the periods of the Bible itself.

In *Naughty Marietta* Rida Johnson Young wrote: "Ah! sweet mystery of life, at last I've found thee" and "And 'tis love, and love alone, that can repay." In *Sweethearts* Robert B. Smith wrote: "Unto my won'ring heart/ And unto the darkness light impart."

This sort of thing was in style early on in the present century. Carrie Jacob Bond's famous standard "The Rosary" had for its opening: "The hours I spend with thee, dear heart."

I understand from this not only an intended religious atmosphere but also an attempt to create a kind of pseudo-elegance. The employment of thee, thou, thine, unto, and many other similar words by lyricists was not uncommon.

In line with this practice, but at the very opposite end of the spectrum, was Lorenz Hart's song "Thou Swell" in *A Connecticut Yankee* (1927). "Thou" was certainly *meant* to indicate the knightly period, but by the mere juxtaposition of "swell" immodestly following it, we are given a nearly impossible relationship at once funny and outrageously at war with itself. In the same score there was another song, "On a Desert Isle with Thee," also a sequence of words that made strange and original bedfellows.

The achievements of both metrical balance and perfect rhyme have, separately or together, always caused considerable concern to lyricists. One of the poorer practices of attempted metrical balance is the frequent use of filler words, unessential words employed for the sole purpose of providing an extra syllable in the rhythm when a beat would otherwise have been missing. The following lines from early musicals will illustrate:

It may be *very* near to you
Sometimes love is *very* trying
But you *really* must not mind it.

Softly the Angelus to prayer *now* calls.

Still our wages are *but* small.

With lords and ladies *great* to kneel.

Hope as my guiding star and perfect love to find *at last* a
fond reward to soothe my heart.

Oh, our lectures and addresses are *just* lovely.

Come *then* close to me.

Then a visit he *did* plan.

Actually the list is endless and it unfortunately extends too frequently into many thoughtless lyrics of our own time. Seventy years ago the use of these filler words provided in all likelihood an unconscious and easily acceptable remedy for a pint-size dilemma. Today when writers have become more conscious of their craft it is less excusable for them to behave so cavalierly when what they need is a more intelligent and thoughtful solution.

It is a curious fact that the earlier American theatre lyricists did indeed have models but the best of these remained cloaked in obscurity or were considered irrelevant. W. S. Gilbert was certainly known in America since his operettas flourished here from 1879.

While the cliché images flourished and the cliché rhymes appeared predictably line after line, at least two distinguished and thoroughly original American poets had lived, written, and died—Emily Dickinson and Walt Whitman. Though it is true that their works were little known at the turn of the century, the drive for newer and fresher images and rhymes had become somewhat urgent, everywhere except in our theatre. It was certainly mirrored in the works of other English and American poets but it in no way affected or influenced our early theatre lyricists.

I should like to list here a few of the images taken more or less at random from the poetry of Emily Dickinson and Walt Whitman. All of them are still new and fresh approximately a century after they were conceived. Observe that all of them relate to everyday things, mostly to nature. How shabby, by comparison, are the common ones that have been in general use for too long.

From Emily Dickinson (1830–1886):

Has it feet [morning] like water lilies?

Bring me the sunset in a cup,

Write me how many notes there be
In the new Robin's extasy....

... who laid the Rainbow's piers,

Until the daffodil
Unties her yellow bonnet

"Hope" is the thing with feathers—

I'll tell you how the Sun rose—
A ribbon at a time—

Good Morning—Midnight—

The Crickets sang
And set the Sun

A cloud withdrew from the sky

Blossoms will run away

Autumn overlooked my knitting

Arrows enamored of his heart

It is easy to work when the soul is at play

From Walt Whitman (1819–1892):
(from "Song of Myself")

... I guess it [grass] is the handkerchief of the Lord,
A scented gift and remembrances designedly dropt,
Bearing the owner's name somewhere in the corners,
That we may see and remark, and say WHOSE?

[grass] the beautiful uncut hair of graves.

It may be you [grass] transpire from the breasts of young men,

The smallest sprout shows there is really no death

Smile O voluptuous cool-breath'd earth!
Earth of the slumbering and liquid trees!
Earth of departed sunset—earth of the mountain's misty-top!
Earth of the limpid gray of clouds brighter and clearer for my sake!
Far-swooping elbow'd earth—rich apple-blossom'd earth!
Smile, for your lover comes.

I hear bravuras of birds, bustle of growing wheat, gossip of flames, clack of sticks cooking my meals,

What is less or more than a touch?

I believe a leaf of grass is no less than the journey-work of the stars,
And the pismire is equally perfect, and a grain of sand, and the egg of the wren,
And the tree-toad is a chef d'oeuvre for the highest,
And the running blackberry would adorn the parlors of heaven.

These excerpts from Dickinson and Whitman are not only filled with fresh images but all of them are *specific*. In earlier days the use of generalities was commonly accepted, and even today most "pop" (non-theatre) lyrics have been little affected by the passage of time. The desirability of the specific as opposed to the general should be obvious. General descriptive words and phrases can hold little interest for the listener because they are vague, and they will almost certainly also be repetitive, resembling every other lyric in the marketplace. The use of general images is ineffective in specifying character or situation; everybody and everything remains the same: plain vanilla. It is the *particularization* of people and situations, epitomized in words, which is at the very root of all theatre and especially of musical theatre. The maturing lyricist in the American musical theatre has become more specific in his use of images and in his conscious effort to find new means of expression, rhymes, and other materials of his trade that have not been used previously.

The fact must not be overlooked that the expressions, foibles, imagery, taste, and customs of each period are, intentionally or otherwise, inevitably mirrored in all creative work, whether it is the product of a genius or an untalented bungler. Richard Rodgers said most aptly in his introduction to *100 Best Songs of the 20's and 30's* "a song is the voice of its times" and "They [the songs] log the temper of an entire era."

The period is ever-present in the song lyrics of our theatre. They reflect the tranquillity, the turbulence, the optimism or pessimism of an era. Sometimes they run so counter to prevailing sentiment, that by so doing they indicate their time equally well by reacting against it. Sometimes they speak to us of times past, as Oscar Hammerstein did in "Kansas City" (*Oklahoma!*—1943) when Will Parker tells his friends with amazement about his new discoveries in the city: the telephone, a seven-story skyscraper, a radiator, indoor toilets, and a burlesque show. In this song Hammerstein addresses the audience of his own time, causing it to smile at the wonderment of earlier people unaccustomed to the things we now take for granted. This is another—backhanded—way that an author defines his own position in time.

Perhaps the most common revelation of time is expressed in use of up-to-date words and phrases since these like clothing styles are the very first to go out-of-date. Theatre lyricists in particular, especially during the two decades beginning with the twenties, were an important segment of Tin Pan Alley. The best show songs were the most popular songs of their period and were often created with that popular market in mind. Afterward, many of them joined the list of more or less timeless standards.

In reflecting their own times and appealing for popularity outside the confines of the shows in which the songs were birthed, lyricists consciously kept their vocabularies up-to-date. This practice imparted to their work a sense of newness, but frequently condemned it afterward to time past. This constant resorting to newness also included an attempt to steer clear of the past.

Noble Sissle and Eubie Blake with "I'm Just Wild About Harry" from *Shuffle Along* (1921) used "vamps" and "heav'nly blisses." Otto Harbach and Oscar Hammerstein II in "Indian Love Call" from *Rose-Marie* (1924) used "blue" ("I will be blue"), which was common in the twenties. Ira Gershwin used "Guardian Angel," "Prince Charming," "flappers," "wizard," "naughty," "sweet," "fond caress," "paradise," "romancin'," "fond embrace," "swell," "coo," "papa" (not in the paternal sense), and many others. It is interesting to note that while "Guardian Angel," for example, seems to be from the twenties and thirties, the same expression was employed more timelessly by T. S. Eliot in *Murder in the Cathedral* (1935)—the middle of the same period under discussion, in a couplet:

Now my good Angel, whom God appoints
To be my guardian, hover over the sword's points.

Cole Porter specified his era not only with words and phrases, but by the inclusion of then famous names, many of them his personal friends, a practice that imparts to his lyrics a sense of their having been intended for performance at a private party. This roster includes Mrs. Ned McLean, Lady Mendl, Mimsie Starr, Cholly Knickerbocker, Fannie Hurst, Fanny Brice, Monty Woolley, Liz Whitney, Dorothy Parker, Michael Strange, and many others. The period words include gigolos, sweetheart, chums, thrill, by cracky, little fool, break my heart, and many more. Nearly all these phrases used by Porter, Gershwin, and the others have been replaced today. Porter wrote in 1934:

Good authors too who once knew better words
Now only use four-letter words. . .

Though contemporary language is less obvious and more subtly employed in nonpopular art, it is nevertheless inevitably present to some degree in all creative works.

Some lyricists have made their own fun by creating words to aid them in their rhyme schemes. Harbach made "dareful" to rhyme with "careful" in *No No Nanette* (1925). Porter in "Friendship" from *DuBarry Was a Lady* (1939) used "blendship" with "friendship," "fergit it" with "it," and "crick" [creek] with "slick." Ira Gershwin made up "laceable" (not really a new word, but seldom called upon) to rhyme with "embraceable," "Gar-a-field" (the president) with "far afield," "vel-a-vit"

with "tell of it." There are many others, usually employed comically, but these examples will suffice.

By 1925, some theatre greats in the lyric department had already created monuments. Among these were Otto Harbach, who had worked with and helped to "bring up" Oscar Hammerstein II, and Irving Caesar, who shared with Harbach the lyric writing for Youmans's *No No Nanette*.

I should like to quote here two of Caesar's *Nanette* lyrics and two of Harbach's from Kern's *Roberta* (1933). In my opinion these four lyrics reached pinnacles in our lyric-writing history. Anything I would add as explanation would be both gratuitous and impertinent.

"TOO MANY RINGS AROUND ROSIE"

VERSE ONE
In an early childhood day,
When December seemed like May;
Ring-around-a-Rosie with the boys I used to play.
Tommy, Andy, Harold, Joe,
Ate my candy, then would go.
I tried to please them all you know;
That's why not one became my beau.

REFRAIN
Too many rings around Rosie
Never got Rosie a ring.
Too many beaux when she should have one,
You know will never bring her
A ring around her finger:
One little name to remember
Is better than having a string.
It doesn't hurt to flirt a bit, but use it as bait.
Make your catch,
Make your match before it's too late.
For too many rings around Rosie will never get Rosie a ring!

VERSE TWO
Men are only grown-up boys,
Pretty ladies are their toys;
Here today, tomorrow they're in search of other joys.
It is nice to have a few
To go loco over you;
But still, one ring to call your own
Is worth a dozen on the phone.

REFRAIN REPEATED

"TEA FOR TWO"

VERSE ONE
I'm discontented with homes that are rented so I have invented my own;
Darling this place is a lover's oasis, where life's weary chase is unknown.
Far from the cry of the city where flowers pretty caress the streams,
Cozy to hide in, to live side by side in, don't let it abide in my dreams.

REFRAIN
Picture you upon my knee just tea for two and two for tea,
Just me for you and you for me alone.
Nobody near us to see us or hear us,

No friends or relations on weekend vacations,
We won't have it known, dear, that we own a telephone, dear,
Day will break and you'll awake and start to bake a sugar cake
    for me to take for all the boys to see.
We will raise a family,
A boy for you,
A girl for me,
Oh can't you see how happy we would be?

VERSE TWO
You are revealing a plan so appealing, I can't help but feeling
    for you.
Darling, I planned; can't you understand, it is yours to com-
    mand it, so do.
All of your schemes I'm admiring, they're worth desiring; but
    can't you see,
I'd like to wait, dear, for some future date, dear.
It won't be too late, dear, for me.

REFRAIN REPEATED

"YESTERDAYS"

Yesterdays,
Yesterdays.
Days I knew as happy, sweet sequester'd days.
Olden days, golden days.
Days of mad romance and love,
Then gay Youth was mine,
Truth was mine,
Joyous free and flaming life forsooth was mine.
Sad am I,
Glad am I,
For today I'm dreaming of
Yesterdays!

"SMOKE GETS IN YOUR EYES"

They asked me how I knew
My true love was true.
I of course replied
"Something here inside,
Cannot be denied."

They said "Some day you'll find
All who love are blind,
When your heart's on fire,
You must realize
Smoke gets in your eyes."

So I chaffed them and I gaily laughed to think they could doubt
    my love.
Yet, today my love has flown away I am without my love.

Now laughing friends deride tears I cannot hide,
So I smile and say "When a lovely flame dies,
Smoke gets in your eyes."

It would be improper to conclude this section without pointing out some dangers, which we should have learned something about from the past. First, unclear meanings:

To know perchance that on the morrow,
For love and smiles come doubts and tears.

We are aware of what the writer is trying to convey but it is his obligation to say it clearly. As a matter of fact, the above quotation is from a solo line in *Mlle. Modiste* (Henry Blossom). Later in the same piece the chorus says it clearly:

To know perchance the morrow may bring doubts and
    tears.

Two other examples. The first is obviously ungrammatical:

I'm happier far than the married men are,
Who are cursed with the shrew of a wife.

The second is correct, but rather far out:

Where the tropics bloom so rare,
Breathe their languor on the air.

Breathing languor seems strange and it it's *"on* the air," it seems fixed there like a kite and inhalable only with the greatest difficulty.

Word associations that wrench the listener's attention to some point unconnected with the song should be avoided. Take, for example, a simple innocuous word such as "sunbeam." Today, it is the brand name of a series of electrical appliances. Anyone hearing the word is apt to recall the fact that his electric razor is a Sunbeam. "Weed" will call up "marijuana," and so on.

As the theatre lyricist, as opposed to the poet, is addressing himself solely to the ear of the listener, he becomes confusing when he employs avoidable but similar sounds that are not intended to rhyme. Because of their proximity to one another, they *appear* almost to rhyme, and they snag the listener's attention, even briefly, and interrupt the flow of sound and meaning while he pauses to reflect. The most accomplished lyricists usually avoid similar vowel sounds at close range when a rhyme is not intended. In most such cases the lyricists seem to have been innocent of any wrongdoing but I feel that unconscious or sloppy craftsmanship is again at issue, especially when it happens today. From the past, I quote four such examples:

She laughs to *scorn* the usual *form*
She must be *won* by storm!

In my opinion the vowel sounds employed in "scorn" and "won" should be almost any other imaginable sound.

Wine and *song*
Ah! *Come,* ah come! Come *along!*

I dream of floods of human blood.

Rhyming singular with plural is common today in popular song, but it is, strictly speaking, incorrect. In the above example they were not meant to rhyme. Here are three similar sounds, none of which is intended to rhyme with the other.

I used to *scoff*
At this *sort* of a *sport* of flirtation.

In line with these listening problems, there is yet another confusion that our language itself causes: the sound-alikes, which have different and usually unassociated meanings. Take words like "two" and "too," "rain" and "reign," "rough" and "ruff" for example. Inasmuch as writers address themselves totally to the ears, it is important that they not employ words whose exactly similar sounds can possibly raise even a momentary question as to their intended meanings. In the end the meaning may be made incontrovertibly clear, that is, when the one or two lines that complete the thought have been heard totally, but meanwhile, even a small distracting element in a lyric causes an interruption of attention that will inevitably be destructive.

I should like to point out one final characteristic commonly found in earlier lyric writing—unconnected with listening—which was in quite general practice at the time: the last line of verses leading into the choruses—the main event! "And this is the song that they hear" *(Rose-Marie*—1924); "That is how the blues really began" *(George White's Scandals*—1926); "So I say to all who feel forlorn" *(Hit the Deck*—1927); "For I'm just the same as you" *(Hit the Deck*—1927); ". . . until I find what would make your eyes glisten like mine with love divine" *(Good Boy*—1928); "For example take my case" *(Crazy Quilt*—1931); and "Let me tell you girls what he said" *(Sweethearts*—1913).

The best lyricists of the last forty years shy away from such obvious lead-ins. (Examples will follow in this volume.) The verse today normally sets up the chorus and merges with it, not needing to provide pointing index fingers.

Theatre lyricists today have made remarkable advances during the last forty-odd years. Many of them have found definable personal styles. They have long ago discovered the need for new and more specific methods of expression, and have often reveled in unaccustomed rhyme schemes and, most of all, have found for the very first time ways to create genuine comedy songs—not arch, cute, clever, coy, self-conscious songs, but songs that can be laughed at aloud and are universal enough not to become unstylish and tired in a few months or years. This is a not inconsiderable achievement.

The pages that follow are in no way exhaustive but will hopefully lead the reader to examine other lyrics not included here. Read. Read aloud. Recognize the accomplishments. Enjoy.

two

THE AMERICAN MUSICAL THEATRE FROM 1925 TO 1972

The lyricists who have had the largest hand in bringing lyric writing in the theatre to its most mature state are represented in this chapter, each in a separate section, with a wealth of examples of their contributions. Each has excelled in his own way. Each was or is unique.

These are the lyricists who are at the heart of the American musical theatre and who advanced lyric writing toward perfection. Most of their work will remain as models to the future.

A special note is necessary concerning some of the very important lyricists whose lyrics are not represented here, because for a variety of reasons they did not wish to grant the author permission to quote from their songs. Included in this group are Johnny Mercer, the authors of *Hair,* and, perhaps the greatest loss, Irving Berlin.

It is unfortunate that Irving Berlin will not allow this or any other writer permission to quote his lyrics or his music. But this book representing the lyricists of the American musical theatre would indeed be incomplete without at least a mention of his contributions and achievements.

Between 1909 and 1962 Berlin produced totally or in part (early in his career) fifty-one shows—music and lyrics. His style was always marked by a simplicity that never seemed elementary, maudlin, or foolish, because sincerity was one of his most obvious qualities.

If I were to point out one show that I believe was most memorable, I should name *Annie Get Your Gun* (1946), which contained an incredible number of unforgettable songs, including "Anything You Can Do," "Doin' What Comes Natur'lly," "The Girl That I Marry," "I Got Lost in His Arms," "I Got the Sun in the Morning," "I'm an Indian Too," "Moonshine Lullaby," "My Defenses Are Down," "There's No Business Like Show Business," "They Say It's Wonderful," "Who Do You Love, I Hope," "You Can't Get a Man with a Gun," and others! Among this plethora of matchless songs, the variety is also endless.

It is my profound hope that Mr. Berlin will someday issue a complete anthology of his incredible lyrics.

Courtesy Museum of the City of New York

Cole Porter (1893–1964)

With the exception of *Kiss Me Kate,* the lyrics of Cole Porter were far more autobiographical than those of any other writer for the musical theatre. This is not to say that the events of his life are spelled out or arranged in any chronological order, but the things he liked, the people, his points of view and many special attitudes toward living and loving are peculiarly defined and developed.

Porter was born into wealth, which was accompanied by social position, and continued to live with both throughout his life. These facts mark Porter as unusual among all other distinguished lyricists. Ira Gershwin, E. Y. Harburg, Irving Berlin, and Harold Rome were the sons of poor immigrants. Stephen Sondheim and Alan Jay Lerner are the only other distinguished lyricsts born into wealthy and educated families. Of the leading lyricists, Porter was the only non-Jew! Porter's wealthy, social, non-Jewish background made him unique, for these facts were in themselves responsible in large measure for the special style, color, gaiety, imagery, and even the subject matter of a majority of his lyrics.

It is indeed curious that almost all our theatre lyricists were the children of immigrants or were themselves new arrivals in the United States. This fact suggests several ideas to me. That the English language had to be learned, that it was not a household language, the basis of everyday communication, makes me wonder that such a situation may have been, perhaps *must* have been, a distinct advantage. The language of our early lyricists was acquired and cultivated. They relished words and did not see them just as a tool of everyday life and work. Besides, as most of our chief lyricists came from Orthodox Jewish homes, they would have had exposure to and intimate familiarity with the rhythmic metrical cantillations employed in daily and holiday Hebraic ceremonies.

The business of reserving the use of language (almost exclusively) for working purposes as opposed to commonplace communication may also account in large measure for the work of the expatriates of the twenties who lived in Paris in voluntary exile: Gertrude Stein, e.e. cummings, James Joyce, Samuel Beckett, and many more. They produced what became English-language models. Their day-to-day living and speaking was conducted in a different tongue.

On reading the words of Cole Porter's songs, I am given the distinct feeling that he was perpetually trying to *please,* not merely to entertain and amuse. I have already referred to his use of proper names as though his songs were intended for performance at a private party. I repeat that contention here. However, more than that, the lyrics try to please. We hear in just a single song:

Mrs. Ned McLean, God bless her,

If Mae West you like
Why, nobody would oppose!

Have you heard that Mimsie Starr
Just got pinched in the Astor Bar?
Well, did you evah?
What a swell party this is.

It's tops, it's first,
It's DuPont, it's Hearst!

Farming, that's the fashion!

Kit Cornell is shelling peas,
Lady Mendl's climbing trees,
Dear Mae West is at her best in the hay!

They tell me cows who are all feelin' milky
All give cream when they're milked by Willkie. . . .

In the preceding song, "Farming," there are compliments to Fannie Hurst, Fanny Brice, Garbo, Margie Hart, Steinbeck, Guy Lombardo, Cliff Odets, Monty Woolley, Michael Strange, and Liz Whitney.

It seems possible that one of two conclusions may be drawn from Porter's use of these names, all of them personal friends. Either he counted on the public's familiarity with them ("Why not?" he might have asked, "they're always in the columns.") or he never seriously considered the possibility that his work would have a broad general success, or more especially an afterlife beyond the precise time in which he and they lived.

There are evidences of other practices peculiar to Porter. One is his preoccupation with words relating to money; another is his frequent reference to places at that time known almost exclusively by people of wealth who spent their money lavishly in the pursuit of pleasure.

The money words and phrases used frequently include: millionaires, rich, tycoon, gigolos, money, Cadillac, Cartier's, castle, keen to give me checks, gold-digging, marble swimming pool, sable, and so on. Typical are the lyrics: "Other girls' luxuries/ Are my necessities. . . ."

The reference to places that at the time Porter named them were indeed "caviare to the general," or visited by well-off Americans, included Taormina, Pitti Palace, Il Duomo, the Riviera, Devonshire, the Arabian Sea, a box at the Garden, the Plaza's Persian Room, Park Avenue, the Ritz, Newport, the Stork Club, El Morocco, and the Lido. There were expensive French champagne brand names, Camembert, and other specialties during the depression years when other lyricists were involved with the more realistic present. He also wrote of yachts and planes when planes were not an everyday means of transportation, and polo, a sport practiced almost exclusively by the rich.

Porter, contrary to general lyric practice, employed complex words, many of them little used elsewhere. These included: cayuse, hobbles, pailletted, espouse, virago, and many more. This would seem to indicate a disregard for general communication. In addition to these rare words, he used many polysyllabic ones—better known, but as words not regular inhabitants of lyrics. But he used them well! These included: pessimistic, chaperone, contagious, incompatibility, objets d'art, disillusioned, affinity, astronomy, antimacassars, transmigration.

Porter was able to combine a general feeling of elegance combined with naturalness when he so desired. Separated into phrases, his kind of elegance included: "you descended," "sportsman abhors," "bathing suit to plus fours," "although I'm disinclined," "fortunate mortals," "learned reliance," "dispense the joys," "someone sympathetic to have about," "You're such a one plus ultra creature," "love affairs among gentility."

Many of Porter's songs were amusing and spirited. His rhyming technique was developed to an almost incredible degree. He seems to have always been in command of *how* he wished to say anything and appears to have delighted in making things work as he wished them to.

His love songs raise psychological questions that do not seem relevant to his other songs. In my opinion, upon reading one ballad after another, Porter was predominantly sad about love. These love songs are largely expressions of frustration, nostalgia, and hopelessness. Often when they seem happy, they generate an unreal storybook quality that I find difficult to believe in, nor can I believe that Porter himself could have really subscribed deeply to their sentiments as real ones.

"Easy to Love":

. . . it does seem a shame
That you can't see
Your future in me. . . .

"I've Got You under My Skin":

Don't you know, little fool, you never can win?

"Let's Be Buddies":

But many's the time I'm blue . . .
What say? How's about it?
Can't I be a buddy to you?

"So Near and Yet So Far" ends:

My condition is only so-so,
'Cause whenever I feel you're close, oh
You turn out to be oh, so
Near and Yet So Far.

"In the Still of the Night":

Do you love me
As I love you?
Are you my life to be?
My dream come true?
Or will this dream of mine fade out of sight
Like the moon growing dim
On the rim of the hill, In the chill
Still of the night?

"Just One of Those Things":

So goodbye, dear, and Amen,
Here's hoping . . . now and then,

"Get Out of Town":

Just disappear,
I care for you too much,

"Ev'ry Time We Say Good-Bye":

Ev'ry time we say good-bye,
I die a little.

"When Love Comes Your Way":

For just when you are sure
That love has come to stay . . .
Love flies away.

These lines are only a very few from the serious songs pertaining to love, but the sentiments of losing, frustration, and the rest are also to be found in the lighter, more playful songs.

"Anything Goes":

So though I'm not a great romancer
I know that you're bound to answer
when I propose,
Anything goes

"Why Shouldn't I?":

Why wait around,
When each age
Has a sage
Who has found
That upon this earth
Love is all that is really worth thinking of?

It must be fun, lots of fun,
To be sure when day is done
That the hour is coming when
You'll be kissed and then . . .
You'll be kissed again!

All debutantes say it's good
And ev'ry star
Out in far Hollywood seems to give it a try,
So why shouldn't I?

"Nobody's Chasing Me":

The clams are almost a mixin',
The hams are chasing T.V.,
The fox is chasing the vixen,
But nobody's fixin' me.

"Since I Kissed My Baby Good-Bye":

Oh, Lord, I've taken such a beatin',
I'm no good, even cheatin',
Since I kissed my baby good-bye.

"Down in the Depths":

Why even the janitor's wife
Has a perfectly good love-life,
And here am I, facing tomorrow,
Alone with my sorrow . . .
Down in the depths on the ninetieth floor.

It must not be supposed that, by pointing out these various unusual aspects of Porter's lyrics, I am attempting to expose weaknesses. Rather, I isolate them here as comprising much of the quintessence of Porter's style, theme, and perhaps representative of his very cause. Over and beyond these qualities there are the lyrics themselves, which burst on our world some forty-five years ago announcing and celebrating a fresh new voice.

Considering Porter's unusual accomplishments in relation to his life, it is my feeling that, as is the case with many profoundly creative artists, what he managed to do was both *because* of his life and *in spite* of it. His wealth and his society-oriented existence often limited his productivity, while also providing his mill with its essential grist. The jauntiness and fun of what he wrote might have been part of a basic attitude that forced him not to appear boring or unamusing at any cost. (He had a superb model in Noël Coward.) I believe that his basic attitude toward romance was his sincerest and represented his true self. As it turned out, so much of his later life was spent enduring great physical pain, his laughter became his public face (perhaps it always had been) and his inner frustrations more and more reflected his real torture.

But his creative mastery was unquestionably nearly always present. His ability to say what he set out to say, and in his own very personal way, was his achievement. He fulfilled the obligation with which his talent charged him.

The music in which he clothed his lyrics is perhaps even more remarkable. Certainly the two elements together always added up to a single satisfying entity. I would here make a very personal observation, which is that when one studies the lyrics without the music the latter is sorely missed. Songs like "Night and Day," "Begin the Beguine," and "I Get a Kick Out of You," which comprise the cornerstone of Porter's achievement, are not particularly remarkable as lyrics alone. However, considered as they were intended as entities *with* their dancing music, they are remarkable and unique.

The songs from *Kiss Me Kate* are, in my opinion, the breakthrough in all aspects of Porter's talent. The lyrics are more truly sophisticated and the music is created on a plane high above the earlier, more facile exercises.

Most of the rhymes in "Where Is the Life That Late I Led?" are obvious, though a few warrant comment. The like sounds (assonances), as opposed to the rhymes in the interludes should be pointed out. In the first interlude there is a consistent liquidity due to the use of *l* sounds: Mi*l*ano, sti*ll*, se*ll*ing, Ca-ro*l*ina, *L*ina, pedd*l*ing, A*l*ice, *L*ucretia, scanda*l*ous. There are also eighteen sibilants *(s* sounds) and eight *p* features: *p*ictures, scri*p*tures, *p*eddling, *p*izza, *p*retty, *P*itti *P*alace, *P*ompeii, and much resonance through the use of *m* and *n* sounds. All this, in addition to the actual rhymes, adds up to considerable music.

The second interlude features an abundance of *k* sounds: Rebe*cc*a, Be*c*ky-we*c*ky-o, *c*ruising, Ve*cc*hio, lu*c*ky, Chi*c*ago, *c*ould, drin*k*in', stin*k*in', pin*k*. The complex rhyme scheme in both interludes is almost completely consistent.

"WHERE IS THE LIFE THAT LATE I LED?"

Since I reached the charming age of puberty
And began to think of feminine curls,
Like a show that's typically Shuberty,
I have always had a multitude of girls.

But now that a married man, at last, am I,
How aware of my dear departed past am I!

Where is that life that late I led?
Where is it now? Totally dead!
Where is the fun I used to find?
Where has it gone? Gone with the wind!

A married life may all be well,
But raising an heir
Could never compare
With raising a bit of hell,

So I repeat what first I said . . .
Where is the life that late I led?

INTERLUDE
In dear Milano, where are you, Momo(1)?
Still selling those pictures(2) of the Scriptures(2) in the
Duomo(1)?
And Carolina, where are you, Lina(3)?
Still peddling your pizza(3) in the streets a' Taormina(3)?
And in Firenze, where are you, Alice(4)?
Still there in your pretty(5) itty-bitty(5)-Pitti(5) Palace(4)?
And sweet Lucre(6)tia, so young and gay(6)-ee(7),
What scandalous doin's(8) in the ruins(8) of Pompeii(7)

Where is the life that late I led?
Where is it now? Totally dead!
Where is the fun I used to find?
Where has it gone? Gone with the wind!

The marriage game is quite all right.
Yes, during the day
It's easy to play,
But oh, what a bore at night!

So I repeat what first I said . . .
Where is the life that late I led?

INTERLUDE
Where is Rebecca, my Becky-wecky-o(9)?
Could still she be cruising(10) that amusing(10) Ponte
  Vecchio(9)?
Where is Fedora, the wild virago(11)?
It's lucky I missed her(12) gangster sister(12) from
  Chicago(11)!
Where is Venetia, who loved to chat so(13)?
Could still she be drinkin'(14) in her stinkin'(14) pink
  palazzo(13)?
And lovely Lisa, where are you, Lisa(15)?
You gave a new meaning(16) to the Leaning Tower of Pisa(15)!

Where is the life that late I led?
Where is it now? Totally dead!
Where is the fun I used to find?
Where has it gone? Gone with the wind!

I've oft been told of nuptial bliss,
But whatta ya' do at quarter-to-two
With only a shrew to kiss?

So I repeat what first I said . . .
Where is the life that late I led?

The fun of "Friendship," from *DuBarry Was a Lady* (1939),
is a result of the non sequiturs. The singer of the song is clearly
endowed with a character: he is a braggart and a coward.

"FRIENDSHIP"

If you're ever in a jam, here I am.
If you're ever in a mess, S.O.S.!
If you ever feel so happy you land in jail, I'm your bail,
It's friendship, friendship,
Just a perfect blendship . . .
When other friendships have been forgot,
Ours will still be hot!

If you're ever up a tree, phone to me.
If you're ever down a well, ring my bell.
If you ever lose your teeth when you're out to dine, Borrow
  mine!
It's friendship, friendship,
Just a perfect blendship . . .
When other friendships have been fergit,
Ours will still be it!

If they ever black your eyes, put me wise.
If they ever cook your goose, turn me loose.
If they ever put a bullet through your br-rain, I'll complain!
It's friendship, friendship,
Just a perfect blendship . . .
When other friendships go up in smoke,

Ours will still be "oke"!

If you ever lose your mind, I'll be kind.
If you ever lose your shirt, I'll be hurt.
If you're ever in a mill and get sawed in half, I won't laugh!
It's friendship, friendship,
Just a perfect blendship . . .
When other friendships are up the crick,
Ours will still be slick!

If they ever crack your spine, drop a line.
If you ever catch on fire, send a wire.
If you ever take a boat and get lost at sea, Write to me.
It's friendship, friendship,
Just a perfect blendship . . .
When other friendships have ceased to jell,
Ours will still be swell!

Most of the fun in the lyrics of "The Physician," from *Nymph
Errant* (1933), is due to the use of technical physiological terms
and their rhyming organization. In strong contrast is "My
Heart Belongs to Daddy," from *Leave It to Me* (1938), written
five years later, in which the words are fairly elemental. However, the rhymes in "The Physician" are unadorned, whereas in
the later song they are much more complex.

"My Heart Belongs to Daddy" starts off with two sets of
triple rhymes framed by one double one. Much of the rest of
the song consists of rhymed couplets, but there is a long list of
words rhyming with "Daddy," which in a sense, helps to tie the
entire song together.

"THE PHYSICIAN"

Once I loved such a shattering physician,
Quite the best-looking doctor in the state.
He looked after my physical condition
And his bedside manner was great!

When I'd gaze up and see him there above me,
Looking less like a doctor than a Turk,
I was tempted to whisper, "Do you love me?
Or do you merely love your work?"

He said my bronchial tubes were entrancing,
My epiglottis filled him with glee,
He simply loved my larynx
And went wild about my pharynx,
But he never said he loved *me*.

He said my epidermis was darling
And found my blood as blue as can be,
He went through wild ecstatics
When I showed him my lymphatics,
But he never said he loved *me*.

And though, no doubt,
It was not very smart of me,
I kept on a-rackin' my soul
To figure out
Why he loved ev'ry part of me
And yet not me as a whole!

With my esophagus he was ravished,
Enthusiastic to a degree . . .
He said 'twas just enormous
My appendix vermiformous,
But he never said he loved *me!*

He said my cerebellum was brilliant
And my cerebrum far from N.G.
I knew he thought a lotta
My medulla oblongata,
But he never said he loved *me*.

He said my maxillaries were marvels
And found my sternum stunning to see,
He did a double hurdle
When I shook my pelvic girdle,
But he never said he loved *me*.

He seemed amused
When he first made a test of me
To further his medical art,
Yet he refused,
When he fixed up the rest of me,
To cure that ache in my heart!

I know he thought my pancreas perfect
And for my spleen was keen as could be . . .
He said of all his sweeties
I'd the sweetest diabetes,
But he never said he loved *me!*

He said my vertebrae were "sehr schone"
And called my coccyx "plus que gentil" . . .
He murmured "molto bella"
When I sat on his patella,
But he never said he loved *me*.

The things he whispered in my tympanum
Were quite enough to leave me at sea,
I felt extremely silly
When he tickled my papillae,
But he never said he loved *me*.

But being sure
That, with all I'd to offer him,
I somehow could make him come through,
Just as a lure,
I attempted to proffer him
Some parlor tricks that I knew . . .

He seemed to love my Spanish fandango
And to adore my "Mother Machree" . . .
He cried, "May heaven strike us!"
When I played my umbilicus,
But he *never* said he loved *me!*

"MY HEART BELONGS TO DADDY"

I used to fall
In love with all
Those boys who maul
Refined ladies,
But now I tell
Each young gazelle
To go to hell . . .
I mean Hades.

For since I've come to care
For such a sweet millionaire . . .

While tearin' off

A game of golf,
I may
Make a play
For the caddy,
But when I do,
I don't follow through
'Cause my heart belongs to daddy.

If I invite
A boy some night
To dine
On my fine
Finnan haddie,
I just adore
His asking for more,
But my heart belongs to daddy.

Yes, my heart belongs to daddy,
So I simply couldn't be bad!
Yes, my heart belongs to daddy . . .
Da-da-da, da-da-da, da-daddy-ad!

So I want to warn you, laddy,
Though I think you're perfectly swell,
That my heart belongs to daddy
And my daddy, he treats it so well!

Saint Patrick's Day
Although I may
Be seen
Wearing green
With a paddy,
I'm always sharp
When playing the harp
'Cause my heart belongs to daddy.

Though other dames,
At football games,
May long
For a strong
Undergraddy,
I never dream
Of making the team
'Cause my heart belongs to daddy.

Yes, my heart belongs to daddy,
So I simply couldn't be bad!
Yes, my heart belongs to daddy . . .
Da-da-da, da-da-da, da-daddy-ad!

So I want to warn you, laddy,
Though I simply hate to be frank,
That I can't be mean to daddy
'Cause my da-da-daddy might spank!

The words of "Brush Up Your Shakespeare" are pure fun words. The author delighted in taking liberties with titles of plays and proper names: Sappo-ho, Othella, Much Ado About Nussing, embessida (British accent indicated) to rhyme with Cressida, Twelf' Night. All of it is fun for the sake of rhymes and is impersonal.

"BRUSH UP YOUR SHAKESPEARE"

The girls today in society
Go for classical poetry,
So to win their hearts one must quote with ease

Aeschylus and Euripides . . .
One must know Homer and believe me, bo,
Sophocles and Sappo-ho . . .
Unless you know Shelley and Keats and Pope,
Dainty debbies will call you a dope . . .
But the poet of them all,
Who will start 'em simply ravin',
Is the poet people call
"The Bard Of Stratford-on-Avon."

Brush up your Shakespeare,
Start quoting him now!
Brush up your Shakespeare
And the women you will wow.
Just declaim a few lines from "Othella"
And they'll think you're a hell of a fella,
If your blonde won't respond when you flatter 'er,
Tell her what Tony told Cleopatterer,
If she fights when her clothes you are mussing,
What are clothes? "Much Ado About Nussing!"
Brush up your Shakespeare, and they'll all kow-tow!

With the wife of the British "embessida" *
Try a crack out of "Troilus And Cressida" . . .
If she says she won't buy it or "tike" † it,
Make her "tike" it, what's more, "As You Like It!"
If she says your behavior is heinous
Kick her right in the "Coriolanus!"
Brush up your Shakespeare, and they'll all kow-tow!
Thinkst thou?
Odds bodkins!
They'll all kow-tow!

Brush up your Shakespeare,
Start quoting him now!
Brush up your Shakespeare
And the women you will wow.
Better mention "The Merchant Of Venice"
When her sweet pound o' flesh you would menace,
If her virtue at first, she defends . . . well,
Just remind her that "All's Well That Ends Well."
When your baby is pleading for pleasure
Let her sample your "Measure For Measure!"
Brush up your Shakespeare, and they'll all kow-tow!

If your goil is a Washington Heights dream,
Treat the kid to "A Midsummer Night's Dream,"
If she then wants an all-by-herself night,
Let her rest ev'ry 'leventh or "Twelf' Night,"
If because of your heat she gets huffy,
Simply play on and "Lay on, MacDuffy!"
Brush up your Shakespeare, and they'll all kow-tow!
Forsooth!
I' faith!
They'll all kow-tow!

The following two songs "I Get a Kick Out of You," from *Anything Goes* (1934), and "Nobody's Chasing Me," from *Out of This World* (1950), illustrate Porter's you-don't-love-me

* "ambassador" with an Oxford accent
† Cockney for "take"

syndrome. They are both graceful, they eschew a feeling of depression, and yet they clearly tell of unrequited love. The flowing rhythms and the amusing rhymes are employed to maintain a breezy feeling in the face of unhappy sentiments.

"I GET A KICK OUT OF YOU"

VERSE
My sto(1)ry is much too sad to be told(2),
But practic'ly ev'rything leaves me to(1)tally cold(2).
The only exception I know(1) is the case(3)
When I'm out on a quiet spree(4)
Fighting vainly the old ennui(4),
And suddenly turn and see(4)
Your fabulous face(3).

CHORUS
I get no kick from champagne(5),
Mere alcohol(6) doesn't thrill me at all(6),
So tell me why should it be true(7),
That I get a kick out of you(7)?

Some(8) get a kick from(8) cocaine(5).
I'm sure that if(9)
I had even one sniff(9)
It would bore me te*rrif*(9)ic'lly, too(7),
Yet I get a kick out of you(7).

I get a kick ev'ry time I see(4)
You're standing there before(10) me(4).
I get a kick tho' it's clear to me(4)
You obviously don't adore(10) me(4).

I get no kick in a plane(5),
Fly(11)ing too(7) high(11) with some guy(11) in the sky(11)
Is my(11) i(11)dea of nothing to do(7).
Yet I(11) get a kick out of you(7).

In the two-line opening of this verse there are two end rhymes, but also two eye rhymes, *sto*ry and *to*tally, which are juxtaposed with the perfect end rhymes "told" and "cold."

Also note that the ō sound is reiterated often throughout the entire lyric. In addition to the four instances pointed out above, Porter also wrote in the verse: *o*n(ly), know, *o*ld, *yo*ur, and in the chorus:

(A1) line 1—*no*
line 2—alc*o*hol
line 3—*So*

(A2) line 1—c*o*caine
line 4—b*o*re

(B) line 2—be*fo*re
line 3—*tho'*
line 4—ad*o*re

(A) line 1—*no*

In the final A section the long *i* sound takes over and we hear: fly, high, guy, sky, my, *i*(dea). Note that the first lines of all three A sections rhyme: champagne, cocaine, plane. The continuous and intricate assonances make an interesting fabric of music throughout. Also note Porter's careful consideration in the musical setting of words with abrupt consonant endings, which are always to be sung briefly: kick (eight times), sniff, *terrific'*-lly. Note also the consistency of the triple rhymes of the verse (lines 4, 5, and 6): spree, ennui, see. The pattern is repeated in A2: if, sniff, ter*rif*ic'lly, and again (plus added fireworks) in the last A, in line 2: high, guy, sky.

"NOBODY'S CHASING ME"

The breeze is chasing the zephyr,
The moon is chasing the sea,
The bull is chasing the heifer,
But nobody's chasing me.

The flood is chasing the levee,
The chimp some champ chimpanzee,
The Ford is chasing the Chevvy,
But nobody's chasing me.

Nobody wants to own me,
And I object.
Nobody wants to phone me,
Even collect!

The dove each moment is bolder,
The lark sings "Ich Liebe Dich,"
Tristan is chasing Isolde,
But nobody's chasing mich.

The cock is chasin' the chicken,
The pee-wee some wee pee-wee,
The cat is takin' a lickin',
But nobody's takin' me.

The snake with passion is shakin'
The pooch is chasin' the flea,
The moose his love call is makin',
But nobody's makin' me.

Each night I get the mirror
From off the shelf
Each night I'm getting nearer
Chasing myself!

The clams are almost a mixin',
The hams are chasing T.V.,
The fox is chasing the vixen,
But nobody's fixin' me.

The llama's chasing the llama,
Pa-pa is chasing ma-ma,
Monsieur is chasing madame,
But nobody's chasing moi.

While Isis chases Osiris,
And Pluto, Proserpine,
My doc is chasing my virus,
But nobody's chasing me.

I'd like to learn Canasta,
Yet how can I?
What wife without her "masta"
Can multiply?

The rain's pursuing the roses,
The snow, the trim Christmas tree,
Big dough pursues Grandma Moses,
But no one's pursuing me!
Nobody!
Nobody's chasing me!

The rhymes here are obvious, but what is less so is the nearly incredible list of *k* sounds throughout: obje*c*-t, colle*c*-t, Di*ch*, mi*ch*, *cock*, *chick*en, *c*at, li*ck*in', ta*k*in', sna*k*e, sha*k*in', *c*all, ma*k*in' (twice), *c*lams, mi*x*in', fo*x*, vi*x*en, fi*x*in'. Twenty times within six quatrains!

In contrast to the two preceding songs the next three concern *fulfilled* love. This sentiment in Porter lyrics is rare.

"You Don't Remind Me" from *Out of This World* (1950) is an oblique love song. "Love" is mentioned only once.

"YOU DON'T REMIND ME"

You don't remind me
Of the iris in Spring,
Or of dawn on the mountain
When the bluebird starts to sing.

You don't remind me
Of the breeze on the bay,
Or of stars in the fountain,
Where the silver fishes play.

To the moonglow
In September,
You reveal no resemblance.
Of the first snow
In November,
You've not even a semblance!

No, you don't remind me
Of the world around me, or behind me,
For so much does my love for you blind me,
That, my darling, you only remind me
Of you, of you, of you!

In "I Love You" from *Mexican Hayride* (1943) note the consistent phrase transposition in both first lines of the two-quatrain verse: "If a love song I could only write" and "But alas, just an amateur am I." Note the tricky rhymes in the chorus. In the first section there are triple outer rhymes in lines 1, 3, and 4. In the second stanza the triple rhymes are *interior* rhymes as in lines 1, 2, and 3. The lyric form is unusual because it is uneven. Porter made it fit quite easily into the usual eight-bar musical phrases. The consistent presence of clichés was undoubtedly intentional: consent to be mine, April breeze, golden dawn, birds on the wing, old melody, and so on.

"I LOVE YOU"

If a love song I could only write(1),
A song with words and music divine(2),
I would serenade you ev'ry night(1),
'Til you'd relent(3) and consent(3) to be mine(2).
But alas, just an amateur am I(4),
And so I'll not be surprised, my dear(5),
If you smile and politely pass it by(4),
When this, my first love song, you hear(5) . . .

"I love you," hums the April breeze(6) . . .
"I love you," echo the hills(7)!
"I love you," the golden dawn agrees(6)
As once more she sees(6) daffodils(7).

It's Spring(8) again
And birds on the wing(8) again

Start to sing(8) again
The old melody(9) . . .
"I love you!"
That's the song of songs(10) and it all belongs(10) to you and
  me(9)!

In "Only Another Boy and Girl" from *Seven Lively Arts*
(1944) the rhymes are incredibly complex and fascinating.

"ONLY ANOTHER BOY AND GIRL"

To be in love is so new(1) to me,
It's difficult to believe(2)
That it hasn't been(3) an original sin(3) since the days of Adam
  and Eve(2).

I can't explain what you do(1) to me,
But I know that now we've combined(4),
Ev'ry hour is so breath-taking(5),
So soul-shaking(5), so epoch-making(5),
That it's mighty hard to bear in mind(4) . . .

We're only another boy and girl,
We're only two(1) kids in love(6).
Folks who(1)'ve been through(1) the mill(7),
Say our chances are nil(7), but we'll still(7) climb our hill(7)
Hand in glove(6).

We're only another Spring romance,
But baby, we'll see it through(1)!
We're only another boy and girl,
But we'll God-bless our break(8),
Take a lot more pains than our elders take(8),
And make(8) love's young dream come true(1).

In "Don't Look at Me That Way," from *Paris* (1928), in
addition to the perfect rhymes, there is a continuous use of ō
sounds:

line 1: oh and so	l. 22: *nobody's*
l. 7: so and *those*	l. 25: home
l. 8: *forget*	l. 26: don't
l. 9: so	l. 28: don't, hold
l. 11: *ado*re and *your*	l. 29: don't
l. 12: *your*	l. 31: won't
l. 13: don't	l. 32: don't
l. 14: *your*	l. 35: show
l. 15: oh, so	l. 36: *hocus pocus*
l. 16: don't	l. 37: *focus*
l. 20: *those*	l. 39: propose
l. 21: *your*	l. 42: don't

It's difficult to believe in thirty accidents.

"DON'T LOOK AT ME THAT WAY"

Oh, I'm so mad(1) about the lad(1) it's too deep to express(2),
And when he tries(3) to use his eyes(3) he has instant success(2).
So full of passions those pupils(4) are
That girls forget what their scruples(4) are,
So when he tur(5)ns them on me(6),
I mur(5)mur tenderly(6) . . .
"I just adore your loving arms(7),
In fact, they're two of your greatest charms(7),
But don't look at me that way!

"Your peepers, too, are heavenly(6),
And oh, so full of variety(6),
But don't look at me that way!

"When you tell me sweetly(6)
You're mine completely(6)
I always give a long cheer(8) . . .
But those sudden flashes(9)
Behind your lashes(9)
Are nobody's business, dear(8)!

"I feel a thrill when you arrive(10)
And when I'm with you, I simply thrive(10),
But if you want to get home alive(10),
Don't look at me that way!"

"I think you're great, I think you're grand(11),
And I don't mind if you hold my hand(11),
But don't look at me that way!

"I'm very mild and very meek(12),
My will is strong but my won't(13) is weak(12),
So don't(13) look at me that way!

When that strange expression(14)
Of indiscretion(14)
Begins to show in your stare(15),
There's a hocus(16) pocus(16)
About your focus(16)
That gives me a terrible scare(15).

"When you propose, the altar calls(17)
And I start living in marble halls(17) . . .
But 'til we get to Niagara Falls(17),
Don't look at me that way!"

Although the style of music invariably indicates its age
(usually by decades), words have such specific meanings that
the young listener or reader does not understand references to
people in time past or, if they are old enough, they recognize
them as belonging to an earlier period.

This use of proper names belonging to earlier eras or references to once-famous events or situations is one thing of which
writers of plays, librettos, and lyrics have become more acutely
aware. Their use helps to create an insurmountable problem
relevant to reviving once-successful musicals of which only the
scores are today understandable.

The three following songs are in this sense period pieces.
Only "Love for Sale" needs no footnotes and it is the one of the
three songs in which no proper names occur.

I would qualify "I've Still Got My Health," from *Panama
Hattie* (1940), as a period piece because of its use of proper
names. "Mrs. Astor" (today, which *one*?) hasn't been called just
that for at least three decades. Lucius Beebe flourished in the
thirties. Minsky's burlesque was banished in 1939 when Billy
Rose was at the height of his career.

"I'VE STILL GOT MY HEALTH"

I wasn't born to stately halls(1) of alabaster(2),
I haven't given any balls(1) for Mrs. Astor(2) . . .
But all the same, I'm in the pink(3),
My constitution's made of zinc(3),
And you never have to give this goil(4)
Oil(4)
Castor(2)!

I'm always a flop(5) at a top(5)-notch affair(6),
But I've still got my health, so what do I care(6)?
My best ring, alas(7), is a glass(7) solitaire(6),
But I've still got my health, so what do I care?

By fashion and fopp'ry(8)
I'm never discussed(9),
Attending the op'ry(8)
My box would be a bust(9)!

When I give a tea(10) Lucius Bee(10)be ain't there(6),
But I've still got my health, so what do I care(6)?

The hip that I shake(11) doesn't make(11) people stare(6),
But I've still got my health, so what do I care(6)?

The sight of my props(12) never stops(12) thoroughfare(6),
But I've still got my health, so what do I care?
I knew I was slipping(13)
At Minsky's one dawn(14) . . .
When I started stripping(13),
They hollered, "Put it on(14)!"

Just once, Billy Rose(15) let me pose(15) in the bare(6),
But I've still got my health, so what do I care(6)?

In "Love for Sale," from *The New Yorkers* (1930), note the deliberate repetition of words: "heavy" twice in stanza 1 and "wayward ways" and "wayward" in stanza 2. This powerful song was written shortly after the Great Depression began.

"LOVE FOR SALE"

When the only sound in the empty street
Is the heavy tread of the heavy feet
That belong to a lonesome cop, I open shop.
When the moon so long has been gazing down
On the wayward ways of this wayward town
That her smile becomes a smirk, I go to work.

Love for sale,
Appetizing young love for sale,
Love that's fresh and still unspoiled,
Love that's only slightly soiled,
Love for sale.

Who will buy?
Who would like to sample my supply?
Who's prepared to pay the price
For a trip to Paradise?
Love for sale.

Let the poets pipe of love
In their childish way,
I know ev'ry type of love
Better far than they.

If you want the thrill of love,
I've been through the mill of love;
Old love, new love,
Ev'ry love but true love.

Love for sale,
Appetizing young love for sale.
If you want to buy my wares,
Follow me and climb the stairs,
Love for sale.

"Let's Fly Away," also from *The New Yorkers*, has a strong sense of unreality. It is about money at a time, one year after the Great Crash, when few people had any. I would call attention to the overall six rhymes/assonances and the tricky rhymes in the second and third lines before the end.

"LET'S FLY AWAY"

Let's fly away(1)
And find a land that's warm and tropic(3),
Where Roosevelt is not the topic(3),
All the livelong day(1).

Let's fly away(1)
And find a land that's so provincial(4)
We'll never hear what Walter Winchell(4)
Might be forced to say(1).

I'll make(7) your life sublime(5),
Far across the blue(6).
I'll take(7) up all your time(5),
Compromising you.(6)

Let's not delay(1)!
Make Mother Nature our messiah(2)!
New York is not for us, let's fly a(2)way(1)!

There is ample evidence to indicate Porter's disregard for money; nothing so ordinary could stand in the way of romance. This would seem to imply that, even in the Depression years when these songs were written, he had no need to consider it, having no financial worries, and that the world he inhabited was a thoroughly unreal storybook world. And these *were* the same days when, especially in New York, we had breadlines, apple sellers on street corners, and so on. These facts of life triggered other writers in other ways: Harburg, for example, wrote "Brother, Can You Spare a Dime?"

"Love for Sale" seems to have contained Porter's sole nod to the economic situation of the thirties, although "Gigolo" and the other songs about money-grabbing such as "I've Come to Wive It Wealthily in Padua" and "Always True to You in My Fashion" are songs that illustrate need, however playfully Porter expressed it.

Porter's use of the image of money in his lyrics was both playful and serious, the latter illustrated by "Love for Sale." The following selection takes note of some more playful aspects, although the pressure of necessity can often be found lurking.

In addition to the indicated rhymes, I should like to call attention to the strong use of the long *ā* sound: *pla*ces, *bra*ces, *la*bor, *la*dies, *fa*ces, *ba*by, *fa*ded, *tai*lors, *wa*y. This song and "Love for Sale" are two that particularize the singer. The character here, besides being a gigolo, tells us he is homosexual.

"I'M A GIGOLO"

I should like you all to know(1)
I'm a famous gigolo(1),
And of lavender my nature's got just a dash in it(2).
As I'm slightly undersexed(3),
You will always find me next(3)
To some dowager who's wealthy rather than passionate(2).
Go to one of those night club places(4)
And you'll find me stretching my braces(4),
Pushing ladies with lifted faces(4)
'Round the floor(5).

But I must confess to you(6)
There are moments when I'm blue(6)
And I ask myself whatever I do(6) it for(5).

I'm a flower that blooms in the winter,
Sinking deeper and deeper in "snow"(1).
I'm a baby who has(7)
No mother but jazz(7) . . .
I'm a gigolo(1).

Ev'ry morning when labor is o(1)ver,
To my sweet-scented lodgings I go(1) . . .
Take the glass from the shelf(8)
And look at myself(8) . . .
I'm a gigolo(1).

I get stocks and bonds(9)
From faded blondes(9)
Ev'ry twenty-fifth of December(10),
Still I'm just a pet(11)
That men forget(11)
And only tailors remember(10).

But when I see the way all the ladies
Treat their husbands who put up the dough(1),
You cannot think me odd(12)
If then, I thank God(12)
I'm a gigolo(1)!

"I've Come to Wive It Wealthily in Padua," from *Kiss Me Kate* (1949), evokes Shakespeare's era *(The Taming of the Shrew)* through the use of such words as zounds, loathsome, Gadzooks, good gad, oft, and honey nunny (for hey nonney).

"I'VE COME TO WIVE IT WEALTHILY IN PADUA"

I've come to wive it wealthily in Padua.
If wealthily, then happily, in Padua.
If my wife has a bag of gold(1),
Do I care if the bag be old(1)?
I've come to wive it wealthily in Padua(2)!

He's come to wive it wealthily in Padua!

I heard you mutter, "Zounds! A loathsome lad you ah(2)!"
I shall not be disturbed one bit(3),
If she be but a quarter-wit(3),
If she only can talk of clo'es(4)
While she powders her goddam nose(4)!
I've come to wive it wealthily in Padua(2)!

He's come to wive it wealthily in Padua!

I heard you say, "Gadzooks! Completely mad you ah(2)!"
'Twouldn't give me the slightest shock(5),
If her knees now and then should knock(5),
If her eyes were a wee bit crossed(6),
Were she wearing the hair she'd lost(6),
Still the damsel I'll make my dame(7) . . .
In the dark they are all the same(7)!
I've come to wive it wealthily·in Padua(2)!

He's come to wive it wealthily in Padua!

I heard you say, "Good gad(8), but what a cad(8) you ah(2)!"
Do I mind if she fret and fuss(9)?
If she fume like Vesuvius(9)?
If she roar like a winter breeze(10)
On the rough Adriatic seas(10)?
If she scream like a teething brat(11)?
If she scratch like a tiger cat(11)?
If she bite like a raging boar(12)?
I have oft stuck a pig before(12)!
I've come to wive it wealthily in Padua(2)!

With a honey nunny nunny(13) and a hey, hey, hey(14)!
Not to mention money, money(13), for a rainy day(14) . . .
I've come to wive it wealthily in Padua(2)!

In "Always True to You in My Fashion," from *Kiss Me Kate* (1949), the idea comes from Ernest Dowson: "I've been faithful to thee, Cynara! in my fashion." The rhymes are marked. I know of no other lyric in which the rhyme pattern set up by the writer was more strictly adhered to. The overall $\bar{a}$ assonance is heard *twenty* times—the last two provided near the end by translating faithful into fidèle.

"ALWAYS TRUE TO YOU IN MY FASHION"

If a custom-tailored vet(1)
Asks me out for something wet(1),
When the vet(1) begins to pet(1) I cry "Hooray(2)!"
But I'm always true to you, darlin', in my fashion,
Yes, I'm always true to you, darlin', in my way(2).

I enjoy a tender pass(3)
By the boss of Boston, Mass(3).
Though his pass(3) is middle-class(3) and not Back Bay(2),
But I'm always true to you, darlin', in my fashion,
Yes, I'm always true to you, darlin', in my way(2).

There's a mad man known as "Mac"(4)
Who is planning to attack(4).
If his mad attack(4) means a Cadillac(4), okay!(2)
But I'm always true to you, darlin',
In my fashion . . .
Yes, I'm always true to you, darlin', in my way(2).

I've been asked to have a meal(5)
By a big tycoon in steel(5).
If the meal(5) includes a deal(5), accept I may(2),
But I'm always true to you, darlin', in my fashion,
Yes, I'm always true to you, darlin', in my way(2).

I could never curl my lip(6)
To a dazzlin' diamond clip(6),
Though the clip(6) meant "let 'er rip(6)," I'd not say "nay(2),"
But I'm always true to you, darlin', in my fashion,
Yes, I'm always true to you, darlin', in my way(2).

There's an oil man known as "Tex"(10)
Who is keen to give me checks,(10)
And his checks, I fear, mean that sex(10) is here to stay(2),
But I'm always true to you, darlin',
In my fashion . . .
Yes, I'm always true to you, darlin', in my way(2).

From Ohio, Mister Thorn(7)
Calls me up from night to morn(7),

Mister Thorn once cornered corn(7) and that ain't hay(2),
But I'm always true to you, darlin', in my fashion,
Yes, I'm always true to you, darlin', in my way(2).

From Milwaukee, Mister Fritz(8)
Often moves me to the Ritz(8).
Mister Fritz(8) is full of Schlitz(8) and full of play(2),
But I'm always true to you, darlin', in my fashion,
Yes, I'm always true to you, darlin', in my way(2).

Mister Harris, plutocrat(9),
Wants to give my cheek a pat(9).
If a Harris pat means a Paris hat(9), Bébé(2)!
Mais, je suis toujours fidèle(2), darlin',
In my fashion,
Oui, je suis toujours fidèle(2), darlin', in my way(2)!

"Two Little Babes in the Wood" from *Paris* (1928) is a narrative ballad that, like "Jenny" by Ira Gershwin, is in story-book style, and consists of two verses and two choruses. It is curious that the verses are each fourteen lines long and the choruses only nine lines. This pattern, unusual today, was quite common in Viennese operetta where verses were often two or three times longer than refrains.

"TWO LITTLE BABES IN THE WOOD"

There's a tale of two(1)
Little orphans who(1)
Were left in their uncle's care(2),
To be reared and ruled(3),
And properly schooled(3)
Till they grew(1) to be ladies fair(2).
But, oh, the luckless pair(2)!
For the uncle, he(4)
Was a cruel trustee(4);
And he longed to possess their gold(5);
So he led them thence(6)
To a forest dense(6),
Where he left them to die(7) of cold(5).
That, at least, is what we're told(5).

They were two little babes in the wood(8),
Two little babes, oh, so good(8)!
Two little hearts, two little heads(9),
Longed to be home in their two little beds(9).
So two little birds built a nest(10),
Where the two little babes went to rest(10),
While the breeze, hov'ring nigh(7),
Sang a last lullaby(7) to the two little babes in the wood.

They were lying there(2)
In the freezing air(2),
When fortunately there appeared(11)
A rich old man(12)
In a big sedan(12)
And a very, very fancy beard(11).
He saw those girls(13) and cheered(11)!
Then he drove them down(14)
To New York town(14),
Where he covered them with useful things(15),
Such as bonds and stocks(16)
And Paris frocks(16)
And Oriental pearls(13) on strings(15),
And a showcase full of rings(15)!

Now those two little babes in the wood(8)
Are the talk of the whole neighborhood(8),
For they've too many cars, too many clo'es(17),
Too many parties and too many beaus(17)!
They have learned that the Fountain of Youth(18)
Is a mixture of gin and vermouth(18) . . .
And the whole town's agreed(19)
That the last thing in speed(19)
Is the two little babes in the wood.

I should like to conclude this section on Cole Porter's lyrics with three songs that belong to no particular category, although each in its own way is related to one of those previously listed.

"Miss Otis Regrets" (1934), written for no show, is a lyric representative of black comedy. "Cherry Pies Ought to Be You" from *Out of This World* (1950) is an example of complex rhyming. This song is a love song that, as it develops, becomes playfully antithetical to all love songs. It also is a period piece by virtue of the names that must eventually lock it in: Super Chief drawing rooms, Eleanor, Errol Flynn, Truman's Bess, Milton Berle.

"It's Delovely," from *Red, Hot and Blue* (1936), like many other songs evokes an echo of Noël Coward. It is a narrative ballad that tells of an affair, a marriage, and a birth. One of its chief features is its progressive and playful lengthening of the title line. Note the created word "tin-pantithesis," which tacitly explains itself, and the seemingly pointless mixture of senseless but amusing dialects at the end of the second chorus. Incidentally, this song is one of several in which Porter reemploys the champagne-plane rhyme.

In the second refrain I should point out the succession of three *ee* sounds in one phrase: seems, sweet, we. In the same refrain there is a formidable parade of *p* sounds: proud, parson, plopped, perch, peeling. Porter again used *p* sounds near the very end of the song: appears, appalling, appealing, polywog, paragon, Popeye, panic, pip.

"MISS OTIS REGRETS"

Miss Otis regrets she's unable to lunch today,
Madam.
Miss Otis regrets she's unable to lunch today.
She is sorry to be delayed,
But last evening down in Lover's Lane she strayed,
Madam.
Miss Otis regrets she's unable to lunch today.

When she woke up and found that her dream of love was gone,
Madam,
She ran to that man who had led her so far astray,
And from under her velvet gown,
She drew a gun and shot her lover down,
Madam.
Miss Otis regrets she's unable to lunch today.

When the mob came and got her and dragged her from the jail,
Madam,
They strung her up on that old willow across the way,
And the moment before she died,
She lifted up her lovely head and cried . . .
Madam . . .
"Miss Otis regrets she's unable to lunch today."

"CHERRY PIES OUGHT TO BE YOU"

HE   Oh, by Jove and by Jehovah(1),
You have set my heart aflame(2)!
SHE   And to you, you Casanova(1),
My reaction is the same(2)!
HE   I would sing thee tender verses,
But the flair, alas, I lack(3).
SHE   Aw, go on and try(4) to versify(4), and I(4)'ll versify(4) back(3)!

Cherry pies(5) ought to be you . . .
Autumn skies(5) ought to be you . . .
Romeo in disguise(5) . . .
Mister Pulitzer's prize(5) . . .
Ought to be you!
Columbine(6) ought to be you . . .
Sparkling wine(6) ought to be you . . .
All of Beethoven's nine(6) . . .
Ev'ry Will Shakespeare line(6) . . .
Ought to be you!
You are so enticing(7),
I'm starting to shake(8).
You are just the icing(7)
To put on my cake(8).
To continue(9),
Heaven's blue(9) ought to be you(9) . . .
Heaven, too(9), ought to be you(9) . . .
Ev'rything su(9)per-do(9)ought to be you(9)!

French perfumes(10) ought to be you . . .
Texas booms(10) ought to be you . . .
Early Egyptian tombs(10) . . .
Super Chief drawing rooms(10) . . .
Ought to be you!

Sweet Snow White(11) ought to be you . . .
Ambrose Light(11) ought to be you . . .
Eleanor, wrong or right(11) . . .
Errol Flynn, loose or tight(11) . . .
Ought to be you!

You may come a cropper(12)
You're losing your breath(13)
Were I not so proper(12),
I'd squeeze you to death(13)!
To continue(9),
Tru(9)man's Bess(14) ought to be you(9) . . .
His success(14) ought to be you(9) . . .
All except Tru(9)man's press(14) ought to be you(9)!

Shootin' pains(15) ought to be you . . .
Addled brains(15) ought to be you . . .
Florida when it rains(15) . . .
Pinchers in subway trains(15) . . .
Ought to be you!

Withered grass(16) ought to be you . . .
Lethal gas(16) ought to be you . . .
Sour old apple sass(16) . . .
Gabby old Balaam's ass(16) . . .
Ought to be you!

You, you look so fearful(17).
You give me the joiks(18)!

Kid, if you ain't "keerful(17),"
I'll give you the woiks(18)!
To continue(9),
Horse meat steak(8) ought to be you . . .
Pickled snake(8) ought to be you . . .
Ev'rything I can't take(8) ought to be you(9)!

Corn that's tough(19) ought to be you . . .
In the rough(19) ought to be you . . .
Ev'ry old powder puff(19) . . .
Ev'rything not enough(19) . . .
Ought to be you!

No one's bride(20) ought to be you . . .
No one's pride(20) ought to be you . . .
Just an old chicken fried(20) . . .
Cyanide(20) on the side(20) . . .
Ought to be you!

That's the darndest get-up(21)
That I've seen in years(22)!
Kid, if you don't shet up(21),
I'll pull off your ears(22)!

To continue(9),
No one's girl(23) ought to be you . . .
Milton Berle(23) ought to be you . . .
Salad with castor erl(23) ought to be you!

"IT'S DELOVELY"

I feel a sudden urge to sing(1)
The kind of ditty that invokes the Spring(1),
So control your desire to curse(20),
While I crucify the verse(2)!

This verse I've started seems to me(3)
The tin-pantithesis of melody(3),
So to spare you all the pain(4),
I'll skip the darned thing(5)
And sing(5) the refrain(4) . . .
Mi mi mi mi(3),
Re re re re(6),
Do sol mi do la si(3),
Take it away(6)!

The night(7) is long, the skies are clear(8),
And if you want to go walking, dear(8)
It's delight(7)ful, it's delicious, it's delovely(3)!

I understand the reason why(9)
You're sentimental, 'cause so am I(7) . . .
It's delightful, it's delicious, it's delovely(3)!

You can tell(10) at a glance(11)
What a swell(10) night this is for romance(11),
You can hear(8) dear(8) Mother Nature murmurin' low(12):
"Let yourself go(12)!"
So(12) . . .
Please be sweet, my chickadee(3),
And when I kiss you, just say to me(3),
"It's delightful, it's delicious, it's delectable,
It's delirious, it's dilemma, it's delimit, it's deluxe, it's delovely(3)!"

Time marches on(13) and soon it's plain(4)

You've won(13) my heart and I've lost my brain(4),
It's delightful, it's delicious, it's delovely(3)!

Life see(3)ms so swee(3)t that we(3) decide(14)
It's in the bag to get unified(14)
It's delightful, it's delicious, it's delovely(3)!

See that crowd(15) in the church(16),
See that proud(15) parson plopped on his perch(16),
Get the sweet(17) beat(17) of that organ pealing our
    doom(18) . . .
Here goes the groom(18)!
Boom(18)!

How they cheer and how they smile(19),
As we go gallop(20)ing down the aisle(19),
It's divine, dear, it's diveen, dear, it's duh vunderbar,
It's duh victory, it's duh vallop(20), it's duh vinner,
It's duh voiks,
It's delovely!

The knot is tied and so we take(21)
A few hours off to eat wedding cake(21),
It's delightful, it's delicious, it's delovely!

It feels fine to be a bride(14),
And how's the groom? Why, he's slight(7)ly fried(14)!
It's delight(7)ful, it's delicious, it's delovely!

To the pop(22) of champagne(23),
Off we hop(22) in our plush little plane(23),
'Til a bright(7) light(7) through the darkness cozily calls(24) . . .
"Niag'ra Falls(24)!"
All's(24)

Well, my love, our day's complete(17),
And what a beautiful bridal suite(17)!
It's dr-reamy, it's dr-rousy, it's de-reverie,(3)
It's de-rhapsody, it's de-regal, it's de-royal.
It's de-Ritz,
It's delovely(3)!

We settle down as man and wife(25)
To solve the riddle called "married life(25),"
It's delightful, it's delicious, it's delovely!

We're on the crest, we have no cares(26),
We're just a couple of honey bears(26),
It's delight(7)ful, it's delicious, it's delovely!

All's as right(7) as can be(3),
'Til one night(7) at my window I see(3)
An absurd(27) bird(27) with a bu(31)ndle hu(31)ng on his
    nose(28) . . .
"Get baby clo'es(28)!"
Those(28)
Eyes(29) of yours are filled with joy(30)
When Nurse appears and cries(29), "It's a boy(30)!"
He's appalling, he's appealing, he's a polywog,
He's a paragon, he's Popeye, he's a panic,
He's a pip,
He's delovely(3)!

Cole Porter's contribution to musical theatre is unique in that it defines a style that is exclusively Porter's and, taken as a whole, it describes its creator's life-style in both subtle and obvious ways. For the most part his lyrics are designed for fun and his achievement is lasting.

Courtesy ASCAP

Lorenz Hart (1895–1943)

I can think of no better way to begin this section than to quote phrases from the foreword to the *Rodgers and Hart Song Book* by Oscar Hammerstein II.

> The essence of the work they [Rodgers and Hart] did together was its youth . . . a couple of lively New York kids, products of their town and their time.

> The quick rise of Rodgers and Hart is a perfect illustration of how eagerly the public runs to meet something new and good, surfeited as they are with stale and imitative professionalism.

Hammerstein described Hart as "skipping and bouncing . . . alert and dynamic and fun to be with."

This writer knew Larry Hart slightly near the end of his too short and unhappy life when he was morose and tearful, the antithesis of the bright witty lyricist who, full of romantic emotionalism, was in his work also "skipping and bouncing."

His wit, accomplished through tremendous skill and complemented by soaring melodies that Rodgers invariably provided, always hit its target head on. And in no way did its profound craftsmanship ever interfere with the ideas and the feelings inherent in the songs. Cleverness, in one form or another, was ever present but it could easily be overlooked—at least momentarily—because what Hart had to say basically superseded his ingenious manner of saying it.

The lightheartedness of a great many of Hart's lyrics is a clue to his real character: they expressed his inner dreamworld. More often, they reflected the unrestrained happiness of youth, which was incapable of accepting disappointment and frustra-

tion. Sometimes, in more reflective moments, these lyrics mirrored the unhappiness that I personally find in many of them. Even so, Hart's manner of stating this frustration made it shine on the surface while suggesting suffering on the inside. One example of such a complex mélange of feeling is to be observed in

> Here in my arms it's adorable!
> It's deplorable
> That you were never there.

Hart was born in 1895 and died forty-eight years later, leaving the world a poorer place. While he lived, he was Richard Rodgers's sole collaborator. Their first published song, "Any Old Place with You," appeared in 1919. Rodgers was seventeen, Hart twenty-four. Their first score *You'd Be Surprised,* for amateur production, appeared the following year. Their first professional show after four amateur productions was *Poor Little Ritz Girl,* which also appeared in 1920. Lew Fields (Weber and Fields) was the producer. Rodgers shared the music with Sigmund Romberg, and Hart shared lyric honors with Alex Gerber. Rodgers and Hart wrote twenty-eight musicals together for the stage and eight for films, one play (also collaborating with Herbert Fields), and one nightclub score.

In 1925, the year of the first *Garrick Gaieties* that was destined to focus attention on the young new writing team of Rodgers and Hart, the approaching thirty-year-olds already with amateur productions to their credit and two professional shows also wrote *Dearest Enemy,* with a book by Herbert Fields.

I should like to begin this section by quoting Hart's lyrics for one of the team's indestructible songs, "Here in My Arms."

One of the outstanding features of the lyrics is the totally unexpected emergence of the subject matter in the *third* line of the refrain. The song has begun with an eight line verse, which says telescopically:

I know a merry place

. . . .

But it's new to you.

The chorus begins "Here in my arms [the place] it's adorable!" but in the third line we are stunned with ". . . you were never there." This is the most original way I've ever heard of a love song's revelation of an unrequited affair. In a sense it's a heartbreaker because it is idiot-bright in the face of nothingness.

Already in 1925 Hart was a magician with complex rhyming. "Here in My Arms" consists of two verses and chorus.

A rhyme factor that Hart employs elsewhere ("Ten Cents a Dance," for instance) is the use of two adjacent words each of which rhymes with a word in the preceding line and in the line ahead of that.

"Only air" rhymes with "lonely" and "share"—occurring in three consecutive lines.

It should also be noted that many of the rhyme words, especially in the two verses, are penultimate rather than the more usual ultimate (end line) words.

"HERE IN MY ARMS"

VERSE ONE
I know a merry(1) place
Far from intrusion(2).
It's just the very(1) place
For your seclusion(2).
There you(3) can while(4) away
Days as you smile(4) away,
It's not a mile(4) away
But it's new(3) to you(3).

REFRAIN
Here in my arms it's adorable(5)!
It's deplorable(5)
That you were never there(6).
When little lips are so kissable(7)
It's permissible(7)
For me to ask my share(6)
Next to my heart it is ever so lonely(8),
I'm holding only(8) air(6),
While here in my arms it's adorable(5)!
It's deplorable(5)
That you were never there(6).

VERSE TWO
I know a pretty(9) place,
At your command(10), sir;
It's not a city(9) place,
Yet near(11) at hand(10), sir;
Here(11), if you loll away,
Two(3) hearts can toll(12) away.
You'd never stroll(12) away,
If you(3) only knew(3)!

REFRAIN

The *Garrick Gaieties* "Opening," also in 1925, presents an extraordinary labyrinth of rhymes that go merrily on their way, in spite of a very solid form and thoroughly appropriate content.

The verse tells the audience at once "We bring drama to your great metropolis" and it concludes with "Each son of us/ Will welcome you at the gate!"

It should be recalled that this show was a kind of Off Broadway weekend bonus for patrons of the new Theatre Guild. No one suspected remotely that it might be a hit and enjoy a respectable run. It was and it did.

The sense of the opening verse—addressed directly as it is to the audience—betrays signs of youth, but its lyrical execution is complex and masterful.

The form is unusual and purposeful. The verse introduces the show and welcomes the audience. This is followed by three patters. The first deals with one fellow Off Broadway theatre, the Neighborhood Playhouse, which produced serious plays not yet seen in commercial houses. The theatre, situated on Grand Street, reflected the taste of its founders, Irene and Alice Lewisohn, who not only produced plays but dance productions, oriental mélanges, pantomimes, and so on. Ultrasophisticated audiences came from "uptown" while the residents of Grand Street—largely poor immigrants—had little if any connection with what went on inside the Grand Street Playhouse. All of this is referred to in the first patter.

The second concerns the Provincetown Playhouse, which eventually evolved into the Theatre Guild. There Eugene O'Neill's plays were first unveiled and the great designer-theatremind Robert Edmond Jones was an influential mentor.

The third patter concerns the Actors Theatre where important and experimental plays could be seen, where the then-current lightweight "bedroom dramas" were eschewed. (An added feature of these lyrics is the offering of "subscription blanks.")

The closing section of this long and fascinating lyric is a chorus: the raison d'être and the least significant part of the whole—a light brouhaha extolling the *Garrick Gaieties'* producer, the Theatre Guild.

In this lyric the fusion of history, deft wit, and a show's opening statement is prodigious.

GARRICK GAIETIES "OPENING"

At rise: Three men are pacing the back curtains, turn toward the audience as they begin.

ALL THREE
We bring drama to your great metropolis(1),
We are the little theatre group(2).
Each of us has built a small acropolis(1)
To hold our little theatre troupe(2).
We'll be very glad to meet(3) you, to greet(3) you, to seat(3) you,
And treat(3) you just great(4),
Help us save the art of your cosmopolis(1)
If you'll be one(5) of us
Each son(5) of us
Will welcome you at the gate(4)!
THE PROVINCETOWN PLAYHOUSE
The Provincetown Playhouse still owns(6)

The art of Robert Edmond Jones(6);
From the classic drama we're a notable secessionist(7)!
The verity of Gene O'Neill,
Then meaning doesn't matter if the manner is expressionist(7);
Our greatest contribution(8)
To art is revolution(8),
Our mood is very Rooshin(8),
You can tell it at a glance(9);
Our bare stage may look funny(10),
But it saves us lots of money(10),
And we're sure of what we do
Because we always take a chance(9).

THE NEIGHBORHOOD PLAYHOUSE

The Neighborhood Playhouse can shine(11)
South of the Macy-Gimbel line(11),
It was built to make a ride for people on Fifth Avenue(12)!
To Yeats, and Synge, and Shaw, and such(13),
We add an Oriental touch(13);
We bring out the aesthetic soul that you don't know you have in you(12)

We like to serve a mild dish(14)
Of folk-lore, quaintly childish(14)
And sometimes, Oscar Wildish(14)
In a pantomime or dance(4);
Grand Street folk, we never see 'em(15).
They think the building's a museum(15),
And we don't know what we do(12),
But then we like to take a chance(9).

THE ACTOR'S THEATRE

For your attention, many thanks(16);
I've brought along subscription blanks(16)
For the Actor's Theatre where the audience can glory in(17)
The dear old Servant In The House(18),
The pride of Mister Rankin Towse(18),
And plays of Henrik Ibsen in a manner quite Victorian(17);
We spurn the bedroom dramas(19)
With heroes in pajamas(19)
For things that pleased our mamas(19),
Such as Candida's romance(9);
We wear our sock and buskin(20)
To the taste of dear John Ruskin(20),
And we're sure of what we do
Because we never take a chance(9).

CHORUS

Gilding the Guild!
Gilding the Guild!
We possess a fine artistic touch(13);
Money doesn't count—not much(13)!
Shubert may say(21)
Art doesn't pay(21),
But we built that cozy little shack(22)
Though we lack(22)
Shubert's jack(22)
In this cute little building(23)
We're gilding(23) the Guild!
(A Girl steps out from Center, and begins:)

GIRL

We suppose you wonder(24)—
Wonder what in thunder(24)
This revue is all about(25).
If this entertainment(26)
Is for art or gain meant(26)

We'll remove your ev'ry doubt(25).
When summer comes we get mutinous(26),
And it's very cute in us(26).
Promise you won't begin shootin' us(26)
If we start stepping out(25)!

CHORUS

Poor old Guild, no one talks about us(27)!
Critics never make a big fuss(27)!
Aleck Woollcott's a cagey old bird(30),
He never gives us a word(30)!
We complain we only can get(31)
More subscribers than the Met(31)ropolitan.
Shows may crash(32),
The Guild has got your cash(32).
If the show(33) is slow(33) you can look at the building(23).
We're gilding(23) the Guild!

In the same *Garrick Gaieties* (1925), Rodgers and Hart created one of their all-time hits, "Manhattan," a jaunty song with a single verse and four choruses. Again, the subject matter comes in the verse. This is a happy song about youth. The verse establishes the couple's decision to stay at home in New York for the summer. Chorus 1 extols the pleasure of New York. Chorus 2 includes an expedition to Greenwich and other nearby adventurous places. Chorus 3 visits still other spots in the vicinity. The final chorus (4) returns to Manhattan and nearer environs.

Many of the rhymes are mind-boggling. Among them "Manhattan—Staten," "what street—Mott Street," "Greenwich—men itch," and so on. Again, Hart employs two consecutive words to rhyme separately with two preceding words. "Abie's Irish Rose" goes with "babies" earlier in the same line and "see it close" in the following one.

It is interesting to note that in each of the four choruses, the fourth from the final line concerns "the city."

1. "The great big city's a wond'rous toy"
2. "The city's bustle cannot destroy"
3. "The city's clamor can never spoil"
4. "But Civic Virtue cannot destroy"

All, of course, have "oi" diphthongs to rhyme with the oncoming "boy" and in 3, due to a transposition, "spoil" rhymes with "goil."

I'd like to point out a series of vowel rhymes in 2: (long *a*'s—bathe, bathing, make, take, Jam*ai*ca, Bay, Lake.

There is also a series of short *a* assonances in 2: *Jamaica, Canarsie, cannot, Manhattan.*

"MANHATTAN"

VERSE

Summer journey to Niag'ra(1),
And to other places aggra(1)vate all our cares(2);
We'll save our fares(2);
I've a cozy little flat in(3) what is known as old Manhattan(3),
We'll settle down(4) right here in town(4).

CHORUS ONE

We'll have Manhattan(3),
The Bronx and Staten(3) Island too(5);
It's lovely going through(5) the Zoo(5);
It's very fancy(6)
On old Delancey(6) Street, you know(7);

The subway charms us so(7),
When balmy breezes blow(7)
To and fro(7);
And tell me what street(8) compares with Mott Street(8) in
    July(9),
Sweet pushcarts gently gliding by(9);
The great big city's a wond'rous toy(10)
Just made for a girl and boy(10),
We'll turn Manhattan(3)
Into an(3) isle of joy(10).

CHORUS TWO
We'll go to Greenwich(11)
Where modern men itch(11)
To be(12) free(12);
And Bowling Green(12) you'll see(12) with me(12);
We'(12)ll bathe at Brighton(13),
The fish you'll frighten(13)
When you're in(14);
Your bathing suit so thin(14)
Will make the shell-fish grin(14)
Fin to fin(14);
I'd like to take a(15) sail on Jamaic(15)a Bay with you(16);
And fair Canarsie's Lake(15) we'll view(16);
The city's bustle cannot destroy(10)
The dreams of a girl and boy(10),
We'll turn Manhattan(3)
Into an isle of joy(10).

CHORUS THREE
We'll go to Yonkers(17)
Where true love conquers(17)
In the wilds(18);
And starve together, dear in Childs'(8)
We'll go to Coney(19)
And eat bologny(19) on a roll(20);
In Central Park, we'll stroll(20)
Where our first kiss we stole(20),
Soul to soul(20);
Our future babies(21) we'll take to Abie's(21) Irish Rose(22),
I hope they'll live to see it close(22);
The city's clamor can never spoil(23)
The dreams of a boy and goil(23),
We'll turn Manhattan(3)
Into an isle of joy(10).

CHORUS FOUR
We'll have Manhattan(3)
The Bronx and Staten(3) Island too(5);
We'll try to cross Fifth Avenue(5);
As black as onyx(24)
We'll find the Bronnix(24) Park Express(25);
Our Flatbush flat I guess(25)
Will be a great success(25).
More or less(25);
A short vacation(26)
On Inspiration(26) Point we'll spend(27)
And in the station(26) house we'll end(27)
But Civic Virtue cannot destroy(10)
The dreams of a girl and boy(10),
We'll turn Manhattan(3)
Into an isle of joy(10).

One year later Rodgers and Hart wrote the score for *The Girl*

Friend (1926). One of the hit songs, "Blue Room," consists of two verses and one chorus. This is another "young" song expressing elation over a happy life after marriage. The first two lines of the first verse announce the topic: "All my future plans,/ Dear, will suit your plans."

The twelve-line verse hasn't a single end rhyme, but a great many interior ones and a single first-word rhyme.

In verse 1 there is also a series of vowel rhymes: pan(try), planned, grand, can.

"BLUE ROOM"

VERSE ONE
HE   All my future(1) plans,
Dear(2), will suit your(1) plans,
Read the little blue(3) * prints;
Here(2)'s your mother's(4) room,
Here(2)'s your brother's(4) room,
On the wall are two(3) prints.
Here(2)'s the kiddies'(5) room,
Here(2)'s the biddy's(5) room,
Here(2)'s a pantry lined with shelves(6), dear,
Here(2) I've planned(7) for us,
Something grand(7) for us,
Where we two can be ourselves(6), dear;

REFRAIN
We'll have a blue(3) room,
A new(3) room,
For two(3) room,
Where ev'ry day's a holiday(8)
Because you're married to me(9).
Not like a ball(10) room
A small(10) room,
A hall(10) room,
Where I can smoke my pipe away(8),
With your wee(9) head upon my knee(9).
We will thrive on(11), keep alive on(11)
Just nothing but kisses(12),
With Mister and Missus(12)
On little blue(3) chairs(13).
You sew(14) your trou(3)sseau(14),
And Robinson Crusoe(14) is not so far from worldly cares(13)
As our blue(3) room far away upstairs(13)!

VERSE TWO
SHE   From all visitors(15)
And inquisitors(15),
We'll keep our apartment(16);
I won't change(17) your plans,
You arrange(17) your plans
Just the way your heart meant(16);
Here, we'll be(9) ourselves
And we'll see(9) ourselves
Doing all the(9) things we're scheming(18),
Here's a certain(19) place,
Cretonne(20) curtain(19) place,
Where no one(20) can see us dreaming(18):

REFRAIN REPEATED

* (3) rhymes with the first syllable of (1)

"Ten Cents a Dance" (1930) was Rodgers and Hart's direct observance of their times. Porter made his obeisance in "Love for Sale."

This is a bitter song. Its hard expressions of an unbearable life-style nevertheless are never self-pitying. This, in itself, is a large accomplishment.

Hart gives us one of his very best two-word rhymes here. "Hero" rhymes with two syllables of "queer romance." The final syllable alone rhymes two lines later with "dance."

There are fairly obscure vowel rhymes. In the patter there is a series of ō sounds: *chorus*, *beaux*, *porous* (a *real* rhyme), holes, toes, closing. This is followed and climaxed by "hero," which is an integral element in the unique perfect rhyme described above.

Also in the patter there is a considerable *k* sequence: tickets, luck, chorus, stockings, closing, thick, queer, come.

In the verse there are ēē rhymes: gee, sleep, and cheap, and teachers and features (perfect rhymes).

The song's form is verse, refrain, and patter, which concludes with the last section of the refrain.

In 1935 Billy Rose produced an enormous spectacle *Jumbo* at the Hippodrome with Jimmy Durante, Gloria Grafton, and Paul Whiteman and his Orchestra. The music and lyrics were by Rodgers and Hart. It is curious that such an enormous show should have included a song as tender and intimate as "Little Girl Blue." This is a truly sad song consisting of a refrain and interlude (trio) followed by a repeat of the refrain. The form of the latter is:

A1—12 bars
A2—11 bars
B—9 bars
A3—4 bars

The trio is in waltz time consisting of:

A1—8 bars
A2—9 bars
transition—8 bars

The title occurs during the final line of each of the three A sections of the refrain. With all the opulent rhyming, the opening refrain or chorus line, "Sit there and count your fingers," which occurs twice, is not rhymed.

In the refrain there are ten oō rhymes; several of these are repetitious and one which I would include is u/se. I feel that the vowel sounds clearly as a rhyme with the preceding "blue" and the musical setting makes us hear "u—seold girl." There are also four "ender" rhymes. The word "count" (unrhymed) is used four times.

"TEN CENTS A DANCE"

VERSE
I work at the Palace Ball(1)room,
But, gee, that palace is cheap(2);
When I get back to my chilly hall(1) room
I'm(3) much too tired to sleep(2),
I'm(3) one of those lady teachers(4)
A beautiful hostess, you know(5),
One that the palace features(4)
At exactly a dime(3) a throw(5).

REFRAIN
Ten cents a dance;
That's what they pay me(6).
Gosh, how they weigh me(6) down(7)!
Ten cents a dance,
Pansies and rough guys(8),
Tough guys(8) who tear my gown(7)!
Seven to midnight, I hear drums(9).
Loudly the saxophone blows(10).
Trumpets are tearing my eardrums(9).
Customers crush my toes(10).
Sometimes I think
I've found my hero(11)
But it's a queer ro(19)mance(12),
All that you need is a ticket;
Come on, big boy, ten cents a dance(12)!

PATTER
Fighters and sailors(13) and bowlegged tailors(13)
Can pay for their tickets and rent me(14)!
Butchers and barbers(15) and rats from the harbors(15)
Are sweethearts my good luck has sent me(14).
Though I've a chorus(16) of elderly beaux(17)
Stockings are porous(16) with holes(17) at the toes(17).
I'm here till clos(17)ing time(18),
Dance and be merry, it's only a dime(18).
Sometimes I think
I've found my hero(19)
But it's a queer ro(19)mance(12),
All that you need is a ticket!
Come on, big boy, ten cents a dance(12)!

"LITTLE GIRL BLUE"

REFRAIN
(A1) Sit there and count your fingers, what can you do(1)?
Old girl, you're through(1).
Sit there and count your little fingers,
Unlucky little girl blue(1).
(A2) Sit there and count the raindrops falling on you(1).
It's time you knew(1) all you can count on is the raindrops
That fall on little girl blue(1).
(B) No u(1)se, old girl, you may as well surrender(2).
Your hope is getting slender(2),
Why won't somebody send a(2) tender(2)
(A3) Blue(1) boy to cheer up little girl blue(1)?

INTERLUDE
When I was very young(3) the world was younger than I(4),
As merry as a carousel(5).
The circus tent was strung(3) with ev'ry star in the sky(4)
Above the ring I loved so well(5);
Now the young world has grown old(6).
Gone are the tinsel and gold(6).

REFRAIN REPEATED

Rodgers and Hart wrote a charming ballad for *Jumbo* called "There's a Small Hotel" but the producer, Billy Rose, thought it unsuitable and refused to keep it in the show. As this was during the height of American musical theatre development when songs had not yet begun to be written for specific characters in situations, "There's a Small Hotel" was easily inserted in the next Rodgers and Hart show *On Your Toes* the following year, 1936.

This song is indeed a charmer. It is impossible to disassociate the words from the music; each seems so irrevocably wedded to the other. The loving languorous mood seems to become a kind of ensign for happiness-in-love.

Though the mood is indeed languorous, Hart's lyrics are incredibly busy. Read them aloud without giving a thought to anything except mood and meaning. Then examine them for assonance and rhyme and see how complex they are. Such complexity cannot be the result of happenstance.

The form is verse, refrain, and refrain with coda (ending).

I would point out first an ingenious set of rhymes in the refrain, which has a melting transition to a different set. The $\overline{ee}$ sound of "suite," "neat," "complete," and "see" becomes "steeple," "people," and finally "sleep." However, "steeple" becomes coupled with "bell" in the process and "steeple bell" rhymes with "sleep well," which finally sheds "sleep," leaving "bell" to rhyme with "hotel" at the very end.* This development is astonishing. In addition, the same chorus has begun with "hotel—well" and so a long progression of rhymes has come full circle.

In the verse we find "(Ju)nior," "you," "(Ju)nior," and "two"—also "Frankie" and "One, Two, Three." Also in the verse we hear "where" three times and these become a rhyme with the first word of the chorus "There 'sa."

"THERE'S A SMALL HOTEL"

VERSE

SHE I'd like to get away(1), Ju(2)nior,
Somewhere alone with you(2).
It could be oh(3), so gay(1), Ju(2)nior!
You need a laugh or two(2).
HE A certain place I know(3), Frankie(4),
Where funny people can have fun.
That's where we two(2) will go(3), Darling,
Before you can count up One, Two, Three(4).

REFRAIN

There's a small hotel(5) with a wishing well(5);
I wish that we were there(6) together.
There's a bridal suite(7);
One room bright and neat(7), complete(7) for us to share(6) together.
Looking through the window you can see(8) a distant stee(8)ple(9);
Not a sign of peo(8)ple(9),
Who wants people(9)?
When the steeple(9) bell(5) says
"Goodnight, sleep well(5)," we'll thank the small hotel(5) together.

REFRAIN WITH CODA

There's a small hotel(5) with a wishing well(5);
I wish that we were there(6) together.
There's a bridal suite(7);
One room bright and neat(7), complete(7) for us to share(6) together.

---

* In the coda this is expanded by the additions of "creep" and "shell"!

Looking through the window you can see(8) a distant stee(8)ple(9);
Not a sign of people(9),
Who wants people(9)?
When the steeple(9) bell(5) says
"Goodnight, sleep(10) well(5)," we'll thank the small hotel(5) together.

CODA

We'll creep(10) into our little shell(5)
And we will thank the small hotel(5) together.

Babes in Arms (1937) contains a formidable list of—by now—standard songs, five of which I should like to examine here lyrically. First (and taken in no special order), there is "My Funny Valentine," a wistful love song, somewhat in the general category (as lyrics) with "Bill" from *Show Boat*, a decade earlier. In both songs the object of affection and devotion is not thought to be attractive or smart, but is especially loving.

A fun aspect of these otherwise simple lyrics is the use in the verse only of archaic and grandiose words: behold, doth, thou knowest not, vacant brow, thy, thou—coming to an end with slightly dopey gent, making it all a joke. The refrain lyrics make no reference to this archaism.

"MY FUNNY VALENTINE"

VERSE

Behold the way our fine feathered friend his virtue doth parade(1).
Thou knowest not, my dim-witted friend,
The picture thou(2) hast made(1),
Thy vacant brow(2) and thy tousled hair conceal thy good intent(3).
Thou noble, upright, truthful, sincere and slightly dopey gent(3), you're

REFRAIN

My funny Valentine,
Sweet comic Valentine,
You make me smile with my heart(4).
Your looks are laughable(5),
Unphotographable(5),
Yet you're my fav'rite work of art(4).
Is your figure less than Greek(5)?
Is your mouth a little weak(5), when you open it to speak(5),
Are you smart(4)?
But don't change a hair(6) for me,
Not if you care(6) for me,
Stay(7), little Valentine, stay(7)!
Each day(7) is Valentine's day(7).

"The Lady Is a Tramp" (also from *Babes in Arms)* is a "list" song, in that each of the refrains contains a long line of often disconnected reasons why the lady is a tramp.

Although the song (very lighthearted) seems to denigrate the "lady," it really makes her an adorable independent person who spurns "society" (the attitude opposite to Porter's) and all the things, places, customs, and habits that at the time were generally accepted as desirable.

Hart's made-up word "Hobohemia" should be elected to membership in the special vocabulary of Lewis Carroll.

The word "tramp" of the title occurs three times in each chorus and as in "My Heart Stood Still," Hart waits until the last one to rhyme it.

"THE LADY IS A TRAMP"

VERSE

I've wined(1) and dined(1) on mulligan stew(2)
And never wished for turkey(3);
As I hitched and hiked and drifted too(2) from Maine to Albuquerque(3).
Alas I missed the Beaux-Arts Ball and what is twice as sad(4),
I was never at a party where they honored Noel Ca'ad(4).
But social circles spin too fast for me(5),
My bohemia is the place to be(5).

REFRAIN

I get too hungry
For dinner at eight(6),
I like the theatre but never come late(6).
I never bother with people I hate(6),
That's why the lady is a tramp.
I don't(7) like crap-games
With Barons and Earls(8),
Won't(7) go to Harlem
In ermine and pearls(8)
Won't dish the dirt with the rest of the girls(8),
That's why the lady is a tramp.
I like the free fresh wind in my hair(9),
Life without care(9),
I'm broke(10), it's oke(10),
Hate California,
It's cold and it's damp(11),
That's why the lady is a tramp(11).

In "Where or When?," also from *Babes in Arms*, there is a kind of classical balance in the very first line of the verse in "things you think" and "dreams you dream." Not only do the phrases balance metrically but the repetition of the opening consonants in each *(th* twice and *d* twice) is also musically lovely.

The song is wistful and frustrated. The sentiment emerges strongly. The rhymes are of secondary and minor importance. The sense of sincerity and meaningfulness is paramount. *W* and *wh* sounds (the latter giving a feeling of breath exhalation) are heard frequently: we, where, (each three times), wearing, wore, awake, wings, what, way, when, were, who. There are also many word repetitions in the verse, which make for both economy and emphasis: think (twice), thought, things (three times), live, lived. In the chorus there are more of the same.

The sentiment—especially in the verse—is both general and philosophical (as opposed to specific), but it always holds the interest.

"WHERE OR WHEN?"

VERSE

When you're awake the things(1) you think come from the dreams you dream(2).
Thought has wings(1),
And lots of things(1) are seldom what they seem(2)
Sometimes you think you've lived before
All that you live today(3).

Things you do(4) come back to you(4),
As though they knew(4) the way(3).
Oh, the tricks your mind can play(3)!

REFRAIN

It seems we stood and talked like this before(5),
We looked at each other in the same way then(6),
But I can't remember where or when(6).
The clothes you're wearing are the clothes you wore(5).
The smile you are smiling you were smiling then(6),
But I can't remember where or when(6).
Some things that happen for the first time,
Seem to be happening again(6).
And so it seems that we have met before, and laughed before, and loved before(5),
But who knows where or when(6)!

"You Are So Fair" *(Babes in Arms)* for some mysterious reason is almost unknown and is not included in the published vocal score, although I was able to use it in my Columbia recording of the show some years ago.

This is a strange song with a verse and three choruses. It is somewhat wistful but it is also extremely playful. The principal feature of the lyrics is the use of "fair," which, in various spellings, combinations, and placings, has seven different meanings. It is the use of "fair" that provides the chorus lyrics with a continuous development in meaning so that the first and last lines reach quite different conclusions: "You are so fair" versus "You're only fair."

"YOU ARE SO FAIR"

VERSE

You're a siren if there ever was one.
And there was one.
You're a Lorelei;
I'm a dope(1)
You're a baddie if I ever saw one.
And I've seen one.
Darling Lorelei,
I've no hope(1).
I'm at the end of my rope(1).

REFRAIN

You are so fair,
Like an oriental vision(2);
But you won't make that decision(2).
You're not quite fair.
I'd pay your fare
To Niagara Falls and back, too(3):
But you never will react to(3)
This love affair.
You are the crepes suzette(4)
I should get(4)
On my bill of fare(5).
But if you love me not(6),
Flower-pot(6),
See if I care(5)!
See how you'll fare
If you keep on playing Rover(7).
When I come to think it over(7),
You're only fair.

II

You are so fair—
But you know you're no Apollo(8),
And to say you're hard to swallow(8)
Is only fair.
I'd pay your fare
All around the world and back too(3),
For I'd like to give a sack to(3)
This love affair(5).
You are the camembert(5)
I can't bear(5)
On my bill of fare(5),
So if you love me not(6),
See if I care(5).
See how you'll fare(5)
If you keep on playing Rover(7),
When I come to think it over(7),
You're only fair.

III

Your hair(5) ain't fair(5)
And you got no style in dressing(9).
I'm afraid you ain't possessing(9)
No savoir faire.
I'd pay your fare
To the tropic of New Guinea(10)
For I'd like to yell "C'est finis"(10)
To this affair.
You are the freak event(11)
In the tent(11)
Of a county fair(5).
So, if you love me not(12),
Polka dot(12)
See if I care(5).
See how you'll fare
If you keep on playing Rover(7)
When I come to think it over(7),
You're only fair.

"Johnny One Note" *(Babes in Arms)* is a straightforward playful rhythm song. It is for pure fun. There are two rhymes that feature the same device: *"gusto"—overlorded"* and *"Aïda"—"Indeed a."*

There is a brief verse, refrain, interlude, and a second refrain with coda. In the refrain there are two sets of triple rhymes and another set inhabits the interlude, with a third set in the coda.

"JOHNNY ONE NOTE"

VERSE
Johnny could only sing one note and the note he sang was this:
Ah————————

REFRAIN
Poor Johnny One Note
Sang out with gusto(1)
And just o(1)verlorded the place(2).
Poor Johnny One Note yelled willy-nilly(3),
Until he(3) was blue in the face(2),
For holding one note was his ace(2).

Couldn't hear the brass(4),
Couldn't hear the drum(5),
He was in a class(4)
By himself, by gum(5)!
Poor Johnny One Note
Got in Aïda(6),
Indeed a(6) great chance to be brave(7).
He took his one note,
Howled like the North Wind(8),
Brought forth wind(8) that made critics rave(7),
While Verdi turned round in his grave(7)!
Couldn't hear the flute(9) or the big trombone(10)
Ev'ryone was mute(9),
Johnny stood alone(10).

INTERLUDE
Cats and dogs stopped yapping(11),
Lions in the zoo all were jealous of Johnny's big trill(12).
Thunderclaps stopped clapping(11),
Traffic ceased its roar, and they tell us Niag'ra stood still(12).
He stopped the train-whistles,
Boat-whistles,
Steam-whistles,
Cop-whistles;
All whistles bowed to his skill(12).

REFRAIN TWO/CODA
Sing Johnny One Note,
Sing out with gusto(1)
And just o(1)verwhelm all the crowd(13).
Ah!
So sing, Johnny One Note, out loud(13)!
Sing, Johnny One Note!
Sing, Johnny One Note, out loud(13)!

Rodgers and Hart wrote two hit shows in 1938: *I Married an Angel* and *The Boys from Syracuse.* From the former I would like to quote the "Spring Is Here" lyric, which is a sad, lonely love song. The rhymes are apparent. The song can be summed up in two lines, of course, in addition to the title: "Maybe it's because nobody needs me" and "Maybe it's because nobody loves me."

"SPRING IS HERE"

VERSE
Once there was a thing(1) called spring(1), when the world was
    writing verses like yours and mine(2)
All the lads and girls would sing(1),
When we sat at little tables and drank May wine(2).
Now April, May and June(3) are sadly out of tune(3),
Life has stuck the pin in the balloon(3).

REFRAIN
Spring is here!
Why doesn't my heart go dancing(4)?
Spring is here!
Why isn't the waltz entrancing(4)?
No desire,
No ambition leads me(5),
Maybe it's because nobody needs me(5).
Spring is here(6)!
Why doesn't the breeze delight me(5)?

Stars appear(6)
Why doesn't the night invite me(5)?
Maybe it's because nobody loves me,
Spring is here I hear(6)!

"Come with Me" from *The Boys from Syracuse* (1938) is a comedy song in the form of a conversation. Three characters participate and a chorus reprise is sung by a male ensemble.

The musical and lyrical styles are quite properly those of the composer and lyricist working in their own time, although the book, adapted by George Abbott, is based on Shakespeare's *The Comedy of Errors*.

The feature of "Come with Me" as a comedy song is that until the very last word of the first chorus, the listener does not know that the "where" of the song is jail.

"COME WITH ME"

SERGEANT

Come with me(1) where the food is free(1),
Where the landlord never comes near(2) you.
Be(1) a guest(3) in a house of rest(3),
Where(4) the best(3) of fellows can cheer(2) you.
There(4)'s your own little room(5)
So cool, not too much light(6),
Where you're one man for whom(5)
No wife(7) waits up at night(6).
When day ends(8) you have lots of friends(8)
Who will guard you well while you slumber,
Safe from battle and strife(7),
Safe from wind and gale(9).
Come with me to jail(9).

ANGELO

You never have to fetch the milk
Or walk the dog at early(10) dawn(11).
There's no "get up, you're late for work"
While you rest in the pearly(10) dawn(11).

SERGEANT

You're never bored by politics.
You're privileged to miss a row(12)
Of tragedies by Sophocles
And diatribes by Cicero(12).

ANTIPHOLUS

Your brother's wife will never come
On Sunday noon to bring(13) you
Her lit(14)tle son, who plays the lute,
Her lit(14)tle girl to sing(13) to you.
You can commit(14) your lit(14)tle sins
And relatives won't yell "fie!"(15)
You needn't take that annual trip
To the oracle at Delphi(15),
You snore and swear and stretch and yawn(11)
In this, your strictly male house(16).
The only way that sinners go to heaven
Is in the jailhouse(16).

REFRAIN *(Men)*

In "Give It Back to the Indians" (1939) from *Too Many Girls,* Hart creates in part of the refrain a feeling that has persisted for well over a century as to the way Indians spoke. This he does by word omissions as well as transpositions. Examples:

On the boxes made for soap.

Whites, on Fifth Avenue,
Blues down in Wall Street losing hope.
Big bargain today,

The lyricist also borrowed from his own work of fourteen years earlier, the famous Manhattan-Staten rhyme.

I'd like to point to a single rhyme "threw" and "knew" in the verse only to illustrate a point in craftsmanship: each occurs on identical beats, four lines apart. The ear easily picks up "And they threw/ . . . For he knew"

This may seem to be a routine part of lyric writing but it is something that is too often ignored.

The many rhymes are indicated.

"GIVE IT BACK TO THE INDIANS"

VERSE

Old Peter Minuit had nothing to lose(1),
When he bought the Isle of Manhattan(2)
For twenty-six dollars and a bottle of booze(1)
And they threw(3) in the Bronx and Staten(2).
Pete thought that he had the best of the bargain(4),
But the poor red man just grinned(5).
And he grunted "Ugh!" meaning O.K. in his Jargon(4),
For he knew(3) poor Pete was skinned(5).
We've tried to run the Cit(6)y,
And now, Peter Minuit(6),
We can't continue it(6)!

REFRAIN

(A1) Broadway's turning into Coney(7),
Champagne Charlie's drinking gin(8),
Old New York is new and phoney(7),
Give it back to the In(8)dians.
(A2) Two(9) cents more to smoke a Lucky(10),
Dodging busses keeps you thin(8).
New(9) New York is simply ducky(10),
Give it back to the In(8)dians.
(B) Take all the reds,
On the boxes made for soap(11).
Whites, on Fifth Avenue,
Blues(12) down in Wall Street los(12)ing hope(11).
Big bargain today(13),
Chief, take it away(13)!
(A3) Come, you busted City slickers(14),
Better take it on the chin(8).
Father Knick has lost his knickers(14),
Give it back to the In(8)dians!

The production of *Pal Joey* (1940) marked Rodgers and Hart's next to final collaboration. They wrote *By Jupiter* in 1942 and worked on revisions for *A Connecticut Yankee,* which was revived in 1943, the year in which Lorenz Hart died. While *Pal Joey* and *By Jupiter* marked the tragic end of a great collaboration, a new era in American musical theatre was ushered in.

Pal Joey had a sophisticated book with three-dimensional characters. It was the first of its kind, and was to be followed by the equally sophisticated Rodgers and Hammerstein collaborations.

Nothing in the *Pal Joey* score illustrates better a sharp sense of characterization—something brand new and deeply significant—than the duet "Den of Iniquity." The music is stylishly elegant and suggests to me in feeling an eighteenth-century court dance. It has elegance and charm.

Pal Joey

The situation for the song is properly opposite. There is no elegance. Vera Simpson is happily ensconced with Joey, her younger lover, in their pied-à-terre, which, like everything else, Vera has bought. She is completely conscious of what she has, what she is doing, and why. She is intelligent, has been around, and above all she is not fooling herself.

Joey is ignorant and naïvely stupid. He has no background but offers Vera the precise physical chemistry that she wants.

In "Den of Iniquity" it is desirable to note exactly who sings what. Vera is joking about herself and the situation when she begins "Just two little love birds. . ." She knows she is not "little" in the age sense, and that there is no love here.

Joey's contributions are all either obtuse or stupid and their dullness for Vera is apparent. His "remarks" include "Artificial roses round the door,/ They are never out of bloom." A *fascinating* comment: "I haven't caught a cold all year."

After Vera's factual if slightly vulgar "A canopy bed has so much class," Joey adds a gaucherie "And so's a ceiling made of glass."

The duet evokes for me a feeling of nostalgia: a sense of satisfaction in a situation momentarily attractive but basically chancy, temporary, and, in the end, unworkable.

"DEN OF INIQUITY"

VERSE

VERA Just two little love birds all alone(1)
In a little cozy nest(2).
With a little secret telephone(1),
That's the place to rest(2).
JOEY Artificial roses round the door(3),
They are never out of bloom(4);
VERA And a flowered carpet on the floor(3)
In the loving room(4).

REFRAIN ONE

BOTH In our little den of iniquity(5)
Our arrangement is good(6).
V It's much more healthy living here(7);
This rushing back home is bad, my dear(7).
J I haven't caught a cold all year(7).
V Knock on wood(6)!
BOTH It was ever thus, since antiquity(5),
Down to you and to me(8).
V The chambermaid is very kind(9),
She always thinks we're so refined(9).
J Of course, she's deaf and dumb and blind(9).
BOTH No fools we(8)
In our little den of iniquity(5).

REFRAIN TWO

BOTH In our little den of iniquity(5)
For a girly and boy(10).
V We'll sit and let the hours pass(11);
A canopy bed has so much class(11).
J And so's a ceiling made of glass(11),
V Oh, what joy(10)!
BOTH Love has been that way,
Since antiquity(5),
All the poets agree(8).
V The radio I used to hate(12),
But now when it is dark and late(12).
J Ravel's Bolero works just great(12).

BOTH That's for me(8)
In our little den of iniquity(5).

REFRAIN THREE

J We're very proper folks, you know(13).
V We've sep'rate bedrooms "comme il faut."(13)
There's one for play and one for show(13)!
BOTH You chase me(8)
In our little den of iniquity.(5)

"Bewitched, Bothered and Bewildered," also from *Pal Joey*, is a comedy song sung by Vera Simpson, the wealthy aggressive socialite who has recently found and bought her Joey. "Bewitched, Bothered and Bewildered" is a model of what I term a "short-joke" comedy song. The term applies to the fact that there are "jokes" at the end of each A and B section, or approximately four for each refrain. Hence, the collaboration of Rodgers with Hart is especially noteworthy. Following each of the three A "jokes," the lyrics "Bewitched, bothered and bewildered. . . ." are heard. After the first time, the listener is aware of when it recurs, and that he is to hear repetition. This fact allows him to laugh more easily since he need not fear that new material is being sung after the joke.

Also, Rodgers's music at the end of this recurrent line allows a pause if necessary (that is, if the laugh continues), and so there is no reason for the audience to feel apprehensive lest it not hear something.

Again—in my opinion—the music of a comedy song should first of all serve the lyric and not intrude upon it. Carried to limits, this implies that the music might reasonably be of secondary importance. However, in "Bewitched, Bothered and Bewildered," although the music never obtrudes or impedes the lyric's meaning, it nevertheless turns out to be of such quality that it can be and frequently is heard alone.

The lyrics themselves require no explanation. The "jokes," as I call them, are, of course, not jokes but "whimsies" manufactured out of this particular character in this particular situation. Unlike "jokes," their repetition out of context would be productive of nothing. Also, they do not and (mostly) will not go out of style. They bear rehearing. One chuckles not only because of the song itself, but because of the outlandish character who soliloquizes so unabashedly and truthfully about herself.

There are a verse, three choruses, and an encore plus a reprise near the end of the show when Vera has decided to leave the temporarily unconscious Joey, to whom she sings.

Note the sometimes overlooked end words of the title line, which change from "like me" to "am I" and finally "no more."

Vera Simpson, through the medium of this song, figuratively undresses herself.

"BEWITCHED"

VERSE

He's a fool and don't I know it(1),
But a fool can have his charms(2),
I'm in love and don't I show it(1),
Like a babe in arms(2).
Love's the same old sad sensation(3),
Lately I've not slept a wink(4),
Since this half-pint imitation(3),
Put me on the blink(4).

REFRAIN ONE
I'm wild(5) again,
Beguiled(5) again,
A simpering(6), whimpering(6), child(5) again,
Bewitched, bothered and bewildered am I.
Couldn't(7) sleep,
And wouldn't(7) sleep,
Until I could sleep where I shouldn't(7) sleep.
Bewitched, bothered and bewildered am I.
Lost my heart, but what of it?
My mistake, I agree(8).
He's a laugh, but I love it
Because the laugh's on me(8).
A pill(9) he is
But still(9) he is
All mine and I'll keep him until(9) he is
Bewitched, bothered and bewildered like me.

REFRAIN TWO
Seen(10) a lot;
I mean(10) a lot!
But now I'm like sweet seventeen(10) a lot.
Bewitched, bothered and bewildered am I.
I'll sing(11) to him
Each spring(11) to him
And worship the trousers that cling(11) to him.
Bewitched, bothered and bewildered am I.
When he talks
He is seeking(12)
Words to get off his chest(13).
Horizontally speaking(12),
He's at his very best(13).
Vexed(14) again,
Perplexed(14) again,
Thank God I can be over-sexed(14) again.
Bewitched, bothered and bewildered am I.

REFRAIN THREE
Sweet(15) again,
Petite(15) again,
And on my proverbial seat(15) again.
Bewitched, bothered and bewildered am I.
What(16) am I?
Half shot(16) am I.
To think that he loves me,
So hot(16) am I.
Bewitched, bothered and bewildered am I.
Though(17) at first we said "No, sir(18)."
Now we're two little dears(19).
You might say we are closer(18)
Than Roe(17)buck is to Sears(19).
I'm dumb(20) again
And numb(20) again,
A rich, ready, ripe little plum(20) again.
Bewitched, bothered and bewildered am I.

ENCORE
It is really quite funny(21)
Just how quickly he learns(22)
How to spend all that money(21)
That Mister Simpson earns(22).
He's kept(23) enough,
He's slept(23) enough,

And yet, where it counts, he's adept(23) enough.
Bewitched, bothered and bewildered am I.

FINAL REPRISE
Wise(24) at last,
My eyes(24) at last
Are cutting you down to your size(24) at last.
Bewitched, bothered and bewildered no more.
Burned(25) a lot,
But learned(25) a lot.
And now you are broke though you earned(25) a lot.
Bewitched, bothered and bewildered no more.
Couldn't eat;
Was dyspeptic(26).
Life was so hard to bear(27).
Now my heart's antiseptic(26)
Since he moved out of there(27).
Romance(28) . . . finis;
Your chance(28) . . . finis;
Those ants(28) that invaded my pants(28) . . . finis.
Bewitched, bothered and bewildered no more.

"My Heart Stood Still" was written for a revue in London, produced by Charles B. Cochran, called *One Dam Thing After Another* (1927), when it was sung with great success by Jessie Mathews. Later in the same year it was included in the score of *A Connecticut Yankee* when, in a completely different context, it was just as popular. The tale is often repeated that Hart got the idea for the title during a near taxi accident when someone made a similar remark. As a lyric, it took on a romantic meaning.

Most of the song's rhymes are clearly apparent. Hart employed his incredible ability to rhyme consecutive words with others on different lines, and here it happens twice. In verse 1 "rise in Spain" rhymes separately with "eyes" one line before and "domain" a line earlier. In verse 2 "Missus Glyn" goes with "kiss" one line above and "sin" two lines earlier.

There is a series of not-so-obvious vowel rhymes in verse 2: *ha*ted, *A*pril, *Pla*to. In verse 1 the only line that contains no rhyme is "A house in Iceland." This fact seemed curious to me since Hart was fond of rhyming and the "house" might have been anywhere. *Except,* the idea is: "Was my heart's domain." (It was cold.) Afterward, Hart concludes the idea: "I saw your eyes;/ Now castles rise in Spain!"

Another of Hart's devices includes *not* rhyming titles until the very end of a refrain. This he does here.

The refrain ends with a triple rhyme: "Until the thrill of that moment when my heart stood still." This repetition creates a sense of satisfaction and dramatic climax.

"MY HEART STOOD STILL"

VERSE ONE
HE I laughed at sweethearts(1)
I met at schools(2);
All indiscreet hearts(1)
Seemed romantic fools(2).
A house in Iceland
Was my heart's domain(3).
I saw your eyes(4);
Now castles rise(4) in Spain(3)!

REFRAIN

I took one look at you(5),
That's all I meant to do(5);
And then my heart stood still!
My feet could step and walk(6),
My lips could move and talk(6),
And yet my heart stood still!
Though not a single word was spoken,
I could tell(7) you knew,
That unfelt clasp of hands
Told me so well(7) you knew.
I never lived at all
Until(8) the thrill(8) of that moment when my heart stood still(8).

VERSE TWO

SHE   Through all my schooldays(9)
I hated boys(10);
Those April Fool days(9)
Brought me loveless joys(10).
I read my Plato,
Love, I thought a sin(11);
But since your kiss(12),
I'm reading Miss(12)us Glyn(11)!

REFRAIN REPEATED

For the revival of *A Connecticut Yankee* in 1943, the last of the marvelous Rodgers and Hart collaborations, "To Keep My Love Alive" was created. This is first of all a comedy song of enormous wit and skill. There is a single verse with two refrains. The "jokes" are incredible, not simply because of *what* they say, but more especially because of how they are said.

The verse sets up a multimarital situation. The two refrains deal comedically with murder. In both, the series of murders are related by being cast in identical form. In each of the three A sections that tale is related in series of triple rhymes. Each B section consists of only a single couplet. The first has end rhymes. The first line of the second is not rhymed while the other contains one set of single rhymes and one set of triple ones!

"TO KEEP MY LOVE ALIVE"

VERSE

I've been married and married, and often I've sighed(1),
I'm never a bride(1)smaid, I'm always the bride(1);

I never divorced them, I hadn't the heart(2),
Yet, remember these sweet words,
"Till death do us part."(2)

REFRAIN ONE

(A1) I married many men, a ton of them(3), because I was untrue to none of them(3),
Because I bumped off ev'ry one of them(3)/to keep my love alive.
(A2) Sir Paul was frail, he looked a wreck to me(4). / At night he was a horse's neck to me(4),
So I performed an appendectomy(4),/to keep my love alive!
(B) Sir Thomas had insomnia, he couldn't sleep at night(5),
I bought a little arsenic, he's sleeping now all right(5).
(A3) Sir Philip played the harp, I cussed the thing(6),
I crowned him with his harp to bust the thing(6),
And now he plays where harps are just the thing(6),/to keep my love alive, to keep my love alive.

REFRAIN TWO

(A1) I thought Sir George had possibilities(7), but his flirtations made me ill at ease(7),
And when I'm ill at ease, I kill at ease(7)/to keep my love alive.
(A2) Sir Charles came from a sanatorium(8),/and yelled for drinks in my emporium(8).
I mixed one drink, he's in memoriam(8),/to keep my love alive!
(B) Sir Francis was a singing bird, a nightingale, that's why(9)
I tossed him off my balcony(4) to see(4) if he(4) could fly(9).
(A3) Sir Athelstane indulged in fratricide(10),
He killed his dad and that was patricide(10).
One night I stabbed him by my mattress side(10),/To keep my love alive, to keep my love alive.

The art of Lorenz Hart achieved memorable heights. His seemingly effortless skill at original rhyming was unmatched, but this never interfered with the sentiments and ideas of the songs.

Most of his lyrics are gay and amusing but his deep personal unhappiness comes clearly to light in such songs as "Little Girl Blue," "Where or When?," and "Here in My Arms." Even in some of the happier ones, such as "Spring Is Here" and "There's a Small Hotel," there is an abundance of wistfulness that shows a sense of wishful dreaming as opposed to fulfillment.

The Hart gift was enormous and in combination with Richard Rodgers's music will remain one of the most memorable contributions to our music theatre library.

Courtesy Museum of the City of New York

Oscar Hammerstein II (1895–1960)

No single person in the American musical theatre absorbed so extensive and wide a variety of experience as Oscar Hammerstein II. Over a period of forty years, marked by great changes and the maturation of our leading indigenous art form, Hammerstein was constantly an important part of the mainstream. As colyricist and coauthor—an appropriate kind of apprenticeship for a young man of twenty-five—he was involved in thirty-four shows. As lyricist on his own, he contributed memorable ones to more than fifteen shows. As author/adapter and lyricist, he was involved in twenty others. Although he collaborated with composers Stothart, Youmans, Romberg, Friml, and Kern, his best remembered work was with Richard Rodgers, with whom he did his most important and most mature work during the last sixteen years of his life.

Hammerstein acknowledged Otto Harbach as his "teacher," and in spite of Harbach's twenty-year seniority and his earlier successes, they worked together as collaborators on eight shows.

Hammerstein came from a distinguished musical theatre family. His grandfather, Oscar Hammerstein I, was impresario of the Manhattan Opera House, where many important American premieres were given. His father, William, was manager of a vaudeville house. His uncle Arthur was a distinguished producer who gave him his first job as assistant stage manager after Oscar had graduated law school at Columbia.

It was during this period of work for his uncle that Oscar's collaboration with Harbach began, and it is to this association that Oscar attributed so much of his development. In the preface to Hammerstein's book on his lyrics, the author gives much invaluable advice on lyric writing and makes many noteworthy comments of which every young lyric writer should take cognizance. He, in the main, eschews the idea of "inspiration" and adds that "some of us do work every day," suggesting that writers do not wait to be "inspired." He says that he and Rodgers "can write words and music best when they are required by a situation or a characterization in a story." He further claims that he and Rodgers "have agreed on a very definite and complete outline, and we have decided how much of the story should be told in dialogue and how much in song" before they begin writing. Hammerstein wrote very astutely that "the song is the servant of the play," saying that it is wrong to write a song first and then try to "wedge it into a story."

He greatly admired W. S. Gilbert and Lorenz Hart, and never felt that in the "field of brilliant light verse" he could compete with them. To this he added, "my inclinations lead me to a more primitive style of lyric." He felt that "if a listener is made rhyme-conscious, his interest may be diverted from the story of the song." To illustrate this he cited his own "Ol' Man River," which contains no rhymes until the ninth and tenth lines. He set great store by the singableness of songs, musically and lyrically. I would like to quote two more of Hammerstein's aphorisms: "The most important ingredient of a good song is sincerity" and ". . . every song that has a long life says something fundamental, and says it in an attractive way musically and lyrically."

It is a great privilege to be able to say of any creative artist as deeply talented as Oscar Hammerstein II that his knowledge, skill, and taste matched his talent. It is this very special combination of natural and acquired gifts that distinguishes the work of Hammerstein. He achieved his own particular goals and helped conspicuously to bring the American musical theatre to the high maturity it reached during his participation.

I should like to begin with some samplings of Hammerstein's lyrics prior to his collaboration with Rodgers. Among his earlier successes was *New Moon* (1928), which he wrote with Sigmund Romberg.

"Lover, Come Back to Me!" is special in that the lyric lines are brief and were obviously dictated by the fragmented musical phrases, most of which commence after a "breathy" rest on many of the downbeats. Take the first line "The sky was blue," for example. The measure begins (the downbeat occurs) just *ahead* of the first word. In fact *all* lines begin *after* the downbeat except the title lines and the release. For the rest, Hammerstein's words (as always) sing and the rhymes are simple and sparse.

"LOVER, COME BACK TO ME!"

The sky was blue,
And high above
The moon was new
And so was love.
This eager heart of mine was singing:
"Lover, where can you be?"
You came at last,
Love had its day,
That day is past,
You've gone away.
This aching heart of mine is singing:
"Lover, come back to me!"
Rememb'ring every little thing you used to say and do,
I'm so lonely,
Ev'ry road I walk along I've walked along with you,
No wonder I am lonely.
The sky is blue,
The night is cold,
The moon is new,
And love is old,
And while I'm waiting here,
This heart of mine is singing:
"Lover come back to me!"

Hammerstein worked with Kern for the third time in 1932 when they wrote *Music in the Air*. One of the loveliest songs in this score is "There's a Hill Beyond a Hill," although some other popular ones from the same show are "I've Told Ev'ry Little Star," "The Song Is You," and "And Love Was Born."

Although I have indicated the rhymes, which really announce themselves quite clearly, it is also important to point out the wide avoidance of similar word sounds—both with vowels and consonants—when the words are *not* intended to rhyme. Such a comment may, on the face of it, seem absurd, but all too often lyricists mislead the ear by placing words with similar sounds in such juxtaposition that the listener wonders whether or not a rhyme is intended. I feel that Hammerstein was acutely aware of such a danger and fought clear of it by using such diverse-sounding end words as world, thing, day, road, walk, mountain, river, life, and so on, which end all of the unrhymed lines in the long verse. This is an important accomplishment.

"THERE'S A HILL BEYOND A HILL"

The world can be a wonderful world
When the thrill of adventure comes(1).
If you don't like that kind of thing,
Stay home and twiddle your thumbs(1).
A day can be a wonderful day
When you're out on the open road.
There is no road too long to walk
If you can sing to pass the time(2).
There is no road too long to walk,
No mountain peak too high to climb(2)!
To climb the highest mountain,
To ford the deepest river,
Will make you feel the zest(3) of life.
Come on and get the best(3) of life,
Come on—
The best of life is farther on!

There's a hill beyond a hill
Beyond a hill beyond a hill—
If your limbs are young and strong(4),
Follow along(4),
Follow along(4)!

There's a dream beyond a dream
Beyond a dream beyond a dream—
If your heart is young and gay(5),
Follow along our way(5)!

Just one year before *New Moon*, Hammerstein enjoyed one of his biggest successes in collaboration with Jerome Kern in *Show Boat* (1927). Although most histories of our musical theatre attribute the integration of song, plot, and character to musicals beginning in the forties, it is my feeling that *Show Boat*, some thirteen years earlier, shows traces of this new "seriousness" as a natural extension of Kern's avowed leanings in this direction.

The black singer of "Ol' Man River" is, according to Hammerstein, a "rugged and untutored philosopher." He further calls this a "song of resignation with a protest implied." Hammerstein consciously avoided rhymes so as not to distract attention from the song's meaning. However, he compensated by the use of balancing words: "sumpin' " and "nuthin' " and "taters" and "cotton."

My own feeling is that what Hammerstein created was a supergod character who watches the events of the world from above, and though impotent to change things nevertheless sees them happen. Despite these events, he says of the river (is it life?), "He jes' keeps rollin' along."

"OL' MAN RIVER"

Dere's an ol' man called de Mississippi;
Dat's de ol' man dat I'd like to be!
What does he care if de world's got troubles?
What does he care if de land ain't free?
(A1) Ol' Man River,
Dat Ol' Man River,
He mus' know sumpin'
But don' say nuthin',
He jes' keeps rollin',
He keeps on rollin' along.

THERE'S A HILL BEYOND A HILL

PEGGY FEARS PRESENTS

music in the air

BOOK AND LYRICS BY
OSCAR HAMMERSTEIN 2ND.

MUSIC BY
JEROME KERN

And Love Was Born
One More Dance
I Am So Eager
There's A Hill Beyond A Hill
We Belong Together
In Egern On The Tegern See
The Song Is You
I've Told Ev'ry Little Star
When The Spring Is In The Air
I'm Alone
Selection

T. B. HARMS
COMPANY
NEW YORK
SOLE SELLING AGENT
HARMS
INCORPORATED

OL' MAN RIVER

➤LOW C (G-E)   ORIGINAL E♭ (B♭-G)

FLORENZ ZIEGFELD

PRESENTS

SHOW BOAT

ADAPTED FROM EDNA FERBER'S NOVEL OF THE SAME NAME

BOOK & LYRICS BY
Oscar Hammerstein II
MUSIC BY
Jerome Kern

ENSEMBLES & DANCES BY
SAMMY LEE
SETTINGS BY
JOSEPH URBAN

PRICE
85c

Also Published Separately
from the Score:
Bill (Words by P. G.
Wodehouse and Oscar
Hammerstein II)
Can't Help Lovin' Dat Man
I Have The Room Above
I Might Fall Back On You
I Still Suits Me
Life Upon The Wicked
Stage
Make Believe
Nobody Else But Me
Ol' Man River
Why Do I Love You?
You Are Love

T. B. HARMS COMPANY
Sole
Distributor CPI CIMINO PUBLICATIONS INCORPORATED
436 Maple Avenue   Westbury, L.I., N.Y. 11590

(A2) He don' plant taters,
He don' plant cotton,
An' dem dat plants 'em
Is soon forgotten,
But Ol' Man River,
He jes' keeps rollin' along.
(B) You an' me, we sweat an' strain,
Body all achin' an' racked wid pain—
Tote dat barge!
Lif' dat bale!
Git a little drunk,
An' you land in jail. . . .
(A3) Ah gits weary
An' sick of tryin';
Ah'm tired of livin'
An' skeered of dyin',
But Ol' Man River,
He jes' keeps rollin' along.
Colored folks work on de Mississippi,
Colored folks work while de white folks play,
Pullin' dem boats from de dawn to sunset,
Gittin' no rest till de Judgment Day—
(B) Don' look up
An' don' look down—
You don' dast make
De white boss frown.
Bend your knees
An' bow your head,
An' pull dat rope
Until yo' dead.
Let me go 'way from de Mississippi,
Let me go 'way from de white man boss;
Show me dat stream called de river Jordan,
Dat's de ol' stream dat I long to cross.
(A1) Ol' Man River,
Dat Ol' Man River,
He mus' know sumpin'
But don' say nuthin',
He jes' keeps rollin',
He keeps on rollin' along.
(A2) He don' plant taters,
He don' plant cotton,
An' dem dat plants 'em
Is soon forgotten,
But Ol' Man River,
He jes' keeps rollin' along.
(B) You an' me, we sweat an' strain,
Body all achin' and racked wid pain—
Tote dat barge!
Lif' dat bale!
Git a little drunk,
An' you land in jail. . . .
(A3) Ah git weary
An' sick of tryin';
Ah'm tired of livin'
An' skeered of dyin',
But Ol' Man River,
He jes' keeps rollin' along.

Also in *Show Boat* in the song "You Are Love" Hammerstein accomplishes something unique. The title ends with the word "love." Many other songs have titles ending with "love," and perhaps the most restrictive aspect of using the word is the limited number of words that rhyme with it. In Clement Wood's *Rhyming Dictionary*, the editor gives basically only "above," "glove," and "dove." Hardly a wide selection, leaving little room for lyric freshness. Most lyricists have found themselves trapped by this restriction and many have simply gone on using only what is possible again and again. Hammerstein faced the problem head on and did not rhyme anything with "love."

"YOU ARE LOVE"

You are love
Here in my arms,
Where you belong,
And here you will stay(1),
I'll not let you away(1),
I want day after day(1)
With you(2).
You are spring,
Bud of romance unfurled(3);
You taught me to see(4),
One truth forever true(2).
You are love,
Wonder of all the world(3).
Where you go with me(4),
Heaven will always be(4).

The collaboration of Hammerstein with Richard Rodgers (1943–1959) brought forth magnificent accomplishments. There were nine shows, most of them record-breaking successes, and several films, chief of which was *State Fair* (1945).

The first of their shows was *Oklahoma!* Hammerstein tells us that in his collaboration with Rodgers, he nearly always wrote the lyrics first, a method he had seldom practiced before. He usually found himself slaving over the words and was often discouraged at finding Rodgers able to match a song to a lyric in a matter of one or two hours. This is, of course, not only a tribute to Rodgers's talent and technique, but also to Hammerstein's master craftsmanship, musical feeling, and ability to select subject matter that stimulated the composer.

Sometimes this subject matter (this is true of some other lyricists as well) was stated to a degree by the original author of the play that was being adapted for musical theatre. This was often true of Alan Jay Lerner in transforming Shaw into *My Fair Lady,* and equally so of Hammerstein in translating Lynn Riggs's *Green Grow the Lilacs* into *Oklahoma!* Nowhere in the latter play is it more evident than in the lyrics of "The Surrey with the Fringe on Top." Lynn Riggs wrote:

CURLY   A bran' new surrey with fringe on the top four inches long—and *yeller!* And two white horses a-rarin' and faunchin' to go! You'd shore ride like a queen settin' up in *that* carriage! Feel like you had a gold crown set on yer head, 'th diamonds in it big as goose eggs. . . . .

I ain't astin' you, I'm *tellin'* you. And this yere rig has got four fine side-curtains, case of a rain. And isinglass winders to look out of! And a red and green lamp set on the dashboard, winkin' like a lightnin' bug! . . . .

Don't you wish there *was* such a rig, though? Nen you could go to the party and do a hoe-down till mornin' 'f you was a mind to. Nen drive home 'th the sun a-peekin' at you over the ridge, purty and fine.

The song, which derives its inspiration from Riggs's dialogue, is extraordinary in many ways. The lyrics are in narrative form. They first describe the imaginary surrey. In the second chorus the couple are en route to the party, and in the final one, which gets slower and slower (more and more tired), the couple are returning home very late at night. I would describe this song as a rhythm ballad and a charm song.

It is no small accomplishment that two verses and three choruses continue to hold the listener's interest, and with this kind of exposure it is no wonder that the song becomes instantly familiar and memorable. Hammerstein, in creating a thoroughly delightful and humorous picture, resorts to rhymes more than usual. I have indicated these.

"THE SURREY WITH THE FRINGE ON TOP"

VERSE I

When I take you out tonight with me(1),
Honey, here's the way it's goin' to be(1):
You will sit behind a team of snow-white horses
In the slickest gig you ever see(1)!

CHORUS I

Chicks and ducks and geese better scurry(2)
When I take you out in the surrey(2),
When I take you out in the surrey with the fringe on top(3).
Watch that fringe and see how it flutters(4)
When I drive them high-steppin' strutters(4)—
Nosey-pokes'll peek through their shutters(4) and their eyes
    will pop(3)!
The wheels are yeller, the upholstery's brown(5),
The dashboard's genuine leather(6),
With isinglass curtains y' c'n roll right down(5)
In case there's a change in the weather(6);
Two bright side lights winkin'(7) and blinkin'(7),
Ain't no finer rig, I'm a-thinkin'(7);
You c'n keep yer rig if you're thinkin' 'at I'd keer to swap(3)
Fer that shiny little surrey with the fringe on the top(3).

VERSE II

Would y' say the fringe was made of silk(8)?
Wouldn't have no(9) other kind but silk(8).
Has it really got a team of snow-white horses?
One's like snow(9)—the other's more like milk(8).

CHORUS II

All the world'll fly(10) in a flurry(2)
When I(10) take you out in the surrey(2),
When I take you out in the surrey with the fringe on top(3).
When we hit that road, hell(11) fer leather(6),
Cats and dogs'll(11) dance in the heather(6),
Birds and frogs'll(11) sing all together(6), and the toads will
    hop(3)!
The wind'll whistle as we rattle along(12),
The cows'll moo in the clover(13),
The river will ripple out a whispered song(12),
And whisper it over and over(13):
Don't you wisht y'd go on ferever?
Don't you wisht y'd go on ferever(14)?
Don't you wisht y'd go on ferever and ud never(14) stop(3)—
In that shiny little surrey with the fringe on the top(4)?

CHORUS III

I can see the stars gittin' blurry(2)
When we ride back home in the surrey(2),
Ridin' slowly home in the surrey with the fringe on top(3).
I can feel the day gittin' older(15),
Feel a sleepy head near my shoulder(15),
Noodin', droopin' close to my shoulder till (16) it falls,
    kerplop(3)!
The sun is swimmin' on the rim of a hill(16),
The moon is takin' a header(17),
And jist as I'm thinkin' all the earth is still(16),
A lark'll wake up in the medder(17) . . .
Hush! You bird, my baby's a-sleepin'(18)—
Maybe got a dream(19) worth a-keepin'(18).
Whoa! You team(19), and jist keep a-creepin'(18) at a slow
    clip-clop(3);
Don't you hurry(2) with the surrey(2) with the fringe on the
    top(3).

There are many less obvious assonances in this lyric. First, there is a plethora of *ee* sounds: me, be, see, team, geese, peek, wheels, keep, keer, really, team (these are in the two verses and chorus 1; chorus 2 omits them almost entirely. They are resumed in chorus 3: see, we, feel, sleepy, a-sleepin', dream, a-keepin', team, a-creepin'.

There are other similar features. In chorus 1 there are many vowel rhymes almost squeezed together: drive, high, eyes, genuine, isinglass, bright, side, lights, finer, I'm, I'd, shiny. In chorus 2 the liquid *l* sounds are one feature: world'll, fly, flurry, hell, leather, dogs'll, frogs'll, all, will, wind'll, whistle, along, cows'll, clover, ripple, little. In the same chorus there are many *w* consonances: world'll, when, with, will, wind'll, whistle, whispered, whisper, wisht. In chorus 3 *o* comes to the fore: home, slowly, older, shoulder, close, whoa, slow. In the same chorus *ur* is another feature: blurry, surrey, bird, worth, hurry.

As a kind of aside, I should like to make the personal comment that in the shape of Rodgers's initial theme, with its repeated notes and phrase ends going quickly upward, I am reminded of the sound of chickens cackling. Could this have been somewhat suggested, consciously or otherwise, by "chicks and ducks and geese better scurry"?

"I Cain't Say No," also from *Oklahoma!*, is a comedy song sung by the flirtatious Ado Annie. If the actress who performs this truly comprehends the seriousness, not the cuteness, of the song, it is always amusing. Ado Annie in all sincerity is telling her friend Laurey that she is the victim of a terrible irresistible disease.

The form of the song is unusual. It consists of a verse, chorus 1, trio (a kind of interlude), and choruses 2 and 3. Though the rhymes are amusing, it is the steady buildup of the idea that marks this as a unique comedy song.

"I CAIN'T SAY NO"

VERSE

It ain't so much a question of not knowin' what to do(1),
I knowed whut's right and wrong since I been ten(2).
I heared a lot of stories—and I reckon they are true(1)—
About how girls're put upon by men(2).
I know I mustn't fall into the pit(3),
But when I'm with a feller—I fergit(3)!

CHORUS I

I'm jist a girl who cain't(4) say no(5),
I'm in a turrible fix(6).
I always say, "Come on, le's go(5)!"
Jist when I orta say, "Nix(6)!"
When a person tries to kiss a girl
I know she orta(7) give his face a smack(8).
But as soon as someone kisses me
I somehow sorta(7) wanta kiss him back(8).
I'm jist a fool when lights are low(5).
I cain't(4) be prissy and quaint(4)—
I ain't(4) the type thet c'n faint(4)—
How c'n I be whut I ain't(4)?
I cain't say no(5)!

TRIO

Whut you goin' to do when a feller gits flirty(9)
And starts to talk purty(9)?
Whut you goin' to do?
S'posin' 'at he says 'at yer lips're like cherries(10),
Er roses, er berries(10)?
Whut you goin' to do?
S'posin' 'at he says 'at you're sweeter'n cream
And he's gotta have cream er die(11)?
Whut you goin' to do when he talks thet way?
Spit in his eye(11)?

CHORUS II

I'm jist a girl who cain't say no(5),
Cain't seem to say(12) it at all(13).
I hate to disserpoint a beau(5)
When he is payin'(12) a call(13).
Fer a while I ack refined and cool(14),
A-set(21)tin' on the velvet(21)een set(21)tee(15)—
Nen I think of thet(21) ol' golden rule(14),
And do fer(16) him whut he would do fer me(15).
I cain't resist a Romeo(5)
In a sombrer(16)o and chaps(17).
Soon as I sit on their laps(17)
Somethin' inside of me snaps(17)—
I cain't say no(5)!

CHORUS III

I'm jist a girl who cain't say(12) no(5).
Kissin's my favorite food(18).
With er without the mistletoe(5)
I'm in a holiday(12) mood(18).
Other girls are coy and hard to catch(19),
But other girls ain't havin' any fun(20).
Ev'ry time I lose a wrestlin' match(19)
I have a funny feelin' that I won(20).
Though I c'n feel the undertow(5),
I never make a complaint(4)
Till it's too late fer restraint(4),
Then when I want to I cain't(4),
I cain't say no(5)!

In "Lonely Room" Jud "paints a savage picture of his solitary life, his hatred of Curley and his mad desire for Laurey. This is self-analysis, but it is emotional, not cerebral. No dialogue could do this dramatic job as vividly or quickly as does the song." *

* *Lyrics*, by Oscar Hammerstein II (New York: Simon and Schuster, 1949).

This song gives another dimension to *Oklahoma!* in the character of Jud. In the original play Jud (or Jeeter as he was called) is a one-dimensional, filthy, fearsome villain. Because of "Lonely Room" he becomes a human being with understandable desires and hates. It is dramatic and lyrical. Jud's suffering arouses our sympathy, and his desires arouse our fears.

"LONELY ROOM"

The floor(1) creaks(2),
The door(1) squeaks(2),
There's a field mouse a-nibblin' on a broom(3),
And I set by myself(4)
Like a cobweb on a shelf(4),
By myself in a lonely room(3).

But when there's a moon in my winder
And it slants down a beam(5) 'crost my bed(6),
Then the shadder of a tree(7) starts a-dancin' on the wall(8)
And a dream(5) starts a-dancin' in my head(6).
And all(8) the things that I wish fer
Turn out like I want them to be(7),
And I'm better'n that smart-aleck cowhand
Who thinks he is better'n me(7),
And the girl that I want
Ain't afraid of my arms,
And her own soft arms keep me warm(10)
And her long, yeller hair
Falls acrost my face
Jist like the rain in a storm(10) . . .

The floor(1) creaks(2),
The door(1) squeaks(2),
And the mouse starts a-nibblin' on the broom(3).
And the sun flicks my eyes(11)—
It was all a pack o' lies(11).
I'm awake in a lonely room(3).

Not instantly apparent in this lyric is the use of repetition. In the first section "by myself" occurs twice. In the second "a-dancin' " and "better'n" occur twice; also "arms" occurs twice. In the third section hard *k* sounds abound: creaks, squeaks, flicks, pack, awake.

Rodgers and Hammerstein musicalized the so-called Bench Scene of Molnár's *Liliom* in *Carousel* and the musical version, I believe, is a masterpiece. If this is not opera American style, I don't believe we shall ever have anything closer. Hammerstein said that "we [he and Rodgers] try to use music as much as we can." He went on to say that "certain subject matters are not good to be sung," an idea that led to a small discussion of grand opera in which everything is sung. He felt that Americans who try to follow this formula are "not writing American operas at all. They are writing European operas governed by European traditions."

The subject matter of the Bench Scene amounts to a circuitous examination of love—something to sing about. The music goes through many changes in this scene but it continues vocally and/or instrumentally throughout. Characterwise, what happens in this scene is subtle and staggering! Julie Jordan, a kind of mouse, deliberately stays on in a park at night with the liar braggart Billy Bigelow. In so doing she has lost her job (she will be locked out of the mill boardinghouse, which closes at ten), she may be in physical danger, and her entire

future life is at once uncertain. What happens ever so slowly and bit by bit is that the apparently weak Julie snares the secure strong Billy. She is in love with him and she masters him by insisting that she isn't in love with him and that she would not marry him! She doesn't even refer to these possibilities except negatively and in answer to his direct questions.

There are five songs and necessary connecting music in this scene. The first and third have been sung earlier in this scene by Julie's friend and co-worker Carrie. The second, third, fourth, and fifth are each sung twice during the Bench Scene. The third, "When I worked in the mill," is a verbatim repeat of what Carrie has sung earlier about Julie. Now, in this scene with Billy, Julie is repeating it (about herself) as though (Miss Innocence!) she has just thought it up. This third song, a direct quote from Carrie, is only one of several pretenses in this scene. A second is "I'm never goin' to marry." A third:

JULIE "If I loved you—"
BILLY "But you don't."
JULIE "No I don't. . . ."

She repeats this shortly afterward, and then, later:

BILLY ". . . are you tryin' t'get me to marry you?"
JULIE "No."

Twice when Julie feels she's made Billy uneasy, she changes the subject abruptly by referring to blossoms falling from the trees. Although Billy is a rough-and-tumble fellow with no education, Hammerstein at high emotional moments gives him lyrics that cause him to transcend himself. Even so, these words never violate his character.

I would like to direct attention to one thing more. There are rhymes and rhythms in the songs and none whatsoever in the spoken dialogue. It is my feeling that this is precisely as it should be. When I hear unsung rhyming and rhythmic dialogue I have the uncomfortable feeling that the lyricist intended that it be set to music but the composer refused. Although this may seldom be the case, I feel that rhythm and rhyme without music in a musical show (unlike the plays of Molière, for example) are like riders without horses.

"IF I LOVED YOU"

BILLY *(Singing softly, shaking head)*
You're a queer one, Julie Jordan.
Ain't you sorry that you didn't run away?
You can still go, if you wanta—
JULIE *(Singing, looking away so as not to meet his eye)*
I reckon that I keer t'choose t'stay.
You couldn't take my money
If I didn't *hev* any,
And I don't hev a penny, that's true!
And if I *did* hev money
You couldn't take any
'Cause you'd ask, and I'd give it to you!
BILLY *(Singing)*
You're a queer one, Julie Jordan. . . .
Ain't y'ever had a feller you give money to?
JULIE No.
BILLY Ain't y'ever had a feller at all?
JULIE No.
BILLY Well y'musta had a feller you went walkin' with—
JULIE Yes.

BILLY Where'd you walk?
JULIE Nowhere special I recall.
BILLY In the woods?
JULIE No.
BILLY On the beach?
JULIE No.
BILLY Did you love him?
JULIE No! Never loved no one—I *told* you that!
BILLY Say, you're a funny kid. Want to go into town and dance maybe? Or—
JULIE No. I have to be keerful.
BILLY Of what?
JULIE My character. Y'see, I'm never goin' to marry. *(Singing)*
I'm never goin' to marry.
If I was goin' to marry,
I wouldn't hev t'be sech a stickler.
But I'm never goin' to marry,
And a girl who don't marry
Has got to be much more pertickler!
(Following lines spoken)
BILLY Suppose I was to say to you that I'd marry you?
JULIE You?
BILLY That scares you, don't it? You're thinkin' what that cop said.
JULIE No, I ain't. I never paid no mind to what he said.
BILLY But you wouldn't marry anyone like me, would you?
JULIE Yes, I would, if I loved you. It wouldn't make any difference what you—even if I died fer it.
BILLY How do you know what you'd do if you loved me? Or how you'd feel—or anythin'?
JULIE I dunno how I know.

BILLY Ah—
JULIE Jest the same, I know how I—how it'd be—if I loved you. *(Singing)*
When I worked in the mill, weavin' at the loom,
I'd gaze absent-minded at the roof,
And half the time the shuttle'd tangle in the threads,
And the warp'd get mixed with the woof . . .
If I loved you—
BILLY *(Spoken)* But you don't.
JULIE *(Spoken)* No I don't. . . . *(Smiles and sings)*
But somehow I ken see
Jest exackly how I'd be . . .
If I loved you,
Time and again I would try to say
All I'd want you to know.
If I loved you,
Words wouldn't come in an easy way—
Round in circles I'd go!
Longin' to tell you, but afraid and shy,
I'd let my golden chances pass me by.
Soon you'd leave me,
Off you would go in the mist of day,
Never, never to know
How I loved you—
If I loved you.
(Pause)
BILLY Well, anyway—You don't love me. That's what you said.
JULIE Yes. . . . I can smell them, can you? The blossoms. The wind brings them down.
BILLY Ain't *much* wind tonight. Hardly any. *(Singing)*

You can't hear a sound—not the turn of a leaf,
Nor the fall of a wave, hittin' the sand.
The tide's creepin' up on the beach like a thief,
Afraid to be caught stealin' the land.
On a night like this I start to wonder what life is all about.

JULIE   And I always say two heads are better than one, to
figger it out.

BILLY   *(Spoken over short musical interlude)* I don't need you
or anyone to help me. I got it figgered out for myself. We ain't
important. What are we? A couple of specks of nothin'. Look
up there. *(He sings)*

There's a helluva lot o' stars in the sky,
And the sky's so big the sea looks small,
And two little people—
You and I—
We don't count at all.

*(They are silent for a while, the music continuing. BILLY looks
down at her and speaks)*

You're a funny kid. Don't remember ever meetin' a girl like
you. You—are you tryin' t'get me to marry you?

JULIE   No.

BILLY   Then what's puttin' it into my head? You're different
all right. Don't know what it is. You look up at me with that
little kid face like—like you trusted me. I wonder what it'd be
like.

JULIE   What?

BILLY   Nothin'. I know what it'd be like. It'd be awful. I can
just see myself— *(He sings)*

Kinda scrawny and pale, pickin' at my food,
And lovesick like any other guy—
I'd throw away my sweater and dress up like a dude
In a dickey and a collar and a tie . . .
If I loved you—

JULIE   *(Speaking)* But you don't.

BILLY   *(Speaking)* No I don't. *(Singing)*

But somehow I can see
Just exactly how I'd be.
If I loved you,
Time and again I would try to say
All I'd want you to know.
If I loved you,
Words wouldn't come in an easy way—
Round in circles I'd go!
Longing to tell you, but afraid and shy,
I'd let my golden chances pass me by.
Soon you'd leave me,
Off you would go in the mist of day,
Never, never to know
How I loved you—
If I loved you.

*(He thinks it over for a few silent moments. Then he shakes his
head ruefully. He turns to JULIE and frowns at her. The rest of
the scene is spoken over music)*

I'm not a feller to marry anybody. Even if a girl was foolish
enough to want me to, I wouldn't.

JULIE   *(Looking right up at him)* Don't worry about it—Billy.

BILLY   Who's worried!

(She smiles and looks up at the trees)

JULIE   You're right about there bein' no wind. The blossoms
are jest comin' down by theirselves. Jest their time to, I
reckon.

*(BILLY looks straight ahead of him, a troubled expression in his

eyes. JULIE *looks up at him, smiling, patient. The music rises
ecstatically. He crosses nearer to her and looks down at her.
She doesn't move her eyes from his. He takes her face in his
hands, leans down, and kisses her gently. The curtains close as
the lights dim)*

In *The King and I*, Rodgers and Hammerstein wrote a
beautiful song for the heroine, Anna Leonowens, which characterizes her vividly. In "Hello, Young Lovers" she is suddenly
the queen of the whole world. She is a lady. She *projects*
emotion but indicates that she feels none. It is as though she
were high up somewhere, looking down on all lovers everywhere. She understands them, embraces, and counsels them.
She speaks of her now-dead love but with no self-pity. She tells
of a "chance that you'll meet," which is "not really by chance."
In this song Anna has the grandeur and coolness of a goddess.

One of Hammerstein's unusual devices in this lyric is the use
of repetition: sometimes the repetition is exact, sometimes approximate. The rhymes here are few and apparent and I will
not indicate them. Above all else, the expression of a unique,
strong and brave woman is clearly articulated.

"HELLO, YOUNG LOVERS"

When I think of Tom
I think about a night
When the earth smelled of summer
And the sky was streaked with white,
And the soft mist of England
Was sleeping on a hill—
I remember this,
And I always will . . .
There are new lovers now on the same silent hill,
Looking on the same blue sea,
And I know Tom and I are a part of them all,
And they're all a part of Tom and me.

Hello, young lovers, whoever you are,
I hope your troubles are few.
All my good wishes go with you tonight—
I've been in love like you.
Be brave, young lovers, and follow your star,
Be brave and faithful and true,
Cling very close to each other tonight—
I've been in love like you.
I know how it feels to have wings on your heels,
And to fly down a street in a trance.
You fly down a street on the chance that you'll meet,
And you meet—not really by chance.
Don't cry, young lovers, whatever you do,
Don't cry because I'm alone;
All of my memories are happy tonight,
I've had a love of my own,
I've had a love of my own, like you—
I've had a love of my own.

Also from *The King and I*, Lady Thiang, the "favorite wife,"
is given a song, "Something Wonderful," which clearly characterizes her, although the subject of the song actually is her
husband, the king. Through her description and attitudes concerning him, one perceives her own self clearly. She is warm,
sensitive, loyal, mature, and loving. The prominent feature of
the lyrics in this song, as in Mrs. Anna's "Hello, Young

Lovers," is Hammerstein's effective use of repetition. Again, the rhymes are sparse and apparent. Incidentally, the musical theme of the chorus, that is, the first two notes, are very close musical transcriptions of normal pleading speech. Try it!

In addition to characterizing the singer, this song has a plot function: Lady Thiang is trying to persuade Mrs. Anna to help the King. Repetition is used for emphasis.

"SOMETHING WONDERFUL"

This is a man who thinks with his heart,
His heart is not always wise.
This is a man who stumbles and falls,
But this is a man who tries.
This is a man you'll forgive and forgive,
And help and protect, as long as you live . . .
He will not always say
What you would have him say
But now and then he'll say
Something wonderful.
The thoughtless things he'll do
Will hurt and worry you—
Then all at once he'll do
Something wonderful.
He has a thousand dreams
That won't come true.
You know that he believes in them
And that's enough for you.
You'll always go along,
Defend him when he's wrong
And tell him, when he's strong
He is wonderful.
He'll always need your love—
And so he'll get your love—
A man who needs your love
Can be wonderful!

One of the many jewels in *South Pacific* is a very simple song, "Some Enchanted Evening," given to Emile De Becque, the hero. In this song the words and music are so inseparable that (as Hammerstein once wrote, speaking generally) you can scarcely think of one without the other.

Within this simple lyric Hammerstein's style of repetition is again at work. The song consists of a regular chorus (AABA) with a coda (ending). The rhymes are few and completely consistent: the last two lines of each of the three A sections rhyme. The B section (release) is half the length of one A section, and the coda is a repetition of B. The first time the B section is used lines 2 and 4 rhyme. The coda repetition has no rhymes.

For me the most remarkable feature of this lyric is its simple organization. In each A section there is a key verb that in itself tells the entire tiny narration: see, hear, feel. Each is a progressive experience "across a crowded room." Hammerstein, for this one, completely sets the stage.

"SOME ENCHANTED EVENING"

Some enchanted evening
You may see a stranger,
You may see a stranger
Across a crowded room.
And somehow you know,

You know even then,
That somewhere you'll see her again and again.

Some enchanted evening
Someone may be laughing,
You may hear her laughing
Across a crowded room—
And night after night,
As strange as it seems,
The sound of her laughter will sing in your dreams.

Who can explain it?
Who can tell you why?
Fools give you reasons—
Wise men never try.

Some enchanted evening,
When you find your true love,
When you feel her call you
Across a crowded room—
Then fly to her side
And make her your own,
Or all through your life you may dream all alone.

Once you have found her,
Never let her go.
Once you have found her,
Never let her go!

Lieutenant Cable, the young lover in *South Pacific*, has a song that contains unusual lyrics, particularly for a love song. First of all there is the image "lovely face." Otherwise, "love" is not mentioned. Second and most interesting, there is only one rhyme in the entire chorus! Hammerstein employs a different device: he creates a rhythmic lilt with one small exception, consistent throughout the song. This takes the form of a two-syllable adjective at the start of a line, invariably followed by "than," which then makes a comparison with another two-syllable word.

"YOUNGER THAN SPRINGTIME"

I touch your hand,
And my arms grow strong,
Like a pair of birds
That burst with song.
My eyes look down
At your lovely face,
And I hold the world
In my embrace.

Younger than springtime are you,
Softer than starlight are you;
Warmer than winds of June are the gentle lips you gave me.
Gayer than laughter are you,
Sweeter than music are you;
Angel and lover, heaven and earth
Are you to me.
And when your youth and joy invade my arms
And fill my heart, as now they do,
Then, younger than springtime am I,
Angel and lover, heaven and earth,
Am I with you.

It is difficult to conclude this section on the distinguished work of Oscar Hammerstein II, since he left us such a large amount of marvelous material. Because of space limitations it is necessary that I do conclude and I should like finally to quote what appears to be a simple lyric from *State Fair,* a film that Rodgers and Hammerstein wrote the music and lyrics for in 1945. In "It Might as Well Be Spring" one of the principal features of both words and music is the graceful sense of "jumpiness." Both are "angular" and restless.

Hammerstein achieves this effect in his lyrics by the juxtaposition of hard dissimilar consonants. In spite of his having worked to arrive at such an effect, he nevertheless employed rhymes. The words here do not melt into each other but rather require considerable articulative gymnastics. This is, of course, intentional. Try reading the words aloud!

"IT MIGHT AS WELL BE SPRING"

CHORUS

I'm as restless as a willow in a windstorm,
I'm as jumpy as a puppet on a string!
(I'd say that I had spring fever,
But I know it isn't spring.)
I am starry-eyed and vaguely discontented,
Like a nightingale without a song to sing.
(Oh, why should I have spring fever
When it isn't even spring?)
I keep wishing I were somewhere else,
Walking down a strange new street,
Hearing words that I have never heard
From a man I've yet to meet.

I'm as busy as a spider, spinning daydreams,
I'm as giddy as a baby on a swing.
I haven't seen a crocus or a rosebud
Or a robin on the wing,

CODA

But I feel so gay—in a melancholy way—
That it might as well be spring . . .
It might as well be spring.

Hammerstein's growth in forty years was enormous. Obviously he was possessed of a distinguished talent, and continually strove to do better in whatever it was he felt he did not do well enough. He was blessed with great and sensitive collaborators and his contributions to our theatre are measureless.

I should like to close this section with Hammerstein's own advice about song writing.

The most important ingredient of a good song is sincerity. Let the song be yours and yours alone. However important, however trivial, believe it. Mean it from the bottom of your heart, and say what is on your mind as carefully, as clearly, as beautifully as you can. Show it to no one until you are certain that you cannot make one change that would improve it. After that, however, be willing to make improvements if someone can convince you that they are needed.

Ira Gershwin
(b. 1896)

Ira Gershwin's work is almost invariably associated with that of his brother George. However, after a collaboration on eighteen theatre and motion picture scores, George's tragic death in 1937 left Ira without a composer. As good lyricists are hard to come by, Ira was in demand and he worked both earlier and subsequently with Vincent Youmans, Arthur Schwartz, Jerome Kern, Vernon Duke, Harry Warren, Kurt Weill, Harold Arlen, and Burton Lane. Although much of this work was for the theatre, a large part also involved movies.

In spite of his indispensability, Ira Gershwin, like other lyricists, has occupied a position secondary to composers with whom he worked. In this connection it is a curious fact that although George Gershwin began his theatre contributions in 1916 with *The Passing Show* for which he wrote a single song in collaboration with Sigmund Romberg, he worked with many well-established lyricists in those early years but wrote only two single songs utilizing Ira's lyrics (written under the pseudonym "Arthur Frances"): "The Real American Folk Song" in 1918 and "The Sweetheart Shop" in 1920.

George is credited with single songs and the entire scores of thirty shows from 1916 to 1924 at which time the two brothers began a long and memorable collaboration with *Lady, Be Good.* In only one of these, *Primrose,* produced in London in 1924, Ira was listed as a colyricist, receiving billing second to Desmond Carter. Of these thirty pre-Ira shows, only *The Perfect Fool* (1921), starring Ed Wynn, and *George White's Scandals of 1920* were real successes. *The Scandals,* I note incidentally, boasted at least five reigning stars—a fact that might have accounted for its success.

But George's first real success did occur in 1924 with *Lady, Be Good* in which the brothers collaborated. From that time

onward they worked together through twenty-three productions, in only one of which, *The Song of the Flame,* Ira was not an important part.

In Ira Gershwin's informative book *Lyrics on Several Occasions* (Alfred A. Knopf, 1959), the author concluded a foreword with a postscript:

"Since most of the lyrics in this lodgement were arrived at by fitting words mosaically to music already composed, any resemblance to actual poetry, living or dead, is highly improbable."

Ira Gershwin to a greater degree than any other lyricist with whose work I have become familiar was occupied *first* with arriving at a title. (We will observe different preoccupations in the work of other strong lyricists.) He refers to this in his book almost continuously in describing his work-in-progress. There is nothing wrong with such a preoccupation but in Ira Gershwin's case the extent of it is nearly unique and it is understandable on a number of levels. Since music itself says nothing specifically but only suggests mood or character on a fairly broad basis, the lyricist faced with making appropriate words fit it must decide what these words will be about. Naturally they must not violate the already written music's mood or rhythmic design and they must indeed say something specific.

It is interesting to note in connection with Ira Gershwin's concern with titles the variety of title placements he came up with. Though this is often true of other fine lyricists, there has nevertheless crept into being a limiting and erroneous concept that titles *should* occur as first or last lines in each of the three A sections of a refrain. I would like to point out a few exceptions to this notion that Gershwin employed.

In "My Son-in-Law" from *Park Avenue* (1946), music by Arthur Schwartz, the title is used as the second and fourth lines in each of two refrains and altered to "Dear son-in-law" in the same position in a third refrain.

> He will be six foot two,
> My son-in-law;
> His haircut will be crew,
> My son-in-law.

In "Sure Thing" from *Cover Girl* (1944), music by Jerome Kern, the title is nearly buried in the first line of the refrain.

> Somehow I'm sure I've found a sure thing in You.

Later on he uses "I'm sure I'm sure," and in the last two lines:

> If love can figure out a sure thing,
> That sure thing is you.

In "My Ship" from *Lady in the Dark* (1941), music by Kurt Weill, the title words appear at the start of the first stanza and of the second ("My ship's aglow"); at the end of the second stanza "When my ship comes in" and lastly in the third line of the final six-line stanza "If the ship I sing," of course substituting "the" for "my."

"MY SHIP"

CHORUS

(A) My ship has sails that are made of silk,
The decks are trimmed with gold;
And of jam and spice
There's a paradise
In the hold.

(A) My ship's aglow with a million pearls,
And rubies fill each bin;
The sun sits high
In a sapphire sky
When my ship comes in.

(B) I can wait the years
Till it appears—
One fine day one spring.
But the pearls and such,
They won't mean much
If there's missing just one thing:

(A) I do not care if that day arrives—
That dream need never be—
If the ship I sing
Doesn't also bring
My own true love to me—
My own true love to me.

There are countless other examples, but I believe these three illustrate sufficiently the point I wish to make: there is no hard rule for placement of a title in a lyric and considerable freedom is practiced by skilled technicians.

In the forties, fifties, and sixties the subject matter of a theatre song was somewhat more prescribed and, in general, more narrowed down because of its increasingly closer relationship to character and situation. However, in the twenties and thirties librettos were less important, characters less well defined (more generalized), and songs more freely interpolated. It was easier during that period for a song—often a very good one—having been written with neither character nor situation in mind, to be inserted almost anywhere in a score and assigned to nearly any character, or to the one—according to cast—who was apt to perform it best. These independently conceived songs were frequently first written to stand alone, to suit the needs of the extracurricular pop market, and then mated as well as possible with the elements and needs of the show.

Another lyric practice characteristic of the twenties and thirties was the employment of names and places as subject matter, often in series, of historical, fictional, and biblical celebrities and their habits. Ira Gershwin and Cole Porter used this device most often. Viewed today, they seem to be period hallmarks. Gershwin, for example, employed Salome, Circe, Venus, Cleo, Psyche, Jezebel, Gardens of Old Babylon, Good Queen Bess, Wellington, Waterloo, Columbus, Edison, and many many others. And many of these names, or others in sequence, became the very point of the song.

In viewing the broad canvas of Ira Gershwin's work, the temptation arises to think first of his cleverness, wry sense of humor, and apparent facility at rhyme. However, on more sober reflection, one is confronted by so much more, so much variety, such depth of feeling that our earlier conclusion in regard to his predominant cleverness has to be revised.

Gershwin's sense of feeling can be noted to a marked degree. His methods of expressing it are diverse and in many ways unique. I should like to quote four lyrics that bespeak emotions, or feelings, as opposed to playful frivolity, as their guiding force. All are gentle but their differences will be noted.

The first—"Embraceable You"—was incorporated into *Girl Crazy* (1930) but, characteristic especially of that period, was originally written for another show, *East Is West*, which failed to materialize. Ira Gershwin points out his "four-syllable rhymes—unusual in a sentimental ballad."

> embraceable you
> irreplaceable you
> silk and laceable you
>
> tipsy in me
> gypsy in me
>
> glorify love
> "Encore!" if I love

What Gershwin has not called attention to is the smooth singableness of the words: the rich resonance in the pivotal *m* sounds. This device, probably unconsciously created, literally resonates the chorus. Actually it appears eleven times.

It is also interesting to note the sharp disjointed conversational verbiage in the verse, which is in contrast with the smooth flowing feeling of the chorus. The verse—considering the lyrics alone—"sings" itself as quick and fragmentary (stopping abruptly at each line's end), with many interior breaks due to the employment of sharp consonants—sometimes at the beginnings of words and often at the end. I refer to words like "up," "lock," "what," "kept," "intuition told," "rhythm of my heart beat," "get just what," and so on. The first verse and first chorus (there are two of each) follow:

"EMBRACEABLE YOU"

VERSE

Dozens of girls would storm up;
I had to lock my door.
Somehow I couldn't warm up
To one before.
What was it that controlled me?
What kept my love-life lean?
My intuition told me
You'd come on the scene.
Lady, listen to the rhythm of my heart beat,
And you'll get just what I mean.

CHORUS

Embrace me,
My sweet embraceable you!
Embrace me,
You irreplaceable you!
Just one look at you, my heart grew tipsy in me;
You and you alone bring out the gypsy in me!
I love all
The many charms about you;
Above all
I want my arms about you.
Don't be a naughty baby,
Come to papa, Come to papa, do!
My sweet embraceable you!

A second emotional lyric is "A Foggy Day" from *A Damsel in Distress* (1937). Ira Gershwin says that the words and music of the chorus were completed in less than an hour. The verse with its "wistful loneliness" was composed next day.

It is my own notion that while the verse and the chorus of a song should have an integral functional relationship, they should also contrast with each other. This difference has been achieved in dozens of ways by many different writers. The verse-chorus differential in "A Foggy Day," as in "Embraceable You," is arrived at similarly in that both verses possess a hasty chatty quality as opposed to the fluency of their choruses. However, the chorus of "A Foggy Day" is brighter. Ira Gershwin says that the verse of "Embraceable You" is marked "whimsically," that of "A Foggy Day" is labeled "rather freely," while the chorus of the first bears the motto "rhythmically" and that of the second advises "brighter but warmly." Once again, the lyrics of the warm if bright rhythmic song abound in *m* and *n* resonances that are important in helping to create a vocal mellifluousness.

"A FOGGY DAY"

VERSE

I was a stranger in the city.
Out of town were the people I knew.
I had that feeling of self-pity:
What to do? What to do? What to do?
The outlook was decidedly blue.
But as I walked through the foggy streets alone,
It turned out to be the luckiest day I've known.

CHORUS

A foggy day in London Town
Had me low and had me down.
I viewed the morning with alarm.

The British Museum had lost its charm.
How long, I wondered, could this thing last?
But the age of miracles hadn't passed,
For, suddenly, I saw you there—
And through foggy London Town
The sun was shining ev'rywhere.

The third of the emotional (romantic) quartet selected here is "Someone to Watch Over Me" from *Oh, Kay!* (1926)—the first total collaboration between the brothers. Ira Gershwin writes that the chorus was first conceived as "fast and jazzy," that one day George played it—with no apparent purpose—slowly, and that both of them instantly agreed that the slower "wistful and warm" version was the proper one.

The verse-chorus contrasts are in practice here.

"SOMEONE TO WATCH OVER ME"

VERSE

There's a saying old
Says that love is blind,
Still we're often told
"Seek and ye shall find."
So I'm going to seek
A certain lad I've had in mind.
Looking ev'rywhere,
Haven't found him yet;
He's the big affair
I cannot forget.
Only man I ever
Think of with regret.
I'd like to add his initial to my monogram.
Tell me, where is the shepherd for this lost lamb.

CHORUS

There's a somebody I'm longing to see.*
I hope that he
Turns out to be
Someone who'll watch over me.

I'm a little lamb who's lost in the wood.
I know I could
Always be good
To one who'll watch over me.

† Although he may not be the man some
Girls think of as handsome.
To my heart he'll carry the key.

Won't you tell him, please, to put on some speed,
Follow my lead,
Oh, how I need
Someone to watch over me.

The last of the "feeling" quartet to be quoted here is "Bidin' My Time," also from *Girl Crazy* (1930). Ira Gershwin characterizes it accurately as "lazy, lethargic." This song, unlike the others, was performed by a quartet, The Foursome.

---

* Observe the triple rhymes in all three A sections of the chorus with a fourth rhyme in A¹.
† The use of "although" at the start of the release, or B, section points to the section's contrasting point of view.

The two verses of "Bidin' My Time" consist of four lyric lines, in each of which there is a well-known song title. The undulating lazy mood begins with the refrain, or chorus. The title appears four times in one chorus. The well-known feature of these lyrics is the wry rhyme "I'm" with "Time," which accentuates the lazy mood. Besides—and importantly—the consistent dropping of the final *g*, characteristically southern or midwestern (country style), contributes invaluably to a feeling of indolence and folksiness.

One curious phenomenon of this song is the quiet, implied humor embedded in the laziness.

> Somethin's bound to happen;
> This year, next year,

gives the feeling of nothing *ever* happening and such nothingness being in no way significant. And

> Chasin' 'way flies,
> How the day flies,

paints a marvelous ironic picture of life racing by despite uneventfulness. It creates at least in this listener a sense of envy: contentment with a slow-motion or even a no-motion life.

Last I should like to call attention to the fourth lines of the second stanzas in each of the two choruses: a real relationship exists. In chorus 1 the line is "I'll just keep on nappin'—" and in chorus 2 the corresponding line is "Dream like Rip Van Winkle." This device adds a nice sense of unity to the song.

"BIDIN' MY TIME"

VERSE I
Some fellers love to Tip-Toe Through The Tulips;
Some fellers go on Singing In The Rain.
Some fellers keep on Paintin' Skies With Sunshine.
Some fellers must go Swingin' Down The Lane.
But

CHORUS I
I'm Bidin' My Time,
'Cause that's the kinda guy I'm,
While other folks grow dizzy
I keep busy
Bidin' My Time.

Next year, next year,
Somethin's bound to happen;
This year, this year,
I'll just keep on nappin',

And Bidin' My Time,
'Cause that's the kinda guy I'm.
There's no regrettin'
When I'm settin',
Bidin' My Time.

VERSE II
Some fellers love to Tell It To The Daisies;
Some stroll beneath The Honeysuckle Vines;
Some fellers when they've Climbed The Highest Mountain
Still keep A-Cryin' For The Carolines.
But

CHORUS II
I'm Bidin' My Time,

'Cause that's the kinda guy I'm.
Beginnin' on a Monday
Right through Sunday,
Bidin' My Time.

Give me, give me,
A glass that's full of tinkle;
Let me, let me,
Dream like Rip Van Winkle.

He Bided His Time
And like that Winkle guy I'm
Chasin' 'way flies,
How the day flies,
Bidin' My Time.

I have chosen three songs in a mood opposite to the preceding gentle ballads. All of them are rhythm songs, all exuberant, bustling, and bright: "Love Is Sweeping the Country" from *Of Thee I Sing* (1931), "I Got Rhythm" from *Girl Crazy* (1930), and "Oh, Lady, Be Good!" from *Lady, Be Good* (1924).

The first is a geyser of unbridled joyous energy that erupts at the outset of the refrain. In contrast to this rhythmic binge is the more contemplative verse. The idea of the song comes very literally from the theme of the book *Of Thee I Sing*, in which the presidential campaign platform has only a single plank: love.

The chorus form is unusual in that A1 is sixteen bars, A2 is eight bars, and I would term the final sixteen, a development "pushing to an ending." Because of the music's odd shape, the design of the lyrics is correspondingly odd.

An interlude follows the refrain. This consists of four four-line stanzas, which return to a chorus repetition.

Ira Gershwin says that the music of this patter was another bit of salvaging from the abandoned *East Is West*.

In the lyrics of the patter the tricky vowel pattern in the second stanza must be noted especially. Ira Gershwin has

> Cal-
> Ifornia
> festi*val*
> Of or*anges*

He also amusingly rhymes "hapless" with "Minneap'lis!" and in his third stanza "zones" of line 1 must of necessity rhyme with "Cohns" of line 3, creating additional humor through an essential reversal of the usual meaning: "And I hear the Cohns/ Are taking up the Cabots."

"LOVE IS SWEEPING THE COUNTRY"

VERSE
Why are people gay(1)
All the night and day(1),
Feeling as they never felt before(2)?
What is the thing(3)
That makes them sing(3)?

Rich man, poor man, thief(4),
Doctor, lawyer, chief(4),
Feel a feeling that they can't ignore(2);
It plays a part(5)
In ev'ry heart(5),

And ev'ry heart is shouting "Encore(2)!"

CHORUS
(A1) Love is sweeping the country;
Waves are hugging the shore(2);
All the sexes(7)
From Maine to Texas(7)
Have never known such love before(2).

(A2) See them billing and cooing
Like the birdies above(6)!
(B) Girl and boy(8) alike,
Sharing joy(8) alike,
Feel that passion'll(9)
Soon be national(9).
(A3) Love is sweeping the country—
There never was so much love(6)!

PATTER
Spring is in the air(10)—
Each mortal loves his neighbor(11);
Who's that loving pair(10)?
That's Capital and Labor(11).

Florida and Cal-(12)
Ifornia get together(13)
In a festival(12)
Of oranges and weather(13).

Boston upper zones(14)
Are changing social habits(15),
And I hear the Cohns(14)
Are taking up the Cabots(15).

Cities are above(6)
The quarrels that were hapless(17).
Look who's making love(6):
St. Paul and Minneap'lis(17)!

CHORUS REPEATED

In connection with "I Got Rhythm" I would like to quote liberally from Ira Gershwin's own interesting comments, which delineate phases of the creative process.

Filling in the seventy-three syllables of the refrain wasn't as simple as it sounds. For over two weeks I kept fooling around with various titles and with sets of double rhymes for the trios of short two-foot lines. I'll ad lib a dummy to show what I was at: "Roly-Poly,/ Eating solely/ Ravioli,/ Better watch your diet or bust./ Lunch or dinner,/ You're a sinner./ Please get thinner./ Losing all that fat is a must." Yet, no matter what series of double rhymes—even pretty good ones—I tried, the results were not quite satisfactory; they seemed at best to give a pleasant and jingly Mother Goose quality to a tune which should throw its weight around more. Getting nowhere, I then found myself not bothering with the rhyme scheme I'd considered necessary (aaab, cccb) and experimenting with non-rhyming lines like (dummy); "Just go forward;/ Don't look backward;/ And you'll soon be/ Winding up ahead of the game." This approach felt stronger, and finally I arrived at the present refrain (the rhymed verse came later), with only "more—door" and "mind him—find him" the rhymes. Though

there is nothing remarkable about all this, it was a bit daring for me who usually depended on rhyme insurance.

But what *is* singular about this lyric is that the phrase "Who could ask for anything more?" occurs four times—which, ordinarily and unquestionably, should make that phrase the title. Somehow the first line of the refrain sounded more arresting and provocative. Therefore, "I Got Rhythm."

In the title and refrain of this song (also in "I Got Plenty o' Nuthin'") "got" is heard in its most colloquial form—the one used for the present tense instead of "have," and the one going back to my childhood: e.g., "I got a toothache" didn't mean "I had a toothache," but only "I have" one. Thumbing through many authorities on usage, style, and dialect, I find no discussion of "got" as a complete substitute for "have." This is somewhat surprising when one considers, say, how often and for how many years the spiritual "All o' God's Chillun Got Shoes" ("I got shoes, you got shoes") has been heard.

On my own, I should like to point out the train-of-thought connections used in each A section, which help enormously to create a sense of unity. In the first A the key topic words are "rhythm," "music," and "man"; in the second "daisies," "pastures," and "man"; in the final A we have "starlight," "sweet dreams," and "man." The connections between the first two words in each section seem obvious. The invariable employment of "man" is germane to the basic idea. Its repetition after each of the first two lines ties it in meaningfully to "music," "pastures," and "dreams," which modify it.

"I GOT RHYTHM"

VERSE
Days can be sunny(1),
With never a sigh(2);
Don't need what money(1)
Can buy(2).

Birds in the tree(3) sing
Their dayful of song(4),
Why shouldn't we(3) sing
Along(4)?

I'm chipper all the day(5),
Happy with my lot(6).
How do I get that way(5)?
Look at what I've got(6):

CHORUS *
(A1) I got rhythm,
I got music
I got my man—
Who could ask for anything more(7)?

(A2) I got daisies
In green pastures,
I got my man
Who could ask for anything more(7)?

(B) Old Man Trouble,

* The rhymes in this chorus are fewer than in most other Gershwin lyrics.

I don't mind(8) him
You won't find(8) him
'Round my door(7).

(A3) I got starlight,
I got sweet dreams,
I got my man
Who could ask for anything more(7),
Who could ask for anything more(7)?

Ira Gershwin wrote "I Can't Get Started" with Vernon Duke, for the *Ziegfeld Follies of 1936,* a film. The song is contained within an amusing sketch involving a man and a woman. The man's complaint is voiced in the song title. After the song in the sketch, the man kisses the woman and she exclaims, "Heavens! You're Wonderful! Just marvelous! Marvelous!" He: "That's all I wanted to know. Well, good night." (Blackout as he leaves her and walks off jauntily.)

In my opinion this is an unusually delightful lyric in addition to its containing a number of technical virtues, which, added together, emerge as a kind of rhyming tour de force. The song is witty and the words are so ordered and colored that they are easy to sing.

"I CAN'T GET STARTED"

VERSE
I'm a glum one(1); it's explainable(2):
I met someone(1) unattainable(2).
Life's a bore(3),
The world is my oyster no more(3).
All the papers(4), where I led(5) the news
With my capers(4), now will spread(5) the news:
"Superman(6)
Turns Out To Be A Flash In the Pan(6)."

CHORUS
(A) I've flown around the world in a plane(7);
I've settled revolutions in Spain(7);
The North Pole I've charted(8),
But I can't get started(8) with you.

(A) Around a golf course I'm under par(9),
And all the movies want me to star(9);
I've got a house, a show-place(10)—
But I get *no* place(10) with you.

(B) You're so supreme(11),
Lyrics I write(15) of you;
Scheme(11)
Just for the sight(15) of you(12);
Dream(11)
Both day and night(15) of you(12),
And what good does it do(12)?

(A) When J. P. Morgan bows, I just nod(13);
Green Pastures wanted me to play God(13).
But you've got me down-hearted(14)
'Cause I can't get started(14) with you(12).

Note the wide variety of line lengths in this lyric and the use of interior as well as line-end rhymes.

In "One Life to Live" from *Lady in the Dark* with music by Kurt Weill (1941), Gershwin wrote words for a most urbane and witty ballad. The feeling is triste.

There are one verse and two choruses. The chief features are—in the verse—a quadruple interior rhyme. (Most, host, ghost, toast.) In the refrain, or chorus, in *all* three A sections lines 2 and 5 rhyme *throughout.* In the first chorus a rhyme is made by reducing "river" to "riv," and in the second, "oblivion" is reduced to "obliv"—a device that gives jauntiness to the meaning and a certain savoir faire to the character of the singer (the heroine).

In addition to elaborate feux d'artifice of all kinds, the song presents clearly the character of the heroine or more accurately her feelings about her character: jaded, sophisticated, brittle, yet somewhat sad.

"ONE LIFE TO LIVE"

VERSE
There are many minds in circulation(1)
Believing in reincarnation(1).
In me you see(2)
One who doesn't agree(2).
Challenging all possible affronts(3),
I believe I'll only live once(3),
And I want to make the most(4) of it:
If there's a party I want to be the host(4) of it;
If there's a haunted house I want to be the ghost(4) of it;
If I'm in town I want to be the toast(4) of it.

CHORUS I
(A1) I say to me ev'ry morning:
You've only one life to live(5),
So why be done in(6)?
Let's let the sun in(6),
And gloom can jump in the riv'(5).

(A2) No use to beat on the doldrums;
Let's be imaginative(5).
Each day is numbered(7)—
No good when slumbered(7)—
With only one life to live(5).

(B) Why let the goblins upset you(8)?
One smile and see how they run(9),
And what does worrying net you(8)?
Nothing(10)!
Tha thing(10)
Is to have fun(9).

(A3) All this may sound kind of hackneyed,
But it's the best I can give(5).
Soon comes December(11),
So, please remember(11),
You've only one life to live(5),
Just—one life to live(5).

CHORUS II
(A1) She says to her ev'ry morning:
She's only one life to live(5);
No time like Now-time(12)
For that big Wow-time(12),
And gloom can jump in the riv'(5).

(A2) What you collect at the grindstone
Becomes a millstone in time(12).
This is my thesis(13):

Why go to pieces(13)?
Step out while you're in your prime(12).

(B) They may say I'm an escapist(14),
But I would rather, by far(15),
Be that than be a red tape-ist(14).
Lead me(16),
Speed me(16),
Straight to the bar(15)!

(A3) Just laugh at Old Man Repression—
He'll fade out into obliv'(5)—
And you're the winner(16)!
I'm off to dinner(16)!
I've only one life to live(5),
Just—one life to live(5).

Note that the title line "One Life to Live" occurs in changing positions; in chorus 1, for example, it is line 2 of A1, line 5 of A2, and 5 and 6 of A3.

"The Princess of Pure Delight" (also from *Lady in the Dark*) is a fairy tale saga in the tradition of *Turandot*. Ira Gershwin in his *Lyrics on Several Occasions* tells an interesting tale, which accounts for the genesis of the idea.

...one Sunday night Richard Rodgers, who had been weekending at nearby George Kaufman's, offered us a ride back to the city [we had come by train], a convenience gladly accepted. We were to leave about nine p.m., but it was decided to wait until city-bound traffic died down a bit. To pass the time, Dick picked an old quiz-and-conundrum book of the Twenties from Moss's shelves; and all present spent an hour or so answering quiz questions, correcting twisted quotations, solving riddles, &c. End of Part One.

Some weeks later when Kurt and I were on the Second Dream Sequence we came to a spot where Liza and some children were alone on the stage. I suggested—and Kurt liked the notion—that here a sung fairy tale might be incorporated. So next day I got hold of some Andersen and the Brothers Grimm, and leafed through for something not too well known to base a narrative on—any short one that could be transformed into a song. In my anxiousness to find something quickly, probably much possible was overlooked; my hurried impressions pictured mainly young princes turning into frogs and vice versa. Which form of corporeal alchemy seemed too complicated and farfetched. Metamorphosis out, I began thinking of other legendary musical gimmicks and concluded that the kind used so frequently in *The Arabian Nights' Entertainments* might do the trick: one where an in-a-spot young man answers brilliantly one or several loaded questions, and reaps, from a delighted and amazed potentate, rewards of non-decapitation, bushels of diamonds and rubies, and other desiderata. It was then that I remembered the Sunday night mentioned above and *my* brilliant answer to a conundrum Dick put: "What word of five letters is never spelled right?" This seemed short, sweet and possible for a device; so, having something to head for, I started.

"The Princess of Pure Delight" is a narrative ballad as distinguished from a love ballad.

There are eight four-line stanzas with an added fifth line that provides a droll grown-up comment—un-fairy-tale-like in style. Only the final stanza lacks the commenting fifth line. The rhyme scheme is simple AABB throughout. The meter, iambic tetrameter, is unchangeable. While the four-line stanza is elementary fairy-tale jingle in style—in no way attempting to sound archaic, the commenting fifth line is obviously contemporary and spoken.

Ira Gershwin says that the comment on stanza 3, "That will be twenty gulden, please," was written "because several of my friends were being analyzed at 20 dollars a session."

"THE PRINCESS OF PURE DELIGHT"

(A) The Prince in Orange and the Prince in Blue,
And the Prince whose raiment was of Lavender hue—
They sighed and they suffered and they tossed at night
For the neighboring Princess of Pure Delight . . . .
(Who was secretly in love with a Minstrel)

(B) Her father, the King, didn't know which to choose;
There were two charming suitors he'd have to refuse.
So he called for the Dean of his Sorcerers and
Inquired which one was to win her hand.
(Which they always did in those days)

(A) "My King, here's a riddle—(you test them tonight):
'What word of five letters is never spelled right?
What word of five letters is always spelled wrong?'
The one who can answer will be wedded ere long.
That will be twenty gulden, please."

(B) The King called the three and he told them the test,
The while his fair daughter kept beating her breast.
He put them the riddle. They failed (as he feared).
Then all of a sudden the Minstrel appeared!
(Quite out of breath)

(C) "I'll answer that riddle," cried the Singer of Song.
"What's never spelled 'right' in five letters is 'wrong,'
And it's right to spell 'wrong'—w-r-o-n-g!
Your Highness, the Princess belongeth to me.
And I love her, anyway!"

(A) "Be off with you, villain!" the King cried in rage,
"For my Princess a Prince—not a man from the stage."
"But, Sire!" said the Minstrel, "'tis love makes me say
No King who's a real King treats lovers this way!
It isn't sporting.

(B) And if you're no real King, no Princess is she—
And if she's no Princess then she can wed me!"
"By gad," cried His Highness, "you handsome young knave,
I fear me you're right!" and his blessing he gave,
As a trumpeter began to trumpet.

(A) The Princess then quickly came out of her swoon
And she looked at her swain and her world was in tune.
And the castle soon rang with cheer and with laughter.
(And of course they lived happily ever after)

Note that the form of this ballad is *not* AABA. A C, or new section, was added for relief. This form is ABABCABA.

Most of the songs reprinted here were written for shows (and one for a film). Only four are somewhat motivated by char-

acters and libretto situations. The assignment of songs to characters and their placement within situations were in general
practice in our musical theatre until roughly the late twenties.
Jerome Kern seems to have been the first to conceive a theatre
in which the various elements were to be integrated. He was
able gradually to put his ideas into practice in *Show Boat*
(1927), *The Cat and the Fiddle* (1931), and *Roberta* (1933), and
there is no doubt that his leadership in the direction of integration greatly influenced Rodgers and Hart and other later
writers.

"My Ship," "One Life to Live," and "The Princess of Pure
Delight" from *Lady in the Dark* previously quoted belong to
the later period when songs had begun to grow out of character
and situation. "My Ship" stands at the very center of the *Lady
in the Dark* idea: a confused lady undergoing psychoanalysis in
an attempt to discover her true identity. Specifically, she is
trying to recall completely an old song associated with troubled
memories. "My Ship"—finally remembered—represents her
analytic cure.

Neither the music nor the lyrics—lovely as they are—are more
crucial to the lady or her problem than the quiet lyrical mood
they create. They are not required to expose or develop or even
resolve anything. They represent a childhood memory. They
need to be fancifully pretty and they are. The ship of the lyrics
(and the title) brings "my own true love to me." Sufficient as to
function.

"One Life to Live" has to pinpoint characters and it does.
The singer (the lady) is particularly urbane, somewhat jaded,
somewhat disillusioned, a little sad.

"The Princess of Pure Delight" is a complete cameo narrative within the show itself. As such, it has no obligation to
anyone or to any moment. It must interest and entertain: it does
both.

The last of the Ira Gershwin lyrics to be quoted here is from
Porgy and Bess: "There's a Boat Dat's Leavin' Soon for New
York," sung by Sporting Life in the final act. This song (and
many others from the same opera) is thoroughly integrated in
the situation and serves to expose the character of the singer
clearly. From the lyrics alone we know that Sporting Life is
unscrupulous: Satan, the Tempter. The song is a complete
entity and the music describes Sporting Life as slimy and
malignant. He will get what he wants because he has much to
offer (all evil) and he offers it with a kind of pleasant, if dark,
flourish of generosity. The combination of words and music
here reveals Sporting Life as a kind of magician of subtle power
who can do anything. And the audience observes his snakelike
performance in a sort of hypnotic trance. Although he is the
embodiment of evil, I believe that during this song the
audience actually *desires* him to win out. Sporting Life in
"There's a Boat Dat's Leavin' Soon for New York" is fascinating and irresistible.

For the reader who is unfamiliar with the situation in *Porgy
and Bess* at this point: Porgy has been taken to jail for ques-
tioning in connection with a murder. Sporting Life is now
telling Bess that he will never be released, and in a further effort
to seduce Bess into going away with him, he offers her "happy
dust" (dope), which she had formerly used.

This lyric is dramatic and its function in the show is immea-
surably important. Its many virtues in addition to those theatrical ones mentioned above should be obvious. The rhyme
scheme is a model of consistency.

Ira Gershwin has written the following regarding the use of
dialect:

It didn't matter too much if dialect was exact or not,
considering the stylized and characteristic music. All that
was required was a suggestion of regional flavor; and if the
artist preferred—for personal literacy or racial righteous-
ness—to enumerate any words formally rather than colloquially, that was all right.

"THERE'S A BOAT DAT'S LEAVIN' SOON FOR NEW YORK"

There's a boat dat's leavin' soon for New York.
Come wid me, dat's where we belong, sister.
You an' me kin live dat high life in New York.
Come wid me, dere you can't go wrong, sister.

I'll buy you de swellest mansion
On upper Fifth Avenue,
An' through Harlem we'll go struttin',
We'll go a-struttin',
An' dere be'll nuttin'
Too good for you.
I'll dress you in silks and satins
In de latest Paris styles.
All de blues you'll be forgettin',
You'll be forgettin',
There'll be no frettin'—
Jes' nothin' but smiles.

Come along wid me, dat's de place,
Don't be a fool, come along, come along.
There's a boat dat's leavin' soon for New York,
Come wid me, dat's where we belong, sister.
Dat's where we belong!

Ira Gershwin is a talented man who has served our musical
theatre handsomely through a long period of growth and transition. His "mosaics" invariably provided bright color to the
music he complemented. He was seldom serious and never
lugubrious. Through his high technical achievements he was
able to give near-perfect expression to his considerable talent
and his position in history is assured, not only because of his
association with his brother and many other renowned theatre
composers, but also because of his own unique
accomplishment.

In closing, I should point out a few details in connection with
Ira Gershwin's accomplishments that have otherwise been
omitted here.

First, his use of apocopated rhyme, the end of one rhyming
word cut off: "say" to rhyme with the first syllable of "cra"-zy;
"Spain" to rhyme with the first syllable of "gain"-less. Also
"special rhymes"—for example, in *Park Avenue* "divorcement"
and "of course, meant" and "there's no jury" with "Missouri."

A pet hope of mine was to find the lyrics of a love song in
which "love" was not mentioned. "They All Laughed" is such a
song.

And finally, I should like to quote from Ira Gershwin's own
comment regarding lyricists.

Anyone may turn up with a hit song, as evidenced by any
number of one-hit writers. What, however, I hope some of
the notes have succeeded in indicating—if only between
the lines—is that a career of lyric-writing isn't one that

anyone can easily muscle in on; that if the lyricist who lasts isn't a W. S. Gilbert he is at least literate and conscientious; that even when his words at times sound like something off the cuff, lots of hard work and experience have made them so. And I do believe that generally I am speaking not only for myself but for—in any order you like—Porter, Fields, Berlin, Mercer, Lerner, Loesser, Dietz, Wodehouse, Comden and Green, Hammerstein, Hart, Harburg, and two or three others whose work I respect.

Howard Dietz
(b. 1896)

The big revue craze began more than twenty years prior to the turn of the present century. Harrigan and Hart (with "somewhat" books) held the boards from 1879 to 1891. Weber and Fields with their famed Music Hall and great stars (including Lillian Russell) flourished from 1896 to 1903. George M. Cohan (also with "somewhat" books) did his own thing from 1901 to 1919. Ziegfeld, beginning in 1907, died in 1931 in bankruptcy after his final Follies. The Hippodrome, starting in 1909, enjoyed tremendous success with not only girls, but elephants, swimming pools, and big name bands. The various others *(Greenwich Village Follies, George White's Scandals, Passing Show, Music Box Revue, Earl Carroll's Vanities,* and *John Murray Anderson's Almanacs)* ran from 1912 to about 1931.

By that time the big revues had been had. They were no longer profitable. They got bigger and too expensive, but had little by little lost their sense of novelty. There were simply more girls, more costumes, more stars, but nothing was fresh or new.

A different revue, which became a new tradition, was begun in 1924 with the *Grand Street Follies* and in 1925 with the *Garrick Gaieties,* neither of which was large. Nor did they have girls in the Ziegfeld sense or lavishness of any kind.

Howard Dietz—as lyricist—is more representative of the new revue and he contributed more to its success at its height than anyone else in his particular category. He was a graduate of the Columbia School of Journalism and had his first production as a lyricist in 1924 when he was twenty-eight. This was one of his few flops.

Although Dietz's first show was written with Jerome Kern,

his first important one was the first *Little Show* (1929) (there were two) in collaboration with Arthur Schwartz with whom thereafter he worked most often. Like many subsequent shows to which Dietz contributed lyrics or sketches and lyrics, and finally book and lyrics, this had neither the expensive grooming of the big shows nor the pristine modesty of the small ones. *The Little Show,* like other shows Dietz was associated with *(Three's a Crowd, The Band Wagon, Flying Colors, Revenge with Music* (based on *The Three-Cornered Hat), Between the Devil,* and *Inside U.S.A.),* had a thoroughly first-class production minus girls-for-girls'-sake and wasteful lavishness for its own sake. They had intelligent literate sketches (often written by Dietz) and songs that were better set up for character and situation than those that had been employed in the jumbo revues chiefly for scene-change purposes.

Howard Dietz recently said to me that the "book show is the novel, whereas the revue is the short story." I feel that that says a great deal.

Actually Dietz has much in common with Cole Porter and Ira Gershwin. Their lyrics often undertook the difficult task of amusing. They preceded the "message" period. Their ballads mostly sang of love—sometimes bitter love—but their technique was so clever that the message was often secondary. Instead of *commenting* on their time, they frequently went the other way and *expressed* it.

In the first of Dietz's lyrics I should like to quote, I think the point of view I've just iterated is clarified. In "I Guess I'll Have to Change My Plan" (1929) from *The Little Show,* the subject is "love at first sight" with a superb "hook" at the end: "I've found the one girl I lost."

This would-be affair, like the song itself, is attractive and amusing because of the fascinating rhymes Dietz employs. As in the many other later lyrics, there are musical *syllables* that rhyme with *words*. In this song "lit(tle)" rhymes with "fit." (Later on I shall point out some unusual vowel rhymes.) I believe that the levity of this lyric is established in a single word in the title: "guess."

"I GUESS I'LL HAVE TO CHANGE MY PLAN"

I beheld her and was conquered at the start(1),
And placed her on a pedestal apart(1):
I planned the lit(2)tle hideaway(3) that we would share some day(3).
When I met her I unfold(4)ed all my dream(5),
And told(4) her how she'd fit(2) into my scheme(5) of what bliss is(6).
Then the blow came(7), when she gave her name(7) as "Mis-sus(6)."

I guess I'll have to change my plan(8)
I should have realized there'd be another man(8)!
I overlooked that point completely
Until the big affair began(8);
Before I knew where I was at(9)
I found myself(10) upon the shelf(10) and that was that(9)
I tried to reach the moon but when I got there(11),
All that I could get was the air(11),
My feet are back upon the ground(12),
I've lost the one girl I found(12).

I guess I'll have to change my plan(8)
I should have realized there'd be another man(8)!
Why did I buy(13) those blue pajamas
Before the big affair began(8)?
My boiling point is much too low(14)
For me to try(13) to be a fly(13) Lothario(14)!
I think I'll crawl right back into my shell(15),
Dwell(15)ing in my personal H-ll(15).
I'll have to change my plan around(12)
I've lost the one girl I found(12).

But on second thought this resignation's wrong(16)
Most women want the one who comes along(16)
With love that's secret and more true(17)
Than they're accustomed to(17)
And besides it gives a most romantic edge(18)
When one is sort of hanging on the ledge(18) of abysses(6)
So methinks I do not mind if she's a Mrs(6).

I guess I'll have to change my plan(8)
Supposing after all there is another man(8);
I'm glad I bought those blue pajamas
Before the enterprise began(8),
For all is fair in love and war(19)
And love's a war—that makes it fairer all the more(19);
Forbidden fruit I've heard is better to taste(20),
Why should I let this go to waste(20)—my conscience to the wind is tossed((21)—I've found the one girl I've lost((21).

Three's a Crowd (1930) was unforgettable. "Something to Remember You By" became a classic on its opening night. Schwartz's tune as well as Dietz's lyric—both of which go hand in hand—are special without the need of resorting here to anal-ysis. However, the lyric becomes even more admirable when at least one not easily recognizable aspect is understood: the *ee* sound is heard nine times in the verse and eleven in the chorus. The other (perfect) rhymes are indicated and are particularly clever.

"SOMETHING TO REMEMBER YOU BY"

VERSE
You are lea(1)ving me(1),
And I will try to face(2)
The world alone(3).

What will be(1) will be(1),
But time cannot erase(2)
The love we(1)'ve known(3).

Let me(1) but have a token(4)
Through which your love is spoken(4),

You are lea(1)ving me(1),
But it will say you're my own(3).

CHORUS
Oh(5), give me(1) something to re(1)member you by(6),
When you are far away from me(1), dear;
Some little something, mea(1)ning love cannot die(6),
No(5) matter where you chance to be(1).
Though(5) I'll pray(7) for you(8),
Night and day(7) for you(8);
It will see(1) me(1) through(8) like a charm,
Till your re(1)turning.
So(5) give me(1) something to re(1)member you by(6),
When you are far away(7) from me(1).

The Band Wagon (1931) was small by comparison with anything by Ziegfeld or at the Hippodrome, but in its more economical way it was visually elaborate and exquisite. *The Band Wagon* was indeed a distinguished landmark, and its sketches by Dietz and Kaufman were unforgettable. The stars included Fred and Adele Astaire, Clifton Webb, Tilly Losch, Frank Morgan, and Helen Broderick. "Dancing in the Dark" became a great hit and will remain so indefinitely. I recall its accompanying production, which developed into a dance featuring Tilly Losch dressed in a silver sequin gown, surrounded by a dozen or so girls in white costumes. They moved on a somewhat tilted turntable covered with dark blue velvet. The turntable was employed in different ways throughout the show and this concept, which was Dietz's, marked the first time a turntable was used as a "character" in a show.

The lyrics are classic, uncomplex, and extraordinarily distinguished. One of their chief features is their superb singableness. They are legato—connected—so that each seems to push the one ahead of it on. They are perfect concomitants to the music, demanding little articulative energy. In the chorus, in most lines, one single consonant is emphasized by its repetition:

1. Dancing—dark
2. Till—tune
3. dancing—dark
5. We're waltzing—wonder (3 times)
6. Why we're
9. Looking—light
11. brigh*ten* up *the* ni*ght*

13. the—together
14. Dancing—dark

The title line is never rhymed.

"DANCING IN THE DARK"

CHORUS
Dancing in the dark
Till the tune(1) ends,
We're dancing in the dark
And it soon(1) ends.
We're waltzing in the wonder
Of why(2) we're(3) here(3).
Time hurries by(2)—we're here(3)
And gone
Looking for the light(4)
Of a new(5) love
To bright(4)en up the night(4)
I have you(5), love,
And we can face the music together
Dancing in the dark.

INTERLUDE
What though love is old?
What though song is old?
Through them we can be young!
Hear(6) this heart(7) of mine
Make yours part(7) of mine!
Dear(6) one,
Tell me that we're(6) one!

CHORUS REPEATED

Also in *The Band Wagon,* "I Love Louisa" was staged on a merry-go-round, another employment of the turntable. It is a charmer of a song. In verse 1 there are only two sets of rhymes, and in verse 2, four. In the chorus, however, in addition to some clear rhymes, Dietz has made sixteen $\overline{ee}$ rhymes in thirteen lines! The *i* in Lou-i-sa accounts for eight of them, and they are made to assonate with me (three times), we (twice), plus she, free, and be.

"I LOVE LOUISA"

FIRST VERSE
HE   How I love a glass of beer!
BOYS   More beer!
HE   Beer goes very good with beer.
BOYS   More beer.(2)
HE   When I'm drinking(1)
Beer I'm thinking(1)
Ach—Life is dear(2)
But there's someone I love
Even more than beer(2):

REFRAIN
I love Loui(3)sa(4),
Loui(3)sa(4) loves me(3).
When we(3) rode on the merry-go-round,
I kissed Loui(3)sa(4),
And then Loui(3)sa(4) kissed me(3).
We(3) were so happy, so happy and free(3).
Ach Gott! but she(3)'s a(4)
Beautiful Loui(3)sa(4)—

Ach, when I choose 'em(5)
I love a great big boosom(5)!
Some day Loui(3)sa(4), Loui(3)sa(4) will be(3)
More than just a fraulein to me(3).

SECOND VERSE
HE   Frenchmen love a glass of wine(6).
BOYS   More beer!
HE   English think(7) that whiskey's fine(6).
BOYS   More beer!
HE   When I comb(8) off
All the foam(8) off
I drink(7) a toast(9)
To the Germans and the Madchen I love most(9).

REFRAIN REPEATED

"Miserable with You," also from *The Band Wagon,* has two verses in dialogue form with one chorus for the girl and one for the boy. This is a fun song and quite naturally it is about personal misery. The rhymes are numerous and complex.

"MISERABLE WITH YOU"

VERSE I
SHE   I just came back from a fu(1)neral.
HE   How was it?
SHE   It was nice.
HE   I'm glad you(1) had a chance to enjoy(2) yourself
SHE   I hear you bought a gun
And you're planning to destroy(2) yourself.
HE   Mm-hmm—
That's true(1)
And how about you(1)?

REFRAIN
CHORUS I
SHE   You talk about your trouble(3)
The trouble(3) I've got is double(3)
Oh when will this depression be thru(1)?
Each day it's getting tougher(4),
But since I have to suffer(4)
I might as well be miserable with you(1).

This cough I've got is hacking(5),
The pain in my head is wracking(5),
I hardly need to mention my flu(1).
The Board of Health has seen me(6),
They want to quarantine me(6),
I might as well be miserable with you(1).

Father, Father went and forged a check(7)
So they put him away(8).
Mother, Mother fell and broke her neck(7) today(8)
Hey, hey(8)!

Between my aches and sneezes(9),
My groans and my grunts and wheezes(9),
I guess you see(10) the rea(10)son I'm blue(1).
The doctor says that maybe(11)
I'm going to have a baby(11),
I might as well be miserable with you(1).

VERSE II
HE   I've been run over by a taxicab.
SHE   How was it?

HE   It was nice.
SHE   I'm hoping that at least they will operate(12).
HE   I'd like to get the name
Of the poison that your popper ate(12).
SHE   Okay(8)—what say(8)
We ta(9)ke it today(8)?

CHORUS II
HE   You talk about your trouble(3),
The trouble(3) I've got is double(3),
I'm wanted for a murder or two(1).
It seems that during Lenten(13)
I killed a guy in Trenton(13),
I might as well be miserable with you(1).

The outlook sure is gloomy(6),
The landlord's about to sue me(6)
To get the rent that's long overdue(1).
There's nothing quite as mean as(14)
Avoiding those subpoenas(14).
I might as well be miserable with you(1).

Sis(15)ter, sister, stole a string of pearls(16),
She is funny that way(8).
Brother's wanted 'cause he raped two girls(16), they say(8),
Hey, Hey(8)!

My mis(15)ery is utter(17),
I'm practically in the gutter(17),
And yesterday I heard something new(1)
Mama, when she was plastered(18)
Admitted I'm a bastard(18),
I might as well be miserable with you(1).

The year after the opening of *The Band Wagon*, Dietz and Schwartz wrote another success, *Flying Colors*, and Dietz also collaborated on the book.

"Alone Together" has simple lyrics with clear and consistent rhymes. One feature of the song has to do with its title "Alone Together," which constitutes the entire first line of the first two stanzas, and the final two words (though they are not together on the last line) of the song. "Together" is heard seven times and has no rhyme until after the *sixth* time when it rhymes with "weather." This device seems to tie the chorus into a single entity. As if this were not enough, the sixth "together" is the last word of A2 and the "weather" rhyme is the last word of the first line of A3 with a two-line release interposed.

"ALONE TOGETHER"

Alone together(1),
Beyond the crowd(2),
Above the world.
We're not too proud(2)
To cling together(1)
We're strong(3) as long(3) as we're together(1).

Alone together(1),
The blinding rain(4),
The starless night,
Were not in vain(4)
For we're(5) together(1),
And what is there to fear(5) together(1).

Our love is as deep as the sea(6),
Our love is as great as a love can be(6)

And we(6) can weather(1)
The great unknown(7)
If we're alone(7)
Together(1).

Three years after *Flying Colors* in 1935 Dietz and Schwartz wrote *At Home Abroad*, a hilarious revue starring Beatrice Lillie in which Dietz doubled as lyricist and sketch writer. One of the unforgettable songs, "Geisha," was additionally funny because it was performed by a line of chorus girls in traditional Japanese (à la Madame Butterfly) attire, moving identically except that a single one of them—Beatrice Lillie—spoke the tag-line solo: "It's better with your shoes off." The phraseology of this lyric swings back and forth between ordinary "American": "She's free and Japanesy" and "You can take her home and maybe carry on" versus what might pass for translated oriental poetry: "And sleep in the forest of cherry blossoms."

The rhymes are clear and for the most part simple.

"GEISHA"

If you have merely looked at a Japanese print(1),
Hokasai, Hiroshige, Hokasai,
The chances are you have but a casual hint(1),
Hokasai, Hiroshige, Hokasai,
Of how—of how we live in Japan.

If you have only read Lafcadio Hearn(2),
His books—his books upon Japan,
We don't see how on earth you could possibly learn(2)
Anything about the isle of Nippon(3).
It's an island you should take a trip on(3),
Do you mind if we give you a tip on(3)
The way you should really see Nippon(3)?

CHORUS
Get yourself a Geisha—a gay little Geisha,
A Geisha girl's the surest(4),
The surest(4) guide for the tourist(4).
If the tourist(4) is no purist(4)
He can have a lot of fun(3)
Doing what he ought to do in Tokio.

Get yourself a Geisha—a gay little Geisha,
She(5)'s free(5) and Japane(5)sy(6),
She(5)'s debonairy and bree(5)zy(6),
And she(5) dances hot-strip-teasy(6),
E(5)ven in Japan it's done(3).

She will take you on the town from dark till dawn(7),
You'll drink a lot of Japanese gin.
When you've had enough of Japanese gin
You can take her home and maybe carry on(7)
When you enter a house you take your shoes off
It's better with your shoes off.

Get(8) yourself a Geisha(9)—but only in case ya(9)
Would pass up what's in guidebooks(10);
The tourist knows if he's tried books(10)
That the best things aren't in guidebooks(10);
Let(8) yourself go—go get(8) yourself a Geisha girl.

She will shower you with Oriental charm(11)
In the land of the Radiant sun(3);
You'll wait up nights for the radiant sun(3),

Then together you will wander arm in arm(11),
And sleep in the forest of cherry blossoms.

SHE It's better with your shoes off.
ALL Get yourself a Geisha(9). The flower of Asia(9),
She's one(3) with whom to take up(12).
At night your bed she'll make up(12),
And she'll be there when you wake up(12).
Let yourself go. Go get yourself a Geisha.
Let yourself go. Go get yourself a Geisha.

For the film version of *The Band Wagon* (1953), Schwartz and Dietz wrote another song, "That's Entertainment." The subject matter runs the gamut from classical theatre to farce. Technically, the separate lines of the lyrics go from a single foot to lines of four feet. The rhymes are indicated here, but a few special ones require mention.

The word "entertainment" is made to rhyme in separate positions and in part. We have in the first chorus "vill*ain*" and "enter*tain*ment." In the second chorus we have "her" opposite "en*ter*tainment." In the last section of the second chorus we find "swain" and "slain" in the second line, flirting with "enter*tain*ment" in the last. Then "say" and "way" with "enter*tain*ment" in the first stanza of the final chorus. In the final A of chorus 1 the *ir* rhymes are prevalent. We have clerk and work, skirt and dirt—two sets of real rhymes interconnected by the vowel rhymes. *Then* in the final two lines we have a similar sound twice in "world."

These added attractions make for truly complex amusement.

"THAT'S ENTERTAINMENT"

VERSE
Everything that happens in life
Can happen in a show(1).
You can make 'em laugh,
You can make 'em cry,
Anything—anything can go(1).

FIRST CHORUS
The clown(2)
With his pants(3) falling down(2)
Or the dance(3)
That's a dream of romance(3)
Or the scene(4)
Where the villain(36) is mean(4),
That's entertain(36)ment.

The lights(5) on,
The lady in tights(5),
Or the bride(6)
With the guy on the side(6),
Or the ball(7)
When she gives you her all(7),
That's entertainment.

The plot(8) can be hot(8)—simply teeming with sex(9),
A gay divorcee(10) who is after her 'ex(9).
It could be(10) Oedipus Rex(9),
Where a chap kills his father(11)
And causes a lot of bother(11).
The clerk(12)
Who is thrown out of work(12)
By the boss(13)

Who is thrown for a loss(13)
By the skirt(12)
Who is doing him dirt(12).
The world is a stage
The stage is a world of entertainment.

SECOND CHORUS
The doubt(14)
While the jury is out(14)
Or the thrill(15)
When they're reading the will(15)
Or the chase(16)
For the man with the face(16),
That's entertainment.

The dame(17) who is known as the flame(17),
Or the king(18)
Of an underworld ring(18),
He's an ape(19)
Who won't let her escape(19),
That's entertain(22)ment.

It might(20) be a fight(20), like you see on the screen(21),
A swain(22) getting slain(22), for the love of a queen(21),
Some great Shakespearean scene(21)
Where a ghost and a prince meet(23)
And everyone ends in mincemeat(23).
The gag(24)
May be waving the flag(24)
That began(25)
With a Mister Cohan(25)
Hip Hurray(26)
The American way(26).
The world is a stage,
The stage is a world of entertain(22)ment.

FINALE CHORUS
A show
That is really a show(1)
Sends you out
With a kind of a glow(1)
And you say(26)
As you go(1) on your way(26),
That's entertainment
A song(27)
That is winging along(27)
Or a dance(3)
With a touch of romance(3)
Is the art(28)
That appeals to the heart(28),
That's entertainment.

Admit(29)
We're a hit(29)
And we'll go on from there(30).
We played(31) a charade(31)
That was lighter than air(30),
A good old fashioned affair(30),
As we sing this finale(32),
We hope it was up your alley(32).
No death(33)
Like you get in Macbeth(33),
No ordeal(34)
Like the end of Camille(34),

This goodbye(35)
Brings a tear to the eye(35).
The world is a stage, the stage is a world
Of entertainment.

"New Sun in the Sky" *(The Band Wagon)* besides being a joyous song has, from start to finish, a long list of *oo* rhymes. They are sparked by the use of "new" eleven times. In addition to clear rhymes, "to," "view," and "blue," there is a less obvious partial rhyme in the very first line, "gloo-my," which also clearly rhymes with "to me." Then there is "horizon," "I" rhymes with "sky" and "high," "zon" with "sun." We also have a vowel rhyme in two consecutive lines—"sung" and "hum." Three other vowel rhymes are "reached," "cheery," and "greets." What seems to be a free, open, celebrative song is in fact a complex of innumerable interesting organisms.

"NEW SUN IN THE SKY"

Yesterday, things were so gloomy(1),
But today, yes sir, they're shining and new(2).
Oh, what a change has come to me(1)!
I've been dusted off the shelf(3),
I am not myself(3);
What a diff'rent world I view(2).

I see a new(2) sun(5)
Up in a new(2) sky(4),
And my whole hori(4)zon(5)
Has reached a new(2) high(4)!
Yesterday, my heart sang a blue(2) song,
But today, hear it hum a cheery new(2) song!
I dreamed a new(2) dream,
I saw a new(2) face(6),
And I'm spreading sunshine
All over the place(6),
With a new(2) point of view(2),
Here's what greets my eye(4):
New(2) love, new(2) luck,
New(2) sun in the sky(4)!

In "High and Low" *(The Band Wagon)* there are two sets of unusual bi- and tri-verbal rhymes that should be noted. "Investigator" goes with "made a" plus "greater," and these form a continuous phrase, "made a greater." Also "excitement" relates to both "night meant" and "right meant."

"HIGH AND LOW"

BOY   My life has been devoted to unraveling(1)
A mystery that's old, but ever new(2)—
I've tried to find(3)
The kind(3) of girl who(2)'ll do(2).
GIRL   I've done about a million miles of traveling(1),
I've sailed on all the blue(2);
And now at last
I've hit on you(2)!

REFRAIN
BOY   High(4) and Low(5),
Low(5) and High(4),
I've been looking for you.
You've been hiding, or you'd
Have come to me(6);
My(4) oh(5) me(6),

Me(6) oh(5) my(4),
No(5) investigator(7)
Ever made a(7) greater(7) discovery(6).
I(4) cannot tell you what excitement(8)
That night meant(8) when I met you(9).
And what wrong or right meant(8)
Our hearts only knew(9).
I was low(5),
Now I'm high(4),
High upon a stee(6)ple(9),
Telling all the people(9)
You(8)'ve come to me(10).

"By Myself" from *Between the Devil* (1937) startles one with its very first line, "The party's over," which is, of course, the theme and first line of Comden and Green's song of that name from *Bells Are Ringing* (1956). This sort of thing is not unusual but always surprising. In Dietz's song, the line sets up the verse, which graduates to a chorus, which is in quite another mood from that of the Comden and Green song.

The *y* sounds pervade the first three quatrains of the chorus. In the entire chorus we find *I'll* six times, *I'm* and *I've* once each, and *I* once. By themselves, they would be meaningless but they accentuate the music of by *my*self, deny *my*self, sky, my, try, fly high, I *my*self, and by *my*self.

"BY MYSELF"

VERSE
The party's over,
The game is ended(1),
The dreams I dreamed
Went up in smoke(2),
They didn't pan out
As intended(1).
I should know
How to take a joke(2).

CHORUS
I(3)'ll go my(3) way by(3) my(3)self,
Here's how the comedy ends(4),
I(3)'ll have to deny(3) my(3)self,
Love(17) and laughter and friends(4).

Grey clouds in the sky(3) above(17)
Have put a blot on my(3) fun(5);
I(3)'ll try(3) to fly(3) high(3) above(17)
For a place(6) in the sun(5).

I(3)'ll face(6) the unknown(7),
I(3)'ll build a world of my(3) own(7);
No one knows better than I(3) my(3)self
I(3)'m by(3) my(3)self alone(7).

I(3)'ll have to pass up
All the dinner parties
I(3)'ve been asked to attend(9).
Parties are now at an end(9),
But one comforting consolation(10),
I(3) won't have to listen to the boring conversation(10).

Have to pass up all(11) the shooting weekends
In Gloucester, Worcester and Kent(12);
Oh, the weekends I've spent(12)
Makes me want to yell from St. Paul(11)'s steeple(13),
The people(13) I'd like to shoot are the shooting people(13).

PATTER

I'm in the dog house,
Persona non grata(14),
Receiving snubs(15) at all the clubs(15).
Let me give you a little more data(14),
I'll go no more on the Gay Riviera
Turning Winter to Spring(16)—an unforgivable thing(16),
Put an end to my fling(16).

The first and title line of "I See Your Face Before Me" from *Between the Devil,* as in many of Dietz's lyrics, does not rhyme (except internally) until it appears as the song's last line when "face" rhymes with "erase" in the preceding line. The sentiment is sad but in no sense tortured. The form is unusual.

"I SEE YOUR FACE BEFORE ME"

I see your(1) face before(1) me
Crowding my every dream(2).
There(3) is your(1) face before(1) me,
You are my only theme(2).
It doesn't matter where(3) you are(4),
I can see how fair(3) you are(4),
I close my eyes and there(3) you are(4),
Always

If you could share(3) the magic(5),
If you(6) could see me too(6),
There(3) would be nothing tragic(5)
In all my dreams of you(6).
Would(7) that my love could(7) haunt me so(8),
Knowing I want you so(8),
I can't erase(9)
Your(1) beautiful face(9) before(1) me.

"Triplets" from *Between the Devil* is a curious kind of comedy song, a narrative ballad in which Dietz has employed somewhat made-up names for cities and people. What is curious is that these names might easily have been created for rhyming purposes but such is not the case. The use of Baden Baden Baden and Walla Walla Walla, of course, suggests that each of the triplets says one of the words.

The proper names are matched syllabically as to length but are in no way meant to rhyme: Mrs. Whiffenpoofer, Mrs. Hildendorfer, Mrs. Hassencooper, and Mrs. Goldenwasser, plus later, Doctor Heimerdinger.

The layout is also somewhat unusual. There are a verse, chorus, interlude, and two choruses. At the same point in the three choruses (eighth and ninth line ends) we have words ending with "les" or "els," which make the same sound: measles (twice), vittels (*sic*), bottles, battles, rattles. There is a curious *ā* rhyme in the interlude: day, *ma*jor, *La*ne, day.

"TRIPLETS"

Three(1) little unexpected children simultaneously(1),
The doctor brought us and you can see(1)
That we(1)'ll be three(1) forever and aye-e-i———Oo(2).
You wouldn't know how agonizing being triple can be(1);
Each one is individually(1)
The victim of the clinical day—e-i—oo(2).
Every summer we go away to Baden Baden Baden,
Every winter we come back home to Walla Walla Walla.

We do everything alike,
We look alike, we dress alike,
We walk(3) alike, we talk(3) alike,
And what is more
We hate each other very much.
We hate our folks(4). We're sick of jokes(4).
Oh what an art(5) it is to tell us apart(5).
If one of us gets the measles,
Then all of us get the measles,
And mumps and croup.
How I wish I had a gun(6),
A little gun(6)—it would be fun(6)
To shoot the other two
And be only one(6).

Mrs. Whiffenpoofer loves to talk to Mrs. Hildendorfer
Of the day(7) she went to Sloan's and had her silly(8) Willie(8).
Mrs. Hassencooper loves to talk to Mrs. Goldenwasser
Of her ma(7)jor opera(7)tion when she had her twins.
But when mother comes along she silences the others(9),
She accomplished something that is very rare in mothers(9).
For example(10) just to prove that she was more than ample(10)
She admits La(7)ne Bryant(11) thought they were measuring a giant(11).
Doctor Heimerdinger(12) almost broke his middle finger(12)
On the day(7) that he(1) first looked upon us three(1).

We do everything alike,
We look alike, we dress alike,
We walk(3) alike, we talk(3) alike,
And what is more,
We hate each other very much. We hate our folks(4).
We're sick of jokes(4).
Oh what an art(5) it is to tell us apart(5).
We eat the same kind of vittels,
We drink the same kind of bottles,
We sit in the same kind of highchair (highchair, highchair).
How I wish I had a gun(6)—a little gun(6).
It would be fun(6) to shoot the other two
And be only one(6).

We do everything alike,
We look alike, we dress alike,
We walk(3) alike, we talk(3) alike,
And what is more,
We hate each other very much.
We hate our folks(4). We're sick of jokes(4).
Oh what an art(5) it is to tell us apart(5).
We play the same kind of soldiers,
We fight the same kind of battles(13),
We shake the same kind of rattles(13).
How I wish I had a gun(6)—a little gun(6),
It would be fun(6) to shoot them other two
And be only one(6).

One of the most beautiful ballads among the Schwartz-Dietz creations is "If There Is Someone Lovelier Than You" from *Revenge with Music* (1934), a book-show that Dietz adapted from the Spanish *The Three-Cornered Hat.* The form of this song is verse and chorus (ABA¹ foreshortened). The "hook" at the song's end is quite inventive: "If there is someone lovelier than you . . . [it] can't be true." The rhymes are apparent.

"IF THERE IS SOMEONE LOVELIER THAN YOU"

Every day is a brand new day(1)
When you are mine(2)
But the moment that you go away(1)
No sun will(3) shine(2).
Your love is my reward(4),
Each night I thank the Lord(4).
Tell me till(3) time is done(5)
We'll be one(5).

If there is someone lovelier than you,
Then I am blind(6),
A man without a mind(6);
If there is someone lovelier than you.

But no, I am not blind(6),
My eyes have travelled ev'rywhere(7)
In hope that I might find(6)
A creature half so fair(7).

If there is someone lovelier than you(8),
By all that's beautiful,
Such beauty can't be true(8).

"You and the Night and the Music," also from *Revenge with Music,* has an unusual rhyme feature in that six rhymes appear in places other than at the ends of lines. Also the *ill* sound (prominent among the beginning line rhymes) occurs eight times. There are also many internal and end-line rhymes. There is a unique set of rhymes in: pa(le) light—daylight—may, away.

"YOU AND THE NIGHT AND THE MUSIC"

VERSE
Song is in the air(1)
Telling us romance is ours to share(1).
Now at last we've found one another alone(2).

Love like yours and mine(3)
Has the thrilling glow of sparkling wine(3),
Make the most of time ere it has flown(2).

CHORUS
You and the night and the music
Fill me with flaming desire(5),
Setting my being completely
On fire(5)!

You and the night and the music
Thrill me(4) but will we(4) be one(6),
After the night(7) and the music
Are done(6)?

Until the(4) pa(8)le light(7) of dawning(9) and day(8)light
Our hearts will be(4) throbbing guitars(10)
Morning(9) may(8) come without warning(9),
And take away(8) the stars(10)

If we must live for the moment,
Love till the(4) moment is through(11)!
After the night and the music die
Will I have you(11)?

REPRISE
Tell me, Maria, how could you(11)
Destroy what was more than divine(12)?

I am no longer your lover
For you're no longer mine(12).
I'll give my heart to another
Tear out this feeling for you(11)
And with the morning you'll find
What my revenge will do(11).

CHORUS

"Confession" from *The Band Wagon* (1931) is a dialogue between girls and boys. The form is verse, chorus (dance interlude), and a repetition of the final verse with different lyrics.

This is a delightful "naughty" song, which will always remain a barometer of its time.

"CONFESSION"

BOYS Let me be your father confessor(1)
GIRLS Yes sir, yes sir(1)!
BOYS Tell your innermost thoughts to me(2).
GIRLS That will be hard to do(3).
BOYS Would you mind if I gathered closer(4)?
GIRLS No sir, no sir(4)!
BOYS Let your innermost thoughts come free(2),
It will comfort you(3).
GIRLS If you find you are shocked at the truth(5),
Excuse it on the grounds of youth(5).

REFRAIN
GIRLS I never kissed a man before. . . . .
BOYS Oh isn't that a shame(6)!
GIRLS I never kissed a man before . . .
Before I knew his name(6).

GIRLS I never had a taste for wine . . .
BOYS Oh isn't that a sin(7)!
GIRLS I never had a taste for wine . . .
For wine can't compare with gin(7).

BOYS It's nice as nice(8) can be
Our faith is at last restored
To find that vice(8) can be
Its own reward.

GIRLS I always go to bed at ten . . .
BOYS Oh, isn't that a bore(9)?
GIRLS I always go to bed at ten . . .
But I go home at four(9).

[There will be a dance movement for one-half a chorus, then they will return to the lyric as follows:]

GIRLS It seems quite shockable(10)
Accepting a gif(11)t from men(12).
BOYS But if(11) it's hockable(10)
GIRLS It's dif(11)ferent then(12)
I don't go in for topless gowns
BOYS No that would never do(13)
GIRLS I don't go in for topless gowns
Unless they're bottomless too(13).

It is difficult today to contemplate "Smokin' Reefers" from *Flying Colors* (1932), since that song appeared forty-two years ago! The lyric is a clear meaningful expression of a miserably unhappy black person's attempt to escape from the tribulations of the real world. It paints an accurate picture of the attitude of acceptance as opposed to today's militancy: 1932 versus 1974.

"SMOKIN' REEFERS"

O weed—cigarette that we must all depend on—Marawanna!
O weed—once begin it and you're sure to end on Marawanna!
It's the kind of thing that dreams are made of—
It's the thing that white folks are afraid of—
Up in Harlem
We go on a
Marawanna
Jag

Smokin' reefers
To puff away the misery—
Go away misery—
Blow away,
Blow away!
Smokin' reefers
To get beyond the worryin'—
Go away worryin'—
Blow away!
Blow away!
Must wake up and work in the mornin'
Must get by the broodin' at night—
You can't change the world you were born in
But I declare
You can be walkin' on air. . . .
Smokin' reefers—
You hear the angels sing away
Helping you fling away
Your worry and trouble and care.

An excellent example of Dietz's wry social comment is to be found in "We Won't Take It Back," from *Inside U.S.A.* (1948), a fun song with a thesis.

"WE WON'T TAKE IT BACK"

Long ago the white man come
And he take the country from
The Indian
That's why Redskin he is blue
White man give the finger to
The Indian
But when things get black
He say: "Let's give it back—
Let's give it back to the Indian."
That's how white man feel
But Indian no schlemeel.

Looking inside the country today
Indian see and Indian say
We won't take it back
We won't take it back
Everyone itch and make a big pitch
Try to get wampum, try to get rich
We won't—no we won't—take it back

(Business, Business—all the time Business)

Kaiser Frazer
Schick Injector Razor
Pepsodent Bulova
That's what the country is fulova
They got a machine for every new use
Even know how not to make a papoose
We won't—no we won't—take it back

Chungala boom, Chungala boom
Women wear falsies in the bosoom

Radio when it give you the news
Mix it up with hair tonic you use
We won't take it back
We won't take it back
Columnists pull things out of their sleeve
Announce your baby—before you conceive
We won't—no we won't—take it back

(Gossip, Gossip—all the time Gossip)

Louella Hedda
They both shoulda stooda in bedda
Bromo Seltzer
You take with a column by Elsa

Everyone know what everyone do
Television show who sleeping with who
We won't—no we won't—take it back

Chickasaw char, Chickasaw char
You can't make love in a Studebaker car

Paleface man he true to his bride
But he have something else on the side
We won't take it back
We won't take it back
Feminine sex have many affairs
Marriage is game like musical chairs
We won't—no we won't—take it back

(Husband, Husband—all the time Husband)

Barbara Hutton
Button Button who's got Hutton
Lana Turner
What's cooking on her burner

Masculine sex he measure up short
Indian read the Kinsey Report
We won't—no we won't—take it back

Chickasaw chew, Chickasaw chew
It's better with your beads off.

Women buy dress at Hattie Boshay
Making them look like bundle of hay
But once off the rack
They won't take it back
Two-way stretch is what women wear
Pull it in here and it comes out there
We won't—no we won't—take it back

(New Look, New Look—all the time New Look)

Short skirt, long skirt
The right skirt look like the wrong skirt
Hokus Pokus
Barrel effect in the tokus

Backless strapless evening gown
Can't figure out why it doesn't fall down
We won't—no we won't—take it back

Chickasaw chick, Chickasaw chick
The best things in life are very expensive.

Finally, I should like to quote from "Before I Kiss the World Goodbye" from *Jennie* (1963), music by Arthur Schwartz. This song begins with chorus 1 and subsequently has two verses and another chorus. In a broad sense this belongs in the "September Song" category, except that the Schwartz-Dietz song is less serious and sentimental. There are several special rhymes and examples of assonance here: *use*, true, Blue, Danube (used twice) and *ha*ppy, *ma*tter, *pa*stures.

"BEFORE I KISS THE WORLD GOODBYE"

The days are few,
I dare not waste(1) them.
I want to see and hear
And touch and taste(1) them;
I want to sing(2),
I want to dance(3),
And have a fling(2) in Paris, France(3),
Before I kiss the world goodbye.

I'll do the town
With roller skates on(4);
I'll be my lady fair
A footman waits on(4);
I'll have him cater to my needs(5);
I'm putting on my fancy beads(5),
Before I kiss the world goodbye,
Before I kiss the world goodbye.

Before I go to meet my maker(6)
I want to u(7)se
The salt left in the shaker(6);
I want to find out if it's true(7)
The Blue(7) Danu(7)be is really blue(7),
Before I kiss the world goodbye.

I want my share of love and laughter(8);
I want it here
And not in some hereafter(8);
Don't want the pie(9)
That's in the sky(9),
I want the pie(9)
Before I die(9);
Before I kiss the world goodbye(9),
Before I kiss the world goodbye(9).

VERSE
Whenever I see wagon wheels(10)
Or carriage wheels
Or any kind of wheels,
I think they must be going somewhere,
Else they wouldn't be wheels(10).
It doesn't matter how young you are,
How old you are,
As long as you are
Spiritually kicking up your heels(10).

Before I take the trip to pastures green(11),
I mean(11) to spend the time enjoying the scene(11).

The days are few,
I dare not waste them(12).
I want to see and hear,
And touch and taste them(12).
With all my plans gone up in smoke(13),
It might as well be "go for broke(13),"
Before I kiss the world goodbye.

I'll play the clown
With cap and bells on(4).
I'll buy a park with
Fifty carrousels on(4).
I'll crash the cymbals,
Drum(14) the drums(15),
Be ready when my num(14)ber comes(15),
Before I kiss the world goodbye,
Before I kiss the world goodbye.

Before I go to meet my maker(6),
I want to use the salt left in the shaker(6).
I want to find out if it's true(7)
The blue(7) Danu(7)be is really blue(7),
Before I kiss the world goodbye.

VERSE
Today has been a gala day,
A hopeful day, a happy day.
The gods look down and smile.
How good it feels(10).
It doesn't matter how young you are,
How old you are,
As long as you are
Spiritually kicking up your heels(10).
Before I take the trip to pastures green(11),
I mean to spend the time enjoying the scene(11).

Dietz, Harburg, and Rome flowered in an era that was bankrupt. Each in his own way mirrored and embodied it in satire. Dietz helped to carry the bankrupt revue into a new state and furthered the interest of revues that intended to amuse. He ran parallel to Ira Gershwin and overlapped Cole Porter. Laughter was the name of the game, and this was laughter —often caustic—in the face of disaster. Schwartz and Dietz helped to reclaim that audience that had been disillusioned by Ziegfeld, Carroll, George White, and the others. They revitalized a form that had fallen into disrepute. All artists react with or against their own periods. In his lyrics Howard Dietz frequently created a playful happy world in which the battle of the sexes allowed nothing to interfere, and he accomplished it with considerable dexterity. But his reaction to the real world in upheaval around him was also included and mocked.

E. Y. Harburg
(b. 1898)

Every creative artist reacts in one way or another to the conditions of his own life. Porter went along with the attractiveness of the wealthy social set—café society—which he knew and enjoyed. Most artists are born into far more modest circumstances. Many have known poverty from the start. Some of these have looked back on it in later years with a kind of peaceful cheerfulness. Others—because of less than modest circumstances—have reacted sharply against it.

It seems to me that E. Y. ("Yip") Harburg belongs somewhere between these two latter groups. He was born of Russian immigrant parents and endured a growing-up fraught with poverty and insecurity. He adored his brother Max, the head of a college physics department, who died at twenty-eight leaving Yip, who was twelve, to help support the family. Yip's brother was always his inspiration.

He began writing parodies of popular songs for his Tompkins Square Park baseball team and poems for his high school paper. His teachers wanted him to become an actor and he was chosen to play the most important roles in school productions. His parents objected to his going on the stage because he would be required to act on Jewish holidays!

Having to help support his family, Harburg worked for the Edison Company lighting street lamps and he also delivered newspapers. In high school he sat next to Ira Gershwin and together they wrote a column in the Townsend Harris High School paper called "Much Ado."

In college they also started a column called "Gargoyles" by Yip and Gersh. Ira, however, in his sophomore year left college and joined his father who was operating a Turkish bath, where Ira became cashier. Yip graduated from City College with a Bachelor of Science degree. From time to time he saw his

poems published in F.P.A.'s column "The Conning Tower" in the New York *Tribune* along with other embryo talents like George S. Kaufman, Dorothy Parker, Marc Connelly, Deems Taylor, and many others who were later to become famous.

After graduating college Yip went into the electric appliance business with a classmate Harry Lifton, father of Yale's famous professor Robert Lifton. They did well in the twenties and were on the road to affluence. During this time George Gershwin came into sudden success and so it was only natural that a few years later the brothers should team up in a collaboration that set the musical theatre ablaze for many decades. All this time Yip kept watching the progress of his buddy Ira, and was relieved in 1929 when the great Depression hit and left him with the only real asset he ever had, his fountain pen.

Ira was there to encourage him, buy him a rhyming dictionary, and introduce him to composer Jay Gorney. To survive the Depression, Yip sold watches by day and worked with Gorney through the night.

After a few months they had enough songs to start *Earl Carroll's Sketchbook* starring Patsy Kelly, George Gibbert, and Will Mahoney. Although the show was an immediate hit, Yip did not give up his job for fear this was all a dream, but continued writing songs. These soon found their way into Paramount Pictures in Astoria, New York, and in the third edition of *The Garrick Gaieties,* produced by the Theatre Guild. The next year the Guild rehired him to do the lyrics for a show called *Americana,* written by the humorist J. P. McEvoy. It was a stinging satire on the state of our economy, its booms, and its depressions. Vincent Youmans was hired to do the music. After writing the opening number Youmans disappeared and was never found again, so Harburg was commissioned to meet the deadline of the opening. This was the beginning of his collaboration with Harold Arlen who, together with Dick Myers and Jay Gorney, furnished the tunes for Harburg's lyrics. Gorney came up with the music for the now classic "Brother, Can You Spare a Dime?," which stamped the era, and became the slogan of the Depression.

Harburg's credo is that art must have its roots in social survival. He has contributed songs to many shows and has worked with some of the great composers. His principal collaborator has been Harold Arlen. His classic *Finian's Rainbow* was however written with Burton Lane, and the score of *Walk a Little Faster,* which included the song "April in Paris," was written with Vernon Duke, starring Beatrice Lillie and Bobby Clark. *Jamaica,* starring Lena Horne, and *Bloomer Girl,* starring Celeste Holm, were written with Arlen; *The Happiest Girl in the World,* based on *Lysistrata,* was an unusual experiment. Harburg selected highlight arias from Offenbach operettas, wrote new lyrics, and made them indigenous to the theme.

Life Begins at 8:40 was one of the first sophisticated revues, with Bert Lahr and Ray Bolger in the cast. He and Ira Gershwin both collaborated on the lyrics to Harold Arlen's music. He also wrote the music to Yip's hilarious satire on war, *Hooray for What,* starring the great Ed Wynn. His worldwide classical and perennial hit with Arlen for the movies was *The Wizard of Oz,* starring Judy Garland, Bert Lahr, Jack Haley, Ray Bolger, Billie Burke, and Margaret Hamilton.

Although many of Harburg's lyrics reflect a strong sense of social consciousness, his range is wide and spans the rainbow from comic to cosmic. His first song quoted here was Harburg's first hit from J. P. McEvoy's revue *Americana* (1932), with music by Jay Gorney, "Brother, Can You Spare a Dime?" This lyric captured the atmosphere of disillusionment of the American people, their loss of faith in the Great American Dream. It is not a cry of self-pity or a plea for a handout, but it states an important economic question: How can a person who produces the wealth of the country not share in that production?

As in the case of all the best lyricists, such general conditions find expression in specific images: "Once I built a railroad" and "Once I built a tower."

The sudden switch from the high sense of accomplishment into the line "Brother, Can You Spare a Dime?" is the ironic surprise that gives the lyric its dramatic impact. His heroism in the war, fighting for the system he believed in, that Yankee Doodle-de-dum, the cheering for him, the kid with the drum, have all been reduced to bewilderment. "Don't you remember, They called me Al. . . . I'm your pal!" How could this dream of peace and glory, which he was building, have collapsed so suddenly?

What keeps the lyric from being a maudlin personal ballad is that it poses a social question still to be answered by the parliaments of man. The words are simple, the rhyme scheme is straightforward and clear.

"BROTHER, CAN YOU SPARE A DIME?"

They used to tell me I was building a dream,
And so I followed the mob
When there was earth to plough or guns to bear
I was always there
Right there on the job.

They used to tell me I was building a dream
With peace and glory ahead
Why should I be standing in line
Just waiting for bread?

REFRAIN
Once I built a railroad,
Made it run,
Made it race against time.
Once I built a railroad,
Now it's done
Brother can you spare a dime?

Once I built a tower,
To the sun.
Brick and rivet and lime,
Once I built a tower,
Now it's done,
Brother, can you spare a dime?

Once in khaki suits
Gee, we looked swell
Full of that Yankee Doodle-de-dum.
Half a million boots went sloggin' thru Hell,
I was the kid with the drum.

Say don't you remember,
They called me Al
It was Al all the time
Say, don't you remember
I'm your pal!
Buddy, can you spare a dime?

The next quoted single song—a lasting hit—demonstrates a sharp change of pace. "April in Paris" is an apostrophe to feeling—personal feeling of an aesthetic experience. What gives it another dimension, however, is that it is about a person who has never been in love or never ever needed to be in love, and finds himself confronted by such overwhelming beauty that now he must share the feeling with someone. No description of stones and trees could possibly convey the beauty of Paris as profoundly as these last lines: "April in Paris,/ Whom can I run to/ What have you done to my heart?"

"APRIL IN PARIS"

April's everywhere,
But here in Paris,
April wears a diff'rent gown
You can see her waltzing down the street.
Her tang of wine is in the air—
She takes my hand, and ev'ryone's my relative,
Never dreamed it could be so exciting to live.

REFRAIN
April in Paris,
Chestnut in blossom,
Holiday tables under the trees.

April in Paris,
This is a feeling
No one can ever reprise.

I never knew the smile of spring,
Never met it face to face.
I never knew my heart could sing,

Never missed a warm embrace,
Till—

April in Paris,
Whom can I run to?
What have you done to—my heart?

"It's Only a Paper Moon," with music by Harold Arlen and words by Harburg and Billy Rose, from *The Great Magoo* (1932) has become—reinforced in recent years—a great American classic. Even two years ago (1972) Peter Bogdanovich used its title for his superior film and the music and lyrics as its theme. Tennessee Williams incorporated it importantly in his greatest play *A Streetcar Named Desire* (1947). "It's Only a Paper Moon" is a philosophic song. It looks at life honestly and realistically. We are all perishable inhabitants on a temporary planet, acting in a movie called life. Tomorrow the scenes are struck and dismantled, and the actors gone. Everything is unreal and ersatz. The "Barnum and Bailey world" is "phony" and "a temporary parking place," "a bubble for a minute." The moon is paper, the sea is cardboard, the sky is canvas, the tree is nylon. It's a "honky-tonk parade," but in spite of it all nature has provided us with a force called love, which is mightier than reality itself. Once we achieve that intercommunication and feeling between people we begin to experience life as if there is no tomorrow.

The eight-line verse contains only two pairs of rhymes. (The world is an abrasive place.) In the three A sections of the refrain there are only three rhymes—all relating to me: sea, tree, be. One couplet in the release rhymes. The softness of sound is lean.

"IT'S ONLY A PAPER MOON"

I never feel a thing is real,
When I'm away from you,
Out of your embrace,
The world's a temporary parking place.
Ho hum, ho hummmm—
A bubble for a minute,
But then you smile.....
The bubble has a rainbow in it.

REFRAIN
Oh, it's only a paper moon,
Sailing over a cardboard sea,
But it wouldn't be make-believe,
If you believed in me.

Yes, it's only a canvas sky,
Hanging over a nylon tree,
But it wouldn't be make-believe,
If you believed in me.

Without your love,
It's a honky-tonk parade,
Without your love,
It's a melody played in a penny arcade.

It's a Barnum and Bailey world,
Just as phony as it can be,
But it wouldn't be make-believe,
If you believed in me.

It is curious to note that in the theatre Harburg has twice been concerned with women's rights. The first time was in 1944 when he and Arlen wrote *Bloomer Girl*, book by Saidy and Herzog, a first-rate hit, and in every way topical. Set in post-Civil War America, it uses Dolly Bloomer and her early women's lib movement as a background not only for that cause, but the show is also concerned with black liberation as well for freedom is indivisible.

"The Eagle and Me," sung by a black slave, has considerable power. It has the feeling and simplicity of a fable. The rhymes are simple. There are neither tricks nor complexities of any kind in the lyrics. Harburg employs one device near the end in summarizing the images requiring freedom: bumble bee, river, eagle, and one that is time-honored: the earliest example of which—as far as I know—occurs traditionally in the Passover service (Seder) in the song about "an only kid"—"Had Gad Ya."

"THE EAGLE AND ME"

What makes the gopher leave his hole,
Tremblin' with fear and fright?
Maybe the gopher's got a soul,
Wantin' to see the light.

That's it!
Oh yea, oh yea, that's it,
The scripture has it writ.
Betcha life that's it.
Nobody likes hole, nobody likes chain,
Don't the good Lord all aroun' you make it plain?

REFRAIN
River it like to flow,
Eagle it like to fly.
Eagle it like to feel its wings
Against the sky.

Possum it like to run,
Ivy it like to climb.
Bird in the tree and bumble bee
Want freedom
In Autumn and summer time.

Ever since that day
When the world was an onion,
'Twas natural for the spirit to soar and play
The way the Lord wanted it.

Free as the sun is free
That's how it's gotta be
Whatever is right for bumble bee
And River and Eagle
Is right for me.
We gotta be free,
The Eagle and me.

What follows is a fun song with serious overtones.

T'MORRA, T'MORRA

T'morra is that better day
With rainbows in the sky.
That's the picture people like to paint.

But while I seek that better day,
The years keep flying by.
And lots of things that should be happening ain't.

Till finally there comes this revelation:
T'morra is the curse of civilization

REFRAIN
T'morra, t'morra,
Livin' for t'morra,
Why is t'morra better than today?

T'morra, t'morra,
Lookin' for t'morra,
My aunt became a spinster that way.

The future, the future,
It's always in the future. . .
What's the matter with now?

Postponin', postponin',
A girl can bust postponin'
Take your t'morra and get!

I'd rather, I'd rather
Have somethin' to remember,
Than nothing to regret.

T'morra, t'morra,
It dawns on me with horra,
Love's gettin' far away and out o'sight.

T'morra, t'morra,
Why can't a lady borra'
A little of t'morra tonight?

The present, the present,
The present is so pleasant,
What am I savin' it for?

Progressive, progressive,
I'd rather be caressive,
My heart is raising a row.

Utopia, Utopia,
Don't be a dope, ya' dope ya',
Get your Utopia now.

Aunt Dora, Aunt Dora,
Kept tellin' Jawn t'morra,
So Jawn married Flora; he was a lusty lad.

Now Flora, now Flora,
Has got a score or more o' of more o'
Little Floras Dora shoulda' had.

T'morra, t'morra,
Oh, isn't it deplora—
Ble, the way a girr-l does fade?

Delayin', delayin',
Is driving me in-say-yne,
My dialectics are clear.

I'll have-ta', I'll have-ta',
Give up here-afta'
For what I'm afta' here!

The women's lib idea was stated directly and wittily in "It Was Good Enough for Grandma." The form is different here. There are three three-stanza verses and three one-stanza refrains that are exact repeats. Each of the three-verse stanzas is five lines, the chorus stanza has six. Since the rhyme schemes are inconsistent and somewhat complex, I have pinpointed them.

"IT WAS GOOD ENOUGH FOR GRANDMA"

When Grandma was a lady,
She sewed and cleaned and cooked(1).
She scrubbed her pots(2),
And raised her tots(2),
The dear old gal was hooked(1).

She stitched her little stitches(3),
Her life was applesauce(4);
That thing that wore the britches(3)
Was boss(4). . . .
Yes, the thing that wore the britches
Was boss.

She had no voice in guvment(5),
And bondage was her fate(6).
She only knew what love meant(5)
From eight to half past eight(6).
And that's a hell of a fate(6)!

REFRAIN
It was good enough for Grandma,
That good old gal
With her frills and her feathers and fuss(7);
It was good enough for Grandma,
Good enough for Grandma—
But it ain't good enough for us(7).

When Grandma was a lassie,
That tyrant known as man(8)
Thought a woman's place(9)
Was just the space(9)
Around a frying pan(8).

He made the world his oyster(10),
Now it ain't worth a cuss(7).
This oyster(10), he can't foist u(10)pon us(7),
No, this oyster, he can't foist upon us.

Our brains against his muscle(11),
Our tea against his rum(12),
Look behind the bustle(11)
For the shape of things to come(12).
Join up with fife and drum(12).

REFRAIN
It was good enough for Grandma,
That good old gal,
With her frills and her feathers and fuss(7);
It was good enough for Grandma,
Good enough for Grandma—
But it ain't good enough for us(7).

We won the revolution
In seventeen-seventy-six(13) . . .
Who says it's nix(13)
For us to mix(13)
Our sex with politics(13)!

We've bigger seas to swim in (14),
And bigger worlds to slice(15).
Oh, Sisters, are we women(14)
Or mice(15)?

Look twice(15) before you step on(16)
The fair(17) sex of the earth(18).
Beware(17) our secret weapon(16),
We could stop giving birth(18)!
Take that for what it's worth(18).

REFRAIN
It was good enough for Grandma,
That good old gal,
With her frills and her feathers and fuss(7);
It was good enough for Grandma,
Good enough for Grandma—
But it ain't good enough for us(7)!

Some sixteen years after *Bloomer Girl* with its message of women's lib and still nearly a decade before the questions it raised were brought into sharp focus, Harburg wrote lyrics for *The Happiest Girl in the World,* a show utilizing various music adapted from the works of Offenbach. This kind of creation raised unusually difficult problems for the lyricist. Because the composer was dead, there could be in no sense any collaboration, yet Harburg completed his own job without any noticeable difficulty. In "Lysistrata's Oath," a problem somewhat larger than women's lib was undertaken—"woman's dissent against war"—a situation closely associated with and deeply pertinent to the then-current undeclared Vietnamese struggle. It was most interesting to note that despite Aristophanes' original authorship (five centuries before the Christian Era), Harburg's language—in my opinion quite properly—is contemporary. He employed words like "nightie" and expressions including "send him packing," "starts cracking," and so on.

"LYSISTRATA'S OATH"

And now on this girdle of Diana,
We take this sacred oath of chastity:

Till there's peace in the air,
We'll abandon Aphrodite.
Not a bed will we share,
Not a bed, not a nightie.

Not a man does there live
Whom we do not vow to scare off,
Not an inch will we give,
For we firmly swear to swear off!

WOMEN
Not an inch, not a hair,
Not a bone . . . will we share;
When he raves with despair
We'll send him packing.
A WOMAN
If he plead or attack
He'll be sacked from the sack—
SECOND WOMAN
And he's not crawling back,
Until he starts cracking.
SEVERAL WOMEN
Not for King or for Crown
Will a Zeus's son seduce us.
Not for King or for Crown,
Shall we girls lay . . . down our arms.
ALL THE WOMEN
So by Venus and by Jove,

And by all the gods above us,
War is hate . . . Love is love,
And a hater cannot love us.
We must turn the fighting leopard,
Back into a gentle shepherd.
Love is love . . . hate is hate,
And the two won't tête-à-tête.
LYSISTRATA
So rise ye legions of rosy lips,
Let loose your curls and your curving hips,
Strike out with fist in velvet glove,
Make way for "Operation Dove."
ECHO
'Ration dove'. . .
ALL
It's war on war through love,
Not either—or,
But love or war,
No less, no more,
Just love or war!

Finian's Rainbow (1947) had a book by Harburg and Fred Saidy, memorable tunes by Burton Lane, and lyrics by Harburg. It concerned an Irish girl and her pixilated father who stole a magic crock of gold from a leprechaun in Ireland. Intrigued by the idea that Americans like to bury all their gold in Fort Knox and grow rich, he migrates to Fort Knox, buries the crock of gold, and waits for success. The crock can grant three wishes. One of them happens to turn a white bigoted senator into a black man. The situation leads, of course, to social satire and hilarious comments on the foibles of racism. It is the first American musical to combine the singing, acting, and dancing of blacks and whites on stage. It is also unique in American musicals in that it is an original story based on no other book or play, and it is that rare thing called fantasy that packs a social wallop. The songs are brilliantly entertaining, and the sermon served with laughter. There is no dead wood in the entire score.

"Glocca Morra" and "Old Devil Moon" are too well known to need quoting here. However, the ebullience and satire of such songs as "Necessity," "Idle Poor, Idle Rich," "The Begat," and "When I'm Not Near the Girl I Love" make *Finian's Rainbow* a landmark in "socially significant" musicals. These lyrics demonstrate Harburg at the peak of his form.

The first, "Necessity," is sung by a group of poor rural southern blacks and whites. The "message" is conveyed with humor.

"NECESSITY"

What is the curse
That makes the universe
So all-bewild'rin'?

What is the hoax
That just provokes
The folks
They call
God's children?

What is the jinx
That gives a body
And his brother

And everyone around,
The run-around?

Necessity, necessity,
That most unnecessary thing, necessity!
What throws the monkey wrench in
A fella's good intention?
That nasty old invention—
Necessity!

My feet want to dance in the sun,
My head wants to rest in the shade.
The Lord says, "Go out and have fun,"
But the landlord says,
"Your rent ain't paid."

Necessity—
It's plain to see
What a lovely old world
This silly old world
Could be—

But, man, it's all in a mess
Account of necess-
Ity.

Necessity, necessity,
There ought to be a law against necessity.
I'd love to play some tennis
Or take a trip to Venice,
But, sister, here's the menace—
Necessity.

Oh, hell is the father of gin,
And Cupid's the father of love.
Old Satan's the father of sin,
But no one knows the father of
Necessity.

(You mean he's a———?
That's what he is?)

Necessity—
That's the maximum
That a minimum
Thing can be.

There's nothing lower than less,
Unless it's necess-
Ity!

The second socially pointed song from *Finian's Rainbow* is "When the Idle Poor Become the Idle Rich." The lyrics speak for themselves.

"WHEN THE IDLE POOR BECOME THE IDLE RICH"

When the idle poor become the idle rich,
You'll never know just who is who—
Or which is which.

Won't it be rich
When everyone's poor relative
Becomes a Rockefellertive
And palms no linger itch?
What a switch!

When we all have ermine and plastic teeth,
How will we determine who's who underneath?
And when all your neighbors are upper class
You won't know your Joneses from your Astors.

Let's toast the day,
The day we drink our drinkie up,
But with the little pinky up,
The day on which
The idle poor become the idle rich.

INTERLUDE
When a rich man doesn't want to work,
He's a bon vivant,
Yes, he's a bon vivant.
But when a poor man doesn't want to work,
He's a loafer, he's a lounger, he's a lazy good for nothin'—
He's a jerk.

When a rich man loses on a horse,
Isn't he the sport?
Isn't he the sport?
But when a poor man loses on a horse,
He's a gambler, he's a spender, he's a low-life,
He's a reason for divorce.

When a rich man chases after dames
He's a man about town,
A man about town.
But when a poor man chases after dames,
He's a bounder, he's a rounder, he's a rotter
And a lot o' dirty names.

But—
When the idle poor become the idle rich,
You'll never know just who is who
Or which is which.

No one will see
The Irish or the Slav in you,
For when you're on Park Avenue,
Cornelius and Mike
Look alike.

When poor Tweedledum is rich Tweedledee,
This discrimination will no longer be.
When we're in the dough and off of the nut,
You won't know your banker from your *but*ler.

Let's make the switch,
With just a few annuities
We'll hide these incongruities
With cloaks from Abercrombie Fitch—
When the idle poor become the idle rich.

Jamaica, costarring Lena Horne and Ricardo Montalban, went on in 1957. Fred Saidy and E. Y. Harburg wrote the book, Harburg the lyrics, and Harold Arlen the music. Much of the music's style suggested calypso and the lyrics likewise have the jerky semiabbreviated patois style of calypso words.

Three amusing songs from *Jamaica* have social overtones that are readily understood. Again, they need no explanation and no comment.

"FOR EVERY FISH"

Man, he eat the barracuda,
Barracuda eat the bass,
Bass he eat the little flounder,
'Cause the flounder lower class.
Little flounder eat the sardine,
That's nature's plan.
Sardine eat the little worm,
Little worm eat the man.

REFRAIN
For every fish there's a little bigger fish
Just a little bigger fish
In the deep blue sea,
And the big big fish
In the deep blue sea
Lives off the fish that's little-er than he.
That's the way things do occur
In the deep blue sea—
That the littler eats the littler-er
'Cause the littler-er is littler-er than her . . .
That's the way things do occur.

For every fish that's a bigger fish,
There's a bigger-er-er-er-er. . . .

To state it
More epi-
Grammatically:
It's a fish's circle for the fisherman
And the fisherman is me.

"PUSH DE BUTTON"

There's a little island on the Hudson,
Mythical, magic and fair,
Shining like a diamond on the Hudson,
Far away from worriment and care.

What an isle!
What an isle!
All de natives relax there in style.
What a life!
What a life!
All de money controlled by de wife.

On this little island on de Hudson
Everyone big millionaire,
With his own cooperative castle
Rising in de air-conditioned air.

Life is easy,
Livin's lazy,
On this isle where crazy dreams come true . . .
All you do is:

REFRAIN
Push de button;
Up de elevator!
Push de button;
Out de orange juice!
Push de button:
From refrigerator
Come banana short-cake and frozen goose!

Push de button;
Wipe de window wiper!
Push de button:
Rinse de baby diaper!
Push de button:
Wanna fry de fish—push de button,
Wash de dish—push de button,
PoooooSH de button.

What an isle!
What an isle!
Where de automat feed ev'ry chile.
Where de brave and de free
Live and love electron-ic-ally.

Push de button;
Don't be small potato.
Be a tycoon,
Big manipulator—
Poooooosh. . . . SH!
Apply de little finger and poosh. . . .
De button.

Button, button, what a button,
Nuttin' but a button,
Everybody got a button,
Glutton for de button.
Barbara got a Hutton button.
Ike he got a puttin' button.
Nixon got a nuttin' button,
All de Dodger fans got button—
All Republicans got button. . . .

Push de button:
Up de helicopter,
Push de button:
Click—de telephone.
Push de button:
From de television
Come de Pepto Bismo with baritone.
Push de button:
Out come Pagliacci,
Push de button:
Also Liberace.
Push de button!
Wanna rock 'n roll—push de button,
Pay de toll—push de button. . . .
Poooo. . . . . SH de button.

What an isle!
What an isle!
Squeeze de tube and get pepsodent smile.
Crack de bank, rob de mail
Turn de knob and get muzak in jail.

Push de button;
Don't be antiquated—
Get de baby
All prefabricated,
Poooooooo. . . . . SH!
Apply de little finger and pooosh. . . .
De button.

"MONKEY IN THE MANGO"

Three monkeys in the mango tree
Were indulging in philosophy,
And as I walked by de mango tree,
One of them addressed himself to me:

"Hey, man. . . . is it true what they say?
Hey, man . . . is it true that today
They claim that my brothers and me
Are the predecessors of humanity?

Hey, man . . . why you give us bad name?
Hey, man . . . it's a blight and a shame
To claim this uncivilized cuss
Could have been descended from
The likes of us!

How can you have de brazen face
To scandalize our noble race?
Don't identify yourself with me,"
Said de monkey in de mango tree.

"Would a monkey do what silly man will do,
Live in de jungle of Mad . . . ison Avenue,
Fight his neighbors with a gun and knife,
Love his horses and divorce his wife?

Would de monkey love a girl in zipper pants,
Mud packs, girdles and deo-dor-ants
Falsies fillin' out de vital spot,
How in hell a feller know just what he got?

Hey, man . . . why you give us bad name?
Hey, man . . . it's a blight and a shame,
To claim—most un-bibli-cal-ly
Dat dis chump could once have been a chimpanzee."

De man he may be clever,
But would a monkey ever:

Analyze his psyche,
Amortize his soul,
Tranquilize his frontal lobes with alcohol?
Televise his follies,
And the life he lives,
Eulogize his gargles and his laxatives?

Simonize his teeth,
Lanolize his hands,
Hormonize his so-and-so's with monkey glands?

Mechanize the Greeks,
Modernize the Turks,
Then with one little atom . . . Poof . . .
Atomize de works?

"Hey, man . . . do you call it fair play,
Hey, man . . . is it cricket to say,
Dat de monkey and his uncles and his cousins and his aunts,
Are de parents of such foolishment and decadence.
Don't you make a human out of me!"
Said de monkey. . . . .
In de mango tree.

It seems especially fitting to conclude this section on the lyrics of E. Y. Harburg with two songs from the classic motion picture *The Wizard of Oz* (1939).

"If I Only Had a Brain," sung by the frustrated Scarecrow (Ray Bolger), is simple and while definitely amusing, is also touching. Harburg took advantage of the situation's lightness to create fun with many of the rhymes:

riddle—individle
thinkin'—Lincoln
nuffin—stuffin'
deserve you—worthy erv you

It is my own conviction that such liberties can only be taken in comedy lyrics where indeed they heighten the humor and characterization.

I would also like to comment on the release (stanza 3 of the refrain). The subject matter is adorably simple and I think there is real genius in the last couplet: "And then I'd sit/ And think some more" because Harburg gives the feeling in the preceding three lines that we will expect the pathetically brainless Scarecrow to come up with something significantly more than telling "why the ocean's near the shore" and "things I never thunk before." What follows, however, suggests a difficult but vain attempt to say something more when, brainless and childlike, the Scarecrow has reached the shallow limits of his thinking.

"IF I ONLY HAD A BRAIN"

SCARECROW
Said a scarecrow swinging on a pole
To a blackbird sitting on a fence,
"Oh! the Lord gave me a soul,
But forgot to give me common sense.
If I had an ounce of common sense. . . ."

REFRAIN
I could while away the hours
Conferrin' with the flow'rs,
Consultin' with the rain.
And my head I'd be scratchin'
While my thoughts were busy hatchin'
If I only had a brain.

I'd unravel ev'ry riddle
For any individle
In trouble or in pain,
With the thoughts I'd be thinkin'
I could be another Lincoln,
If I only had a brain.

Oh, I could tell you why
The ocean's near the shore,
I could think of things I never thunk before,
And then I'd sit
And think some more.

I would not be just a nuffin'
My head all full of stuffin'
My heart all full of pain.
And perhaps I'd deserve you,
And be even worthy erv you,
If I only had a brain.

In closing, I'd like to quote the well-loved song that Judy Garland immortalized in the movie and afterward everywhere else in the world. Though there are no new images in these lyrics, with the exception of "troubles melt like lemon drops," they are so skillfully and honestly put together that simplicity supercedes everything and anything. More would have seemed pretentious and out of place.

"OVER THE RAINBOW"

When all the world is a hopeless jumble
And the raindrops tumble all around,
Heaven opens a magic lane.

When all the clouds darken up the skyway,
There's a rainbow highway to be found
Leading from your window pane
To a place behind the sun,
Just a step beyond the rain. . . .

REFRAIN
Somewhere over the rainbow,
Way up high,
There's a land that I heard of
Once in a lullaby.

Somewhere over the rainbow,
Skies are blue,
And the dreams that you dare to dream
Really do come true.

Someday I'll wish upon a star
And wake up where the clouds are far
Behind me.
Where troubles melt like lemon drops,
Away, above the chimney tops,
That's where you'll find me.

Somewhere over the rainbow,
Bluebirds fly,
Birds fly over the rainbow,
Why then, oh why, can't I?

If any little bird can fly beyond the rainbow,
Why, oh why, can't I?

Throughout all his work Harburg displays humor as opposed to stinging wit. His ideas, whenever possible, are deeply tied in with many of the world's problems. Though the problems are often dark and complex, Harburg's presentation of them and his comments are cheering and hopeful. Though his "sermons" have "texts," they are most importantly never "preached."

Courtesy ASCAP

Dorothy Fields (1904–1974)

It is impossible that anyone could have been born and reared in the midst of a larger and more impressive musical theatre environment than Dorothy Fields. She was the daughter of Lew Fields, the taller and more important member of the Weber & Fields team. Her father split up with his fellow performer at about the time Dorothy was born (1904) and he was well enough off financially to become a producer.

The Fields children, of whom Dorothy was the youngest, consisted of an older sister—the only one who did not go into the theatre—and two older brothers, Joseph and Herbert. This theatre-bound trio began their careers over the protests of their parents.

In addition to blood connections with the theatre, Dorothy's brother Herbert, who eventually collaborated with her in writing books and lyrics for musicals, was a good friend of the promising young Rodgers and Hart duo.

Following the pattern of all writers in the twenties and thirties, Dorothy Fields began her career writing lyrics for songs in revues that, at the outset, were Harlem nightclub productions. Her collaborator-composer at that time and for a decade was Jimmy McHugh. Their first show was a Cotton Club Revue *Hot Chocolates,* which introduced Duke Ellington. When McHugh and Fields wrote the songs for Lew Leslie's *Blackbirds of 1928*, which continued on through the 1930 edition, they enjoyed their first resounding hit with "I Can't Give You Anything but Love."

The lyrics from the then twenty-four-year-old Dorothy were amazingly well developed. These are graceful words. They dance. In addition to the rhymes which I have indicated, there are less apparent but interesting assonances. These include:

*tou*gh—*lu*ck (lines 1 and 3)
*cha*nging—some*day*
*rea*ch—*see*
*Ba*by—*bra*celets—*day*
*bui*lt—*wi*lling

"I CAN'T GIVE YOU ANYTHING BUT LOVE"

VERSE ONE
Gee, but it's tough to be broke(1), kid,
It's not a joke(1), kid, it's a curse(2);
My luck is changing, it's gotten(3)
From simply rotten(3) to something worse(2),
Who knows someday I will win too(4),
I'll begin to(4) reach my prime(5);
Now though I see what our end is(6)
All I can spend is(6) just my time(5):

CHORUS
I can't give you anything but love(7),
Baby,
That's the only thing I've plenty of(7),
Baby,
Dream(8) awhile, scheme(8) awhile,
We're sure to find(9)
Happiness(10) and I guess(10)
All those things you've always pined(9) for,
Gee(11) I'd like to see(11) you looking swell(12),
Baby,
Diamond bracelets Woolworth doesn't sell(12),
Baby,

Till that lucky day, you know darned well(12),
Baby,
I can't give you anything but love.(7)

VERSE TWO

Rome wasn't built in a day, kid(13),
You have to pay, kid(13),
For what you get(14),
But I am willing to wait, dear(15),
Your little mate, dear(15), will not forget(14),
You have a lifetime before you(16),
I'll adore you(16), come what may(17);
Please don't be blue(16) for the present(18),
When it's so pleasant(18)
To hear you say(17):

CHORUS

In Lew Leslie's *International Revue* (1930), the McHugh-Fields team delivered "On the Sunny Side of the Street." Again, although I have indicated the rhymes, I should like to point out the vowel rhymes: ne*ver*, ce*nt*, *Rocke*feller. It should be remembered that this song, written in 1930, is a product of the great 1929 Depression.

"ON THE SUNNY SIDE OF THE STREET"

Walked(1) with no-one(8), and talked(1) with no-one(8),
And I had nothing but shadows.
Then one morning you passed(2)
And I brightened at last(2).
Now I greet(3) the day, and complete(3) the day(4),
With the sun(8) in my heart.
All my worry blew away(4)
When you taught me how to say(4):

Grab your coat, and get your hat(5),
Leave your worry on the doorstep(6).
Just direct your feet(7)
To the sunny side of the street(7).
Can't you hear a pitter-pat(5)?
And that happy tune is your step(6).
Life can be so sweet(7)
On the sunny side of the street(7).
I used to walk in the shade(8),
With those blues on parade(8),
But I'm not afraid(8).
This Rover(9) crossed over(9).
If I never have a cent,
I'll be rich as Rockefeller,
Gold dust at my feet(7),
On the sunny side of the street(7).

In 1935 Dorothy Fields—still writing with Jimmy McHugh —created the songs for the film *Every Night at Eight*. There was one blockbuster—"I'm in the Mood for Love." The *ēē* rhymes in the verse include: *love*ly–d*ear*–swee*theart*–me–dr*eam*–r*eal*, f*eel*, *app*eal, rea*son*.

"I'M IN THE MOOD FOR LOVE"

VERSE

Lovely interlude(1)!
Most romantic mood(1) and your attitude(1) is right(3), dear.

Sweetheart!
You have me under your spell!
Now my dream is real(2)!
That is why I feel(2)
Such a strong appeal(2) tonight(3)!
Somehow!
All my reason takes flight(3)!
Dear

CHORUS

I'm in the Mood for Love,
Simply because you're near me.
Funny, but when you're near me,
I'm in the Mood for Love.
Heaven is in your eyes,
Bright as the stars we're under(4).
Oh! Is it any wonder(4)
I'm in the Mood for Love?
Why stop to think of whether(5)
This little dream might fade(6)?
We've put our hearts together(5),
Now we are one,
I'm not afraid(6)!
If there's a cloud above(7),
If it should rain we'll let it(8),
But for tonight, forget it(8)!
I'm in the Mood for Love(7).

The Fields-McHugh collaboration continued on the West Coast with Walter Wanger's *Every Night at Eight* in 1935. For this film the writers (with George Oppenheimer) produced a great hit song, "I Feel a Song Comin' On." Again—I should like to point out the less obvious vowel rhymes: r*emember*, dr*eam*, *heart*b*eat*, r*equiring*, the*me*, dee*p*, me, Fee*l*.

"I FEEL A SONG COMIN' ON"

VERSE

I remember my days of soli(1)tude when it was folly(1) to dream(2),
When my heartbeat was not requiring(3) a great inspiring(3) theme(2),
But today my dark cloud is breaking(4),
Music deep inside me is waking(4).

CHORUS

I Feel a Song Comin' On
And I'm warning ya.
It's a victorious(5), happy and glorious(5) new strain(6)!
I Feel a Song Comin' On(7),
It's a melody! full of the laughter(11) of children out after(11) the rain(6)!
You'll hear a tuneful story(8),
Ringin' thru ya(9),
Love and glory(8)!
Hallelujah(9)!
And now that my troubles are gone(7),
Let those heavenly drums go on(7) drummin'(10), cause I Feel a Song Comin(10) On!

In "I Dream Too Much," the title song of the 1935 RKO film, Miss Fields collaborated with Jerome Kern. In addition to the indicated perfect rhymes, I should like to point out the more subtle ones. In the long verse the short ĕ sound recurs often: re*st*, st*ep*, sl*e*nder, h*e*r, d*i*sp*e*l, gu*e*ss. In the refrain the $\overline{ee}$ sound is often reiterated: dr*eam* (six times), m*e*, w*e* (three times), st*ea*l.

"I DREAM TOO MUCH"

VERSE
Stars fade out of the skies(1)
Just to rest in her eyes(1),
Her step is like a slender daffodil swaying(2),
Her voice is like a muted violin playing(2);
The light(3) will bloom(4) and quite(3) dispel the gloom(4) on
    sight(3) of her who can charmingly grace a room(4).
You cannot guess what loveliness belongs to you(5);
If you would dance(6), we'd have a chance(6) to share it too(5).
I am not gay enough
To share a waltz(7),
Tonight I boast(8) one of my most(8) unhappy faults(7).

CHORUS
I dream too much(9), but if I dream too much
I only dream to touch(9) your heart again.
I close my eye(10)s to see your hand, your smi(10)le, your joy in
    loving me.
We dance and sing(11), we steal a touch of spring(11),
I dream of ev'rything(11) we two have known(12),
And yet my dreams have shown(12)
Perhaps I dream too much alone(12).

Although Dorothy Fields worked with—besides Jimmy Mc-Hugh and Jerome Kern—Oscar Levant, Fritz Kreisler, Sigmund Romberg, Morton Gould, Harold Arlen, Harry Warren, Burton Lane, Albert Hague, and Cy Coleman, some of her best work was done with Arthur Schwartz. This collaboration began in 1939 with "Stars in Your Eyes" starring Ethel Merman and Jimmy Durante.
In "I'll Pay the Check," the complexity of rhyming is near an all-time high.

"I'LL PAY THE CHECK"

REFRAIN
I'll pay the check,
Without complaining(1)!
I'll pay the check,
I'm entertaining(1)!
This little spree(2) was what I prayed for(3),
It must be paid for(3) by me(2).
Please do(4)n't forget(5)
You owe(4) me nothing;
Have no(4) regret(5),
You are free(2).
I've nothing in sto(6)re.
I'm headed for the mo(6)st enormous wreck(7),
But this is my party,
I'll pay the check(7)!

INTERLUDE
How long can this strange thing last(8)?
I'm getting nowhere and getting there fast(8)!
I love you,

You don't love me(2);
But when it's over you'll see(2) that. . . .

REFRAIN

Most of the virtues of "It's All Yours," also from *Stars in Your Eyes,* are obvious.

"IT'S ALL YOURS"

VERSE
Don't say(1) the dai(1)ly struggle will get you down,
Don't say you're tired fighting it out(2).
Enter reason, exit doubt(2),
There's no blessing,
You must do without(2).

CHORUS
It's all yours
Ev'rything you see(3),
It's all yours
Absolutely free(3).
Just leave your cloister(4),
Baby, stop mopin'(5),
The world's your oyster(4)
Ready to open(5),
It's all(6) yours,
If it's health(7) you want
To call(6) yours
All the wealth(7) you want,
The sun, the moon,
The land and the sea(3) too, me(3) too,
It's all(6) of it yours,
It's all(6) of it yours.

In "A Lady Needs a Change" rhyming consistency is particularly striking. The patterns are adhered to.

"A LADY NEEDS A CHANGE"

VERSE
It is not within our power(1)
To keep love from getting sour(1),
Ask each one who tries it(2)!
Don't be down or broken-hearted(3)
When the cooling-off gets started(3),
Be Big! recognize it(2)!

CHORUS ONE
When arms are not inviting(4),
His kiss is not exciting(4),
When there's no thrill in fighting(4),
A lady needs a change!
When music doesn't floor(5) you,
The moon does nothing for(5) you,
His face begins to bore(5) you!
A lady needs a change!
Once he looked romantic, so romantic!
You fell with a crash(6)!
Now he's just(7) a bust(7), and love is just(7) a
Warmed-up plate of hash(6)!
You yawn at one another(8),
You treat him like a brother(8)!
He treats you like his mother(8)!

I DREAM TOO MUCH

JEROME KERN'S

"I Dream too Much"

STARRING
LILY PONS

WITH
HENRY FONDA
OSGOOD PERKINS
ERIC BLORE

LYRICS BY
DOROTHY FIELDS

AN RKO RADIO PICTURE

T.B. HARMS
COMPANY
1619 BROADWAY NEW YORK
MADE IN U.S.A.

Price 60 cents

When there's no doubt(9) the fire's out(9)!
A lady needs a change!

CHORUS TWO
I buy a dress on Monday,
The dress looks great on Monday(10),
It's on my cook by Sunday(10),
A lady needs a change!
A new chauffeur on Monday,
He drives me all day Monday(10),
I take a taxi Sunday(10),
A lady needs a change!
When love begins to curdle(11)
Some new bird'll(11) help to fill the gap(12)!
Just make(13) up your mind to take(13) that hurdle(11)
Right(14) into his lap(12)!
Let's say you love potatoes,
That's all you'll eat, potatoes(15)!
One night(14) you try tomatoes(15)!
I guarantee(16) that you'll agree(16)!
A lady needs a change!

Dorothy Fields furnished lyrics for the last show of Sigmund Romberg, *Up in Central Park*, produced while he was still alive, in 1945. In 1920 her father had coproduced *Poor Little Ritz Girl* for which her brother Herbert wrote the book, Romberg had collaborated on the score with eighteen-year-old Richard Rodgers.

The idea of "Close as Pages in a Book" is an especially fortuitous one and the complexity of Dorothy Fields's rhymes is especially unusual when one considers the simplicity of her language.

"CLOSE AS PAGES IN A BOOK"

VERSE
My joy in loving you is past understanding(1);
It makes me much too eager, much too demanding(1).
I'm a very selfish lover
With a jealous heart.
If you're across the room, I'd be alone(2)
I've got to feel my cheek against your own(2).

CHORUS
We'll be close as pages in a book(3),
My love and I(4).
So close we can share a single look(3),
Share ev'ry sigh(4).
So close that before I hear(5) your laugh,
My laugh breaks through(6);
And when a tear(5) starts to appear(5),
My eyes grow misty too(6).
Our dreams won't come(7) tumb(7)ling to the ground(8),
We'll hold them fast(10).
Your life is my life and while life beats away in my heart(9)
We'll be close as pages in a book,
Never to part(9).

Arthur Schwartz's most distinguished score was contained in *A Tree Grows in Brooklyn* (1951), starring Shirley Booth. Dorothy Fields furnished the lyrics.

"Love is the Reason" is an amusing charm song. The use of the single unconnected words, "personally" and "obviously,"

one in each refrain, is most effective. In addition to the true rhymes, the constant vowel rhymes in refrain 1 are interesting. In the first half there are $\bar{e}\bar{e}$ rhymes: *rea*son, *glea*m, *peo*ple (three times). In the second half, long and short *i* rhymes. The long *i* rhymes are right, buy, clim*bin'*. The short *i* rhymes are: kick, as*pir*in, flap*pin'*, fins, climb*in'*, it. Hearing the words in passing, most of these elements will go unobserved. However, they create a general feeling of assonance that helps the song to sing better.

"LOVE IS THE REASON"

VERSE
HE   Why am I here?
SHE   Just because I'm here.
HE   Can't make a dime(1) wasting my time(1) here,
SHE   Still you don't go,
HE   I start to say goodbye(2),
       Then I can't say it, but why(2)?
SHE   It's love!
HE   It's love!
SHE   It's love!

REFRAIN ONE
Love is the reason you were born,
Love was the gleam in poppa's eye(3),
People suddenly meet
People suddenly fit(4)
People suddenly hit(4)!
And brother, that's it(4)!
Personally,
Love is a kick right in the pants.
Love is the aspirin you buy(3).
If you're flappin' your fins
If you're climbin' a wall(5)
There must be a reason for it all(5)
What is the reason for it?
Love is the reason for it all.

REFRAIN TWO
Love is the night you can't recall(5),
Love is the extra drink you drank(6).
Love's a shot(7) in the arm,
Love's a poke in the ribs(8),
Buying bot(7)tles and bibs(8),
Filling up cribs(8).
Obviously,
Love is an old established trap.
Ten million suckers walk the plank(6).
If you land on your tail
Ev'ry time that you fall(5)
I can't see the reason(9) for it all(5).
Who needs a reason(9) for it?
Love is the reason(9) for it all(5)
All night the teasin'(9) in the hall(5)
Hallways are lovely for a brawl(5)
Call(5) it the season(9), I say
Love is the reason(9) for it all(5).

These songs for *A Tree Grows in Brooklyn*, coming from a period of high maturity in the American musical theatre, all explore the character of the singer. In "Growing Pains" young people comment on their own changes. Despite the simplicity of attitude and character, the rhyme complexities, instead of confusing, contribute to the charm of the song.

"GROWING PAINS"

One day your mama drops the hem of your skirt(1),
Next day you give up yelling "What's for dessert(1)?"
You can't explain it,
But you're one solid hurt(1).
Baby, you've got Growing Pains.
Your Christmas penny doesn't look half so bright(2),
Papa's not president since, maybe, tonight(2),
When you're not quite(2) so sure that mom's always right(2),
Baby, you've got Growing Pains.
Nothing's wrong(3), just Growing Pains,
And they never hurt too long(3).

My palace in the tree is just the fire escape(4),
I wear a coat, no sky blue cape(4),
Pretending, pretending,
Till ev-rything real looks out of shape(4)
Familiar things look strange(5),
But that's 'cause all of us change(5).
We start to think
We start to look(6)
Beyond a book(6)
I can't play our game(7)
A shame(7) to let it go(8)
Why do we get to know(8) the things we don't want to know?

When there are cobwebs in the dreams that you weave(9),
When there's no magic in the words: "Make Believe(9),"
When Doubt(10) comes peeping out(10) and tugs at your
    sleeve(9),
Baby, you've got Growing Pains.
When you come home from school and don't slam the
    door(11),
Ride down the banisters or slide 'cross the floor(11),
When you don't cry for ev'ry top in the store(11),
Baby, you've got Growing Pains.
They're not bad(12, just Growing Pains,
You'll be awf'lly glad(12 you had (12).

The tender humorous character of "Love Is the Reason" is also present in the next song, "Look Who's Dancing." The rhymes are noted. In addition, however, there is a sense of word balance that contributes enormously to the unification of the lyric. This is a rhythmic attribute. In the verse there are: "wedding with flowers," "standing right here," "music and flowers," "kick my heels," "laugh and sing."

"LOOK WHO'S DANCING"

VERSE
I don't want a wedding with flowers,
All I want is standing right here,
Ev'rywhere there's music and flowers,
Got to kick my heels,
Got to laugh and sing(1),
Here's a girl with ev'rything(1).

CHORUS
Look who's dancing, look who's on air(2),
Sill(3)y and dizzy and too dumb to care(2).
Will(3) you look who's floatin' like a feather(4),
Since she said that we belong together(4).
    he
Look who's dancing, look who's a fool(5),
Young as a chick(6) with a kick(6) like a mule(5).
Look who hasn't got a wrinkle on her brow(7),
Look who's dancing, look who's dancing,
Look, look, look who's dancing now(7).

Look who's dancing, without a blush(8),
Loony(9) and spoony(9) all moonlight and mush(8).
Look who hasn't got a wrinkle on her brow(7),
Look who's dancing, look who's dancing,
Look, look, look who's dancing now(7).

"I'm Like a New Broom" is a ballad from *A Tree Grows in Brooklyn*. It seems quite clear to me from this lyric that the boy singing it is an unsuccessful and somewhat shady character who is so sincerely in love that he himself believes he will be able to change, to become more stable. In the first half of the chorus the $\overline{ee}$ sounds abound: sweep, clean (each twice), feel, be (twice), leaf. The real rhymes are indicated.

"I'M LIKE A NEW BROOM"

VERSE
Twenty-four hours ago(1), my friends,
I was I was real low(1), my friends,
I was a second-rate no(1) good kind of guy(2)!
Here's a respectable new me(3)
Long overdue me(3)
Miracles happening to me(3),
That's why(2) I(2)'m high(2).

CHORUS
I'm like a new broom
I'm gonna sweep clean
And make a clean sweep today(4)
Feel at last I could be(3)
Ev'rything I should be(3)
I turned a new leaf
I'm climbin' up there and when I'm up there I'll stay(4).
Got my girl and nothin's goin' astray(4).
I get a lump in my throat(5) to see the hope in her eye(6)
I gotta take off my coat(5) make her proud I'm her guy(6)!
I'm like a new broom
I'm gonna house-clean,
I want a clean house to start(7)
Then I'll take my girl to live in my heart(7).

"Make the Man Love Me" is a love ballad also from *A Tree Grows in Brooklyn*. The number of short *e* sounds occurring in the verse are particularly musical: *e*lse (twice), *e*nvied, mys*e*lf, gu*e*ss, shamel*e*ss, n*e*ver (twice). Also the recurrence of *m* sounds in the chorus sets up a kind of continual expressive resonance: must, make, man, him, may, dim. Some of these words are used a number of times.

Make The Man Love Me

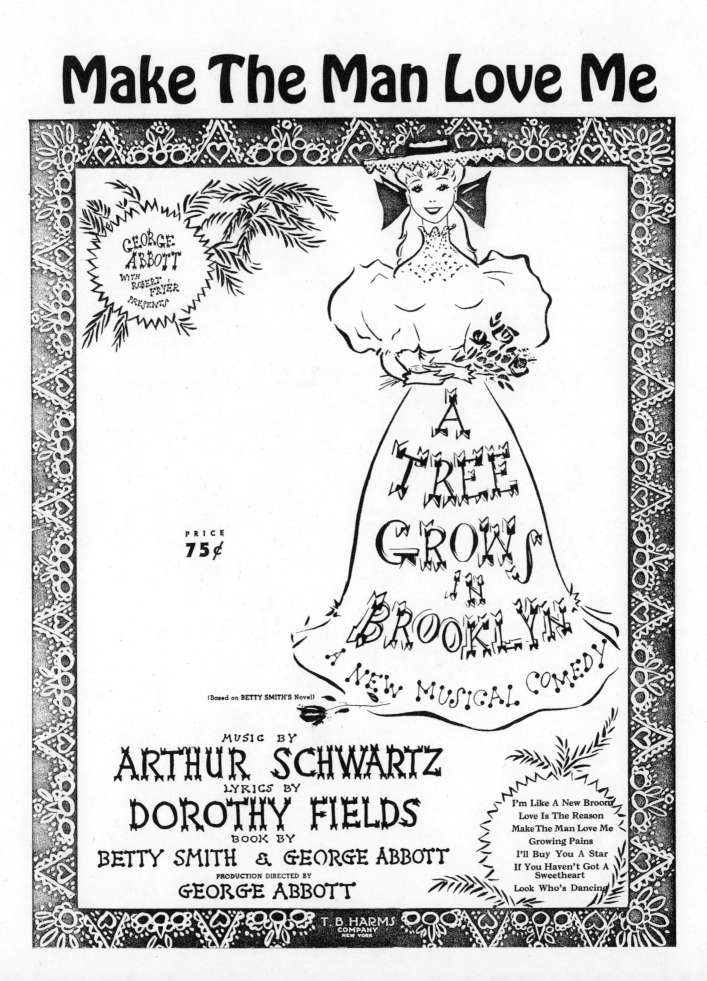

"MAKE THE MAN LOVE ME"

VERSE
You kissed me once by mistake,
Thought I was somebody else.
I felt that kiss and I envied that somebody else.
I wanted you for myself.
I guess I was shameless and bold(1).
But I made a plan in my heart,
I've never breathed,
I've never told(1)

CHORUS
I(2) must try to Make the Man Love Me,
Make the man love me now(3).
Bye(2) and bye, I'll make the man happy, I know how(3).
He must see how badly I want him(4),
Want him just as he is(5).
May(6) I say(6) that should the man ask me(7),
I'll be his(5).
Can I tell the man just how dearly(8) blessed we would be(7)?
All the beauty I see(7) so clearly(8),
Oh, why can't he(7)?
So, I pray to heaven above(9) me(7),
Pray(6) until day(8) grows dim(4),
For a way(6) to Make the Man Love(9) Me as I love him(4).

"I'll Buy You a Star" is a ballad sung by the young hero of *A Tree Grows in Brooklyn*. It contains one of Arthur Schwartz's most beautiful melodies, which is given simple expressive lyrics by Dorothy Fields. Something unusually sensitive transpires in these words, which try to express something extravagant and, of course, literally impossible. I interpret these sentiments as coming from someone who is a failure, unable to buy anything, and therefore willing to offer to his love the stars and the moon. It is emotional, beautiful, and what he offers is necessarily doomed to failure. This song tells us all about the young man and his painful situation in life.

"I'LL BUY YOU A STAR"

VERSE
There's nothing that I know(1) here on this earth(2)
Good enough for you,
So, if I want to show(1) you(3)
All you're worth(2),
I'd have to try(4)
Shopping up in the blue(3).

CHORUS
I'll buy(4) you a star, not just a star, but the best(5) one in the
   sky(4)
You'll have a cloud to sleep on
A cloud as light as an angel's sigh(4)
A fine silver chain(6)
Made from the rain(6) of a summer afternoon(7)
I'll buy you a star,
My darling,
But I won't rest(5) until I buy(4) the moon(7).

Fifteen years after *A Tree Grows in Brooklyn*, Dorothy Fields wrote lyrics for Cy Coleman's music in *Sweet Charity*. Between these shows she wrote the Tony Award-winning *Redhead* (1961)

with Albert Hague. She had collaborated on its book with her brother Herbert, who unfortunately died during their work-in-progress.

The success of *Sweet Charity*, starring Gwen Verdon and directed by Bob Fosse (both of whom had occupied similar positions in *Redhead)*, is well known.

"Big Spender" is an unusual song in that it is sung by several dance-hall girls addressing the audience as though they were potential customers. This is an especially difficult kind of song to write and it succeeds completely. The difficulties are due to its being an ensemble song and that it must represent a group point of view rather than a personal one. It nevertheless pinpoints the attitude: slightly bitter, jaundiced, carelessly needing just anybody, flattering and not precisely in focus as to whom it needs.

The lyrics are as specific as possible under such general circumstances. The rhymes are simple and apparent. There is one chorus, an interlude, and a second chorus.

"BIG SPENDER"

ALL The minute you walked in the joint
I could see you were a man of distinction,
A real big spender,
Good looking, so refined.
Say, wouldn't you like to know what's going on in my mind?
So let me get right to the point.
I don't pop my cork for ev'ry guy I see.
Hey! Big Spender,
Spend a little time with me . . . me . . .
Do you wanna have . . . fun?
How about a few . . . laughs?
I can show you a good time.
Do you wanna have fun . . . fun . . .
Fun . . . fun . . . fun . . . fun . . .
How about a few . . . laughs . . . laughs . . .
Fun . . . laughs . . . fun . . . laughs . . . fun . . . laughs . . . . fun
. . . laughs . . .
I can . . . show you a . . . good time . . .
. . .
Fun . . .laughs . . . good time . . .
Hey! Big spender,
Spend a little time with me.
FIRST GIRL What do you say to a . . .
SECOND GIRL How's about a . . .
ALL Laugh.
THIRD GIRL I could give you some . . .
FOURTH GIRL Are you ready for some . . .
ALL Fun.
FIFTH GIRL How would you like a . . .
SIXTH GIRL Let me show you a . . .
ALL Good time.
Hey! Big spender!
Hey! Big spender!
The minute you walked in the joint
I could see you were a man of distinction,
A real big spender,
Good looking, so refined.
Say, wouldn't you like to know what's going on in my mind?
So let me get right to the point.

I don't pop my cork for ev'ry guy I see.
Hey! Big spender!
Hey! Big spender!
Hey! Big spender,
Spend a little time with me.
Fun, laughs, good time . . .
Fun, laughs, good time . . .
Fun, laughs, good time . . .
NICKIE How 'bout it, palsy?
ALL Yeah.

In "I Love to Cry at Weddings" *(Sweet Charity)* the everyday character of the sentimental singer is well established. It is interesting to note that in the final A section of the refrain, the music is not a melodic repetition of the first two A sections.

The rhyme relationships among words in the second and third lines is quite complex: chapel—*happil*y is clear, but fam*ily* is assonantal with happ*ily* also.

"I LOVE TO CRY AT WEDDINGS"

CHORUS I
I Love to Cry at Weddings, how I Love to Cry at Weddings,
I walk into a chapel(1) and get happil(1)y(2) hysterical,
The ushers and attendants(3), the family(2) dependents(3),
I see them and I start to sniff(4), have you an extra handkerchief(4)?

And all through the service(5) while the bride and groom look nervous(5)
Tears of joy are streaming down my face(6),
I Love to Cry at Weddings, anybody's wedding anytime!
Anywhere, any place(6).

CHORUS II
I Love to Cry at Weddings, how I Love to Cry at Weddings,
I walk into a chapel and get happily hysterical,
The ushers and attendants, the family dependents,
I see them and I start to sniff, have you an extra handkerchief?

And all through the service while the bride and groom look nervous
I drink champagne and sing "Sweet Adeline(7)."
I Love to Cry at Weddings, anybody's wedding just as long as it's not mine(7)!

The setup for "If My Friends Could See Me Now!" *(Sweet Charity)* is unique. Charity is a loser. She is in search of love. When she is picked up by a reigning movie star and taken to his apartment, her reaction is not that at last she has won attention or affection, but only that she wants her friends to believe that she was actually with such a celebrity. *Their* being able to believe in this remarkable encounter is more important to her than the experience itself. The rhymes are unusually complex and are indicated here. Note the rhyme schemes in the three choruses:

CHORUS I
mine—wine
fact—attract
am—jam
tonight—right
bums—chums

CHORUS II
group—coop
her—fur
*traip*sing—*drap*ed
raff—autograph

CHORUS III
gives—lives

In addition to the above, there are forty-eight $\bar{ee}$ sounds (assonances or rhymes) and seventeen *ow* sounds.

"IF MY FRIENDS COULD SEE ME NOW!"

CHARITY Hurricane Hazel could strike, I'm not moving.
(He smiles and nods at her and exits. CHARITY, *very contented with herself, looks around the room. The music starts)* The girls at the Ballroom would never believe me in a million years. *(She sings and dances.)*
If they could see(1) me(1) now(2),
That little gang of mine(3)—
I'm ea(1)ting fancy chow(2)
And drinking fancy(1) wine(3)—
I'd like those stumble-bums(4)
To see(1) for a fact(5)
The kind of top-drawer first-rate
Chums(4) I attract(5)!
All I can say is wow(2)—
Eee(1), looka where I am(6)!
Tonight(7) I landed pow(2)!
Right(7) in a pot of jam(6)!
·What a set-up! Holy(1) cow(2),
They'd never be(1)lie(1)ve it
If my friends could see(1) me(1) now(2)!
They'd never be(1)lie(1)ve it—
They'd never be(1)lie(1)ve—
(VIDAL *comes in.* CHARITY *bumps into him and stops her dance)*
VIDAL *(He has a pop-up top hat which he snaps and "pops up")* I used this in my first picture, Million Dollar Lips.
CHARITY What a beautiful black thing.
VIDAL It's a hat. *(Opens it)* Eccola. *(Smiles)* Wait. There's some more.
(He exits)
CHARITY *(Singing)*
If they could see(1) me(1) now(2),
My little dusty group(8),
Traip(9)sing 'round this
Million-dollar chicken coop(8)!
I'd hear those thrift-shop cats say:
"Brother! Get her(10)!"
Drap(9)ed on a bedspread made from
Three(1) kinds of fur(10)!
All I can say is: "Wow(2)!"
Wait till the riff and raff(11)
See(1) just exactly how(2)
He(1) signed this autograph(11)!
What a build-up! Holy(1) cow(2),
They'd never be(1)lie(1)ve it
If my friends could see(1) me(1) now(2)!

If they could see(1) me(1) now(2),
Alone with Mr. V(1)!

Who's waiting on me(1) like he(1) was a maître d'(1)!
I hear my buddies saying:
"Crazy! What gives(12)?
Tonight she's living like the other half lives(12)!"
To think the highest-brow(2),
Which I must say is he(1),
Should pick the lowest-brow(2),
Which there's no doubt is me(1),
What a step up! Holy(1) cow(2)!
They'd never be(1)lie(1)ve it
If my friends could see(1) me(1) now(2)!

They'd never be(1)lie(1)ve it
They'd never be(1)lie(1)ve it
If my friends could see(1) me(1) now(2).

Hi, girls—it's me(1)—Charity(1)!

"Poor Everybody Else" is another fine song from *Sweet Charity.*

"POOR EVERYBODY ELSE"

Poor ev'rybody else
How I pity ev'rybody else
But me.
I'm sorry they're not loved
Like I'm being loved.
In this world there's no girl alive got the
Goosebumps that I've got
Today feel so rich today
I'd give ev'rything but him
Away.
This town would flip
But they just can't make the contact
He's under exclusive contract to me.
Poor ev'rybody else,
Pity ev'rybody else.
I could sit down and cry for
Poor ev'rybody else but me.

Poor ev'rybody else
My heart aches for you and you and you
And you.
We're spiri'chul'ly tied,
Physically tied.
Like he says we're interdependers
Like pants and suspenders
We match funny how we match
And what's more we hit it off
From scratch.
I love my friends
But just in case you are tempted
Remember the guy's preempted by me.
Poor ev'rybody else,
Lonely ev'rybody else.
Got a lump in my throat for
Poor ev'rybody else but me.

In "Baby, Dream Your Dream" *(Sweet Charity),* Dorothy Fields made a lyric that is so chatty and "in the vernacular" that at first it hardly appears to be a lyric at all. The sentiments clearly mark the singers (it's a duet) as rough-and-tumble realistic people who find it impossible to subscribe sincerely to unrealistic romance. In addition to the considerable rhyming, I should like to point out the many $\overline{ee}$ sounds in the first section: dream (7 times), lease, leave, three, we'll (twice), street, P, cream. And in the second half: three, he's (twice), he, be, me, cream, dream (9 times).

In addition, in the second part, long $\bar{o}$ sounds abound: so, don't, home, going, bowling (twice), rolling, both (twice), exploded, loaded, knows, your, close, only.

Music in words!

"BABY, DREAM YOUR DREAM"

HELENE   Baby, dream your dream;
Close your eye(1)s and try(1) it(2).
NICKIE   Dream of furniture;
Dream that I can buy it(2).
HELENE   That fancy bed you prayed for(3),
Not only bought but paid for(3).
NICKIE   Dream we sign(4) the lease,
Leave a small deposit(5).
HELENE   Three and one-half rooms
With a walk-in closet(5).
BOTH   We'll ask the local Jet Set(6)
To dine(4) on our dinette(6) set
Right across the street.
NICKIE   There's a friend(7)ly bank; you(8)
Make a friend(7)ly loan
HELENE   and the bank says, "Thank you(8)."
BOTH   Every Saturday(9)
We'll spend(7) all our money(10).
HELENE   Join the P.T.A.(9)
NICKIE   They will love you, honey(10).
BOTH   Life will be frozen peaches and cream(11);
Baby, dream your dream(11).
NICKIE   Can't you see that little love nest in three years?
HELENE   Yeah. She's feeding the chicks and he's ready to fly the coop!
BOTH   Three fat, hungry kids,
All in pink condition(12).
HELENE   So! Who's in the red?
NICKIE   That nice obstetrician(12).
BOTH   Big Dad(13)dy's fav'rite(2) pastime(13)
He's had(13) it(2) for the last time(13).
Soon Daddy don't come home;

He says he's going bowling(14),
But a bowling ball
NICKIE   Is not what Daddy's rolling(14).
BOTH   Every night(15) they fight(15);
Once they both exploded(16).
Then they both got tight(15).
HELENE   Tight? Hell, they got loaded(16)!
BOTH   Well, who knows what will sour the cream(11)
When you dream(11)—your—
(Both laugh)
But come(12) to think of it,
How happy I would(13) be(14)
If some(12) day I could(13) find(17)
The kind(17) of guy who'd say(18) to me(14)
"Ba(18)by, dream your dream(11);
Close your eye(1)s and try(1) it."

HELENE   "Dream of three fat kids."
NICKIE   Brother, would I(1) buy(1) it!
BOTH   Life could be frozen peaches and cream(11)
If only I could dream(11),
Dream, dream, dream a dream!

Dorothy Fields, as both librettist and lyricist, had a career spanning more than forty-six years. Perhaps her most important libretto was the one coauthored with her brother Herbert for Irving Berlin's *Annie Get Your Gun*. As recently as two years ago, she was still presented on Broadway with *Seesaw*. Her popular (standard) song catalog is enormous. Her film contri-butions have been numerous. In addition to her collaborations with most of the Broadway greats, she coprovided the vehicles for most of our musical stars, including Merman, Fred Astaire, Danny Kaye, Gwen Verdon, Lawrence Tibbett, Grace Moore, Shirley Booth, and many others.

Like most composers and lyricists beginning in the twenties, Dorothy Fields got her start in revues—at first nightclub revues. She graduated to Broadway and then, in my opinion, she grew, developed, and was able to keep step with the swiftly changing world. Her contributions were nearly endless. For a girl who found "connections" in the theatre a hindrance in the beginning, she went very far indeed.

Marc Blitzstein (1905–1964)

Marc Blitzstein was educated for a career in serious music. Like Kurt Weill, who greatly influenced him, he became almost exclusively a composer for the theatre. In addition, Blitzstein was his own lyricist, and for his operas *Triple-Sec* (1930), *The Cradle Will Rock* (1937), *No for an Answer* (1941), *Regina* (1949), and *Juno* (1959), he was his own librettist.

He wrote much incidental music, a ballet, and a cantata. He also adapted Brecht's book and lyrics for the successful revival of Weill's *The Threepenny Opera.* At the time of his death he was at work on an opera for the Metropolitan based on the Sacco-Vanzetti case.

Blitzstein's interest was always expressed—often bitterly, satirically, or humorously—in matters of social concern. He was involved in this most particularly at the height of the Depression when he wrote what, in my opinion, was his most original work, *The Cradle Will Rock* (1937), which suffered a long and well-known history of production delay. In *The Cradle,* an opera, Blitzstein created a narrative interspersed with flashbacks. Though the whole work takes place basically in a night court, it moves to street corners, a drugstore, a garden, a church, and many other places. It is, indeed, in every sense of the word, revolutionary.

Blitzstein's music and stage ideas drew on every phase of American musical theatre, including vaudeville, minstrel show, operatic scene, torch song, and many others.

I should point out basic differences between the lyrics in *The Cradle Will Rock* and *Regina.* In the first, all the characters are representational. They are wonderful posters that tell us what to think and what to feel. The moll, or prostitute, who sings "Nickel Under the Foot" is, of course, a kind of spunky heroine taken advantage of by society and law enforcement officers whom society employs. Junior and Sister Mister are the frivolous teen-age children of the town's ruthless capitalist, the villain of the piece.

The drugstore scene, though still operating by means of figurative characters, is nevertheless moving. The warm relationship between the druggist and his son Stevie, who is killed at the end of the scene, constitutes an extraordinary achievement on Blitzstein's part. The speaking (nonsinging) gangster stereotype, Bugs, turns the scene into a melodrama, which involves the audience in suspense that might have been but is not ludicrous.

Yasha, the violinist, and Dauber, the painter (what else?), who share the duet "The Rich," are a number of different things simultaneously. They first epitomize "artists" who lend themselves to anything in return for patronage. They are, and yet they are not, caricatures. They are end men in a minstrel show. They are a vaudeville team. By being unreal, they are hilarious and most real. We recognize them intimately.

The characters in *Regina,* on the other hand, while still in a sense enacting a parable, are full three-dimensional people, by turns ruthless, savage, and pathetic. These contrasts of style and character between the two operas are clearly evident.

I should like to quote here from *The Cradle Will Rock* (1937) and from *Regina* (1949), based on Lillian Hellman's play *The Little Foxes.*

"THE RICH"

The Cradle Will Rock

DAUBER   Don't let me keep you, please be on your way.

You must have many things to do.

YASHA No, not at all, an appointment today
Brings me to these parts.

DAUBER Me too.

YASHA But the person I'm about to meet,
I doubt you could have met her.
The kind that grovels at my feet,
She'd stay there if I let her.
She's fabulously wealthy,
And although that's not the reason,
I think she can be counted on
To subsidize me all next season.

DAUBER Your ladyfriend does resemble a lot
Someone, and that's very queer.

YASHA So?

DAUBER Someone who's meeting me here!

YASHA No!

DAUBER Is her Pierce Arrow light blue?

YASHA Yes.

DAUBER Not Missus Mister?

YASHA Well, yes, Missus Mister!

DAUBER Me too.

BOTH O, there's something so damned low about the rich,
They're fantastic, they're far-fetched,
They're just funny.
They've no impulse, no fine feeling, no great itch.

YASHA What have they got?

DAUBER What have they got?

BOTH What have they got?
Money.

DAUBER Stupid woman, Missus Mister.

YASHA Stupid! What she doesn't know about music would
put Heifetz back on his feet again.

DAUBER She asked me to bring El Greco to tea this summer!

YASHA *This* summer!

YASHA O, so she mentioned the summer to *you*.
Did she say where she will be?

DAUBER No, but we both thought that Paris would do,
Or Capri, she calls it Capree.

YASHA Why, she promised me Bar Harbor
With an extra house where I . . .
But of course if she has other plans,
I've other fish to fry.

DAUBER Well, dear lady Duchess desperately wants me at her
place,
She's had ev'ryone do her three quarters,
I'm to do her full face.

YASHA And I just heard from Marchesa Contessa last week.
She was Matilda Magee.

DAUBER Well?

YASHA Now she's divorced the Marquis.

DAUBER Hell,
My Lady Duchess loves me.

YASHA Swell!

DAUBER But to wed wealth, so I fear, would affect my career.

YASHA I agree.

BOTH O, there's something so damned low about the rich,
It's incredible the open way they court you.
All these millionaires I can't tell which is which.

DAUBER What can they do?

YASHA What can they do?

BOTH What can they do?
Support you.

"NICKEL UNDER THE FOOT"

The Cradle Will Rock

Maybe you wonder what it is makes people good or bad,
Why some guy, an ace without a doubt,
Turns out to be a bastard and the other way about;
I'll tell you what I feel, it's just the nickel under the heel.

O, you can live like hearts and flowers
And ev'ry day is a wonderland tour.
O, you can dream and scheme and happily put and take,
Take and put,
But first be sure the nickel's under your foot.
Go stand on someone's neck while you're takin',
Cut into somebody's throat as you put,
For ev'ry dream and scheme's depending on whether all
  through the storm
You've kept it warm
The nickel under your foot.
And if you're sweet then you'll grow rotten,
Your pretty heart covered over with soot,
And if for once you're gay,
And devil may careless,
And o so hot,
I know you've got that nickel under your foot.

"CROON-SPOON"

The Cradle Will Rock

C-rrroon, Croon till it hurts, baby,
Croon
My heart asserts, baby,
Croonin' in spurts, baby is just the nerts for a tune.
Sp-p-oon- in a canoe, baby—
Spoon
One built for two, baby, just me and you, baby
I can, can-oo, baby, spoon?

O, the crooner's life is a bless-ed one, he makes the population
  happy.
For when all one's cares have dis-tress-ed one
O to spoon is grand in the June-day sun,
You spoon and spoon and never get tired;
But it's nicer at night than in the noon-day sun,
'Cause then you're Gary Cooper and I'm Carole Lombard!

Just croon, Even the poor are not immune,
If they're without a suit, they shouldn't give a hoot
When they can substitute—

Find me a dream man, and leave us in dream-land,
Where me and my dream-man can—
When they can substitute—
Croon: Spoon!

DRUGSTORE SCENE

The Cradle Will Rock

DRUGGIST Steve!

STEVE Yes, pop?

DRUGGIST   Those glasses, really clean this time, hah! like that.

STEVE   Hah?

DRUGGIST   That's the way.

(sings) It looks like summer weather,

There's a fine warm sun.

I swear I'd not change places with King Solomon.

I ought to make you pay for ev'ry glass that you drop.

It certainly feels fine to own my shop.

STEVE   O, pop,

You're such a crazy, and how about the mortgage?

DRUGGIST   The mortgage now!

You know how much it worries me.

I saw the man again, told him to let me be.

I'll pay him when I can.

You know who owns the company?

It's Mister Mister; tell me, what does he want with my little cash?

(Speaks) It's a terrible world, Stevie, And I feel fine.

BUGS   *(Speaks)* Are you the guy who runs this joint?

DRUGGIST   *(Sings)* I'm the proprietor.

BUGS   *(Speaks)* Do you know a Polock who comes here ev'ry Sunday?

DRUGGIST   *(Parlando)* A Polock?

BUGS   Sure, a punk! Wid his wife he comes here.

STEVE   You know, that Polish fellow.

DRUGGIST   *(Sings)* He brings his wife here ev'ry week about this time,

She likes our icecream sodas,

Yes, I know them well.

BUGS   *(Speaks)* You know what he looks like?

DRUGGIST   Yes, why?

BUGS   *(Parlando)* Uh, you'd like to keep dis drugstore, wouldn't you?

You wouldn't want any company to clamp down on your mortgage or anything like dat, now would you?

DRUGGIST   What's the idea?

BUGS   Here's the dope when dis Polock comes in today,

You don't say nuttin'.

He goes out,

Dere's a big noise outside,

You don't say nuttin', nuttin', understand?

You keep your trap shut;

But when dey ast you later on who done it,

You remember it's dis here Polock.

DRUGGIST   *(Spoken)* Done what?

BUGS   *(Spoken)* Explosion. Dey're takin' a little piece off Union Headquarters across the street.

DRUGGIST   Who is?

BUGS   None of your darn business! Jeez, I don't know why the boss hadda pick you outa all the stores on dis side—talk about dumb!

STEVE   The boss? Mister Mister's behind this somewhere, Pop!

BUGS   You don't know that name! You never heard that name before! Get me?

DRUGGIST   But, man! I can't say somebody did something if he didn't! Suppose he denies it?

BUGS   Listen! I'll go over it all again! Der's gonna be an explosion. Dis *guy's* gonna be *in* the explosion. He ain't gonna bother you none after dat.

DRUGGIST   And his *wife*, too?

BUGS   Can't help it if his wife never lets him out of her sight.

STEVIE   *(Parlando)* Pop, I heard what he said,

Pop, you're not goin' to let him get away with it?

BUGS   You keep your shirt on,

You don't wanna interfere with your old man!

DRUGGIST   Steve, they got me cornered!

I'll lose the store!

They can do it!

I'll lose ev'rything!

They got me, Stevie!

What shall I do?

STEVIE   Pop!

BUGS   Shut up now, here they come!

(Enter) GUS and SADIE

GUS   *(Sings)* Why don't my Sadie tell me she's gonna have baby?

SADIE   Now Gus, I ast you twice today, don't talk that way.

GUS   What I care what they hear!

SADIE   Okay maybe.

GUS   I make a little bed from wood,

So my son sleep good.

BOTH   So my son sleep good.

We wonder if anyone could be as much in love as we

We wonder if anyone ever was before.

They couldn't be any more than we are.

There never was such a day or such a nighttime;

There never was such a boy as we will have and all in the right time.

(GUS *and* SADIE *start to go.*)

GUS   Wassa matta, Kid?

(GUS *and* SADIE *go out*)

STEVIE   No, wait! wait, they're gonna get you! *(Exit after them)*

DRUGGIST   Stevie! Stevie!

(Explosion. Blackout)

"THE BEST THING OF ALL"

Regina

You know, if you want—if you want—if you want something that's over the wall,

Don't wait—and don't hope—

And don't beg—and don't crawl—

Oh no, you must take what you want.

You must take it in your hand like a ball.

To want and to take is the best thing of all!

Now some in the crowd holler loud how they want something, and want it a lot.

They *don't* know what they want—and they hunt—and for what?

Then there are a few—just a few—

Oh, they knew pretty well what to pursue;

But mumbled and fumbled, and lost it all.

And how about those solemn heroes in the story

Who fought the fight, and died in glory?

They never lived to tell their very heart's desire.

They merely fell into the fire.

We forget them, and we let them fall.

The best thing of all, is to want—

Is to want something with all your heart,

To aim, with no shame,
With a true aim at the start,
And if you are good, very good,
When the moment's nearly upon you—
Take that moment, and you've got the best thing of all!

"BLUES"

Regina

ADDIE
Night could be time to sleep.
Night could be time to weep.
Please, Miss Birdie.
Night could be time of ease,
Rubbing out memories.
Please, Miss Birdie.
Till what the day may be bringing,
Here's singing.

If you was like the night, and you could see the things there are,
If you was like the night, and you could see the things there are,
Then you'd be blue, like you ain't never been before, so far.
Maybe you knows the woes that making folks so blue tonight.
Maybe you knows the woes that making folks so blue tonight.
Then let your own alone, and they'll go out, just like the night.

Night could be time to sleep.
Night could be time to weep.
Please, Miss Birdie.

BIRDIE *(Spoken)* Thank you, Addie.

"WALTZ"

Regina

Do you wish we had wed years ago?
You remember I said we might marry then,
And then you went away.
Do you wish we had wed that day?
If you could, would you care for me now?
Would you sing a sad song, with a soulful art,
To all my heart requires?
Do you dream what my heart desires?

Hail the haggard swain, complete with courtliness and grace.
No one would divine the wispy weakness of your face,
Or note the light whine in your sighs.
Is my beauty still warm in your eyes?
Have my cheeks any charm of enduring youth
For your sweet tooth to crave?
Did you wander on wind and wave,
Still ever my lovesick slave?
Decrepit and brave, my soldier slave?

Youth was one thing, wonderful yearning,
Burning a burning feverish brew.
But childhood is childish and done with!
Sense a new century, too.
If I'm restless, restless for something,
Sorry that something, burning anew, is not you!
You're a wretched reply to my fires.
Now hark back to my heart's desires:

There are diamonds that sparkle and shine.
There are fineries, furs, and a thousand things.

I count those things for mine.
I'm no simpering saint with wings,
To whom Vacuous Virtue clings.
I don't mind handling money, handfuls of money.
Money means things, and the things I can do with things!
For the half-poor are poorer than poor,
Unhappy, unloved, unsure;
More feeble by far than the meek and the weak,
Are the noble, the nibbling, the Not-Quite-Poor.
I'm in love with things.
You've a thousand rivals—things.

"BIRDIE'S ARIA"

Regina

Mama used to say you can stop hiccups
By sipping slowly elderberry wine.
Mama used to say—I can see her now, laughing.
My first party; and hiccups.
My brother kept pounding me on the back, and Mama
  laughing.
Mama always laughed.
Mama always laughed, laughed, laughed.
Holding the elderberry bottle, and laughing.
A lovely party at Lionnet.
A lovely dress, come all the way from Mister Worth in Paris,
  France
La la. . . . .
And me with hiccups.

Lionnet.
Lionnet.
Remember Lionnet.
The lawn down to the river.
Lionnet—the lawn so smooth and lovely to see.
Lovely to see.
Lovely it used to be.
And the music at Lionnet!
The singing on the river
And people came and loved to come, and listen there.
We sang.
How we sang.
La, la, la. . . . .
Oh, if we could all go back!
If only we could, to Lionnet.
People would be better there.
They'd be kind and good, at Lionnet.
I like people to be kind.
Don't you? Of course you do,
Like people to be kind.

Leo isn't kind.
Leo isn't kind.
You all want to know something?
Leo isn't kind.
I don't like Leo.
My very own son, and I don't like him at all!
My, I guess I even like Oscar more.
I thought I liked Oscar.
I thought he liked me too.
I married him.
He was so kind and nice then
So kind.

Yes. I married him.
I thought
I thought
Ev'rybody knew why *he* chose me.
Ev'rybody knew it was true.
Ev'ryone but me.
Ben Hubbard wanted the cotton on Lionnet then.
And Oscar Hubbard married it for Ben!
Why would I not see
What was plain to see?
Ev'rybody knew but me—stupid, stupid me!

Oscar Hubbard married me so that they could take our
  Lionnet!
Headache—headache—I've never had a headache in all my life.
You all know that.
That's just a lie they tell for me.
I drink.
All by myself, in my own room,
By myself, I drink.
Look at me, I drink.
Then they try to hide it:
"Birdie's got a headache, a headache, a headache, a headache
  again."

And now,
Even you won't love me.
Won't love me, won't love me anymore.
And that's good!
Don't love me.
Don't, don't love me.
Because in twenty years
You'll be just like me.
Trailing after them like me,
Hoping they won't see.
Hoping for one day
That they won't be mean,
Or say something to make you feel so bad!
Lionnet.
Lionnet.
Lionnet.
La la la. . . . .

ALEXANDRA
(Spoken) Come, Aunt Birdie. I'll walk you home. Just you and
  me.

BIRDIE
(Whisper) You and me.

Harold Rome
(b. 1908)

Since the composer of *Prince Igor* was a chemist, the man who gave us *Boris Godunov* a surveyor, and Rimski-Korsakov a naval officer, it is not surprising that the composer-lyricist of *Pins and Needles, Call Me Mister, Fanny, Destry Rides Again, I Can Get It for You Wholesale, Wish You Were Here,* and others, began life when he picked up his diploma at Yale as an architect!

It is a fact that creative people are either exactly what they write, that is, they reflect their true selves in their work, or unfortunately, as has often been the case, they lead a double life. They have many times been intolerable human beings who escape from their impossible selves into another, better world that they create. Harold Rome is one of the former. In his best work one finds the simple sweetness that is his dominant personal characteristic. Luckily, sweetness when coupled with invention is capable of generating humor. This is a Rome accomplishment.

There is nothing unusual about a young composer-lyricist beginning his career as a writer for amateurs. Rodgers and Hart wrote six shows that were given nonprofessional productions before this celebrated team wrote great songs for a professionally accredited company provided by the Theatre Guild. This production, a modest revue called *The Garrick Gaieties* in 1925, marked their true beginning. Other writers began similarly in schools and colleges. The difference in Harold Rome's case was that, in my opinion, Rome began at the top of his form in 1937 when he wrote memorable and certainly timely songs for the amateur performers recruited from the membership of the International Ladies Garment Workers Union. The show was the revue *Pins and Needles,* and it rang up a total of 1,108

performances in two runs, between which it enjoyed a successful tour.

We read a great deal in history about times "making the man." Of course, such a happening requires a particular kind of man in possession of a special and appropriate talent and "times" capable of stimulating the proper response from him.

In 1937 the situation on the labor front was very different from the one with which we are familiar today. The ILGWU, already financially strong and boasting an enormous and loyal membership, had largely won its fight against sweatshop conditions, substandard salaries, and many other intolerable employer-employee relationships.

There had to be a second phase in the progressive life of the ILGWU, when it set out to provide cultural advantages for its dues-paying members. These cultural advantages assumed many different forms. Since many of the members had come to the United States as immigrants, there was so much that they could and wanted to learn, especially since, under improved working conditions, they at long last had some leisure time to fill—perhaps for the first time in their lives. In all cultures—and many different ones were represented in this union's membership—there has always existed a burning desire to "go on the stage." For some of the most talented, this desire became a reality with the production of *Pins and Needles.*

Labor Stage, previously called the Princess Theatre when Jerome Kern had filled it a decade earlier, with a seating capacity of only about three hundred, was the home of *Pins and Needles.* Although many different writers and composers at various times contributed material to this little revue, Harold Rome was its chief creator and was, with the aid of Earl Robinson and later Baldwin Bergerson, its copianist. Most of the shifts in material, the exchange of new songs for older ones that occurred from time to time, were due to political changes. Though some of these directly affected conditions close to the parent union, an equal number was caused by larger world conditions: the rise of Hitler, Mussolini, and Fascism. These were indeed perilous times, and *Pins and Needles* always reflected them.

Some playwrights of the same period attacked similar problems with seriousness and a fighting spirit. Clifford Odets, for example, wrote *Waiting for Lefty,* and *Awake and Sing,* both in 1935. Shaw wrote *Bury the Dead* in 1936 and Lawson wrote *Processional* in 1937, the year of Blitzstein's *The Cradle Will Rock.* But Harold Rome almost invariably employed satire as his weapon. Serious situations were knocked down by laughter. Though the hard inner core of the songs provided by Rome was serious, the outer coating was sweet. Spectators responded to a sensible point of view in regard to hideous world situations that were then in the making, but were entertained by his creative method.

In my opinion Harold Rome began his professional life in full maturity. Many of the songs he created for *Pins and Needles* are still, thirty-eight years later, pertinent and permanent. To be able to appreciate humor, years after, without the aid of footnotes, is a difficult and rare achievement. His style, like his nature, is gentle and sweet. The less satiric subjects of songs such as "Nobody Makes a Pass at Me," "Chain Store Daisy," and "It's Better with a Union Man" are lovable. The harder, more bitter songs, such as "Four Little Angels of Peace," about Chamberlain, Hirohito, Mussolini, and Hitler, retained their cool and provided audiences with amusing satire and ridicule in place of anger. In 1937 it was too early for anger.

But Rome's darts hit their targets. They served the world at a time of approaching crisis and they linger on today when most of them are still applicable. Old crises have given way to new but—alas—similar ones. Rome's songs served the needs and desires of the ILGWU, which spawned them, and those needs and desires have become universal.

All lyricists of consequence have reflected in one of a number of ways the worlds in which they lived. I have attempted to point out the styles and peculiarities of each. Harold Rome, a product of the thirties and happily directly involved with a leading movement of that time, was automatically provided with a wealth of pertinent material that he took full and diverse advantage of. It seems obvious that this material was deeply meaningful to him, and having the talent to translate it into a kind of Theatre of Action, he did it, not head on, which would have been far less effective, but with a charm that became irresistible.

I should like to begin by quoting some lyrics from *Pins and Needles.* First from the gentler subjects that directly involved the ILGWU membership and subsequently all working people of that time who were struggling to extricate themselves from the quagmires of impotence.

"Social Significance" sets a pace for most of what follows. Like most of Rome's lyrics, these are straightforward. They say what they have a mind to say: "Let meaning shine from every line."

The rhymes are simple, but in this first song I have indicated them. Note that in the two-word title there are four sibilants *(s* sounds). This element pervades the entire song. In the verse and first chorus alone there are no fewer than 56 *s* sounds!

These lyrics paint a complete picture of life and the prevailing attitudes of the thirties.

"SING US A SONG WITH SOCIAL SIGNIFICANCE"

VERSE
GIRLS We're tired of moon(1) songs,
Of star and of June(1) songs.
They simply make us nap(2).
And ditties romantic(3)
Drive us nearly frantic(3).
We think they're all full of pap(2).
Nations are quaking(4),
History making(4),
Why sing of stars above(5)?
While we are waiting(6)
Time is creating(6)
New things to be singing of(5).

CHORUS I
Sing us a song
With social significance!
All other tunes are taboo(7).
We want a ditty with heat(8) in it,
Appealing(9) with feeling(9) and meat(8) in it.
Sing us a song
With social significance,
Or you can sing 'till you're blue(7).
Let meaning shine(10) from every line(10),
Or we won't love you(7).

Sing us of wars,
And sing us of breadlines(11),
Sing of front page news.
Sing us of strikes,
And last-minute headlines(11).—
Dress your observation(12) in
Syncopation(12).

Sing us a song
With social significance!
There's nothing else that will do(7).
It must be packed(13)
With social fact(13)
Or we won't love you(7)!

CHORUS II BOYS
We'll sing a song
With social significance.
All other tunes are taboo(7).
We'll get a song that's satirical(14).
Putting the "mere" into miracle(14).
We'll sing a song
With social significance.
We'll get a song that will do(7),
Entirely fraught(15) with social thought(15).—
Tell us will that do(7)?

We'll sing of wars,
And conferences martial(16),
Tell you of mills and mines,

Sing you of courts
That aren't impartial(16).
Dress our economics(17)
In the best harmonics(17).

We'll sing a song
With social significance.
There's nothing else that will do(7).
It will be tense(18)
With common sense(18).

GIRLS
Then we will love you(7)!

CHORUS III
Sing us a song
With social significance!
All other tunes are taboo(7).
We want a song to make history(19),
Robbing the great of their mystery(19).

Sing us a song
With social significance
Or you can sing 'till you're blue(7).
It must get hot(20)
With what is what(20)
Then we will love you(7).

Sing us of kings
And of revolutions(21),
Sing us
Of social trends,
Sing us of old
And new constitutions(21),—
What's to be done with 'em(22)
We want it in rhythm(22)!

Sing(23) us a song
With social significance.
There's nothing else that will do(7).
It must ring(23) true(7)
With social view(7),
Or we won't love you(7)!

"Nobody Makes a Pass at Me" presages "Miss Marmelstein," a song Rome wrote twenty-five years later for Barbra Streisand in *I Can Get It for You Wholesale*. The chief difference between the two, both of which make the same point, is in their respective developments. "Miss Marmelstein" expresses a desire to be called pet names. The girl of "Nobody Makes a Pass at Me," a victim of radio commercials, uses all the advertised products, though this produces no improvement in her lonely social life. The humor is triggered by the misfortune of the singer as in Loesser's "Adelaide's Lament," Rodgers and Hammerstein's "I Cain't Say No," and Lerner and Loewe's "The Love of My Life."

"NOBODY MAKES A PASS AT ME"

VERSE
I want men that I can squeeze,
That I can please, that I can tease.
Two or three or four or more!
What are those fools waiting for?
I want love and I want kissing.
I want more of what I'm missing—

Nobody comes knocking at my front door.
What do they think my knocker's for?
If they don't come soon there won't be any more!
What can the matter be?

CHORUS I
I wash my clothes with Lux,
My etiquette's the best.
I spend my hard-earned bucks
On just what the ads suggest.
Oh dear what can the matter be?
Nobody makes a pass at me!

I'm full of Kellogs's bran,
Eat Grape-Nuts on the sly,
A date is on the can
Of the coffee that I buy.
Oh dear what can the matter be?
Nobody makes a pass at me!

Oh Beatrice Fairfax, give me the bare facts,
How do you make them fall?
If you don't save me, the things the Lord gave me
Never will be of any use to me at all.

I sprinkle on a dash
Of Fragrance de Amour
The ads say "makes men rash"—
But I guess their smell is poor!
Oh dear what can the matter be?
Nobody makes a pass at me!

PATTER
I use Ovaltine and Listerine,
Barbasol and Musterole,
Lifebuoy soap and Flit,
So why ain't I got it?

I use Coca-Cola and Mazola,
Crisco, Lesco, and Marmola,
Ex-Lax, and Vapex,
So why ain't I got sex?

I use Alboline and Maybelline,
Alka-Seltzer, Bromo-Seltzer,
Odorono and Sensation,
So why ain't I got fascination?

My girdles come from Best.
The Times ads say they're chic,
And up above I'm dressed
In the brassiere of the week.
Oh dear what can the matter be?
Nobody makes a pass at me!

I use Pond's on my skin.
With Ry-Krisp I have thinned.
I get my culture in—
I began "Gone with the Wind."
Oh dear what can the matter be?
Nobody makes a pass at me!

Oh Dorothy Dix, please show me some tricks, please.
I want some men to hold.
I want attention and things I won't mention—
And I want them all before I get too old.

I use Mum every day
And Angelus Lip-Lure
But still men stay away
Just like Ivory Soap I'm 99 and 44/100ths percent pure!

I don't know!

"Chain Store Daisy," like the preceding song, is a "personal misfortune" ditty. In this one the tribulation belongs to a girl who has graduated from Vassar but finds herself ignominiously employed. Though the song and its humor are personal, the subject matter is much larger in that it reflects a serious general condition of the Depression era. The form and rhyme scheme are clear.

"CHAIN STORE DAISY"

VERSE
When I was young I studied hard and thirsted after knowledge,
And often burned the midnight oil so I could get to college,
They told me my fine education would help improve my situation;
So then I crammed and crammed 'till I was almost in a coma,
And thesised and examed until I got me a diploma,
"Ah-hah," they said,
Now comes admission,
Into a very high position.

Out I went and looked around,
And Macy's is the place I found,
I filled my blanks and application
And went for my examination.

They took my weight and took my height,
And tapped my chest and tested my sight.
Examined my head, took prints of my toes,
Looked at my teeth and up my nose.

Examined my throat and measured my hips,
And even took prints of my finger tips.
They made me say "ah" and told me to grunt.
Examined my back, examined my front.

Then they tested my "I.Q."
And asked me what I'd like to do
And when that exam was thru
What there was to know Macy's knew!
(Spoken) (So I got the job)

CHORUS
Life is a bitter cup of tea,
Now I'm just salesgirl seventy-three,
I used to be on the daisy chain,
Now I'm a chain store daisy.

Once they gave me the honor seat,
Now I stand up with pains in my feet,
I used to be on the daisy chain
Now shoppers drive me crazy.

I sell smart but thrifty
Corsets at three-fifty
Better grade four-sixty nine.
I sell bras and girdles
For Mauds and Myrtles,
To hold in their plump
Behind this counter.

Once I wrote poems, put folks in tears,
Now I write checks for ladies' brassieres,
I used to be on the daisy chain
Now I'm a chain store daisy.

(Spoken)
Oh! yes, madam—Oh! no, madam—
I guess, madam—That's so, madam—
Of course madam—that's the very best,
Exactly the kind that's worn by Mae West.

For you, madam—we do madam—
That's true, madam—in blue, madam—
That one is nineteen-seventy-four.
It ought to be expensive
It's the largest in the store.

Sung
Once I had a yearning
For all higher learning,
Studied 'till I made the grade
I pursued my knowledge
And finished college,
Well look at the
Kind of grade I made.

I'm now selling things to fit in the figure,
(Spoken) Make the big things small and
The small things bigger!
I used to be on the daisy chain
Now I'm a chain store daisy.

"Not Cricket to Picket," also from *Pins and Needles,* creates a character. She is lifelike and hooted at as being outrageously unreasonable, the granddaughter of the very queen who said "Let 'em eat cake." She has background, manners, and everything except comprehension of the problems of less well-off people, and she was a favorite character in the thirties. It should be obvious that she becomes more excited as the song progresses, so that she then confuses the title line. Rome indulges in more rhyming sport in this lyric than in any other.

"IT'S NOT CRICKET TO PICKET"

It's not cricket(1) to picket(1)—not cricket(1).
Oh no, not "Comme il faut(2)" to picket(1).
You haven't any right you know(2); you're acting in great haste(3).
Just think of the predic(4)ament in which your boss is placed(3).
And entre-nous—I think it's in exceedingly bad taste(3)!
Not crick(4)et to picket(1)—not cricket(1)!

It's not cricket(1) to picket(1)—not cricket(1),
Atro(2)cious and quite "gauche(2)" you know(2), to picket(1).
Go home and starve like gentlemen, not like a noisy brood(5).
Real ladies never make a fuss tho(2) they lack clothes and food(5).
And money's never talked about, for that would be quite rude(5)!
(Excited) Not cricket(1) to picket(1)—not cricket(1)!

It's not cricket(1) to picket(1), not cricket(1).
Now, go away or you will get a ticket(1).
You're acting just like foreigners with names like Serge or Olga(6),
Or Rooshians or Italians or like some uncultured Bulgar(6).
You'll pardon me for saying so, but you are being vulgar(6)!
(More excited) Not cricket(1) to picket(1)—not cricket(1)!

It's not cricket(1) to picket(1)—not cricket(1),
Uncultured and unmannerly to picket(1).
You know you're misbehaving—now you mustn't lose your mind(7).
You're being so inelegant, and frankly, quite unkind(7).
Excuse my indiscretion, but you're all darned unrefined(7)!
Not picket(1) to cricket(1), not picket(1)!

(Boiling over)
It's not ticket(1) to sticket(1), not picket(1)
Now officer, give each man there a cricket(1)
Oh dear! *(Shouting)* Where is your decency? No Vanderbilts or Astors(8)
Would act in such a vulgar way, befitting only dastards(8)
I beg you get the hell away, you lousy bunch of bastards(8)!
It's not picket(1) to cricket(1)! not picket(1)!

A final example from *Pins and Needles* is an impersonal satirical quartet, making fun of the unfunny ambitions of Chamberlain, Hirohito, Mussolini, and Hitler, four years before the United States became embroiled in the world holocaust.

"FOUR LITTLE ANGELS OF PEACE"

REFRAIN
Four little angels of peace are we(1),
Loving our neighbors so peacefully(1):
There's really no harm(2) if we do not disarm(2),
For we're always in close harm(2)ony(1).

Four little angels of peace are we(1),
There is one thing on which we agree(1):
With foe or with friend(3) we will fight to the end(3)
Just for Peace! Peace! Peace!

CHAMBERLAIN
Though we butchered the Boers(4) on their own native shores(4),
And slaughtered the Irish no end(3),
Though on India we poured(5), slaying horde(5) upon horde(5),
We were playing the part of a friend(3).

Yes, our arms we increase(6) but we're really for peace(6)
Except in the case of a crook(7).
We conquered both spheres(8), now we're up to our ears(8),
Just trying to keep what we took(7).

REFRAIN
Three(1) little angels of peace are we(1),
Living together so blissfully(1):
Oh, we never fight(9) unless we're in the right(9),
But we're always in the right, you see(1).

Three little angels of peace are we(1).
There is one thing on which we agree(1).—
Until we are wrecks(10) we'll break each other's necks(10)
Just for Peace! Peace! Peace!

HIROHITO
In Japan we delight(9) in our generals' might(9)
But the emperor knows peace is finer(11).
It isn't our fault(12), it's a case of assault(12),
We're picked on and bullied by China(11).

Oh, how we deplore(13) our great need for a war(13)!
We're a nation of poets and thinkers(14).
Though we bomb without pity(15) and lay waste to each city(15),
It's because all the Chinese are stinkers(14).

REFRAIN
Two little angels of peace are we(1),
Living together in amity(1):
Oh, we'll sign any pact saying we won't attack,
But that's just a mere formality(1).

Two little angels of peace are we(1),
There is one thing on which we agree(1).
We try to keep calm(16) when we gas and we bomb(16)
Just for Peace! Peace! Peace!

MUSSOLINI
Now I know that war(13) is a thing to abhor(13)
And that peace will fill our cornucopia(17).
With love from the start(18)
I just did my part(18)
To civilize dear Ethiopia(17).

Though you call me sadistic(19),
Imperialistic(19),
My armies require a quarry(20).
And though we may slay(21) hordes of Spaniards each day(21),
After all, don't we say(21) that we're sorry(20)?

HITLER
Though I fall for the urge(22) of a nice bloody purge(22).
And leave in my wake(23) piles of carrion(24),
Though I clean up my schmutz(25) with a real Nazi putsch(25),
It is all for the sake(23) of the Aryan(24).

My ambitions are small(25),
I want nothing at all(25),
My plans couldn't be any littler(26);
Now that Austria's Nazi(27)
It would be hotsey(27)-totsey(27)
To put the whole world under Hitler(26)!

REFRAIN
Four little angels of peace are we(1),
Reek(28)ing with odor of sanctity(1);
Though we slaughter the meek(28), we confer ev'ry week(28),
And we talk it over peacefully(1).

Four little angels of peace are we(1),
There is one thing on which we agree(1).
With shot and with shell(29) we give each other hell(29)
Just for Peace! Peace! Peace!

Rome's next show after *Pins and Needles* was another revue with political satire as its central thread. *Sing Out the News* contained a particularly beautiful ballad. Its melody might have framed a love song, but as it happens, "One of These Fine

Days," besides having a haunting homey quality, has also more than a pinch of social comment. The complex rhyme system is indicated. As busy as it is, the overall feeling is one of laziness. It also is a detailed dramatic narrative.

"ONE OF THESE FINE DAYS"

Scene: A Harlem Street

VERSE I
Just about around this time of year(1)
When the days are feeling warm and clear(1),
When the park is green and new(2),
And the song of birds comes thru(2) to here(1).
I get weary of this crowded stair(22),
With a yearning for some room to spare(22).
There's a voice that seems to say(3),
Man, you ought to get away(3), out there—out there(22)!

CHORUS I
One of these fine days(4),
When the spring winds blow(5),
Gonna change my ways(4) around(6),
I'll just up and go(5).

Don't care where I'm bound(6),
Don't care where I land(7),
Wanna look around(6) a bit,
Let myself expand(7).

MAN 2
Where folks ain't crowded like flies together,
MAN 1
Where there's a job for me(8),
MAN 2
Where life is right(9)—no black and no(5) white(9),
Where men are free(8)!
MAN 1
One of these fine days
I'll be on my way(3).
One of these fine days I'll go(5)—
But not today(3).

Maybe tomorrow,
Who can say(3)?
One of these fine days,
But not today(3).

CHORUS II
(Old Lady reading young girl's palm)
One of these fine days(4)
He will come for you(10)
With his fancy ways(4), that boy,
But he won't be true(10).

YOUNG GIRL
Then I'll(11) bide my time
Till my true love comes(12).
OLD LADY
Honey chile(11), your kind don't set
Twiddling their thumbs(12).
WOMAN 1
I ain't seen Jim for a month of Sundays
Where did your sweet boy go(5)?

WOMAN 2
Never a word(13), I just haven't heard(13), I miss him so(5)!
One of these fine days
He'll come back to stay(3)
"Never leave your side no more,"
WOMAN 1
But not today(3),
WOMAN 2
Not today(3).

CHORUS III
(Visiting nurse and mother come out)
NURSE
One of these fine days(4)
Your boy, he'll pull thru(10).
MOTHER
You've just got to help us now!
NURSE
God, what can I do(10)!
(Boys have been playing craps—there's a whistle—cop comes strolling on)
OLD MAN TO BOYS
Better mend your ways(4).
Satan's on your trail(14).
COP
Come on break it up, you bums,
Wanna land in jail(14).
(Married couple with carriage and lots of kids)
HUSBAND
Lord, ain't we got enough kids already
What's that you told Mis' Dunn(15)?
WIFE
Yes Joe it's true(10)
(Whispers) A new kid is due(10)
HUSBAND
Another one(15)!
(Sweethearts watching kids go by)
BOY
One of these fine days
Honey, what you say(3),
GIRL
One of these fine days, perhaps,
But not today(3),
Not today(3).

CHORUS IV
(Little girl going on errand stops and looks in beauty parlor)
One of these fine days
Gonna do my hair(1)
Till they make it stay so nice,
(Mother's voice from upper window yells "Mary, hurry up now")
(As girl goes) Like that gal in there(1).
(Boys watch Jim in bar pay for drink with a big roll)
BOY 1
Oh man, look at that dough,
Bango right(9) on the bean,
BOY 2
That's just chicken feed(22)
When I be(23) like Joe Lewis,
Wait and see(23) my speed(22)
(Shadow boxing)
I'll get right into the ring.
(Ice man passing)

That's it, biff 'em.
And every night(9) I'll win a big fight(9)
'Till I'm champeen.
(Man hesitating at door to bar)
One of these fine days,
Gonna stay(3) away(3),
One of these fine days, I will,
Hm———
(Goes in) But not today(3).

CHORUS V
(Man with trumpet starts playing in window)
JIM
Jesus let me go
(GANGSTER)
Nuts, you're in too deep(17)
(Man from another window to trumpeter)
Hey you stop that blowing now!
How'm I gonna sleep(17)!
(Slams window)
(Trumpet keeps playing—muted)
GANGSTER
Better make it fast(18)
It ain't healthy here(1).
WOMAN 2
(Coming over—she's been called by a boy)
Jim, you're back(19) at last(18), thank God!
JIM
Had to disappear(1).
A mob used my hack(19) to pull a stickup.
Then they got(20) in a jam(21),
When things got hot(20)—put me on the spot(20)—
I've got(20) to scram(21)—

One of these fine days
I'll come back to stay(3)
WOMAN 2
But when, Jim when?
JIM
One of these fine days, honey *(ad lib)*
(He's shot)
But not today(3),
Not today(3)
(Cash register in bar rings)
MAN 2
One of these fine days
Judgment's on the way(3).
Gonna be some changes made,
But not today(3),
Maybe tomorrow,
Who can say(3),
One of these fine days
But not today(3).

Rome's social concerns were to be an integral part of at least two other shows and to become his own personal autograph.

The Little Dog Laughed (1940) was a "book show," as opposed to a revue, which saw life first on the Atlantic City boardwalk and, a few short weeks later, breathed its last in Boston without ever reaching Broadway.

"The Fairy Tales Are All Unfair!" carries on the tradition Rome established for himself in "Chain Store Daisy" and "Nobody Makes a Pass at Me." Here, however, the machinery of protest is used by the "older sisters" of fairy tales against writers who traditionally have relegated them to positions of spinsterhood. The form and the rhymes are self-evident. The basic idea and the humor are original.

"THE FAIRY TALES ARE ALL UNFAIR!"

VERSE
There's a very unfair condition,
That you'll find in all fairy tales;
Younger sisters get all the heroes,
While we older ones bite our nails!
We're so tired of seeing them rush off,
Since fairytales began,
While we stand by and get the brush off—
But never get our man!

We don't want to be homely,
We demand a brand new deal,
With improved facial conditions,
And higher sex appeal!

CHORUS
Unfair, unfair!
To every elder daughter,
We don't get what we oughta,
We're nervous wrecks!

In every book,
When princes come to woo us,
They never bill and coo us,
We've got no sex!
A younger sister passes by,
Gives him the eye,
And we're left panting high and dry!
Unfair, unfair!
Cinderellas get the fellas,
And all we get is jealous!
The fairy tales are all unfair!

PATTER
Without a single pang,
We'll picket Andrew Lang,
We strike with all our vim,
Against the brothers Grimm,
We want our wrongs undone,
Hans Christian Andersen,
Don't patronize . . .
These story writing guys!

CHORUS II
Unfair, unfair!
These authors all conspire,
They give us the desire,
But not the men . . .
The story ends . . .
In Denmark something's rotten,
We're always left forgotten . . .
Just foiled again!
We've got demands that must be met,
To kiss and pet
To get what girls like Snow White get . . .
Unfair, unfair!

We've got no plot to kiss in . . .
The fairy tales are all unfair!

It's downright prejudiced, that's what . . .
A dirty plot,
What's Snow White got that we ain't got . . .
Unfair, unfair!
Our sex appeal is zero,
We never get the hero. . . .
The fairy tales are all unfair!

Just after World War II when Rome and writer Arnold Auerbach came out of the service, they wrote a topical revue celebrating the return of military personnel to civilian life. The show, *Call Me Mister* (1946) was a huge success. Most of the cast had also just left the armed forces. The New York company included Betty Garrett, Jules Munshin, Harry Clark, Chandler Cowles, Lawrence Winters, Billy Cahahan, Maria Karnilova, George Irving, David Nillo, and Dodie Goodman in the chorus. A subsequent road company included Bob Fosse, Buddy Hackett, Carl Reiner, and Betty Kean. The producers, Herman Levin and Melvyn Douglas, along with many of the performers, were making their debuts. *Call Me Mister* spoofed the military, spoke of the seriousness of war, lampooned the new civilian changeover, and sang reverently of the late F.D.R.

A memory of battle heroism was echoed in "The Red Ball Express," a dramatic narrative ballad. The lyric form and rhymes are evident. What is perhaps more elusive is the all-pervading ō sound that is heard throughout in words like coast, 44, shore, story, and old, all of which appear in the first quatrain. These sounds continue in the other two verses (eight lines each) and the three choruses.

"THE RED BALL EXPRESS"

VERSE I
There are songs of infantry—of the air corps and the sea—
Of the coast guard and marines in battle dress.
We sing August 44 and the Normandy French shore—
Just the story of the old Red Ball Express.

Driving truck loads night and day—36 hours on the way,
They supplied our hungry armies from the shore.
Steam was hissing from their hoods, when they showed up with
   the goods,
But they turned around and went right back for more.

CHORUS
It's the Red Ball Express, roaring by, roaring by!
It's the Red Ball Express, roaring by!
With one man at the wheel and one man at the gun
And a pride in the job to be done.
With the clashing of gears and the clanking of chains
And a song ringing clear to the sky.
It's the Red Ball Express roaring by,—roaring by!
It's the Red Ball Express roaring by!

VERSE II
In a never ending chain—thru the mud and thru the rain,
Closing up the gaps that shells left in their file,
They kept driving, holding tight, sometimes stopped to dig and
   fight—
Then they highballed on—a song for every mile.

Oh, the way those trucks did hop—would have killed a traffic
   cop.
There was driving out of this world on those runs.
Sometimes one truck would detour-draw the fire to make sure.
That the other loads got safely by the guns.

CHORUS
It's the Red Ball Express, roaring by, roaring by!
It's the Red Ball Express, roaring by!
With one man at the wheel and one man at the gun,
And a pride in the job to be done.
With the clashing of gears and the clanking of chains
And a song ringing clear to the sky.
It's the Red Ball Express roaring by—roaring by!
It's the Red Ball Express roaring by!

VERSE III
So we sing this ballad for the old quartermaster corps.
Just a small part of the team of victory.
Tho you may not know the name, there are plenty all the same
Never will forget that job in Normandy.

To this very day they say, when the night is dull and gray,
Norman farmers hear a strange hullabaloo.
And they peep outside and yell—French for "shut my mouth-
   do tell"
As a ghostly caravan comes bouncing thru!

CHORUS
It's the Red Ball Express, roaring by, roaring by!
It's the Red Ball Express, roaring by!
With one man at the wheel and one man at the gun
With the clashing of gears and the clanking of chains
And a song ringing clear to the sky
It's the Red Ball Express roaring by,—roaring by!
It's the Red Ball Express, roaring by,—roaring by!

F.D.R.'s memory is evoked in a ballad, "The Face on the Dime." Although it is dedicated to the late president through contemplation of the then-new Roosevelt dime, Rome was still creating a singing character identifying himself with "everyman."

I don't know who's on a hundred
Or a thousand dollar bill,
And I don't suppose I ever will.

The rhymes are simple, sparse, and clearly evident.

"THE FACE ON THE DIME"

VERSE
Jefferson's on the nickel.
Washington's on a quarter.
And they both sure oughta be there.

Lincoln is on the penny
Because he thought of the many.
You've got to admit that's fair.

I don't know who's on a hundred
Or a thousand dollar bill,
And I don't suppose I ever will.

But I've got my picture gallery
Of great men right here with me—

Most of the time—
On a cent, a nickel, a quarter and now a dime.

CHORUS
Just a face on the dime,
One shiny new dime.
How can I even start
To tell what's in my heart
At the sight of a dime,
Of a shiny new dime.

He's not long in the past
But his name sure will last down thru time—
Down thru time.

Let the few rant and scandal and doubt him—
They did that to Abe Lincoln before.
As for me, I'll teach my kids about him—
Yes sir! They'll know the score.

When it came to the end,
I knew I'd lost a friend.
Thru the earth us plain guys
Brushed a tear from our eyes, for we knew—
The world was a poorer and colder place
Without that face on the dime—
The face on the shiny new dime.

From *Call Me Mister* I should like to quote a musical scene in its entirety, "Yuletide, Park Avenue." It presents its own cast of characters who are wealthy and represent social elegance. The atmosphere is cheerful, the satire gentle and without animus. The entire scene—a complete entity—is sung as a kind of operetta.

"YULETIDE, PARK AVENUE"

ALL   With a hey nonny nonny nonny.
Hey nonny, nonny nonny.
Hey nonny,
Tra-la-la-la-la,
BUTLER   Tra-la-la.
ALL   Tra-la-la-la-la,
BUTLER   Tra-la-la.
MOTHER   Sing hey for the season of the jolly holly, the merry berry.
The sleigh bell jangle, the shopper's wrangle.
BUTLER   Ho, t'is here, the season of the yuletide.
GIRLS   Season of the Yuletide, season of the Yuletide
ALL   Season of the Yuletide cheer.
SISTER   Sing a hey, nonny, nonny, to the Xmas carol, the gay apparel,
The lights all gleaming, the shop-girl screaming.
MEN   Ho, tis here, the season of the Yuletide cheer.
GIRLS   Season of the Yuletide—season of the Yule.
YOUNG SISTER   Sing an extra nonny to the wreathes and crosses, the Santa Clauses,
The kids that sit up, the trees all lit up.
GRANDMOTHER   *(With a look to the parents)*
The parents likewise lit up
For the gayest season of the year.
ALL   With a hey nonny, nonny, nonny.
Hey nonny, nonny, nonny,
Hey nonny,

Tra-la-la-la,
BUTLER   Tra-la-la-
ALL   Tra-la-la-la-la,
BUTLER   Tra-la-la.
LIEUT.   Sing a hey nonny nonny, to the bells all ringing, the voices singing
The servants hopping, the frantic shopping.
ALL   Ho, tis here, the season of the Yuletide
GIRLS   Season of the Yuletide
ALL   Season of the Yuletide cheer.
BUTLER   And now I think it only fitting that each sir and dame
Should give their thanks, their humble thanks to where
Their presents came from,
ALL   To whence their presents came.
(The uncle returns to his chair)
GRANDMOTHER
(Gives her cup to young sister, rises and moves downstage) Bergdorf Goodman, Bonwit Teller, Henri Bendel, too, oo-oo-oo-oo
All our thanks to you, oo-oo-oo-oo-
ALL
(With a half bow) Heartfelt thanks to you.
GRANDMOTHER   Wanamaker, Lord & Taylor, also Best and Co., o-o-o-o
Thank you, thank you so-o-o-o-much
ALL
(With a half bow) Thank you, thank you so.
GRANDMOTHER   Bloomingdale's and Arnold Constable, also Saks Fifth A-A-A-Ave
All our blessings ha-ha-ha-have.
ALL   *(With a half bow)*
All our blessings have
GRANDMOTHER   Of B. Altman and De Pinna, also Jay Thorpe I-I-I-Inc.
We will kindly thi-i-i-nk
ALL
(With a half bow) We will very, very kindly think
(Before Grandmother can continue, the Butler interrupts with his thanks. Grandmother gives him a withering look.)
BUTLER   And now I think it only fitting that each sir and dame
Should give their thanks, their humble thanks to where their presents come from,
ALL   To *whence* their presents came.
(The Uncle returns to his chair)
(Before Grandmother can continue, the Butler interrupts with his thanks. Grandmother gives him a withering look)
BUTLER   *(All hum)*
Gimbels, Macy's, Milgrim, Hearns,
Benson & Hedges, Jensen, Sterns,
Hammacher Schlemmer, Woolworth, Kress,
With our thanks we bless, yes,
ALL   *(With a half bow)*
With our thanks we bless.
GRANDMOTHER   To all the rest of whom the time allows no recita-a-a-ation
Our fond apprecia-a-a-ation, to each dear corpora-a-a-ation
(Grandmother raises her arms as tho she needed help, and the Lieut. and the Father go to her and help her back to her chair. The young sister rises to give Grandmother her goblet from which she drinks, after sitting)
ALL   To each dear firm and lovely corporation.
GIRLS   *(Men hum)*

Sing hey nonny, nonny, to the Yuletide brightness, the cold politeness

The looks so pleasant, the useless present.

ALL   Ho, tis here. The season of the Yuletide

GIRLS   Season of the Yuletide, season of the Yule.

YOUNG SISTER   Sing an extra nonny to the neighbors calling, the children bawling

The servants goaded, the trees so loaded,

GRANDMOTHER   *(With a look to the parents)*

The parents likewise loaded for

The gayest season of the year.

ALL   With a hey nonny, nonny, nonny,

Hey, nonny, nonny, nonny

Hey, nonny, tra-la-la-la

BUTLER   Tra-la-la.

ALL   Tra-la-la-la-la

BUTLER   Tra-la-la

LIEUT.   Sing a hey nonny, nonny, to the trees that stand out, the bell boys hand out

The stores so hot in, the gift forgotten.

ALL   Ho, tis here, the season of the Yuletide

GIRLS   Season of the Yuletide

ALL   Season of the Yuletide cheer.

OLDER SISTER   To the spirit loving,

HER HUSBAND   The crowds all shoving,

UNCLE   The engraved greeting,

LIEUT.   The overeating,

YOUNG SISTER   The joy exquisite

GRANDMOTHER   Of relatives visit,

FATHER   The mixture disturbin'

MOTHER   Of Scotch and Bourbon,

BROTHER   The guests that show up.

HIS WIFE   The cooks that blow up,

GRANDMOTHER   The mistletoe up,

BUTLER   The kids that throw up.

ALL   *(With a look toward the Butler, then front)*

Oh! Tis here the gayest season of the,—

Gayest season of the, gayest season of the,

Gayest season of the year.

(All rise on the last phrase for the toast as the lights fade and the traveler curtain closes)

The songs in *Fanny* were no less simple because they were written for a larger and star-studded production with an alien setting—different in all these respects from the shows Rome had written earlier.

I would like to quote several lyrics that function as character exposition. First, there is the young hero Marius whose real love is the sea. This is expressed in "My Restless Heart."

"RESTLESS HEART"

I see a silver bird that streaks the sky
And off we fly,
My heart and I,
My restless heart and I.

I see a cloud dance by and fade from view
There we go too.
My heart and I,
My restless heart and I.

CHORUS
I say to each new ship that sails the bay,
"Are you the one it will be?
Have you come at last
This golden day
To set us free?
Take us away with you," we cry.
My restless heart.
My restless, restless, restless, restless, restless, restless heart and I.

Marius's father Cesar, a brittle, feisty, independent old man, is given what in my opinion is the best song in *Fanny*, "Welcome Home." He observes: "Some day, Marius, you will be old enough to know that the best thing about going away is coming back." The treatment of the subject is most original in these lyrics and what is basically a sentimental idea is handled with taste and skill. Rome's customary simplicity makes any explanation unnecessary.

"WELCOME HOME"

(Spoken)
Why, even when I leave this neighborhood for only a day,
To go to the beach or the vineyards across the bay,
No matter what I do or see,
After turning home again,
I get to that corner and then,

(Sung) VERSE
Sweet voices,
I hear sweet voices calling to me!

CHORUS
Welcome home, says the street,
As I hurry on my way.
Welcome home, sings the gate, like a song.
Welcome home, says the door,
Glad to feel your hand once more.
Now you're back where you belong.
Welcome home, says the chair,
Holding out its friendly arms.
Welcome home, says the bed, rest on me.
Now you're back where you should be,
Close your eyes, close your eyes,
And the world will settle down to size.
Welcome home, says the lamp,
Lighting up familiar things.
Look around at your friends good and true.
Get your cares all untied,
While you're warming up inside,
Welcome home to you.
Welcome home to you.

This isn't a place to go away from. It's a place to come back to—a quiet place where things are manageable—where there's a routine you can roll up in like a blanket *(slaps* MARIUS' *cheek)* and the air all around you is humming a familiar song.

Welcome home, ticks the clock,
Now it's time to get undressed.
Welcome home, says the floor to your shoe.
Then you turn out the light

And the darkness says good night.
Welcome home to you . . . my son,
Welcome home to you!

Slightly later in the same scene, Marius, who has lived most of his life with his widowed father, is feeling guilty at the thought of his secret plan to go to sea. He and his father have never been very close in their personal relationship, and here the son tries to express his real feelings to his father with understandable difficulty. Again, this idea is original: a song of love in an unintentionally distant relationship, "I Like You."

"I LIKE YOU"

I like you,
Like you very much,
More than I could ever show.
I like you.
It's not much to say,
But I need to tell you so.
Sometimes you wait to say things,
You wait too late.
Days that once seemed so slow,
How fast they go!
Words spoken
Never mean too much,
Still I just want you to know
I like you.

The impetuous Fanny is distraught, having an uncertain feeling that Marius, with whom she has always been in love, is to be torn away from her. Instinctively she feels that Marius will go away. She bursts in with a brief but frantic song, "I Have to Tell You."

"I HAVE TO TELL YOU"

I have to, I have to, I have to tell you
I have to but I don't know where to start.
I have to, I have to, I have to say
What I'm shouting in my heart.
I love you, I love you,
I'll always love you.
Love you, want you, need you
My life through!
I've said it, I've told you, and now forget it
Unless you have to say it too.
Maybe you do.

Marius's reply becomes the show's title song. He explains that he has always been drawn toward the sea: "I have despised myself for not going before, and now I know why. It's been you."

"FANNY"

Only you, long as I may live, Fanny, Fanny, Fanny,
You, long as I may live, Fanny.
If I could love, that's what I would say.
But my heart isn't mine to give, Fanny, Fanny, Fanny.
No, no, not mine to give, Fanny,
For it is gone, given long away.
To the sea, my one love
In her gray green clothes,
Deep with wonders beyond the shore.

To the isles 'neath the winds
Where the spice wood grows.
I must know them all or sleep no more!
Here's a boy with no heart to give, Fanny, Fanny, Fanny.
Not worth one tear you'll cry, Fanny!
Oh, Fanny, good-bye!

As I conducted *Fanny* (as well as nearly all of Rome's other shows), I must inject here a personal recollection that makes a major point. Panisse (Walter Slezak), the lovable old family friend, on learning of Marius's departure and Fanny's pregnancy, implores Fanny to marry him and let him be the father of the child. She acquiesces and later, in a scene in celebration of their fifth wedding anniversary, Panisse toasts Fanny in "To My Wife."

The song seemed to go well in rehearsal and the cast thought it touching. On opening night in Boston the audience was embarrassingly silent at the end. The feeling at the production meeting afterward was that the song had failed and should be abandoned. I believe it was my idea to try expanding it a bit at the next performance. The orchestra reprised the chorus, and Panisse spoke a toast over the music, singing only the last few bars. We tried this at the second performance and because of the song's increased exposure, it was received cordially and remained in the show.

"TO MY WIFE"

To my wife
Who walks so gently through my thoughts
All day long.
Clean and fresh and white,
Soft and strong.
Makes me feel
That there is nothing I can't do
If I try
With my wife and son
Standing by.
She may scold, say I eat too much,
Find some fault, give free advice.
But a meal needs that added touch of salt and spice.
To be extra nice.
Words won't do.
There's so much I must thank her for.
Where to start?
How am I to say
From the heart
What I owe?
To my critic, my partner,
The flavor of my life—
To my wife.
(Spoken)
Fanny, a famous Greek philosopher once said a wife is one who will stick by you through all the troubles you would not have had if you hadn't married her, but I don't believe that because every night and every morning when I wake up I raise an invisible glass—
(Sung)
To the sunlight that brightens
The autumn of my life,
To my wife.

Cesar, the real grandfather of the child, sings a song of

wonderment about the baby, Marius's baby, whom he adores.
It is a simple waltz.

"LOVE IS A VERY LIGHT THING"

VERSE
When the baby arrived, he weighed eight pounds.
Now he weighs twenty-three.
What are they made of, those extra pounds?
What can they be?
Fifteen pounds of love they are.
Fifteen solid pounds!

CHORUS
Love is a very light thing.
Love is so fragile and frail.
You cannot hold it here in your hand
Or weigh it on a scale.
Cigarette smoke, that's all it is,
Wispy and curling around.
Oh, it takes a lot of love to make a pound.

Fanny gave her measure. I slipped in an ounce or two. But the
big weight . . . the bulk . . . Panisse.

And yet, love is a very light thing.
Light as a song in the air.
How do you start
To fill up a heart?
How many ounces there?
Dragon-fly wings—that's all it is,
Whispering by with no sound.
Oh, it takes a lot of love to make a pound.

Fanny has an amusing and original little song that she sings
to her young child, Cesario.

"BE KIND TO YOUR PARENTS"

VERSE
Here's a piece of good advice
Think it over once or twice.

CHORUS
Be kind to your parents
Though they don't deserve it.
Remember they're grownups,
A difficult stage of life.
They're apt to be nervous,
And over-excited,
Confused from their daily storm and strife.
Just keep in mind,
Though it sounds odd, I know,
Most parents once were children long ago.
Incredible!
So treat them with patience
And sweet understanding
In spite of the foolish things they do.
Some day you may wake up
And find you're a parent too!

The presence in *I Can Get It for You Wholesale* of a talented
young new singer, who was indeed difficult to explain as she
broke (or transcended?) all the rules, was a reason for Harold
Rome's creating a couple of songs that otherwise would not

have been in the score. The singer was Barbra Streisand, and it
was her first show. Streisand played a harassed young secretary,
not attractive, but dedicated and thoroughly efficient. The first
of Miss Marmelstein's songs is "Well Man."

"I'M NOT A WELL MAN"

He's not a well man
And he's getting worse.
If he had any sense he'd be in bed
With a graduate nurse,

A couple big specialists,
High-priced consultations.
And outside, waiting in the hall,
Assorted large and small
Poor relations.

His aches have got aches.
His pains are in pain.
And what sizzles and frizzles inside there
All the smartest professors couldn't explain.

PULVERMACHER *(Removes the thermometer, stares worriedly at
it, and sings:)*
They wouldn't know what.
Be quick as you can.
Time I haven't got,
You're dealing with not,
(A few weak coughs)
With not a well man.

A second section follows shortly afterward.

PULVERMACHER
I should own a pharmacy
For just my prescriptions.
My bills for only pills alone
Would chill you to the bone
With conniptions.

What I have been through,
No man could recite.
It would make a heartbreaking play or story
That only Turgenev, maybe, could write,
A tragical plot.
So how can I plan
You're dealing with not,
With not a well man.

Streisand's big solo, created solely for her, entitled "Miss
Marmelstein," is a comedy song. In it her frustrations, her
desire to be what she never appears to anyone else actually to
be, emerge. Everything she is and everything she longs for—
very simple needs—is voiced here. It is a funny sad song.

"MISS MARMELSTEIN"

Why is it always Miss Marmelstein?
Miss Marmelstein?
Miss Marmelstein?

Other girls get called by their first names right away.
They get cosy, intimay—you know what I mean?

Nobody calls me hey, Baby Doll,
Or Honey Dear,

Or Sweetie Pie.
Even my first name would be prefurable,
Though it's turable,
It might be better—it's Yetta!

Or perhaps my second name—that's Tessye,
Spelled T-e-s-s-y—e!

But, no, no, it's always Miss Marmelstein.
You'd think at least Miss "M"
They could try.
Miss Marmelstein!
Miss Marmelstein!

Oh, I could die!

I'm a very
Willing secretary.
Enjoy my work
As my employer will corroborate.

Except for one disappointment,
One fly in the ointment,
It's great, I mean, simply great!

But the aggravation
Of my situation—
I might as well get it off my chest—
Is the drab appellation,
(Pardon the big words I apply
But I was an English major at CCNY)
The drab appellation
With which I am persistently addressed—
Persistently, perpetually,
Continually, inevitably addressed!
(Believe me, it could drive a person positively psychosomatic!)
Why is it always Miss Marmelstein?
Miss Marmelstein?
Miss Marmelstein?

Other girls get called by their nicknames right away,
Slightly naughty or risqué. You know what I mean.
Nobody calls me hey, Coochy-coo,
Or Boobaleh,
Or Passion Pie.

Even "Hey there, Babe," though not respectable,
Ain't so objectable.
It's kind of crummy,
But chummy.
'Course if I got married, that would do it.
So where's the lucky guy! (Huh!)

Till then it still is Miss Marmelstein.
Every day I get more and more fussed.
Miss Marmelstein
Miss Marmelstein
Ooh, I could bust!

The anti-hero, Harry Bogen, is trying to arrange an affair with an attractive girl, Martha, who is hard and brash and determined to get whatever she can out of anyone to whom she gives favors. Martha and Harry sing (and dance) a duet in which, for a change, both tell the ugly truth.

"THE SOUND OF MONEY"

MARTHA
There's every indication
We two should get together.
We're tuned to the same station,
Birds of a feather.

HARRY
I feel a strange attraction.
We share the same reaction,
Antennas both aware
Of that certain something calling,
Calling to us in the air!

The sound of money,
The lovely sound of money!
I find it quite appealing,
A feeling you may share.

It seems to cheer me,
Whenever it is near me.
It elevates my spirit
To hear it in the air.

What savage splendor,
That mating call of legal tender,
As dollars meet in sweet surrender.
And when the romance ends, dividends!
(The bartender, cigarette girl, and waiter enter. They join in the
    dance)
The sound of money,
Enchanting sound of money!
Here's hoping I keep saying
My whole life long,
"Dear, they're playing our song,"
The sound of money.
(HARRY sings the following counter-melody while the others
    softly sing the chorus)
A chauffeur standing by
Makes me hear angels harmonize.
A penthouse in the sky
Whispers lullabies.

A great big yacht about to dock
Makes such a couth and soothing sound.
A block of blue-chip stock—
Music all around.

What savage splendor
That mating call of legal tender
As dollars meet in sweet surrender
And when the romance mounts
Bank Accounts!

Riding in a Bentley
Or a Rolls, the clock tick-tocks
Much more sentiment'ly
Than a tune of Offenbach's.

"Dear, they're playing our song,"

MARTHA
Listen!
ALL
The sound of money.

Harry and his very real girl, Ruthie from the Bronx, have two duets. The first, a kind of love duet, is called "When Gemini Meets Capricorn."

"WHEN GEMINI MEETS CAPRICORN"

HARRY   Common sense says, "No,
It could not be so."
RUTHIE   But a great many folks keep track
Every single day
What astrologers say
Goes on in the zodiac.
HARRY   Common sense says, "No."
RUTHIE   Why be con or pro?
Keep an open mind, don't choose.
It's kind of fun to half believe it.
What's a person got to lose?
HARRY   What's a person got to lose?
When Gemini meets Capricorn
On her way from the I.R.T.,
Could be coincidence—
RUTHIE   Could be astrology.
When Capricorn meets Gemini
Right across from the Grand Concourse,
HARRY   Could be an accident—
RUTHIE   Could be some heavenly force.
BOTH   Did the planets plan it,
Or was it chance?
Hey, you stars over the Bronx,
Did you know the whole deal
In advance?
HARRY   Know all the while
RUTHIE   How they both would smile,
BOTH   How they both would stop,
Feel their hearts go
Clop—clop—clop.
RUTHIE   When Capricorn met Gemini
On a Hundred and Eighty-third,
HARRY   Relishing every word they found to say.
Could be the whole event was an accident—
RUTHIE   Could be foretold in their horoscope
Plain as day.
BOTH   Could be the whole event was an accident,
Could be foretold in their horoscope
Plain as day,
Plain as day.

Much later in the show Ruthie has come to realize Harry's unfaithfulness to her and his dishonesty in business. This duet, "A Funny Thing Happened," is a song of parting, bitter and recriminating.

"A FUNNY THING HAPPENED"

You don't have to shout.
From now on I'm out
Of the kitchen!

What's more I can't stand
Your cigarette brand,
And I'm switchin'!
I'm unhappy with things the way they've occurred.
It is time to face facts and not mince a word.
Certain parties named Bogen are getting the bird.

Au revoir, fare thee well, and good-bye!
And I'll tell you why!

A funny thing happened
On my way to love,
I lost the young fella
I'd been dreaming of.
He changed while I waited
And hoped for his call
To someone who's no fun at all.

So I'll start forgetting.
What else can I do?
And much thanks for letting
Me practice on you.
It's farewell, my lovely.
Excuse, please, my dust.
Unravel and travel I must.

No tears, no hurt surprise!
It's with a pleasant glow I realize

If I had that much love,
So deep, true and strong
All ready to hand you,
My dead Mister Wrong,

Just think of the treasures,
The joy and delight
I'll give to my own Mister Right,
My own
Mister Right!

HARRY
So hasta la vista,
Ta-ta, toodle-oo,
The world will keep turning.
RUTHIE
But not around you.
There's someone else waiting
Who's more than a friend.
HARRY
Best wishes and dishes I'll send.
RUTHIE   (Sarcastic) Thank you so much.
RUTHIE AND HARRY
So long, I'm on my way.
Thanks for the buggy ride, and may I say.

HARRY   If you had that much love
So deep true and strong,
How come it's so easy
To tell me so long?
HARRY   And hurry to Murray.
How quick can you fall?
Oh, no!
It couldn't be so.
What a stall,
You never loved me at all.

RUTHIE   If I had that much love
So deep true and strong
All ready to hand you,
My dear Mister Wrong,
RUTHIE   Just think of the treasu
The joy and delight
I'll give
As long as I live
Day and night
To my own Mister Right.

The final scene of *I Can Get It for You Wholesale* is a heartbreaking and original one. Harry is bankrupt and in disgrace. He has come home to his mother. (In the original production Elliott Gould played Harry and Lillian Roth his mother.) He joins her in the kitchen. As the scene progresses her hatred and bitterness mount. This is a powerful song scene. The simple song—especially the sentiments of a Jewish mother to someone who doesn't feel well—grows in intensity and continues to the end of the play. Harold Rome wrote the lyrics, music, and words of this scene.

"EAT A LITTLE SOMETHING"

MRS. BOGEN

Eat a little something.
Try a little something.

Things won't look so bad
Once you've had
A bite or two.

Chew a little something.
Touch a little something.

Eat it while it's hot.
So why not?
It's good for you.

Force yourself—
Just a taste!
Go ahead, start in.

Such a home-cooked meal
Who could waste?
It's a sin.

Eat a little something.
Try a little something.

Let the troubles wait.
Clean the plate.
Here, start with these.

Eat a little something.
Please!

Eat a little something.
Try a little something.

Things won't look so bad
Once you've had
A bite or two.

Chew a little something.
Take a little something.

Eat it while it's hot.
So why not?
It's good for you.

Force yourself
Just a taste
Go ahead, start in.
Such a home-cooked meal

Who could waste?
It's a sin.

Eat a little something.
Try a little something.

Let the troubles wait.
Clean the plate.
Here start with these.

Eat a little something, please!
(The music continues)

HARRY *(Talking as* MRS. BOGEN *keeps singing) Ma, listen. Bankruptcy—what you read in Women's Wear—*it ain't so terrible. Ma, it looks bad—what came out at the hearing this afternoon. But only if you don't know the facts. Sure, there was a special bank account, but it was in Meyer's name. All the money from the firm went into the account. And then it was taken out again. The evidence shows it was Meyer took it out. Don't you see, Ma, I'm clean. Meyer says he gave the money to me. So we could fool the income tax department. But there was no proof, Ma, no proof. Nothing to show where the money went. The referee, the judge he understood. That's why, downtown in court—he said it's Meyer, not me, Ma. He ordered Meyer to give back the money. Or Meyer goes to jail. I'm clean, Ma. All perfectly legal. They can't touch me. You understand, Ma, don't you? Nothing to show where the money went. The referee—the judge —he understood. That's why the referee—the judge —downtown in court—that's why he said its Meyer. Not me, Ma. It's Meyer who has to account for the money. He ordered Meyer to give back the money. Or he goes to jail. I'm clean, Ma. All perfectly legal. They can't touch me. You understand, Ma, don't you? You understand?

MRS. BOGEN   Sure I understand. The problem is how can we make Blanche understand? You know how stupid some people are. How selfish.
(Sings) Eat a little something.
All she thinks about, that Blanche, the only thing in her head is Meyer. All she worries about is tomorrow morning he's going to jail.
(Sings) Force yourself, go ahead,
Take a taste, start in.
People who have room in their heads for only little things like that, what chance have they got to get ahead in the world? The way you did, Harry. The way I did through you.
(Sings) Eat a little something!
People like Blanche Bushkin, they don't have closets full of silver foxes. People like Meyer, they don't get marked clean by a judge downtown. But you and me, Harry? We're different. We know what we want. And we know how to get it.
(Sings) Eat a little something!
You'll need your strength. We'll both need it. For the next Meyer who comes along and gets in our way. Who is he, Harry? You got him maybe picked out already? Make it somebody a little bigger than Meyer, yes? This time for my commission I want mink, not silver fox. Harry, eat. It's good. Your mother made it. Just like she made you, she made these.
(Sings) Eat a little something,
Please!
(He sits motionless as the song quietly ends)

Although Rome has written several other shows, my own favorite being *Destry Rides Again*, there is nothing not already represented in the foregoing lyrics. The essence of his style is simplicity flavored with personal tenderness. His craftsmanship is clean. He is possessed of a strong sense of humor that he has employed largely as satire. He is one of a kind.

Courtesy ASCAP

Frank Loesser
(1910–1969)

Early in the present century, before the airplane made travel so swift and far away places so common, our shows were set in exotic, faraway lands with strange people, invariably unlike the real ones. We were then ignorant of their unfaithful representation, but fascinated by the very idea of the faraway and the exotic.

By the thirties "The Girl from . . . " well, just *everywhere,* seemed old-fashioned and she was at last laid to rest. The forties saw the musical theatre in America come of age, and more and more writers turned to American history and American settings for their shows. History was spoofed by Irving Berlin with *Louisiana Purchase* (1940). Rodgers and Hammerstein inspired us with their tale of Oklahoma Territory in 1943. Arlen and Harburg turned to nineteenth-century history in *Bloomer Girl* (1944), as did Styne and Cahn with *High Button Shoes* in 1947. Berlin portrayed Buffalo Bill's show in *Annie Get Your Gun* (1946) and the making of the statue in New York harbor in *Miss Liberty* (1949). Seamy society in Chicago was the subject of *Pal Joey* (1940) and youth in New York was made amusing in *On the Town* (1944). There were other examples of home interest but no one dealt with the fabulous characters of Damon Runyon's Broadway until Frank Loesser cast them in *Guys and Dolls* in 1950. His Italian California grape grower in *The Most Happy Fella* was also an indigenous contribution. These are two of the peripheral contributions to be found in Loesser's bag.

Few creative artists in the American musical theatre left a mark as strongly individualistic as Frank Loesser's. As both composer and lyricist, he was one of a kind. His untimely death at fifty-nine was a tragic loss, and we can only be grateful for the unique works of art he left with us.

The high quality of his work and his intensely personal style aside, the wide variety of his accomplishments is staggering. *Where's Charley?* has enormous charm. In *Guys and Dolls* he translated the special characters of Damon Runyon for the stage where they will continue living for all time. For *The Most Happy Fella* he took a dated play and breathed new life into it through the richness of his music and lyrics, the addition of vital and hitherto nonexistent characters, and a scope far bigger than the original. In *How to Succeed in Business Without Really Trying,* he gave us fun and games. If we consider only these four major works, with all the strength, individuality, wit, and beauty that they contain, we can only conclude that Loesser's unique contribution to our lyric theatre is, in its way, unsurpassed. The colors he used in both music and lyrics were his own and they remain a monument to a unique man.

Loesser was first a writer and then a lyricist. He wrote words for tunes by William Schuman, Irving Actman, Hoagy Carmichael, Burton Lane, Jimmy McHugh, Jule Styne, Arthur Schwartz, and others. His very first song as composer and lyricist was "Praise the Lord and Pass the Ammunition." In addition to his distinguished contributions to the musical theatre, he won an Academy Award for "Baby, It's Cold Outside" from the film *Neptune's Daughter.*

Loesser came up through the ultracommercial Tin Pan Alley school, probably learning first of all what sold. It seems certain that this practical education and experience not only left his poetic nature unbesmirched but strengthened it by relating it firmly to the practical needs of musical theatre. As a lyricist he learned how to characterize and particularize many types of people who had not before and have not since appeared in our musicals. They are uniquely American and uniquely Loesser's.

They by no means fall into any single category and some of them are multifaceted, as I shall attempt to point out.

His first success in the theatre was *Where's Charley?* (1948) based on Brandon Thomas's *Charley's Aunt*, a farce set about the turn of the century at Oxford, and starring Ray Bolger. Loesser's lyrics suggest characters, place, and time without literally reproducing them.

"Make a Miracle" is a comedic duet, the subject of which is, of course, love. The song finds its difference in its exchanges about the marvels of future progress. The audience's amusement comes from its smug feeling of prior knowledge of what was to be. "Make a Miracle" is more than a duet: it is an entire musical scene. Amy's connivance and Charley's love are both well defined.

"MAKE A MIRACLE"

AMY   Our future will be marvelously exciting(1).
CHARLEY   *(Spoken)* Exciting!
AMY   For progress is a thing there is no sense fighting(1).
CHARLEY   Progress!
AMY   They say it will seem like emerging into the light from a dismal penitenti'ry(2).
CHARLEY   *(Spoken)* What are you talking about?
AMY   *(Spoken)* The twentieth century(2).
CHARLEY   *(Spoken)* Amy! Don't change the subject!
AMY   I've just read a book on what's to be expected(3)
They'll have wireless telegraphy perfected(3)
Electric lights, and fountain pens
And machines by which a lie can be detected(3).
CHARLEY   *(Spoken)* Amy, what about us?
AMY   Horseless carriages, on the road(4)
Breakfast cereals that explode(4).
CHARLEY   *(Spoken)* I know. I know. I know. I know. I know—
Someday they'll have horseless carriages that fly(5)
AMY   Horseless carriages that fly
CHARLEY   Horseless carriages that fly—
Someday they'll be roaring all about the sky(5).
AMY   Spelling out slogans(6): "Buy a beer at Hogan's"(6)
CHARLEY   But who knows when that age of miracles will come to be(7)
So meanwhile, darling, make a miracle and marry me(7).
AMY   Horseless carriages!
I can't believe it, no I can't—
CHARLEY   Some day they'll have stereopticons that move(8)
AMY   Stereopticons that move(8)
CHARLEY   Stereopticons appearing in cathedrals larger than the Louvre(8)
AMY   How romantic!(9)
CHARLEY   Colossal!
AMY   Gigantic(9)!
CHARLEY   But who knows when that great great cultural event will shine(10)
So meanwhile, darling,
Make a miracle and say you're mine(10).
AMY   Stereopticons—I can't believe it—no I can't
CHARLEY   And I will see the wonders of the future in your eyes(11)
Brightly gleaming
Wonders that I challenge modern science to devise(11)
Oh yes, I know that—

Someday after we've grown very very old(12)
AMY   Oh so very very old(12)
CHARLEY   Old enough to bury
Someone rather bright will cure the common cold(12)
AMY   *(Spoken)* Not the British. Never the British.
CHARLEY   And someday just a small white pill will feed a family(13)
But meanwhile, let's have steak and kidney pie(14).
And meanwhile, let's be sure our feet are dry(14)
And meanwhile, darling, make that miracle and marry me(13)
AMY   Horseless carriages, I can't believe it
Stereopticons, I can't believe it—No I can't.
CHARLEY   *(Spoken)* Someday—
(Then sings) They'll be wearing(19) skirts way up to here(15).
AMY   Daring(19) skirts way up to here(15).
CHARLEY   Wearing(19) skirts way up to
Someday, with a neckline equally sincere(15)
AMY   Ah, the future, to peer(15) into the future
CHARLEY   A vision that, alas, I may not be alive to see(7)
So meanwhile, darling, make a miracle and marry me(7).
AMY   Wearing skirts way to, to—can't believe it, no I can't.
CHARLEY   Someday life will be one sweet domestic dream
AMY   Be one sweet domestic dream
CHARLEY   Someday life will be one sweet domestic dream
AMY   Be one sweet domestic dream(16)
CHARLEY   On that sweet domestic someday
They'll be heating cottages with steam(16)
AMY   Not the British
Never the British
CHARLEY   But somehow, can't you warm this heart until that dream comes true(17)
Yes, meanwhile, darling, make a miracle and say "I do."(17)
AMY   Heating cottages, I can't believe it, no I can't.
CHARLEY   And I will see the wonders of the future in your eyes(11)
Brightly gleaming
Wonders that I challenge modern science to devise(11)
Oh, yes, I know that
Someday when your mind keeps harboring a grouch(18)
Someday, Doctor Bones will place you on a couch(18)
And listen to your sad sad story for a handsome fee(7)
But meanwhile, let's get one big Morris chair(15)
And meanwhile, tell me all our troubles there(15)
And meanwhile, darling, make that miracle and marry me(7)
AMY   Stereopticons—I can't believe it no I—
CHARLEY   Marry me
AMY   Can't believe it, no I—Heating cottages
I can't believe it no(20)—
CHARLEY   Marry me
AMY   Wearing skirts way up to—
(Dance routine)
AMY   Really, Mr. Wykeham! Oh(20)!

One of the most difficult problems any composer or lyricist can hope to resolve successfully in the musical theatre is the creation of an ensemble song, particularly if it is to be an integral part of the show's action. There are several reasons for the difficulty. First of all, a large number of singers is physically awkward for a stage director to move about for any believable dramatic effect, and so the fewer bodies involved, the easier and more believable the task becomes. Secondly, if such a vocal number is to make any sense to the audience, the lyrics must be comprehensible. This places a heavy responsibility on both the composer and the lyricist. The words have to be simple and easy to articulate. The music has to use the words discreetly so that it will not overpower them, and voices must not be "crossed" so as to make the words unintelligible by superimposing *different* words simultaneously.

Frank Loesser, as both lyricist and composer, had to deal with all these problems and he created a smooth-working model in "The Gossips." This little song scene is charming. It recaps a part of the easily garbled plot, it provides the singing ensemble with a specific character, and allows several of the earlier solo songs to be reprised in part.

"THE GOSSIPS"

3RD GIRL A pity(1)
1ST GIRL A pity(1)
3RD GIRL Poor Amy
1ST GIRL Poor Kitty(1)
3RD GIRL But of course you've all heard?(2)
ALL No—tell us, tell us, tell us
3RD GIRL No I promise I'll never breathe a word(2)
ALL Oh
3RD GIRL (Spoken) However—
(Sings:) It seems that two young ladies
Went visiting two chaps(3).
ALL Went visiting two chaps(3).
3RD GIRL Went visiting—perhaps(3).
1ST GIRL Behaving in a manner
That can hardly be condoned(4)
Unchaperoned(4)
ALL Oh
1ST GIRL Unchaperoned
Unchaperoned
1ST GIRL Unchaperoned
2ND GIRL Unchaperoned
Unchaperoned
Unchaperoned
ALL What a shame, would you imagine it in all your life of those well-brought-up girls?
1ST GIRL (Spoken) And suddenly
(Sings) Old Spettigue, their guardian
Arrived upon the scene(5)
ALL Arrived upon the scene(5)
1ST GIRL So crafty and so mean(5)
2ND GIRL But standing there to greet him
Like a potted rubber plant(6)
ALL Who?
2ND GIRL Charley's Aunt(6)
1ST SOPRANOS Who's Charley's Aunt
Who's Charley's Aunt
Who's Charley's Aunt
Who's Charley's Aunt
2ND SOPRANOS Who's Charley's Aunt
Who's Charley's Aunt
Who's Charley's Aunt
ALTOS I don't know I've never heard of her. In all of my life. I wonder, who she means.
3RD GIRL (Spoken) I know, I know.
(Sung) It's Charley Wykeham's aunt, Lucia
Slightly off her track(7)

Those chaps the girls went visiting today
Were Charley and Jack(7)
ALL Oh, tell us, tell us.
3RD GIRL No, I swore that my silence wouldn't crack(7).
ALL Oh-h-h-!
3RD GIRL (Spoken)
Oh, well.
(Sung) Charley Wykeham's aunt was there
To be the chaperone(8)
But somehow she went wandering away
And left them alone(8).
2ND GIRL I know, I know;
I saw him, I heard him.
ALL (Spoken) Who(14)?
2ND GIRL (Sung) Spettigue(14)!
ALL (Sung) Spettigue—where?
2ND GIRL Under the window singing.
ALL Singing?
2ND GIRL Lucia, Lucia,
You stand at your window and smile(9)
Lucia, Lucia.
Oh, please ask me in for a while(9).
Lucia, Lucia . . .
4TH AND 5TH GIRLS We saw Jack proposing to Kitty.
ALL They saw Jack proposing to Kitty.
What did he say to her?
What did she answer him?
4TH AND 5TH GIRLS My darling, my darling(10),
I fluttered and fled like a starling(10),
My courage just melted away.
6TH GIRL I remember now . . .
ALL (Spoken) What?
6TH GIRL (Spoken) Just this afternoon . . .
(SHE begins to sing as the rest hum)
We heard Charley . . .
ALL (Spoken) Charley?
6TH GIRL (Sung) Saying this to Amy . . .
Marry me, marry(11) me,
Marry me, marry me.
ALL (Sung) Can't believe it, no, I . . .
Horseless carri(11)ages,
I can't believe it, No, I . . .
Stereopticons . . .
1ST GIRL (Sung) A pity, a pity(1),
2ND GIRL (Sung) Poor Amy, poor Kitty(1)
But of course you've all heard(2) . . .
ALL (Sung) No, tell us! tell us!
2ND GIRL (Sung) Well, I promised I'd never say a word(2).
ALL (Spoken) Ohhhh!
2ND GIRL (Spoken) Wellll . . . It's old Spettigue . . .
(Sung) He'll never let them marry
Their money's in his hands.
ALL (Sung) Their money's in his hands(12).
2ND GIRL (Sung) And that's the way it stands(12).
He loses all their money if they take the marriage vow(13).
ALL (Spoken) Shhhhh!
(Sung) Here they come, here they come!
Shhhh!
Here they come now(13)!

Only two years after *Where's Charley?*, Loesser came up with his most original work, *Guys and Dolls* (1950). In subject matter and characters, based on Damon Runyon (book by Jo Swerling and Abe Burrows), he created a new musical theatre. In reality, this was made up of two almost conflicting elements. On the one hand, with his choice of character and setting he entered virgin territory; on the other, the twin boy-girl plots were in themselves basically conventional. The real distinction lay in the style, which was new but in no way startling, only fresh and somehow unexpected.

One of the unique aspects of the book is to be found in the two parallel plots. In my opinion there is no principal plot and no subplot, only two concurrent ones: the gambler and his soul-saving sidewalk evangelist versus another gambler and his longtime paramour nightclub stripper. All four principals are well defined and spectacularly different.

Whereas the songs in *Where's Charley?* tend to be typical of the musical theatre of the time, those of *Guys and Dolls* are individualistic and belong exclusively to the characters and situations of that particular musical.

The lyricist's vernacular is also original. The words *suggest* the people but in some extraordinary way transcend them. In real life these characters do not speak as Loesser has charted them, but through his words we know them clearly. He has theatricalized and poetized them. This evening of gamblers, gangsters, whores, and righteous indignants never threatens but amuses. The audience comprehends and empathizes for these people are truly make-believe; Loesser labels *Guys and Dolls* "A Musical Fable of Broadway." A gun-flourishing mobster from Chicago is a hilarious caricature. A professional gambler is a poet. A lady-reformer is ignorant of life. Another lady who disrobes in public is a pathetic innocent.

Guys and Dolls opens on a choreographed pantomime: Broadway with tourists, cops, molls, pugilists, pitchmen, bobby-soxers, celebrities, nursemaids, etc. This busy mélange melts away and we are left with three secondary male characters, each reading a racing form. Right away, Loesser titillates us with a three-part canon called "Fugue for Tinhorns." In spite of musical and verbal overlapping, we comprehend everything. It is the first musical number and a tour de force.

The rhymes occur in bunches.

"FUGUE FOR TINHORNS"

NICELY
I got the horse right here(1),
The name is Paul Revere(1),
And here's a guy that says if the weather's clear(1),
Can do, can do, this guy says the horse can do.
If he says the horse can do, can do, can do.
Can do—can do—this guy says the horse can do.
If he says the horse can do—can do, can do.
For Paul Revere I'll bite(2),
I hear his foot's all right(2).
Of course it all depends if it rained last night(2).

Likes mud, likes mud, this "X" means the horse likes mud.

If that means the horse likes mud, likes mud, likes mud.

I tell you Paul Revere(1),
Now this is no bum steer(1).
It's from a handicapper that's real sincere(1),
Can do, can do, this guy says the horse can do.
If he says the horse can do—can do, can do.
Paul Revere(1). I got the horse right here(1).

BENNY
I'm pickin' Valentine(3), 'cause on the morning line(3)
The guy has got him figured at five to nine(3).
Has chance, has chance, this guy says the horse has chance.
If he says the horse has chance, has chance, has chance.

I know it's Valentine(3), the morning works look fine(3),
Besides the jockey's brother's a friend of mine(3).
Needs race, needs race, this guy says the horse needs race.
If he says the horse needs race—needs race, needs race.
BENNY
I go for Valentine(3), 'cause on the morning line(3)
The guy has got him figured at five to nine(3).
Has chance, has chance, this guy says the horse has chance.
Valentine(3)! I got the horse right here.
RUSTY CHARLIE
But look at Epitaph(4). He wins it by a half(4),
According to this here in the Telegraph(4)
"Big Threat"—"Big Threat."
This guy calls the horse "Big Threat."
If he calls the horse "Big Threat,"
Big Threat, Big Threat.
And just a minute, boys(5),
I got the feed box noise(5)
Shows class, shows class,
This guy says the horse shows class
It says the great-grandfather was Equipoise(5)
If he says the horse shows class,
Shows class, shows class.
So make it Epitaph(4), he wins it by a half(4),
According to this here in the Telegraph(4).
Epitaph(4), I got the horse right here!

"The Oldest Established," the next song in the show, is an ensemble song. It is clear and humorous. The characters bring to mind the old *Beggar's Opera*. The situation involves gamblers who are desperately in search of a place to hold an important crap game but have no money to pay for it. Nathan Detroit, a lovable, weak-minded blockhead of a gambler, is trying to work matters out. (Nathan is one of the four principals.) The lyrics are entirely appropriate for these shady characters and yet, in reality, they are literate.

"THE OLDEST ESTABLISHED"

BENNY
Nathan, concentrate on the game. The town's up to here with high players. The Greek's in town!
NICELY
Brandy Bottle Bates!
BENNY
Scranton Slim!
NATHAN
I know. I could make a fortune. But where can I have the game?
NICELY
(Sings) The Biltmore garage wants a grand(1).
BENNY
But we ain't got a grand on hand(1).
NATHAN
And they've now got a lock(2) on the door(3)
Of the gym at Public School Eighty-four(3).

NICELY
There's the stock(2)-room behind McClosky's Bar(4).
BENNY
But Missus McClosky ain't a good scout(5).
NATHAN
And things bein'—how they are(4).
The back of the Police Station's out(5).
NICELY
So the Biltmore garage is the spot(6).
ALL THREE
But the one-thousand bucks we ain't got(6).
FIRST CRAP SHOOTER
Why it's good old reliable Nathan.
THREE CRAP SHOOTERS
Nathan, Nathan, Nathan Detroit.
MORE CRAP SHOOTERS
If you're looking for action he'll furnish the spot(6).
STILL MORE CRAP SHOOTERS
Even when the heat is on it's never too hot(6).
ALL THE CRAP SHOOTERS
Not for good old reliable Nathan for it's always just a short
    walk(7).
To the oldest established permanent floating crap game in New
    York(7).

There are well-heeled shooters ev-rywhere, ev-rywhere(8).
There are well(9)-heeled shooters ev-rywhere—
And an awful lot of lettuce(10)
For the fell(9)a who can get us(10) there(8).
NICELY, BENNY, NATHAN
If we only had a lousy little grand we could be a millionaire(8).
ALL
That's—Good old reliable Nathan, Nathan, Nathan, Nathan
    Detroit.

If the size of your bundle you want to increase(11)
He'll arrange that you go broke in quiet(12) and peace(11)
In a hideout(12) provide(12)d by Nathan where there are no
    neighbors to squawk(7).
It's the oldest established permanent floating crap game in New
    York(7).

NICELY, BENNY, NATHAN Where's the action? Where's the
game(13)?
Gotta have the game or we'll die from shame(13).
ALL
It's the oldest established permanent floating crap game in New
    York.

Note the plethora of *ī* sounds in the final section, beginning
with "If the size . . . ," size, quiet, hideout, provided, die.

In the first ballad, an oblique quarreling love ballad, between
Sky Masterson, the fairly introspective gambler, and the evangelist, the two characters are clearly exposed. The banter is
bitter and sardonic. This is a musical scene that serves to further
the plot. Although there are many rhymes, the long *ī* sound is
carried far into the song. The list includes: I've, fibre, pipe,
type, time, ripe, I'll, fly-by-night, guy, mine, surprise, and many
I's.

"I'LL KNOW"

SARAH *(Sings)*.
For I've imagined every bit of him

From his strong moral fibre
To the wisdom in his head
To the homey aroma of his pipe
SKY
You have wished yourself a Scarsdale Gallahad
The breakfast-eating Brooks Brothers type!
SARAH *(Spoken)*.
Yes [*Sings*] and I shall meet him when the time is ripe.
SKY *(Spoken)*.
You've got it all figured out. Haven't you?
SARAH *(Spoken)*.
I have.
SKY *(Spoken)*.
Including what he smokes. All figured out, huh?
SARAH *(Spoken)*.
All figured out.
SARAH *(Sings)*.
I'll know when my love comes along
I won't take a chance
For oh, he'll be just what I need
Not some fly-by-night Broadway romance.
SKY
And you'll know at a glance
By the two pair of pants.
SARAH
I'll know by the calm steady voice
Those feet on the ground
I'll know, as I run to his arms
That at last I've come home safe and sound
And till then I shall wait
And till then I'll be strong
For I'll know when my love comes along.
SKY
No, no . . . no . . . you're talking about love. You can't dope it
    like that. What are you picking, a guy or a horse?
SARAH *(Spoken)*.
I wouldn't expect a gambler to understand.
SKY
Would you like to hear how a gambler feels about the big heart
    throb.
SARAH
No!
SKY
Well I'll tell you . . .
SKY *(Sings)*.
Mine will come as a surprise to me
Mine, I leave to chance—and chemistry.
SARAH *(Speaks)*
Chemistry?
SKY *(Spoken)*.
Yeah, chemistry.
(Singing).
Suddenly, I'll know, when my love comes along
I'll know, then and there
I'll know, at the sight of her face
How I care, how I care, how I care!
And I'll stop and I'll stare
And I'll know long before we can speak
I'll know in my heart
I'll know and I won't ever ask:
"Am I right? Am I wise? Am I smart?"
But I'll stop and I'll stare at that face in the throng
Yes, I'll know when my love comes along.

SARAH
I'll know.
SARAH AND *(Duet)*
SKY *(Kisses her)* When my love comes along.

Miss Adelaide, the somewhat long-in-the-tooth "chantoosie," is given two nightclub production numbers, one in each act. The first, "A Bushel and a Peck," is costumed "à la farmerette."

"A BUSHEL AND A PECK"

ADELAIDE   I love you a bushel and a peck(1)
A bushel and a peck and a hug around the neck(1)
Hug around the neck and a barrel and a heap(2)
Barrel and a heap and I'm talkin' in my sleep(2) about you—
GIRLS   About you?
ADELAIDE   About you—
GIRLS   My heart is leap(2)in', havin' trouble sleep(2)in'
ADELAIDE   'Cause I love you a bushel and a peck(1)
You bet your pretty neck(1) I do—
ADELAIDE   Doodle, oodle, oodle, Doodle, oodle, oodle, Doodle,
AND GIRLS   oodle, oodle, oo.
ADELAIDE   I love you a bushel and a peck(1)
AND GIRLS   A bushel and a peck, tho' it beats me all to heck(1)
ADELAIDE   Beats me all to heck how I'll
Ever tend the farm, ever tend the farm(3),
When I want to keep my arm(3) about you—
GIRLS About you?
ADELAIDE   About you—
GIRLS   The cows and chickens(4) are going to the dickens(4)—
ADELAIDE   'Cause I love you(5) a bushel and a peck(1)
You bet your pretty neck(1) I do(5)—
ADELAIDE   Doodle, oodle, oodle, Doodle, oodle, oodle,
AND GIRLS   Doodle, oodle, oodle, oo.

The second, "Take Back Your Mink," Miss Adelaide's song from Act Two, is in narrative style. It is delivered in outrage and petulance. With each "Take back," the item named is removed. It is a kind of naïve excuse for a striptease. The subterfuge that the lyrics of the song provide is particularly amusing. Miss Adelaide is protesting her innocence in having accepted gifts given in anticipation of immoral returns. Now she is saying "Take back your . . . ," which produces the physical act of undressing.

"TAKE BACK YOUR MINK"

ADELAIDE   He bought me the fur thing, five winters ago
And the gown the following fall(1), Then the necklace
the bag, the gloves, and the hat
That was—late(2) forty-eight(2), I recall(1)
Then last night in his apartment
He tried to remove them all(1)
And I said as I ran down the hall(1):
Take back your mink(3),
Take back your pearls(4),
What made you think(3) that I was one of those girls(4)?
Take back the gown(10), the shoes and the hat(5)
I may be down(10), but I'm not flat(5) as all that(5).

I thought that each expensive gift you'd arrange(6)

Was a token of your esteem(7),
Now when I think of what you want in exchange(6)
It all seems a horrible dream(7)—
So, take back your mink,
To from whence it came(8),
And tell them to Hollanderize it
For some other dame(8)

ADELAIDE AND GIRLS   Take back your mink.
Take back your pearls(4).
What made you think that I was one of those girls(4)—
I'm screaming
Take back the gown, take back the hat(5).
I may be down, but I'm not flat(5) as all that(5).
I thought that each expensive gift you'd arrange(6)
Was a token of your esteem(7)
But when I think of what you want in exchange(6)
It all seems a horrible dream(7), (eek!)
Take back your mink,
Those old worn out pelts(9),
And go shorten the sleeves
For somebody else(9).

Miss Adelaide sings what, in my opinion, is a great classic comedy song, "Adelaide's Lament." Adelaide's lover and for fourteen years her husband-to-be is Nathan Detroit. He is standing her up after her late performance in order to take part in his finally arranged crap game. She is frustrated and has nothing to do. The customers and personnel at "The Hot Box," the honky-tonk nightclub in which she works, have gone. Adelaide, miserable, opens a book in which she seeks consolation, although she does not understand what she is reading. She has "psychosomatic symptoms" that she is trying to comprehend. Every image in this lyric is precise. Although the subject matter is amusing, it is Loesser's manner of expressing it that makes it come off so well. The tempo of the music is slow, Adelaide's delivery is labored, and her accent is usually "Brooklynese."

"ADELAIDE'S LAMENT"

ADELAIDE   *(Reading)*
It says here
(Singing)
The average unmarried female, basically insecure(1)
Due to some long frustration, may react(2)
With psychosomatic symptoms, difficult to endure(1)
Affecting the upper respiratory tract(2).
In other words, just from waiting around
For that plain little band of gold(3)
A person . . . can develop a cold(3)
You can spray her wherever you figure the streptococci lurk(4)
You can give her a shot(5) for whatever she's got(5) but it just
won't work(4).
If she's tired of getting the fish-eye from the hotel clerk(4)
A person . . . can develop a cold(3).
(Reads again)
It says here:
(Sings)
The female remaining single, just in the legal sense(6)
Shows a neurotic tendency, see note, *(Spoken).* note, note(7)
(Looks at note)
(Sings)

Chronic organic syndromes, toxic or hypertense(6)
Involving the eye, the ear and the nose and the throat(7)
In other words, just from worrying whether the
Wedding is on or off(8)
A person . . . can develop a cough(8).

You can feed her all day(9) with the Vitamin A(9) and the
   bromo fizz(10)
But the medicine never gets anywhere near where the trouble
   is(10)
If she's getting a kind of name for herself and the name ain't
   "his"(10)
A person . . . can develop a cough(8).
And furthermore, just from stalling and stalling
And stalling the wedding trip(11)
A person . . . can develop La grippe(11)
When they get on the train for Niagara, and she can hear
   church bells chime(12)
The compartment is air conditioned, and the mood
   sublime(12)
Then they get off at Saratoga, for the fourteenth time(12)
A person . . . can develop La grippe(11).
(H'm).
La grippe,
La post nasal drip(11) . . .
With the wheezes(13) and the sneezes(13).
And a sinus that's really a pip(11)
From a lack of community property and a feeling she's getting
   too old(3)
A person . . . can develop a bad, bad cold(3).

The show's title song is unusual in a special way. Two of the three characters involved in "Fugue for Tinhorns" perform here like a vintage vaudeville act. Its function, like a Greek chorus, is in commenting on Nathan's being "just another victim" due to his infatuation for Adelaide. The verse takes the form of a hilarious recitative (cantillations on a single note, nonmelodic and discursive) that seems particularly absurd since we associate recitatives with grand opera and the two performers are rough unlearned characters. There are three choruses. The philosophy is of the two-penny variety, the music belongs on a stage, and the fun is contagious.

"GUYS AND DOLLS"

NICELY
What's playing at the Roxy?
I'll tell you what's playing at the Roxy(1).
A picture about a Minnesota man, so in love with a Mississippi
   girl
That he sacrifices everything and moves all the way to Biloxi(1)
That's what's playing at the Roxy.
BENNY
What's in the Daily News?
I'll tell you what's in the Daily News(2).
Story about a guy who bought his wife a small ruby,
With what otherwise would have been his union dues(2)
That's what's in the Daily News.
NICELY
What's happening all over?
I'll tell you what's happening all over(3).
Guys sitting home by a television set, who once
Used to be something of a rover(3)

BOTH
That's what's happening all over.
Love is the thing that has licked 'em(4)
And it looks like Nathan's just another victim(4).
NICELY
Yes sir, when you see a guy(5) reach for stars in the sky(5),
You can bet that he's doing it for some doll(6).
BENNY
When you spot a John waiting out in the rain(7)
Chances are he's insane(7) as only a John can be for a Jane(7).
NICELY
When you meet a gent(8) paying all kinds of rent(8)
For a flat that could flatten the Taj Mahal(6)
BOTH
Call it sad, call it funny(9).
But it's better than even money(9)
That the guy's only doing it for some doll(6).
BENNY
CHORUS II
When you see a Joe(10) saving half of his dough(10)
You can bet there'll be mink in it for some doll(6)
NICELY
When a bum buys wine like a bum can't afford(11)
It's a cinch that the bum(12) is under the thumb(12) of some
   little broad(11)
BENNY
When you meet a mug(13), lately out of the jug(13),
And he's still lifting platinum fol-de-rol(6)
BOTH
Call it hell, call it heaven(14),
It's a probable twelve to seven(14)
That the guy's only doing it for some doll(6).
BENNY
When you see a sport(15) and his cash has run short(15)
Make a bet that he's banking it with some doll(6).
NICELY
When a guy wears tails with the front gleaming white(16)
Who the hell do you think(17) he's tickling pink(17) on Satur-
   day night(16)?
BENNY
When a lazy slob(18) takes a good steady job(18)
And he smells from Vitalis and Barbasol(6)
BOTH
Call it dumb, call it clever(19),
Ah, but you can give odds Forever(19)
That the guy's only doing it
For some doll,
Some doll, some doll,
The guy's only doing it for some doll(6)!

A unique fragment of a song appears near the end of Act One. Sung by Sky Masterson, the gambler, it functions somewhat like a verse, or introduction, to the love song "I've Never Been in Love Before." Aside from its placement and shape, which are extraordinary, the melody is more sophisticated than anything else in *Guys and Dolls,* and so are the harmonies and lyrics. It provides a quiet sensitive moment, and is so poetic as to seem at first surprising that it emanates from Masterson. It is as though Loesser gave us a brief look into Masterson's soul. The images are fresh and new. Here is a breath of welcome air in the theatre. Here is a representation of the ordinary city world just before daybreak. It is endowed with a poetic insight created out of small everyday things, which suddenly take on a very personal and special beauty.

"MY TIME OF DAY"

SKY
My time of day is the dark-time
A couple of deals before dawn(1)
When the street belongs to the cop(2)
And the janitor with the mop(2)
And the grocery clerks are all gone(1)
When the smell of the rain-washed pavement
Comes up clean and fresh and cold(3)
And the street lamp light fills the gutter with gold(3)
That's my time of day,
My time of day,
And you're the only doll I've ever wanted to share it with me.

Adelaide and Nathan have a comic song-scene, "Sue Me." They are quarreling as usual because Adelaide is neglected, and Nathan, in his simple guileless way, is trying to put up a defense. In this duet the sense of the two characters is especially strong. Adelaide is accusative; Nathan whines with plea after plea. Her tempo has the swift thrust of machine-gun bullets; he whimpers beseechingly.

"SUE ME"

ADELAIDE
You promise me this(1)
You promise me that(2)
You promise me anything under the sun
Then you give me a kiss(1)
And you're grabbin' your hat(2)
And you're off to the races again.
When I think of the time gone by(3).
NATHAN
Adelaide! Adelaide!
ADELAIDE
And I think of the way I try(3).
NATHAN
Adelaide!
ADELAIDE
I could honestly die(3).
NATHAN
Call a lawyer and
Sue me, sue me(4),
What can you(5) do(5) me(4)?
I love you
Give a holler and hate me, hate me,
Go ahead hate me
I love you.
ADELAIDE
The best years of my life I was a fool to give to you(5).
NATHAN
Alright, already I'm just a no goodnick
Alright already it's true(5), so nu(5)?
So sue me, sue(5) me
What can you do(5) me?
I love you.(5)
ADELAIDE
You gamble it here
You gamble it there(6)

You gamble on everything all except me
And I'm sick of you keeping me up in the air(6)
Till you're back in the money again
When I think of the time gone by(3).
NATHAN
Adelaide! Adelaide!
ADELAIDE
And I think of the way I try(3).
NATHAN
Adelaide!
ADELAIDE
I could honestly die.(7)
NATHAN
Serve a paper and sue me, sue me,
What can you do me?
I love you.
Give a holler and hate me, hate me,
Go ahead hate me
I love you.
ADELAIDE
When you wind up in jail(8) don't come to me to bail(8) you out.
NATHAN
Alright, already so call a policeman,
Alright, already it's true, so nu?
So sue me, sue me.
What can you do me?
I love you.
ADELAIDE
You're at it again.
You're running the game
I'm not gonna play second fiddle to that
And I'm sick and I'm tired of stalling around.
And I'm telling you now that we're through
When I think of the time gone by.
NATHAN
Adelaide! Adelaide!
ADELAIDE
And I think of the way I try.
NATHAN
Adelaide!
ADELAIDE
I could honestly die.
NATHAN
Sue me, sue me,
Shoot bullets through me
I love you.

Finally, from *Guys and Dolls*, I should like to quote the lyrics of a duet sung by Adelaide and Sarah. The two know each other by sight but have never before met. They are poles apart in life-styles but now they are exactly alike: each has told her man to get lost, both are filled with regret and feel that they've acted foolishly.

Though this is a duet, the two identities are preserved. We are still in New York. The girls are miserable, but comedy is usually created out of misery. Besides, *Guys and Dolls* calls itself a fable. These characters, and all the others, are representations. We don't believe them because we are not supposed to believe in their reality. What they are *about* is real and belongs to each of us.

"MARRY THE MAN TODAY"

ADELAIDE *(Spoken)* At Wanamaker's and Saks' and Klein's.
(Sung). A lesson I've been taught(1)
You can't get alterations on a dress you haven't bought(1)
SARAH At any veg'table market from Borneo to Nome(2)
You mustn't squeeze a melon till you get the melon home(2).
ADELAIDE
You've simply got to gamble.
SARAH You get no guarantee(3).
ADELAIDE Now doesn't that kind of apply to you and I?
SARAH You and me(3).
ADELAIDE *(Spoken)* Why not?
SARAH *(Spoken)* Why not what?
ADELAIDE *(Sings)* Marry the man today(4)
Trouble though he may be(5)
Much as he loves to play(4)
Crazy and wild and free(5).
SARAH AND ADELAIDE Marry the man today.
Rather than sigh and sorrow(6)
ADELAIDE Marry the man today
And change his ways tomorrow(6).
SARAH Marry the man today(4)
Maybe he's leaving town(7)
Don't let him get away(4)
Hurry and track(8) him down(7)
ADELAIDE Marry the man today(4)
Maybe he's leaving town(7)
Don't let him get away(4)
Counter-attack(8) him and
SARAH AND ADELAIDE Marry the man today. Give him the
   girlish laughter(9).
SARAH Give him your hand today and
Save the fist for after(9)
ADELAIDE Slowly introduce him to the better things
Respectable, conservative and clean(10).
SARAH Reader's Digest!
ADELAIDE Guy Lombardo!
SARAH Rogers Peet!
ADELAIDE *(Spoken)* Golf!
SARAH *(Spoken)* Galoshes!
ADELAIDE *(Sung)* Ovaltine(10)!
BOTH But marry the man today.
Handle it meek and gently(11).
ADELAIDE Marry the man today(4) and train him subse-
   quently(11).
SARAH Carefully expose him to domestic life
And if he ever tries to stray(4) from you(12)
Have a pot-roast.
ADELAIDE Have a headache.
SARAH Have a baby.
ADELAIDE Have two(12)!
SARAH *(spoken)* Six!
ADELAIDE *(Spoken)* Nine!
SARAT *(Spoken)* Stop!
BOTH *(Sung)* Marry the man today
Rather than sigh and sorrow(6)
Marry the man today
And change his ways, and change his ways, and
   change his ways tomorrow(6)!

Six years after *Guys and Dolls, The Most Happy Fella* opened. The two shows are light-years apart. Whereas *Guys and Dolls* was set in New York, *The Most Happy Fella* takes place in the green of rural California. Loesser fashioned the libretto himself out of Sidney Howard's play *They Knew What They Wanted* (1924), thirty-two years later. In my opinion Loesser rescued the play, which is dated and withered. What he did, besides introducing music and lyrics, was to alter considerably the character of the heroine, who originally was "just a little tired" and quite ordinary. Rosabella (her name in the play was Amy) appears "less used." Loesser introduced (and opens the show with) Cleo, another waitress, Rosabella's best friend. She is a comedian, and later on we meet her opposite number at Tony's ranch, Herman, also a Loesser creation. There is another new character in Marie, Tony's depressing sister.

As the music seldom stops throughout the entire three-act show, *The Most Happy Fella* has often been referred to as an opera. But, in a different way, so are *Oklahoma!, Carousel, West Side Story, Fiddler on the Roof,* and many others with less music.

Openings of musicals have changed greatly during the 1940–1965 period, and the opening of *The Most Happy Fella* is different from all the others. It is a comedy song, "Ooh My Feet," sung by Cleo, the leading lady's coworker. The rhymes come through clearly and so does the humor.

This song serves several purposes. First, it amuses and by so doing puts the audience offguard for what is to become an unusual emotional experience. Further, it indicates the lifestyles and day-to-day feelings of not only Cleo, but her friend Rosabella when we meet her just after the song.

"OOH MY FEET!"

CLEO
Ooh my feet! My poor, poor feet!
Betcha your life a waitress earns her pay
I've been on my feet, my poor, poor feet
All day long today.

Ooh my toes! My poor, poor toes!
How can I give the service with the smile
When I'm on my toes, my poor, poor toes
Mile after mile after mile after mile after mile?

This little piggy's only broken
This little piggy's on the bum
This little piggy's in the middle
Consequently, absolutely numb.

This little piggy feels the weight of the plate
Though the freight's just an order of melba toast
And this little piggy is the littlest little piggy
But the big son-of-a-bitch hurts the most!
Ooh my feet! My poor, poor feet!
Betcha your life a waitress earns her pay
I've been on my feet, my poor, poor feet
All day long today
Doing my blue plate special ballet!

As the two waitresses clear off the tables after closing time, Rosabella discovers a note left her in lieu of a tip by a customer she cannot recall. It is pinned to the tablecloth by a man's amethyst tiepin because the man has felt awkward about leaving her money. He has written his name and address, says he wants to get married, that he owns a grape ranch, and invites her to send him a postcard. This all-important incident leads to an impassioned recitative and arioso, which ends the first scene.

The verse, or recitative, has no rhymes. The chorus, or arioso, has two sets of quadruple rhymes (in both cases one word is a repetition).

"SOMEBODY, SOMEWHERE"

ROSABELLA
Wanting to be wanted,
Needing to be needed,
That's what it is,
That's what it is.
Now I'm lucky that

CHORUS
Somebody, somewhere(1)
Wants me and needs me
That's very wonderful to know(2)
Somebody lonely wants me to care(1)
Wants me of all people to notice him there(1)
Well, I want to be wanted
Need to be needed
And I'll admit I'm all aglow(2)
'Cause somebody somewhere wants me and needs me
Wants lonely me to smile and say hello(2)
Somebody, somewhere(1)
Wants me and needs me
And that's very wonderful to know(2).

Joe, Tony's handsome young foreman, is addicted to wanderlust. Joey's inadvertent involvement with Rosabella in the plot, actually a result of Tony's insecurity, is of paramount importance. Before Rosabella's arrival, Joey tells Tony that he feels the need to move on—nowhere in particular. His song "Joey, Joey, Joey" is image-filled and nostalgia-packed. The feeling of longing is hauntingly conveyed. As full of emotion as the song is, there is only a single set of rhymes in the verse, and three sets in the chorus. The images are always specific and widely diversified. This is a song of high quality.

"JOEY, JOEY, JOEY"

JOE
(VERSE)
Like a perfumed woman,
The wind blows in the bunk-house—
Like a perfumed woman,
Smellin' of where she's been.
Smellin' of Oregon cherries
Or maybe Texas avocado
Or maybe Arizona sugar beet.
The wind blows in
And she sings to me,
'Cause I'm one of her ramblin' kin.

She sings—

(CHORUS)
Joey, Joey, Joey,
Joey, Joey, Joe
You've been too long in one place

And it's time to go, time to go!
Joey, Joey, Joey,
Joey, travel on
You've been too long in one town
And the harvest time's come and gone.
That's what the wind sings to me
When the bunk I've been bunkin' in
Gets to feelin' too soft and cozy,
When the grub they've been cookin' me
Gets to tastin' too good,
When I've had all I want of the ladies in the neighborhood.

She sings—
Joey, Joey, Joey
Joey, Joey, Joe
You've been too long in one place
And it's time to go—time to go!
Joey, Joey, Joe

Considerably later, when Rosabella has married Tony, the good-hearted Italian immigrant ranch owner, she tries to teach him how to behave at a first meeting with a stranger. This duet is both funny and touching.

The first part is between husband and wife. Shortly afterward, Cleo appears. Tony has secretly imported her as a companion for Rosabella, and there is a second, or "applied," section of the lesson. Then the song becomes a trio.

Both the lyrics and the music have a simple lilt. This is an example of a scene that, without music, would seem intolerable. As it is, it has great charm. There is considerable overlapping of the answering phrases.

"HAPPY TO MAKE YOUR ACQUAINTANCE"

ROSABELLA Well,—
When you meet somebody for the first time
There are special things you're supposed to say
Which you may not mean
But they sound polite as can be
Would you like to learn them?
Well then, repeat after me.
Happy to make your acquaintance.
TONY 'Appy to make you acquaintance.
ROSABELLA Thank you so much, I feel fine.
TONY T'ank you so much, omma feel fine.
ROSABELLA Happy to make your acquaintance
TONY —Acquaintance
ROSABELLA And let me say the pleasure—
TONY Da pleasure—
ROSABELLA Is mine.
TONY Da pleasure's-a mine.
ROSABELLA How do you do? Pleased to know you.
TONY 'Ow do you do? Pleased to know you.
ROSABELLA And though my English is poor—
TONY My English is a goddamn' poor!
BOTH Happy to make your acquaintance.
ROSABELLA Now won't you please say, likewise.
TONY Look-a-wise.
ROSABELLA No. Likewise.
TONY Like-a-ways.
ROSABELLA No. Likewise.
TONY Oh, like-a-wise.
BOTH I'm sure.

Excerpt from Act I Scene II

JOEY, JOEY, JOEY

KERMIT BLOOMGARDEN and LYNN LOESSER
present
FRANK LOESSER'S MUSICAL

THE MOST HAPPY FELLA

starring ROBERT WEEDE

with JO SULLIVAN · ART LUND
SUSAN JOHNSON · SHORTY LONG
MONA PAULEE
based on SIDNEY HOWARD'S
"THEY KNEW WHAT THEY WANTED"

orchestra and choral direction by HERBERT GREENE
orchestrations by DON WALKER
choreography by DANIA KRUPSKA
costumes by MOTLEY
scenery and lighting by JO MIELZINER
directed by JOSEPH ANTHONY

from the score
SOMEBODY, SOMEWHERE
JOEY, JOEY, JOEY
STANDING ON THE CORNER
THE MOST HAPPY FELLA
DON'T CRY
BIG D
WARM ALL OVER
MY HEART IS SO FULL OF YOU

PRICE 75 CENTS

Sole Selling Agents:
FRANK MUSIC CORP.
119 West 57th Street · New York, N.Y. 10019

007100 00
Printed in U.S.A.

ROSABELLA *(Spoken)* That's very good. Very—*(While speaking* ROSABELLA *starts to wheel* TONY's *chair.* CICCIO *enters stage* L. *carrying a suitcase and a pair of strangely familiar women's shoes with which he is beckoning someone on.* RO-SABELLA *watches him fascinated and in wonderment. A moment later* CLEO *enters in her stocking feet. They rush toward each other and embrace happily.)* Cleo!

CLEO   Hello, honey. What's the matter? You look like you didn't expect me?

TONY   Surprise! (ROSABELLA *and* CLEO *walk over to* TONY's *chair.)*

ROSABELLA   What happened? Why is she here?

TONY   I sent for her. I give her job pastin' labels on my grape boxes.

CLEO   No walking. It's in my contract.

TONY   'At's-a right. Sit down all day.

ROSABELLA   Gosh, I'm glad to see you!

CLEO   And me, you, baby.

ROSABELLA   That's a new outfit. Turn around.

CLEO   Like it?

ROSABELLA   What did you do to your hair?

CLEO   I rinsed it in the Friday special.

TONY   Hey, now you got old friend keep you company. Do like you say—intrafaduce me.

ROSABELLA   Oh, I'm sorry. This is Tony.

CLEO   How are you?

TONY   'Ow I am?
'Appy to make you acquaintance.

CLEO   Feeling better after the accident?

TONY   T'ank you so much, omma feel fine.

CLEO   Certainly nice to meet you.

TONY   'Appy to make you acquaintance.

CLEO   It's a pleasure.

TONY   An' let me say
Da pleasure she's-a mine.

CLEO   He's cute.

TONY   'Ow do you do? Pleased to know you.

CLEO   And so polite too.

TONY   An' do' my English he's poor.

CLEO   Your English suits me fine.

CLEO AND TONY   Happy to make your acquaintance. . . .

ROSABELLA Now won't you please say, likewise?

TONY   Look-a-wise.

ROSABELLA   No. Likewise.

TONY   Like-a-ways.

ROSABELLA   No. Likewise.

TONY   Oh, likewise.

ALL   I'm sure.

The Broadway-pop element in *The Most Happy Fella* is present in "Big D," a song of joyous recognition. It occurs in Act Two when Cleo, newly ensconced at the ranch in Napa Valley, is greeted in passing by Herman, a worker on the ranch. Nearly all of the following is sung despite the fact that in print much of the beginning appears to be dialogue. This is a wildly raucous song, gutsy and gay. Rhymewise, there is one long series of sibilants, *s*'s, as indicated. Loesser has fun with this as well as with the game of spelling out Dallas in single letters.

"BIG D"

CLEO
Would you mind sayin' that again?

HERMAN
I said, "Ev'nin, Ma'am."

CLEO *(Singing)*
"Ev'nin' Ma'am!"
Mister, you've got a way of sayin' "Ev'nin' Ma'am"
That puts me in a friendly state of mind.

HERMAN
Would you mind sayin' that again.
I mean "friendly state."

CLEO
Friendly state.

HERMAN
Sister, you've got a way of sayin' "friendly state"
That gives me the impression you're my kind.

CLEO
Would you mind sayin' "crazy crystals."

HERMAN
"Crazy crystals!"
Would you mind sayin' "Neiman Marcus."

CLEO
"Neiman Marcus."

HERMAN
Wait a minute!
You're from big D.
I can guess(1)
By the way you drawl and the way you dress.(1).
You're from big D.

BOTH
My, oh yes(1).
I mean, Big D. little A, double L—A—S(1)!
And that spells Dallas
My darlin', darlin' Dallas(1)

HERMAN
Don't it give you pleasure to confess(1).
That you're from Big D.

BOTH
My, oh yes(1).
I mean Big D, little A, double L—A
Big D, little A, double L—A
Big D, little A, double L—A—S(1).
And that spells Dallas(1)
Where ev'ry home's a palace(1).

HERMAN
Cause the settlers settle for no less(1)
Hooray for Big D

BOTH
My, oh yes(1).
I mean Big D, little A, double L—A
Big D, little A, double L—A
Big D, little A, double L—A—S(1)

CLEO
You're from Big D
I can guess(1)
By the way you drawl and the way you dress(1)
You're from Big D

BOTH
My, oh yes.
I mean Big D, little A, double L—A—S(1)
And that spells Dallas(1)

CLEO
Just dig your toe in Dallas(1)
And there's oil all over your address(1)

Back home in Big D
BOTH
My, oh yes(1)
I mean Big D, little A, double L—A
Big D, little A, double L—A
Big D, little A, double L—A—S(1)
And that spells Dallas(1)
I mean it with no malice(1)
CLEO
But the rest of Texas looks a mess(1)
When you're from Big D
BOTH
My, oh yes(1).
I mean Big D, little A, double L—A
Big D, little A, double L—A
Big D, little A, double L—A—S(1).
ENSEMBLE
Big D, Big D
People from Big D, Big D
Talkin' 'bout Big D, Big D.
ONE VOICE
Big what?
ENSEMBLE
"D"!!
Oil! Oil! Oil! Cattle, Cattle, Cattle. My, oh Dallas(1), Dallas,
    Dallas, Dall*AS. BIG D*! little A double L—*A*—S(1)!
CLEO, HERMAN AND CHORUS
And that spells Dallas(1)
My darlin', darlin' Dallas
Don't it give you pleasure to confess(1)
That you're from Big D
My, oh yes(1).
I mean—
Big D
Little A, double L—A
Big D
Little A, double L—A
Big D, little A, double L—A—S(1)!

I should like to include a different kind of duet between the
fictitious Cleo and Herman. This occurs after Cleo has decided
to go away secretly with Rosabella, since Rosabella has discovered her pregnancy by Joey. Cleo sadly has come to say
goodbye to Herman, to whom she has become attached.
Knowing that she plans to leave at once, Cleo's mood is serious.
Herman's maddening responses are just like Herman: not serious, but playful and forever optimistic. The duet is both sad
and innocently playful.

"GOODBYE, DARLIN' "

HERMAN   Hey! Where you goin'?
CLEO   Shhh!
Supposin' I should have to say goodbye, darlin'?
What would you say, darlin'?
HERMAN   I'd say goodbye, darlin'
CLEO   That's not what I mean!
Supposin' I just packed my bag and went, darlin'?
How would you feel, darlin'?
HERMAN   I'd feel content.
CLEO   Content(1)?
HERMAN   Content that you'd be back pretty soon
From wherever it was you went(1).

CLEO   I'm gonna give you one more chance—
I may be leavin' in a little while(2), darlin',
How can you smile(2), darlin'?
HERMAN   Smilin's my style(2), darlin'—
HERMAN   I like ev'rybody
—That I've ever met(3)
I never met anybody
—That got me upset(3)

No chip on my shoulder(5)
Hate in my heart
Or green in my eye(6).

And as I get older(5)
I find that more and more
I like ev'rybody—
—That's my kind of fun(8)
And tho' I strike ev'rybody
—As chump number one(8)
No robber can rob(10)
This good natured slob(10)
Of his private sky of blue(7)
CLEO   Ooh! Smile, smile, smile
That's all you do is smile
You wouldn't shed one tear(4)
If I went miles, miles, miles
From here(4).
Goodbye(6)—
Farewell—
So long,
We're through(7)!
I'm tired—
—of watching you(7).

Smile, smile, smile
That's all you do is smile
You don't get mad(9) or sad(9),
Or just feel bad(9) to hear me say
Goodbye—
Farewell—
So long—we're through(7).
HERMAN   I like ev'rybody
And extra 'specially I like you(7).
CLEO   And extra 'specially I like you(7).

Finally, from *The Most Happy Fella,* I would like to include
lyrics from an ensemble song, begun as a solo by the doctor. It is
tender and touching, carries the function of the classic Greek
chorus, and is another fine achievement of Loesser's in the area
of ensemble writing. This song is simple both lyrically and
musically. As the choral writing is homophonic (the voices sing
chordally, that is, the notes and therefore the words coincide
precisely with one another), there is no problem in com-
prehending the lyrics. Rhyming is sparse and clear. Everything
is quiet and breathless.

"SONG OF A SUMMER NIGHT"

DOC
All nature seems to know
There are two lovers tonight
There are two lovers tonight, hereabouts.
All nature seems to know
And sing her song,

Her tender song
That all is well
And all is right. Listen!
Do you hear what I hear?
ENSEMBLE
Do you hear what I hear?
Song of a summer night(1)
Song of a summer night
Song of a thousand voices
Full of a rare delight(1)
I hear it in the air(2)
It's a kind of lovers' music
Kind of music for the happy, happy pair(2).
Listen! Listen to the
Song of the cricket call(5)
Song of the lazy breeze(3)
Song of the blossom fall(5)ing
Down from the 'cacia trees(3)
I hear it ev'rywhere(2)
It's a kind of lovers' music
Kind of music for the happy lovers.
Listen, listen to it.
Look! Here comes the blushing, blushing bride(4)
Ah look! Here comes the happy, happy groom.
Ah!
Let's all leave them standing side by side(4)
Ah yes, they wanna be alone,
They wanna be alone, alone, alone
Leave 'em alone, alone, alone.
Leave 'em alone to hear the
Song of a summer night(1)
Song of a summer night
Song of a thousand voices
Full of a rare delight(1)
I hear it in the air(2)
It's a kind of lovers' music
Kind of music for the happy, happy pair(2).
Softly, gently playing,
Leave them, let's leave them,
Leave them, let's leave them—
There(2).

Loesser's final show, *How to Succeed in Business Without Really Trying*, a satire on big business and ambition, was a great success. It opened in 1961, five years after *The Most Happy Fella*, and eight years before Loesser's untimely death. I would like to quote only two songs from *How to Succeed*, both comedy songs.

The first, "The Company Way," is a duet between Twimble, head of the mail room, and Finch, his eager assistant, star of the show (played originally by Robert Morse). The song requires no explanation.

"THE COMPANY WAY"

TWIMBLE *(To audience)*
When I joined this firm
As a brash, young man,
Well, I said to myself,
"Now, brash young man
Don't get any ideas(1)."
Well, I stuck to that

And I haven't had one in years(1)!
FINCH You play it safe!
TWIMBLE I play it the company way(2);
Wherever the company puts me,
There I'll stay(2).
FINCH But what is your point of (view)?
TWIMBLE I have no point of view(3),
FINCH Supposing the company thinks . . .
TWIMBLE I think so too(3)!
FINCH What would you say if . . .
TWIMBLE I wouldn't say!
FINCH Your face is a company face(4);
TWIMBLE It smiles at executives, then goes back in place(4).
FINCH The company furniture?
TWIMBLE Oh it suits me fine(5) . . .
FINCH The company letterhead is (so) . . .
TWIMBLE A valentine(5)!
FINCH Is there anything you're against?
TWIMBLE Unemployment!
FINCH When they want brilliant thinking from employees;
TWIMBLE That is no concern of mine(5).
FINCH Suppose a man of genius makes suggestions. . . .
TWIMBLE Watch that genius get
Suggested to resign(5)!
FINCH So you play it the company way(2);
TWIMBLE All company policy is by me okay(2)!
FINCH You'll never rise up to the (top)
TWIMBLE But there's one thing clear(6);
Whoever the company fires,
I will still be here(6)!
FINCH You certainly found a home!
TWIMBLE It's cozy!
FINCH Your brain is a company brain(7);
TWIMBLE The company washed it and now
I can't complain(7).
FINCH The company magazine?
TWIMBLE Boy, what style, what punch(8)!
FINCH The company restaurant?
TWIMBLE Ev'ry day same lunch(8)!
Their haddock sandwich; it's delicious!
FINCH I must try it.
TWIMBLE Early in the week!
FINCH Do you have any hobbies?
TWIMBLE I've a hobby;
I play gin with Mister Bratt(9).
FINCH And do you play it nicely?
TWIMBLE Play it nicely . . . still he blitzes me
In ev'ry game, like that(9)!
FINCH Why?
TWIMBLE 'Cause I play it the company way(2),
Executive policy
Is by me okay(2).
FINCH How can you get anywhere (in the) . . .
TWIMBLE Junior, have no fear(6);
Whoever the company fires,
I will still be here(6)!
FINCH You will still be here(6).
TWIMBLE Year after year(6) after fiscal(10),
BOTH Never take a risk-al(10) year(6)!

Finally, in the second act, the indomitable Finch sings a unique song in the men's washroom. Finch, alone, begins to shave. He sings to his own image in the mirror, which in reality is a glassless frame so that his face is seen *through* it by the audience. Because it is a song of boundless and incredible ego, it makes us laugh uncomfortably. This is while seeing the show. However, the song works *outside* the show when it automatically becomes a love song addressed to anyone else, retaining no hint of the song's original intent.

"I BELIEVE IN YOU"

MEN
Gotta stop that man,
I gotta stop that man
Cold . . .
Or he'll stop me.

Big deal, big rocket(1),
Thinks he has the world in his pocket(1).
Gotta stop, gotta stop, gotta stop that man, that man.

(All MEN *fade* U.S. FINCH *crosses* D. *to* C. *sink, looks at himself in the mirror facing the audience.)*
FINCH
Now, there you are,
Yes, there's that face;
That face that somehow I trust(2).
It may embarrass you to hear me say it,
But say it I must, say it I must(2)!
You have the cool, clear eyes of a
Seeker of wisdom and truth(3),
Yet there's that upturned chin(4), and the
Grin(4) of impetuous youth(3).
Oh, I believe in you, I believe in you.
I hear the sound of good, solid
Judgment whenever you talk(5);
Yet, there's the bold, brave spring of the
Tiger that quickens your walk(5).
Oh, I believe in you, I believe in you.
And when my faith in my fellow man
All but falls apart(6),
I've but to feel your hand grasping mine,
And I take heart, I take heart(6) . . .
To see the cool, clear eyes of a
Seeker of wisdom and truth(7);
Yet, with the slam(8)-bang(8)-tang(8)
Reminiscent of gin and vermouth(7),
Oh, I believe in you, oh, I believe in you.

MEN
Gotta stop that man,
Gotta stop that man . . .
Or he'll stop me.
Big wheel, big beaver(9),
Boiling hot with front office fever(9).
Gotta stop, gotta stop, gotta stop that man.

FINCH
Oh, I believe in you,
MEN
Don't let him be such a hero.
FINCH
I believe in you . . .
MEN
Stop that man, gotta stop him,
Stop that man,
FINCH *(Looking in mirror)*
You . . .
You . . .
MEN
Gotta stop him,
Stop that man,
Gotta stop that man!
Gotta stop that man,
I've gotta stop that man cold . . .
Or he'll stop me.
FINCH
I believe in you,
I believe in you.

Frank Loesser gave us something fresh and new, simple and meaningful. Both his musical and lyrical idioms are uniquely American and they express a wide variety of characters, times, and places without ever imitating or reproducing the mere factual things that they represent. *Where's Charley?* is neither English (it is set in Oxford) nor late nineteenth century, but supports both. *Guys and Dolls* shows us some of the seamier elements in New York. Yet Loesser's gambling mobsters are sensitive, amusing, and even poetic. The music says "Broadway" but in its own particular way *The Most Happy Fella* is a compendium of many different things that, in a most unusual way, mesh. Feeling is often turned into passion, an element found rarely in the commercial theatre of our time. There is a sense of rural America that places *The Most Happy Fella* light-years apart from *Guys and Dolls. How to Succeed* floats in space and we laugh at the foibles we unfortunately have come to know so well in our own time.

Courtesy Comden and Green

Betty Comden and Adolph Green (b. 1915)

Betty Comden and Adolph Green are thought of as a team. As far as I am able to find out, they have never written separately. Both are products of the present century, are not related, write librettos and lyrics, and, in my opinion, most significant, are themselves performers.

They began as part of a nightclub act at the end of 1938 in Greenwich Village where they wrote the material and performed it along with three other unknowns, including a girl named Judy Holliday. Their direction was largely comedic in performance as well as in creativity.

Their start in the theatre was in 1944 when they wrote the book and lyrics along with young Leonard Bernstein's music and Jerome Robbins's choreography for *On the Town*, and they were, with Nancy Walker and Sono Osato, two leading members of the cast.

Since 1944 they have written *Billion Dollar Baby* (1945) with Morton Gould, *Wonderful Town* (lyrics) (1953) with Leonard Bernstein as composer, and book and/or lyrics for Jule Styne for *Two on the Aisle* (a revue) (1951), additional lyrics for Mary Martin's *Peter Pan* (1954), *Bells are Ringing* (1956), starring Judy Holliday, *Say Darling* (1958) with David Wayne (a play with songs), *Do Re Mi* (1960) with Phil Silvers and Nancy Walker, *Subways are for Sleeping* (1960), *Fade Out-Fade In* (1964) with Carol Burnett, *Hallelujah Baby* (1967) with Leslie Uggams, and they wrote the book most recently for *Applause* (1970) (lyrics and music by Strouse and Adams, starring Lauren Bacall).

They also performed in a well-received recital of their own material, *A Party with Comden and Green* (1959), and were writers of nearly a dozen films, among them *Singin' in the Rain*,

The Band Wagon, It's Always Fair Weather (with score by them and André Previn), and films of their shows *On the Town* and *Bells Are Ringing*.

The first lyric I should like to quote is a joyous celebration "New York, New York" from Comden and Green's first show, *On the Town*. Sung by three young sailors on twenty-four-hour leave, the song bursts with anticipation. The rhymes and rhythms are apparent. The chief virtue is its indomitable spirit.

"NEW YORK, NEW YORK"

(Sailors rush off ship into navy yard as six o'clock whistle blows)

OZZIE
Come on, Gabey, hurry up!

CHIP
Twenty-four hours!!!

(GABEY *bumps into another sailor as* HE *looks around*)

SAILOR
Hey, why don'tcha look where ya goin'. You'd think it was your
    first time in New York!—

GABEY
It *is!*

(They see the New York skyline)

ALL THREE
New York—New York—it's a helluva town!

CHIP
We've got one day here and not another minute—
To see the famous sights!

OZZIE
We'll find the romance and danger waiting in it—
Beneath the Broadway lights—

128

ALL
And we've hair on our chest—
So what we like the best—
Are the nights!

CHIP
Sights!

GABEY
Lights!

OZZIE
Nights!

ALL
New York, New York—a helluva town—
The Bronx is up—but the Battery's down
The people ride in a hole in the groun'
New York—New York—it's a helluva town!

CHIP
(Points to Empire State Building)
Hey, Gabey!
(Consulting his guidebook with reverence and excitement)
It says here—"There are 20,000 streets in New York City, not counting MacDougall Alley in the heart of Green-Witch Village—a charming thoroughfare filled with—"
Here we go again!

OZZIE
The famous places to visit are so many
Or so the guide books say
I promised Daddy I wouldn't miss on any
And we have just one day—
Gotta see the whole town—
From Yonkers on down to the Bay—
In just one day!

ALL
New York, New York—a visitor's place—
Where no one lives on account of the pace—
But seven millions are screaming for space—
New York—New York—
It's a visitor's place!
(TWO SAILORS enter, weaving and weary-looking. One happy, one very glum)

GABEY
Hey! Here comes Tom and Andy!—

ALL
Hullo, Tom! Hullo, Andy!

ANDY
'Lo, guys!

TOM
Hullo—

OZZIE
Hey, fellas—how are the New York dames?

ANDY
Wonderful—I don't remember a thing!

TOM
Awful! I remember everything.
(THEY exit)

OZZIE
Manhattan women are dressed in silk and satin—
Or so the fellas say—
There's just one thing that's important in Manhattan
When you have just one day—
Gotta pick up a date—

CHIP
Maybe seven—

OZZIE
Or eight—
On your way—
In just one day—

ALL
New York, New York—a helluva town—
The Bronx is up but the Battery's down—
The people ride in a hole in the groun'
New York, New York—it's a helluva town!

"Come Up to My Place" (On the Town) is sung by Hildy, a female cabdriver who, having just been fired, is selecting her very last fare. Chip, the sight-seeing sailor looking for a cab, is told to hop in beside the driver. This kind of song is known as "special material" inasmuch as it provides viable comedy grist for (usually) "special" performers. These were often Comden and Green themselves.

The lyric here takes the form of a musical scene rather than a song. The humor it contains is its raison d'être. In my opinion it could only have been conceived by performers.

"COME UP TO MY PLACE"

CHIP
My father told me "Chip, my boy, there'll come a time when you leave home
If you should ever hit New York,
Be sure to see the Hippodrome."

HILDY
The Hippodrome?

CHIP
The Hippodrome.

HILDY
Did I hear right?
Did you say the Hippodrome?

CHIP
Yes, you heard right—
Yes, I said the Hip—
(Brake noise)
Hey, what did you stop for?

HILDY
It ain't there anymore—
Aida sang an A and blew the place away—

CHIP (Spoken)
Ah, I wanted to see the Hippodrome!

HILDY (Spoken)
Give me a chance, kid. I haven't got 5,000 seats, but the one I have is a honey! Come up to my place.

CHIP
No, the Forrest Theatre—
When I was home I saw the plays
The Ladies Drama Circle showed.
Now I'm here—I want to get—
Some tickets for "Tobacco Road."

HILDY
Tobacco Road?

CHIP
Tobacco Road.

HILDY
Did I dig that—

Did you say Tobacco Road?
CHIP
Yes, you dug that—
Sure, I said Tobac—
(Brake noise)
Hey, what for did you stop?
HILDY
That show has closed up shop—
The actors washed their feet
And called it "Angel Street"—
CHIP (Spoken)
I wanted to see Tobacco Road—
HILDY (Also spoken)
Stick with me, kid. I'll show you the road to ruin. Come up to
  my place.
CHIP
No—Battery Park
Back home I dreamt of catching fish
So big I couldn't carry 'em.
They told me that they have my size
Right here in the Aquarium—
HILDY
Aquarium?
CHIP
Aquarium—
HILDY
Hold the phone, Joe—
Did you say Aquarium?
CHIP
I'm still ringing—
Yes I said Aquar-
(Brake noise)
Did you stop for what, hey?
HILDY
The fish have flown away—
They're in the Bronx instead—
They might as well be dead—Come up to my place!
CHIP
No—Chambers Street.
They told me I could see New York in all its spreading strength
  and power
From the city's highest spot—
Atop the famous Woolworth Tower—
HILDY
The Woolworth Tower?
CHIP
The Woolworth Tower.
HILDY
Beat me, Daddy—
Did you say the Woolworth Tower?
CHIP
I won't beat you, but I said the Wool-
(Brake noise)
Did you stop for hey what—
HILDY
That ain't the highest spot—
You're just a little late—We've got the Empire State—
Let's go to my place—
CHIP
Let's go to Cleopatra's needle.
HILDY
Let's go to my place.

CHIP
Let's see Wanamaker's store—
HILDY
Let's go to my place.
CHIP
Go to Lindy's—go to Luchow's—
HILDY
Go to my place.
CHIP
Let's see Radio City—and Herald Square—
HILDY
Let's go to my place.
CHIP
Go to Reuben's—
HILDY
Go to my place.
CHIP
Go to Macy's.
HILDY
Go to my place.
CHIP
Roxy—
HILDY
Go to my place.
CHIP
Cloisters.
HILDY
My place.
CHIP
Gimbel's.
HILDY
My place.
CHIP
Flatiron Building.
HILDY
MY PLACE!!!
CHIP
HIPPODROME!!!!
HILDY
My place—

Another "special material" number, "I Get Carried Away," *(On the Town),* was originally performed by Betty Comden as Claire de Loon, an anthropologist and Adolph Green as Ozzie, one of the trio of sailors. They have just met in the museum of Natural History near a realistic statue of *Pithecanthropus erectus,* an ancestor of man. Claire is "carried away" at the sight of Ozzie, who, in her rapturous opinion, is exactly like the statue. Ozzie, at first, mistakes her attention and enthusiasm for interest in his "irresistible charms."

This operatic spoof leads to a catastrophic and hilarious scene end. Again, this lyric, though conforming to a more regular song form than "Come Up to My Place," is nevertheless essentially a comedic scene. The mood of the song is tense and operatic, with an agitato buildup to a climax at the end of each section to convey the excessiveness of the characters.

"I GET CARRIED AWAY"

CLAIRE

I try hard to stay controlled
But I get carried away
Try to act aloof and cold
But I GET CARRIED AWAY.

BOTH

Carried away—carried away
(OZZIE:) You— (CLAIRE:) I . . . *(SIMULTANEOUSLY)* get carried—
just carried away.

CLAIRE

When I go to listen to a symphony
Why can't I just say the music's grand—
Why must I leap upon the stage hysterically—
They're playing pizzicato—
And everything goes blotto—
I grab the maestro's stick—and start in leading the band!

BOTH

Carried away—carried away—
(OZZIE:) You—(CLAIRE:) I—*(SIMULTANEOUSLY)* got carried—
just carried away.

OZZIE

And when I go to see a moving picture show
And I'm watching actors in a scene
I start to think what's happening is really so—
The girl—I must protect her—
The villain don't respect her—
I leap to her defense and knock a hole right through the screen.

BOTH

Carried away—carried away—
(OZZIE:) I—(CLAIRE:) He—*(SIMULTANEOUSLY)*
Gets carried—just carried away.

OZZIE

I try hard to keep detached
But I get carried away.
Try to act less booby-hatched
But I get CARRIED AWAY.

BOTH

Carried away—carried away—
(OZZIE:) I—(CLAIRE:) He—*(SIMULTANEOUSLY)*
Gets carried—just carried away!

OZZIE

When shopping I'm a sucker for a bargain sale
If something is marked down upon a shelf
My sense of what is practical begins to fail
I buy one, then another—
Another and another—
I buy the whole store out and I'm in business for myself!

BOTH

Carried away—carried away—
(OZZIE:) I— (CLAIRE): He— (SIMULTANEOUSLY)
Gets carried—just carried away.

CLAIRE

And when I go to see my friends off on a train
Golly how I hate to see them go
For then my love of traveling I can't restrain
The time has come for parting
The train's already starting—
I hop a freight and in a flash I'm off to Buffalo.

BOTH

Carried away—carried away

We get carried—just carried—a- Ah——!
(They break off abruptly on a wild high note, screaming in each
other's faces—shrug at the hopelessness of their state, and
turn away as the music finishes.)

"Lonely Town" *(On the Town)* is a ballad. It is sung by one of
the sailors who feels lost and deserted in a strange city. It is one
of the loveliest songs in Bernstein's score. The lyrics are simple,
unpretentious, and expressive.

"LONELY TOWN"

Gabey's comin'—Gabey's comin' to town—
So what—who cares?
Back on the ship—it seemed such a snap—
You'd tap a girl on the shoulder—
She'd turn around—
And then she'd say "I love you"—
But once on shore—
It's not such a snap—
You get the cold shoulder—
The old run-around
You're left with no one but you—
Gabey's coming—Gabey's coming to town.

CHORUS

A town's a Lonely Town
When you pass through
And there is no one waiting there for you
Then it's a Lonely Town
You wander up and down
The crowds rush by
A million faces pass before your eye
Still it's a Lonely Town.

Unless there's love
A love that's shining like a harbor light—
You're lost in the night
Unless there's love—
The world's an empty place
And every town's—a Lonely Town.

The romantic sailor Gabey, who sang "Lonely Town," has
another ballad, "Lucky to Be Me," which is graceful and full of
intense happiness. The melody can best be described, I think,
as "angular": it darts about up and down charmingly. The lyric
that accompanies it is largely monosyllabic. In the eight-line
verse, there are only six two- or three-syllable words—all simple. In the sixteen-line chorus there are only fourteen non-
monosyllabic words, three of which are the "lucky" of the title.
Though Comden and Green probably did not intend to use
principally monosyllabic words, the results are especially fortuitous because of the tune: these words are easily sung and
easily comprehended.

The rhymes in both verse and chorus are all end ones, in
couplets, except for the triple rhymes, proud, crowd, and loud,
which occur during the fourth and second lines from the end of
the chorus.

"LUCKY TO BE ME"

I used to think it might be fun to be
Anyone else but me.
I thought that it would be a pleasant surprise
To wake up as a couple of other guys

But now that I've found you—
I've changed my point of view
And now I wouldn't give a dime to be
Anyone else but me.

CHORUS

What a day—
Fortune smiled and came my way—
Bringing love I never thought I'd see—
I'm so lucky to be me.
What a night—
Suddenly you come in sight—
Looking just the way I hoped you'd be—
I'm so lucky to be me.
I am simply thunderstruck
At this change in my luck
Knew at once I wanted you
Never dreamed you'd want me too.
I'm so proud you chose me from all the crowd
There's no other guy I'd rather be—
I could laugh out loud—I'm so lucky to be me.

Near the end of *On the Town*, there is a "sighing" song given two of the couples: Claire, Ozzie, Chip, and Hildy. They are riding the subway to Coney Island. Their day together is nearing its end and they are anticipating parting.

Expression is the chief aim and accomplishment here. Rhymewise, the chorus is divided into one rhyming couplet, one nonrhyming couplet, and the same pattern is repeated in two eight-line stanzas. There is one neat rhyming trick: "gone to" and "want to." It *does* rhyme.

"SOME OTHER TIME"

CLAIRE   VERSE

Twenty-four hours can go so fast
You look around—the day has past—
When you're in love—
Time is precious stuff—
Even a lifetime isn't enough.

CHORUS

Where has the time all gone to?
Haven't done half the things we want to—
Oh, well—we'll catch up—
Some Other Time.
This day was just a token
Too many words are still unspoken
Oh well—we'll catch up—
Some Other Time.

Just when the fun is starting—
Comes the time for parting—
But let's be glad—for what we've had—
And what's to come.
There's so much more embracing—
Still to be done but time is racing—
Oh, well—we'll catch up—
Some Other Time.

HILDY *(Continuing song)*

Didn't get half my wishes—
Never have seen you dry the dishes—
Oh, well—we'll catch up—
Some other time.

Can't satisfy my craving—
Never have watched you while you're shaving.
Oh, well—we'll catch up—
Some other time.
Just when the fun's beginning—
Comes the final inning—comes

CONDUCTOR   *(Spoken, as they embrace)*

Coney Island—all out.

OZZIE

Haven't had time to wake up—
Seeing you there without your make up
Oh, well—we'll catch up some other time.

ALL

Just when the fun is starting
Comes the time for parting
But let's be glad for what we've had—
And what's to come.
There's so much more embracing.
Still to be done but time is racing.
Oh, well—we'll catch up some other time.

The nightclub act, The Revuers, in which Betty and Adolph began their writing and performing before collaborating on *On the Town,* was actually less an act and more a series of satirical revues. One of the opening numbers was about the show business bible *Variety,* called "Variety Says."

The verse has ten lines, only four of which rhyme. The chorus consists of five quatrains and a coda of four lines. Each stanza contains a pair of rhyming couplets.

It is interesting to me to note that since, in my own "theory of opposites," comedy is to be extracted chiefly from tragedy or its parts, each of these five quatrains concerns failure.

"VARIETY SAYS"

BOTH

There's a paper that is read by theatre people,
It's a magazine that's called Variety.
If you want to know what's happening in the show world
Variety's the magazine to see.
But the language that it uses isn't English,
It's a language that's entirely unkown.
We'd be glad to act as your interpreter
Cause Variety has a lingo all its own.
With lengthy stories it has no patience
Variety uses abbreviations.

B.C.

Broadway is dead and the season's a flop
Receipts at the box office start to drop
Deep in despair the theatre is
Variety says "Show Biz Fizz."

A.G.

Now you open a show in Buffalo
You give out passes but business is slow
You give out more passes til it's full enough
Variety says "Buff On Cuff."

B.C.

You open an opera at popular price
But popular price does not suffice
The opera decides to close up shop
Variety says "Pop Op Flop."

A.G.
Now you open a club that's a restaurant
But it isn't just what the patrons want
The food gathers dust so you close the club
Variety says "Grub Club Dub."
BOTH
You open a picture out of town
The reviews come in: all thumbs down
You open five more but none of them clicks
Variety says "Hix Nix Six Pix."

Show Biz Fizz
Buff On Cuff
Pop Op Flop
Variety says

Comden and Green wrote a bag of wonderful songs with Jule Styne's music for *Bells Are Ringing* (1956). The lyricists did a remarkable job in "I Met a Girl." Their problem was very similar to the one they were faced with in "Lucky to Be Me *(On the Town),* only in "Lucky" the melody was "angular," while in "I Met a Girl" it is the machine-gun-like rhythm that they had to accommodate. In spite of the problem, the result bears no sign of a struggle. The words push themselves out, are easy to sing, and make articulation seem quite simple and even inevitable.

There is an infectious steamroller enthusiasm about this song.

"I MET A GIRL"

I met(1) a girl—
A wonderful girl!
She's really got(2) a lot(2) to recommend her for a girl,
A fabulous creature without any doubt(3).
Hey! What am I get(1)ting so excited about(3)?!

She's just a girl—
An ev'ry day girl.
And yet(1) I guess(4) she's really rather spec(4)ial for a girl,
For once you have seen her the others are out(3).
Hey! What am I get(1)ting so excited about(3)?!

But so what? What has she got(2) others have not(2)?
Two eyes, two lips, a nose(5)—
Most girls have some of those(5).
Yet(1) when she looks up at me(6) what do I see(6)?
The most enchanting face(7)! My pulse begins to race(7).
  Hey(8)!

I met(1) a girl—
A marvelous girl(9)!
She's rarer(10) than uranium and fairer(10) than a pearl(9).
I found me a treasure and I want to shout(3)!
This is what I'm get(1)ting so excited about(3)!
I met(1) a girl(9) and I fell in love today(8)!

There is a tender ballad "Long Before I Knew You" in *Bells Are Ringing.* It is sung by the hero and begun as "dictation" to the heroine, who, unknown to him, works for a telephone answering service.

The rhymes are fairly sparse, but what is unusual in these simple lyrics is the variety of verbs in the developing argument of the song: knew you, met you, find you, held you, kissed you, touched you, knew you.

"LONG BEFORE I KNEW YOU"

Dearest—Dearest—
One thing I know(1)—
Everything I feel for you
Started many years ago(1).

Long before I knew you—
Long before I met you—
I was sure I'd find you(2)
Some day, somehow(3).
I pictured someone who'd walk(4) and talk(4) and smile as you
  do(2),
Who'd make me feel as you do right now(3)!

But that was long before I held you,
Long before I kissed you,
Long before I touched you and felt this glow(1);
But now you really are here and now at last I know(1)
That long before I knew you,
I loved you so(1).

In the same score there is an attractive "jump" song, "Just in Time." The lyrics here develop by repetition. "Just in Time" is heard four times in the chorus. The word "time" is repeated again in the line after the second reiteration. In lines four and five we have "lost" and "losing." In each of the next three lines we hear "were," "where," and "here." This device adds emphasis to the stanza.

"JUST IN TIME"

Just in time,
I found you just in time,
Before you came, my time was running low(1).
I was lost,
The losing dice were tossed(2),
My bridges all were crossed(2)—
Nowhere to go(1).
Now you're here(3)
And now I know(1) just where I'm going;
No more doubt or fear(3)—
I've found my way(4).
For love came just in time;
You found me just in time
And changed my lonely life that lovely day(4).

The most memorable song from *Bells Are Ringing* is "The Party's Over," a melancholy ballad. The numerous rhymes are indicated. However, there are many assonantal long ī rhymes, some of which are real rhymes: time (twice), wind, mind, piper, night, right.

The song's statement is simple, musical, and clear. The language is colloquial.

"THE PARTY'S OVER"

He's in love with Melisande Scott(1).
A girl who doesn't exist(2).
He's in love with someone you're not(1).
And so, remember, it was never you he kissed(2).

The party's over—
It's time to call it a day(10)—
They've burst your pretty balloon(3)

And taken the moon(3) away(10).
It's time to wind up(4) the masquerade(5)—
Just make your mind up(4)—
The piper must be paid(5).
The party's over—
The candles flicker and dim(6)—
You danced and dreamed(11) through the night(7)—
It seemed(11) to be right(7) just being with him(6).
Now you must wake up(8)—
All dreams must end(9)—
Take off your make-up(8)—
The party's over—
It's all over, my friend(9).

One of Comden and Green's major achievements is "Christopher Street," the opening number of *Wonderful Town* (1953), which they wrote with Leonard Bernstein. The lyrical framework is delivered by a guide, tourists, and villagers, Periodically, everyone on stage "freezes" while secondary characters are introduced in a few spoken lines. This opening number is particularly appropriate in spirit for this Chodorov-Field's adaptation of their *My Sister Eileen*, an extremely witty play. The time, place, and main characters—as well as the temper of the play—are set up at the outset in this number.

The few rhymes are totally consistent with the lyricists' pattern: the second line of a three-line stanza invariably rhymes with the second line of the next three-line stanza. The last line of the second stanza is a repetition of the first stanza's second line. The few rhymes following this pattern all rhyme with "Street."

"CHRISTOPHER STREET"

On your left,
Washington Square(1),
Right in the heart of Greenwich Village.
TOURISTS
(Looking around ecstatically)
My, what trees—
Smell that air(1)—
Painters and pigeons in Washington Square(1).
GUIDE
On your right,
Waverly Place(2)—
Bit of Paree in Greenwich Village.
TOURISTS
My, what charm—
My, what grace(2)!
Poets and peasants on Waverly Place(2)—
GUIDE
(Reeling off his customary spiel)
Ever since eighteen-seventy Greenwich Village has been the Bohemian cradle of painters, writers, actors, etc., who've gone on to fame and fortune. Today in nineteen thirty-five, who knows what future greats live in these twisting alleys? Come along! *(As the* GUIDE *and group cross to the side, the curtain opens, revealing Christopher Street. The scene looks like a cheery postcard of Greenwich Village, with Village characters exhibiting their paintings, grouped in a tableau under a banner which reads "Greenwich Village Art Contest, 1935.")*

GUIDE
Here you see
Christopher Street(3),
Pleasant and peaceful on Christopher Street(3)?
(Suddenly the tableau comes to life and all hell breaks loose. An angry artist smashes his painting over the head of an art-contest judge who retires in confusion.)
VILLAGER *(Spoken)*
Here comes another judge.
GUIDE *(Sung)*
Here is home,
Christopher Street(3)—
Right in the heart of Greenwich Village.
VILLAGERS
Life is calm,
Life is sweet(3),
Pleasant and peaceful on Christopher Street(3).
(They freeze into another tableau as a cop comes in, a friend of the street, named LONIGAN. *He goes up to one of the artists, a dynamic, explosive character named* APPOPOLOUS.)*
GUIDE
Here's a famous Village type,
Mr. Appopolous—modern painter,
Better known on this beat(3)
As the lovable landlord of Christopher Street(3).
(Music is interrupted.)
APPOPOLOUS
(Breaking out of tableau. To LONIGAN—*violently)*
Throw that Violet woman out of my building!
LONIGAN
What's the beef now, Appopolous?
APPOPOLOUS I'm very broadminded, but when a woman gives rumba lessons all night, she's gotta have at least a phonograph!
GUIDE
Here's a guy known as The Wreck,
Football professional out of season,
Unemployed throughout the heat(3),
Living on nothing on Christopher Street(3).
(Music is interrupted. Freeze breaks. WRECK *kisses* HELEN.)*
HELEN
Hi! Where you goin' with Dicky Bird?
WRECK
Takin' him down to Benny's to see what I can get for him.
HELEN
Oh, no, Wreck! You can't hock Dicky!
WRECK
Take your choice—we either hock him or have him on toast.
(He goes off. VIOLET *comes out of building, followed by* LONIGAN.)*
VIOLET
Let go of me, ya big phony!
GUIDE
Here is yet another type.
Everyone knows the famous Violet,
Nicest gal you'd ever meet(3)
Steadily working on Christopher Street(3).
(Music is cut off.)
VIOLET *(To* LONIGAN)*
Don't shove me, ya big phony!

LONIGAN

On your way, Violet. *(VIOLET is pushed off by LONIGAN.)*

VIOLET *(As she goes)*

You're a public servant—I pay your salary! So just you show a little respect! *(Music resumes.)*

ALL

Life is gay,

Life is sweet(3),

Interesting people live on Christopher Street(3).

A PHILOSOPHER

(Enters, carrying a sign—"MEETING ON UNION SQUARE")

Down with Wall Street! Down with Wall Street(3)!

(He freezes with the others, fist in air)

GUIDE *(Sung)*

Such interesting people live on Christopher Street(3)!

YOGI *(Enters with sign "PEACE")*

Love thy neighbor! Love thy neighbor!

(Another freeze)

TOURISTS *(Sung)*

Such interesting people live on Christopher Street(3)!

(Two MODERN DANCERS enter.)

MODERN DANCERS *(Working hard)*

And one—and two—and three—and four—

And one—and two—and three—and four

TOURISTS

Such interesting people live on Christopher Street(3).

ALL

Look! Look!

Poets! Actors! Dancers! Writers!

Here we live,

Here we love.

This is the place for self-expression.

Life is mad,

Life is sweet(3),

Interesting people living on Christopher Street(3)!

Earlier I spoke of Comden and Green's ability to write "special material." They put this particular talent to use twice in *Wonderful Town.* The first was in "One Hundred Easy Ways to Lose a Man." This was tailored for the star Rosalind Russell, who otherwise had no solo spot in the show. Besides, the star's vocal range was narrow (she had never sung before), and her personal proclivity lay in her ability to perform comedy material.

"One Hundred Easy Ways to Lose a Man" came strictly out of character—the older of the two sisters who had come to New York from Columbus, Ohio, considered herself quite naturally unattractive because Eileen, her younger sister, was always being sought after by men. The lead-in to the song is here quoted in order to present the entire setup.

In each of the three A sections there are three sung rhymes and the last word of the ensuing spoken section adds a fourth.

"ONE HUNDRED EASY WAYS TO LOSE A MAN"

RUTH

Gee, since I've been in New York, I only met one man, and he said, "Why the hell don't you look where you're going?" Maybe it's just as well. Every time I meet one I gum it up. I'm the world's leading expert on discouraging men. I ought to write a book about it. "Girls, are you constantly bothered by the cloying attentions of the male sex? Well, here's the solution for you. Get Ruth Sherwood's new best-seller–'One Hundred Easy Ways to Lose a Man.' " *(EILEEN laughs and goes into house as RUTH sings in a spirit of rueful self-mockery.)*

Chapter one—

Now the first way to lose a man—

(Sings with exaggerated romanticism)

You've met a charming fellow and you're out for a spin(1).

The motor fails and he just wears a helpless grin(1)—

Don't bat your eyes and say, "What a romantic spot we're in(1)."

(Spoken flatly)

Just get out, crawl under the car, tell him it's the gasket and fix it in two seconds flat with a bobby pin(1).

(Sung) That's a good way to lose a man—

He takes you to the baseball game.

You sit knee to knee(2)—

He says, "The next man up at bat will bunt, you'll see(2)."

Don't say, "Oooh, what's a bunt? This game's too hard for little me(2)."

(Spoken)

Just say, "Bunt? Are you nuts?!! With one out and two men on base, and a left-handed batter coming up, you'll walk right into a triple play just like it happened in the fifth game of the World Series in 1923(2)."

(Sung)

That's a sure way to lose a man.

A sure sure sure sure way to lose a man,

A splendid way to lose a man—

Just throw your knowledge in his face(3)

He'll never try for second base(3).

Ninety-eight ways to go.

The third way to lose a man—

The life-guard at the beach that all the girlies adore(4)

Swims bravely out to save you through the ocean's roar(4).

Don't say, "Oh, thanks, I would have dwowned in just one second more(4)"—

(Spoken)

Just push his head under water and yell, "Last one in is a rotten egg" and race him back to shore(4)!

(Sung)

That's a swell way to lose a man

You've found your perfect mate and it's been love from the start(5).

He whispers, "You're the one to who I give my heart(5)."

Don't say, "I love you too, my dear, let's never never part(5)"—

(Spoken)

Just say, "I'm afraid you've made a grammatical error—It's not 'To who I give my heart,' it's 'To whom I give my heart'— You see, with the use of the preposition 'to,' 'who' becomes the indirect object, making the use of 'whom' imperative which I can easily show you by drawing a simple chart(5)"—*(Waving good-bye toward an imaginary retreating figure)*

That's a fine way to lose a man.

A fine fine fine fine way to lose a man,

A dandy way to lose a man—

Just be(2) more well-informed than he(2),

You'll never hear 'O Promise Me(2)"—

Just show him where his grammar errs(6)
Then mark your towels "hers" and "hers(6)"—
Yes, girls, you too can lose your man(7)
If you will use Ruth Sherwood's plan(7)—
One hundred easy ways to lose a man(7)!

The male principal of *Wonderful Town*, Bob Baker, an editor, has an interview with Ruth Sherwood who has brought him some of her unacceptable manuscripts. Other editors join with Baker in several sections of this musical scene.

"WHAT A WASTE"

RUTH
(Looks at pile of manuscripts, then up to BOB*)*
Well, what do you advise me to do?
BAKER
(Sung)
Go home!
Go west!
Go back where you came from!
Oh, why did you ever leave Ohio?
RUTH
Because I think I have talent!
BAKER
A million kids just like you
Come to town every day
With stars in their eyes;
They're going to conquer the city(1),
They're going to grab off the Pulitzer Prize(2),
But it's a terrible pity(1)
Because they're in for a bitter surprise(2).
And their stories all follow one line(3)
(Pointing with his arm to FIRST EDITOR*)*
Like his,
(Pointing to SECOND EDITOR*)*
Like his,
(To himself with both hands)
Like mine(3).
(To RUTH*)*
Born in Duluth,
Natural writer,
Published at seven—genius type(4)—
Wrote the school play,
Wrote the school paper—
Summa cum laude—all of that tripe(4)—
Came to New York,
Got on the staff here—
This was my chance to be heard(5).
Well, since then I haven't written a word(5).
BAKER AND EDITORS
What a waste,
What a waste,
What a waste of money and time(3)!
FIRST EDITOR
Man from Detroit—
Wonderful Artist—
Went to Picasso—Pablo said "Wow(6)!"
Settled in France,
Bought him a beret,
Lived in Montmartre,
Really learned how(6)

Came to New York—had an exhibit,
Art critics made a big fuss(7),
Now he paints those tooth-paste ads on the bus(7)!
EDITORS AND BAKER
What a waste,
What a waste,
What a waste of money and time!
SECOND EDITOR
Girl from Mobile
Versatile actress—
Tragic or comic—
Any old play(11).
Suffered and starved,
Met Stanislavsky.
He said the world would
Cheer her some day(11).
Came to New York,
Repertoire ready,
Chekhov's and Shakespeare's and Wilde's(8)—
Now they watch her flipping flapjacks at Childs'(8).
EDITORS AND BAKER
What a waste,
What a waste,
What a waste of money and time!
BAKER
Kid from Cape Cod,
Fisherman's family,
Marvelous singer—big baritone(9)—
Rented his boat,
Paid for his lessons
Starved for his studies
Down to the bone(9)—
Came to New York,
Aimed at the opera—
Sing "Rigoletto" his wish(10)—
At the Fulton Market now he yells "Fish(10)!"
EDITORS
What a waste,
What a waste,
What a waste of money and time!
BAKER
Go home! Go west!
Go back where you came from!
Go home!

The next musical scene, "Nice People," is "special material": The trombone music is incidental but exactly what is needed, and it serves as a necessary cohesive factor. As it occurs between speeches especially, it somehow manages to spell out boredom and embarrassment, the loud vulgar sound of a ghastly silence.

Each of the guest's characters is spelled out accurately and hilariously. This bringing together of thoroughly disparate people is "photographed" here in this unique piece.

"NICE PEOPLE"

RUTH
I'd like you to meet Mr. Clark—Mr. Lippencott—This is Mr. Baker—
FRANK
Pleased to meet you.
(Holds out his hand, which BAKER *shakes.)*

CHICK
What the hell is this, a block party?
RUTH
You're quite a card, aren't you, Mr. Clark? *(Puts wine on window sill)* Mr. Lippencott brought you some wine, dear.
EILEEN
Oh, how sweet! Shall we sit down? *(She motions the others to join her and there is a general embarrassed shuffling about for chairs. She pulls* BOB *down beside her on her chair.* CHICK *brings a chair forward and* RUTH, *assuming it is for her, goes toward it, but* CHICK *sits on it himself. She gets her own and the five wind up in a tight uncomfortable group facing one another with nothing to say.* EILEEN *after a pause)*
Well—here we are—all together— *(There is a dry discordant vamp in the orchestra expressing the atmosphere of embarrassed silence, which is repeated during every pause in the following song and conversation. It seems to grow more mocking and desperate at each repetition. After another pause they all start speaking at once very animatedly and then dwindle off. Pause again.* EILEEN *giggles nervously. Pause.)*
FRANK *(Starting bravely)*
At the bottom of the vanilla— *(He has a terrific coughing fit.* BAKER *slaps his back, and he sits down—and combs his hair.)*
It's nothing.
(Vamp.)
EILEEN *(Singing, over-brightly, after a pause)*
Mmmm—mmmm—it's so nice to sit around—
And chat—
Nice people, nice talk,
A balmy summer night,
A bottle of wine—
Nice talk—nice people,
Nice feeling—nice talk—
The combination's right
And everything's fine—

Nice talk—nice people
It's friendly—it's gay
To sit around this way.
What more do you need?
Just talk—and people.
For that can suffice
When both the talk and people are so nice—
(She finishes lamely as the vamp is played again. Pause.)
FRANK
(Settling back in chair with a hollow, unconvincing laugh)
Ha ha—Funny thing happened at the counter today—Man comes in—Sort of tall like—Nice looking refined type—Red bow tie—and all. Well sir, he orders a banana split—That's our jumbo special—twenty-eight cents—Three scoops—chocolate, strawberry, vanilla—choice of cherry or caramel sauce—chopped nuts—whipped cream—Well, sir, he eats the whole thing—I look at his plate and I'll be hornswoggled if he doesn't leave the whole banana—doesn't touch it—not a bite—Don't you see?—If he doesn't like bananas, what does he order a banana split for?—He coulda had a sundae—nineteen cents—Three scoops—Chocolate—Strawberry—Vanilla—
(He dwindles off as vamp is played again.)
RUTH *(Making a noble attempt to save the day)*
I was re-reading *Moby Dick* the other day and—Oh, I haven't read it since—I'm sure none of us has—It's worth picking up again— It's about this whale— *(Her futile attempt hangs heavy on the air. Vamp again.)*
CHICK
(Even he is driven by desperation to attempt sociability)
Boy, it's hot! Reminds me of that time in Panama—I was down there on a story—I was in this, well, dive— And there was this broad there—What was her name?—Marquita?—Maroota? *(Warming to his subject)* Ahh, what's the difference what her name was—That dame was built like a brick—
(A sharp drum crash cuts him off and the vamp is played with hysterical speed and violence. The four others spring to their feet horrified and, as CHICK *stands by puzzled, they cover up with a sudden outburst of animated talk and laughter expressed by a rapid rendition of "Nice People, Nice Talk" with* EILEEN *singing an insane coloratura obbligato as the music builds to a thunderous close.)*
ALL
Nice people, nice talk,
A balmy summer night,
A bottle of wine—
Nice talk, nice people,
Nice feeling—nice talk.
The combination's right
and everything's fine.

Nice talk, nice people—
It's friendly, it's gay
To sit around this way.
What more do you need?
Just talk and people.
For that can suffice
When both the talk and people are so nice
It's nice!

In all the library of musical theatre this "Nice People" is special. It is funny and embarrassing, a strange marvelous mixture of music used to comment in the manner of the Greek chorus and with an occasional song. This is a one-of-a-kind achievement.

Comden and Green have written—besides a number of librettos—every kind of lyric. Their particular forte—and I believe (as I said earlier) it is because they have always also been performers—has been their ability to create "special material." In this they have had no peers.

Frederick Loewe and Alan Jay Lerner

Alan Jay Lerner (b. 1918)

The career of Alan Jay Lerner as a lyricist has been almost exclusively tied up with that of composer Frederick Loewe. His three well-known works that did not involve Loewe were *Love Life,* with Kurt Weill, *On a Clear Day You Can See Forever,* written with Burton Lane, and *Coco,* with André Previn. The Loewe shows included *Brigadoon, Paint Your Wagon, The Day Before Spring, My Fair Lady, Camelot,* and *Gigi*—the latter first a film and more recently a musical for the stage.

Though individual songs in each show achieved enduring success, to date the outstanding accomplishments of Alan Jay Lerner are to be found in *Brigadoon,* and then nine years later, the most distinguished of his works, the musical version of Shaw's *Pygmalion, My Fair Lady.*

Lerner has never indulged in cuteness or tricks. His best lyrics first of all sing. Then too they are literate to a very high degree. There is a sense of inevitability about the shape of his songs, and a clear organization of his thought processes. Both rhymes and rhythms are simple as befit the almost classical style of Loewe's music.

Before tackling Lerner's lyrics in his two most distinguished shows, I should like to call attention (in no chronological order) to some single songs in the others.

The title song for *On a Clear Day You Can See Forever* (1965) provides an excellent example to begin with. It is generated by a scene in which the heroine's extrasensory perception is being discussed with her by her psychiatrist friend, Mark. The dialogue lead-in to the song and the verse of the song itself follow.

"ON A CLEAR DAY YOU CAN SEE FOREVER"

MARK I think that extrasensory perception is as normal as being able to see. The trouble is, most people don't see very well. And even then, most of the time you have to tell them what it is they're seeing. Every railroad crossing has a sign, and do you know what it says? "Railroad Crossing." And every bridge has to have a sign that says "Bridge." So far, your sign hasn't been painted, that's all.

DAISY Well, until it is, you won't say anything about me, will you, Doctor? I mean, I don't want my friends to know I haven't got a sign.

MARK Miss Gamble, you mustn't be ashamed of being ahead of us. *(He sings)*

Could anyone among us have an inkling or a clue
What magic feats of wizardry and voodoo you can do?
And who would ever guess
What powers you possess?
And who would have the sense to change his views?
And start to mind his ESP's and Q's?

For who would ever dream of hearing phones before they ring?
Or ordering the earth to send you up a little spring?
Or finding you've been crowned
The Queen of Lost and Found?
And who would not be stunned to see you prove
There's more to us than surgeons can remove?

So much more than we ever knew,
So much more were we born to do.

Should you draw back the curtain
This I am certain
You'll be impressed with you.

The second stanza contains a plethora of fresh images: "hearing phones before they ring," "ordering the earth to send you up a little spring," "crowned The Queen of Lost and Found," and especially "There's more to us than surgeons can remove."

In the same show the same character, the psychiatrist, must make an important decision: will he hand in scientific papers professing his belief in reincarnation (which he *knows* his unusual experiences in the play prove) or, to avoid embarrassment, will he pretend that the experiences never took place?

"MELINDA"

This is a dream, Melinda,
Just a mirage, so they say.
This whole affair,
They all declare,
Was dream'd each step of the way.

You're a mere dream, Melinda,
Out for a gay little spin,
Dealing me lies
Before my eyes
Of days that never have been.

There's no Melinda!
They say for sure.
But don't go, Melinda!
I know and you know
That you're no mere dream, Melinda,
Gone when the dawn glimmers through.
You and I know
That long ago,
Before the dream, there was you.
There once was you.
(Music continues under. He goes to his intercom and turns it on)
MARK *(Into the intercom)* Mrs. Hatch, come in please. *(She enters)* Mrs. Hatch, deliver that case history and these papers to the Board of Trustees of the University. Tonight.
(He hands her the papers)
MRS. HATCH Yes, Doctor.
(She exits)
MARK *(Sings)*
There was Melinda,
I know for sure.
So don't go, Melinda.
I know and you know.
That you're no mere dream, Melinda,
Gone when the dawn glimmers through.
You and I know
That long ago
Before the dream there was you.
There once was you.

Of special interest is the revised point of view between the final two stanzas. In each, Lerner is led by the dramatic situation. Out of the entire ten lines, the ear hears no rhyme until the eighth line, which rhymes with the seventh, and then the ninth rhymes with the sixth. Yet one does not miss the euphony that is normally expected of a lyric. The sense of movement is so strong that the lyric seems, at first, more like a bald statement.

From *Paint Your Wagon* (1951), I should like to quote three lyrics. The first, unlike the two subsequent ones, was not wildly popular. "How Can I Wait?" is sung by a plain country girl, a mid-nineteenth-century American type. It is a love song addressed to her lover's trousers. It is happy, anxious, and fraught with anticipation. The singing character, Jennifer, speaks colloquially and Lerner had to come to grips with this problem of dialect. It is interesting to see his solution. First of all, he chiefly employs, incorrectly, "was" for "were": "I wish his legs was in these pants." In the ten-line verse "wish" occurs five times. Only the last couplet rhymes. In the refrain Lerner retains the slang by dropping the final *g* three times, using "gonna" twice, and "till" for "until" five times. This is quite a sufficient departure from the norm to remind the listener that this is a country girl. The rhymes do not come to the ear until the fifth line, which rhymes with the fourth, then the sixth with the third. Afterward, the rhymes occur in couplets.

"HOW CAN I WAIT?"

I wish his legs was in these pants;
His feet was in these socks.
I wish his arms was in this shirt
And all of him was here.
I wish his hands was in these sleeves,
His face was in this towel.
I wish himself was in this bag
And all of him was here.
I wish I knew why every night
I ache and miss him so . . .

(Spoken.) 'Specially when I'm gonna see him again tomorrow
by the ravine. *(Sings.)*
Where we always go.

How can I wait, can I wait till tomorrow comes?
How can I live till tomorrow comes?
How can I make every minute fly
Till that shinin' moment when
I'll be seein' him again?
I'm gonna die,
Gonna die, or be old and gray!
Why is tomorrow so far away?
How can I talk, can I breathe, can I eat?
What can I do with my hands and my feet?
How can I wait, can I wait till tomorrow comes?

Starlight, go away, fade away, blow away!
Sunrise come again, make a new sunny day!

Oh, what can I do, can I think about?
How can my heart keep from jumpin' out?
How can I sleep, couldn't sleep if I tried!
Where can I run till I run to his side?
How can I wait till tomorrow comes!

The two hit songs from *Paint Your Wagon*, still heard frequently after twenty-three years, are "They Call the Wind Maria" and "I Talk to the Trees." The first has a cowboy flavor. In the lyric its folk quality is accentuated by personifying the wind (Maria), rain (Tess), and fire (Jo). Lerner has invented an interesting kind of narration by describing Maria's attributes: she blows the stars around, sends the clouds a-flyin', and makes the mountains sound.

This simple song typifies the author's very orderly organiza-

Paint Your Wagon

tion of material. And in this particular case the material had to be entirely invented! A part of it follows.

"THEY CALL THE WIND MARIA"

Away out here they got a name
For wind and rain and fire;
The rain is Tess, the fire's Jo,
And they call the wind Maria.
Maria blows the stars around
And sends the clouds a-flyin'.
Maria makes the mountains sound
Like folks were up there dyin'.
Maria! Maria! They call the wind Maria!

There is a strong reason for a writer's coloring speech (or lyrics) in order to indicate locale, especially when or perhaps *only* when he wishes to contrast people who have speech differences. The people in *Paint Your Wagon* are somewhat different from each other and quite apart from ourselves. In *My Fair Lady*, Eliza Doolittle *has* to sound vastly different from Henry Higgins. The heroine of *Brigadoon* and the others who reside there are pure isolated Scottish and must be heard in contrast to the American travelers. However, I believe just as strongly that a change in time or locale should not be expressed by an author's phony attempt to emulate a style of speech that is not his own.

Shaw's elegant speech style, written in 1912, is still an upper-class English speech style today, sixty-three years later. We do not know how King Arthur spoke but even if we could approximate the style, doing so would be the frustrating task of the research specialist and not the artist, whose business it is to create.

In *Camelot*, speech and lyrics are, as we are accustomed to them, normal. They vary only in relation to character dynamics and are not an attempt to imitate a way of life that is alien to us. For example, Arthur says, "When I was a lad of eighteen" etc., while King Pellinore, a comic character in armor, wearing a monocle, says, "Howdyado, Your Majesty will have to forego the bending. Beastly hinges need oiling." The difference in speech is between the characters, not between *their* time and ours.

Incidentally, Tennyson's language in "The Idylls of the King" is also normal. In no way does it attempt to assume an air of antiquity, but viewed today it *appears* to be dated: a lovely expression of Tennyson's own nineteenth-century English:

I found Him in the shining of the stars,
I mark'd Him in the flowering of His fields,
But in His ways with men I find Him not.
I waged His wars, and now I pass and die.

In "Camelot," sung by King Arthur, we hear normal lyrics and speech, and these are used to delightfully puncture the image that the audience brings with it to the theatre of the fairy-tale character of the king as righteous and untouchable. In this song, the first in the show, the king reveals himself as young, joyous, and bouncy, in short, human. This kind of character definition, so contrary to tradition, is one of the many things that Lerner accomplished with grace, ease, and credibility. Such an idea is appropriately conveyed through music and lyrics, and might have been clumsy and cute if entrusted to spoken dialogue.

"CAMELOT"

ARTHUR *(Sings)*
It's true! It's true! The crown has made it clear:
The climate must be perfect all the year.

A law was made a distant moon ago here,
July and August cannot be too hot;
And there's a legal limit to the snow here
In Camelot.

The winter is forbidden till December,
And exits March the second on the dot.
By order summer lingers through September
In Camelot.

Camelot! Camelot!
I know it sounds a bit bizarre;
But in Camelot, Camelot
That's how conditions are.

The rain may never fall till after sundown.
By eight the morning fog must disappear.
In short, there's simply not
A more congenial spot
For happ'ly-ever-aftering than here
In Camelot.

GUENEVERE *(Sarcastically)*
And I suppose the autumn leaves fall in neat little piles.
ARTHUR
Oh, no, Milady. They blow away completely. At night, of course.
GUENEVERE
Of course.
(She moves away from him, as if to leave. He leaps after her and blocks her way.)
ARTHUR
Camelot! Camelot!
I know it gives a person pause
But in Camelot, Camelot
Those are the legal laws.

The snow may never slush upon the hillside.
By nine P.M. the moonlight must appear.
In short, there's simply not
A more congenial spot
For happ'ly-ever-aftering than here
In Camelot.

The correct organization of the time sequence in this song is infallibly present in all of Alan Lerner's lyrics. Note that the months proceed in sequence (this may seem expected, but too often in my experience its absence makes for a sloppy kind of compromise): July, August, December, and March. Note also that the rather regular rhymes frequently overlap. The verse consists of only two lines. The refrain is double the usual length—64 bars. A is 16 bars and is heard twice. B, or the release, is also 16 bars, and then A is repeated again. There is one chorus, followed by dialogue with background music, and then the final two sections are sung. Rhymes with "Camelot" pervade the entire song.

Another song in *Camelot* involving the changing seasons, "If Ever I Would Leave You," is a love ballad sung by Lancelot.

Camelot

This begins with a chorus (two seven-line stanzas) followed by a two-line interlude, which in turn is followed by the second half of the refrain with a new set of lyrics. In the repetition of a refrain or even half of it, a changed developed lyric is desirable since the writer is then taking full advantage of his opportunity to move forward the plot or his character's thinking, and is not content with simple repetition. The listener's interest will also be kept much more alive with the developing thoughts.

Here is an intensely romantic song and out of the two seven-line sections comprising the refrain, there is only one single pair of rhymes—occurring consistently at the ends of lines 5 and 7. In the new reprise after the interlude, the seven lines have been compressed into six and there are two sets of rhymes. The form of this song is quite unusual. It is made of eight-bar blocks in the pattern ABABCAB. A part, from the end, follows.

"IF EVER I WOULD LEAVE YOU"

(A) If ever I would leave you,
How could it be in springtime,
Knowing how in spring I'm bewitch'd by you so?
(B) Oh, no, not in springtime!
Summer, winter or fall!
No, never could I leave you at all.

The most distinguished of all Lerner and Loewe contributions to the theatre are *Brigadoon* (1947) and *My Fair Lady* (1956). The first, now nearly thirty years old, has become a classic and shows few if any signs of age. *Brigadoon* is essentially an exercise in love and death and timelessness, told as a kind of fairy tale. It is highly theatrical, constitutes a high point in the development of our musical theatre from 1940 to 1965, has the necessary romantic ingredients provided by two sets of lovers, and has a comedic pair for contrast. The fairy tale that contains all of this titillates us with questions that have interested us in the plays of Priestley, Cocteau, Pirandello, and the novels of H. G. Wells—all of these to be sure on a more fulsome level. There is drama, melodrama, and a thin sweet philosophical overlay that the music and lyrics make both palatable and attractive.

As if to establish from the outset the feeling of mystery and legend, the sound of a chorus is heard in the darkness:

Once in the Highlands, the Highlands of Scotland,
Deep in the night on a murky brae;
There in the Highlands, the Highlands of Scotland,
Two weary hunters lost their way.

And this is what happened,
The strange thing that happened,
To two weary hunters who lost their way.

The simplicity and clarity of this once-upon-a-time style are refreshing, and theatrically spine-chilling. We are alerted to something strange that is about to unfold.

The style of the prologue is amplified by another invisibly sung choral section following the first brief scene of dialogue—almost predictably opposite to the prologue in every way. The scene is matter-of-fact, contemporary, and humorous. What follows not only involves the audience but arrests the attention of the two American travelers.

Brigadoon, Brigadoon,
Blooming under sable skies.

Brigadoon, Brigadoon,
There my heart for ever lies.
Let the world grow cold around us,
Let the heavens cry above . . .

Afterward we find ourselves in the strange village of Brigadoon, and our travelers, along with the audience, meet everyone in the play in what functions as the opening chorus, set in the marketplace.

The lyrics, in line with what was said earlier regarding time and place, employ two elements that define the inhabitants for the Americans. A single word used many times tells us (along with the costumes) that we have gone back in time. It is "ye." The place words include laddie, ken, and glen. These suggestions of Scotland at an earlier time are to be found throughout the show in all the lyrics sung by the town's inhabitants. The Americans have words belonging to us here and now.

Fiona is the heroine. That fact, plus the assurance—in the event that we would not guess—that she is going to be paired off with the American hero is implied in her first song, "Waitin' for My Dearie." Simple as it is, this is a very functional song. Audiences accepting this milieu must be told even what they may instinctively know already.

"WAITIN' FOR MY DEARIE"

Many a lassie as ev'ryone knows'll
Try to be married before twenty-five.
So she'll agree to most any proposal,
All he mus' be is a man an' alive.

I hold a dream an' there's no compromisin'
I know there's one certain laddie for me.
One day he'll come walkin' o'er the horizon;
But should he not then an old maid I'll be.

Foolish ye may say.
Foolish I will stay.

Waitin' for my dearie
An' happy am I
To hold my heart till
He comes strollin' by.
When he comes, my dearie,
One look an' I'll know
That he's the dearie
I've been wantin' so.

Though I'll live forty lives
Till the day he arrives
I'll not ever, ever grieve.
For my hopes will be high
That he'll come strollin' by;
For ye see, I believe
That there's a laddie weary
An' wanderin' free
Who's waitin' for his dearie;
Me.

The lyric explains not only itself, but the character who sings it (Fiona) and her situation.

In contrast to Fiona and what might be described as her maturity and patience, there is another kind of love song that has charm and bounce and is clearly more youthful. It is sung by Charlie Dalrymple, the male half of a couple about to be

CAMELOT

LERNER & LOEWE'S

MUSIC BY
FREDERICK LOEWE

BOOK AND LYRICS BY
ALAN JAY LERNER

DIRECTED BY
MOSS HART

PRODUCED BY THE MESSRS. LERNER · LOEWE · HART

Also Published Separately from the Score
FOLLOW ME
CAMELOT
HOW TO HANDLE A WOMAN
IF EVER I WOULD LEAVE YOU
I LOVED YOU ONCE IN SILENCE

CHAPPELL & CO., INC., with ALFRED PRODUCTIONS, INC.
609 Fifth Avenue, New York 17, N. Y.

60¢

wed. One surprising aspect of this fast-moving song is that Charlie, a quite young guileless boy, boasts of the others in his premarital life: "So farewell to one an' all." This aspect of the song, a considerable part of it, tells us how really young, inexperienced, and innocent he is. He feels the need to proclaim what he undoubtedly knows nothing whatsoever about. The rhythm dances and the rhymes glide. A section follows.

"I'LL GO HOME WITH BONNIE JEAN"

CHARLIE
I used to be a rovin' lad
A rovin' an' wanderin' life I had.
On any lass I'd frown
Who would try to tie me down.
But then one day I saw a maid
Who held out her hand, an' I stayed an' stayed.
An' now across the green,
I'll go home with bonnie Jean.

Meg Brockie is to *Brigadoon* exactly what Ado Annie is to *Oklahoma!* She is a comic character and the female counterpart of the American Jeff Douglas. Alan Lerner wrote what is in my opinion a model comedy song for her, "The Love of My Life." I call it a "long-joke" song, since the principal laugh occurs at the end of each of four choruses. Everything else builds up to it. The form of this song is unusual and it is a great tribute to Lerner that he could keep things amusing for so long a time. It begins with a verse that becomes an interlude between each of the three succeeding choruses, as well as an ending after the fourth. In other words, this verse, or interlude, occurs five times. Its subject matter concerns the reactions of Meg's father. Meg tells us these in all innocence—one of her comic characteristics—and known to us but unknown to her is the gradually emerging fact that her father wishes to be rid of her.

The choruses not only lead up to jokes at the end of each section (jokes derived solely from the character involved in the situation and in no way liftable), but the first chorus is connected with the second chorus though Meg's encounter with a boy named MacGill, and in the second she sings: ". . . he told me he had heard about me from his friend MacGill."

The third chorus is about a rhymer and the fourth a soldier. These two are connected by a line in the fourth: ". . . I found the sword has more might than the pen."

This model comedy song of the "long-joke" variety is not only timelessly funny but its detailed revelation of Meg's character is also remarkable. She is so naïve that although she tells us repeatedly that her four lovers left her, never to return, it does not occur to her that she alone was the cause of their retreats. She does not realize her father's eagerness to be rid of her, and *we* learn it is her own impatience to find "the real love of my life" that prevents its happening. These truly unprepossessing and innocent characteristics are the stuff that comedy, comedy songs, and comedic performances are made of. The lyrics as such are simple, as are all of Alan Jay Lerner's, but it is the content and ease of this lyric that make it so special.

"THE LOVE OF MY LIFE"

At sixteen years I was o' so sad,
Then father said I should find a lad.
So I set out to become a wife
An' found the real love of my life.

His name it was Chris, an' the last was MacGill.
I met him one night pickin' flowers on the hill.
He had lots of charm an' a certain kind o' touch,
An' a certain kind o' eagerness that pleased me very much.

So there 'neath the moon where romance often springs,
I gave him my heart—an' a few other things.
I don't know how long that I stayed upon the hill
But the moon had disappeared an' so had Christopher MacGill.

So I went home an' I thought I'd die,
Till father said: make another try.
So out I went to become a wife,
An' found the real love of my life.

He came from the lowlands, the lowlands said he,
I saw him an' knew he was perfect for me.
Jus' one thing that puzzled me an' it always will,
Was he told me he had heard about me from his friend MacGill.

We quick fell in love an' went down by the creek,
The next day he said he'd be back in a week.
An' I thought he would, for now how was I to know,
That of all the lowland laddies there was never one as low.

I told my father the awful truth,
He said: What difference? Ye've got your youth.
So out I went mad to be a wife
An' found the real love of my life.

Oh, he was a poet, a rhymer was he.
He read me some verse he had written for me.
He said they would move me these poems from his pen;
An' how right he was because they moved me right into the glen.

We stayed till the dawn came an' lighted the sky.
Then I shook his hand an' I bid him good-bye.
I never went back for what I had heard was true;
That a poet only writes about the things he cannot do.

My pa said: look out for men who think
Ye'll be more certain with men who drink.
So out I went to become a wife,
An' found the real love of my life.

Oh, he was a soldier, a fine Highland son.
He told me about all the battles he'd won.
He wasted his time tellin' me about his might,
For one look at him decided me not to put up a fight.

We skirmished for hours that night in the glen,
An' I found the sword has more might than the pen.
But when I was drowsin' I snored to my dismay,
An' he thought it was a bugle an' got up an' marched away.

Now pa said: daughter there must be one.
Someone who's true or too old to run.
So I'm still lookin' to be a wife
An' find the real love of my life.

Lack of space compels me to skip over many fine songs in *Brigadoon*, but for several reasons I would like to discuss two others. The first, "There but for You Go I; sung by Tommy, the American hero, is distinguished because what it has to say as a

love song is quite original. In addition, Lerner does some very special things with the rhymes and assonances. As some of these are quite complex, I will endeavor to point them out. Incidentally, what I will point out is what I *hear* and I do not know whether Lerner intended them to *harmonize* or not. I believe that this is beside the point. In the verse we have:
lea, *flee*ting, sudden*ly*, free, *being*, lone*ly*, *rea*son
and *mo*ment, *lo*nely, *clo*sed and *eye*s, why.

The last two will cause raised eyebrows. I myself am very much opposed to a practice that can be commonly found in much popular music, that of rhyming singular with plural. In this case, however, I feel that the phrase "Then I closed my eyes and saw" is set to be and in fact *is* sung "Then I closed my eye sand saw" so that the ear hears "eye" without the *s*. According to my own count, in this verse of seven short lines, there are seven $\overline{ee}$ rhymes, three $\overline{o}$ rhymes, and two $\overline{\imath}$ rhymes: eleven rhymes in seven lines. Besides, and of more importance, the idea set in motion by the verse is unique.

The chorus, in conventional AABA form, has regular rhymes—lines 1 with 2 and 3 with 4 in the three A sections; in the B section the rhymes in lines 1 and 3 occur next to the last words, and in lines 2 and 4 end rhymes are used, with a third rhyme (Trying) at the beginning of line 2. Beyond this technical *feu d'artifice*, the sentiments of the song and the way they are expressed make it very beautiful.

"THERE BUT FOR YOU GO I"

VERSE
This is hard to say,
But as I wandered through the lea,
I felt for just a fleeting moment
That I suddenly was free
Of being lonely.
Then I closed my eyes and saw
The very reason why.

CHORUS
I saw a man with his head bowed low.
His heart had no place to go.
I looked and I thought to myself with a sigh,
There but for you go I.

I saw a man walking by the sea.
Alone with the tide was he.
I looked and I thought as I watched him go by,
There but for you go I.

Lonely men around me,
Trying not to cry.
Till the day you found me
There among them was I.

I saw a man who had never known
A love that was all his own.

I thought as I thanked all the stars in the sky,
There but for you go I.

The musical form of the chorus of "From This Day On" is unique. A consists of twelve bars instead of eight or sixteen. These twelve are composed of a musical motif of three bars, which run into one another and overlap three times. As reflected in the lyrics, they go:

You and the world we knew will glow
Till my life is through;
For you're part of me from this day on.

A musical extension of three bars at the end accounts for the total of twelve bars. This A section is repeated with an altered ending.

The B section is eight bars long, in two four-bar phrases. Then A repeats, with an added ending. This structure, musically and lyrically, is one of a kind.

"FROM THIS DAY ON"

You and the world we knew will glow
Till my life is through;
For you're part of me from this day on.
And some day if I should love,
It's you I'll be dreaming of;
For you're all I'll see from this day on.

These hurried hours were all the life we could share.
Still I will go with not a tear, just a prayer.
That when we are far apart you'll find
Something from your heart has gone
Gone with me from this day on.

Through all the years to come and through
All the tears to come I know
I'll be yours from this day on.

In *My Fair Lady*, Eliza's father, Alfred P. Doolittle, the philosophical dustman, is introduced in his native habitat, in front of a bar with two drinking companions in his lower-class neighborhood. This scene does not occur in Shaw. Doolittle, for the purposes of musical theatre, is somewhat more simplified than Shaw's original, but as we find out in this simple music-hall-type song he is lazy, fond of liquor, women, and profoundly irresponsible. A section of the song follows.

"WITH A LITTLE BIT OF LUCK"

The Lord above gave man an arm of iron
So he could do his job and never shirk.
The Lord above gave man an arm of iron—but
With a little bit of luck,
With a little bit of luck,
Someone else'll do the blinkin' work!

With a little bit . . . . with a little bit. . . .
With a little bit of luck
You'll never work!

One of the advances made in modern theatre writing has been the dramatic integration of song and story, as opposed to songs that were formerly loosely inserted at random. This older practice usually meant that some lame and often ridiculous excuse was invented for inserting an attractive song almost anywhere within a show, and its assignment to nearly any character. Today there is a misapprehension that because of the new trend toward better integration, of conceiving songs specifically for a certain character in a particular situation, the songs themselves have become less interesting and less memorable. Such an idea is, of course, absurd. To paraphrase Gertrude Stein, "A good song is a good song is a good song." Its tight fitting to character and situation has nothing whatsoever to do with its quality. This confusion is largely due to the fact that in older shows songs were reprised again and again, then used instrumentally during scene changes and so on, whereas nowadays there are fewer good reasons for reprises and less necessity for time-consuming scene-changing. Songs today are less often repeated, and there are fewer opportunities for drumming them into an audience's consciousness. However, when songs are both very good and very tightly conceived for a specific character and situation, the more pertinent and interesting they become.

"I'm an Ordinary Man" is a case in point. It could only be sung by Higgins, because it reveals certain aspects of his character that are peculiar to nobody else in *My Fair Lady*. The very special thing it tells the audience is that Higgins himself is unaware of his own peculiarities: he honestly believes he *is* an ordinary man. As the lyrics develop we laugh more and more because he tells us that he *is* what we know, beyond any doubt, that he is *not*. What makes this statement really funny is the fact that we know Higgins believes honestly that what he says is true.

"I'm an Ordinary Man" is a song of sharp musical and lyric contrasts and these dictate the form. Each section is divided into "gentle" and "aggressive" parts, the latter nearly three times as long as the former. These sequences occur three times, each time with new lyrics.

The rhyming conforms to no set pattern. There are two sets of rhymes in the first stanza and these occur at the ends of the seventh and tenth lines and the eighth and ninth lines. The second stanza is in four sections, and though it does not *sound* like a chorus, in fact it *is* one in AABA form. Each A is seven lines long and B has only four. There are three sets of rhymes in the first two As, one set in B.

What is impressive is the whole style of the song, built as it is on two strongly contrasting elements, with a chorus that is anything but lyrical. Its viciousness helps to create its comedic qualities.

"I'M AN ORDINARY MAN"

HIGGINS
Have you ever met a man of good character where women were
    concerned?
PICKERING
Yes. Very frequently.
HIGGINS
(Dogmatically) Well, I haven't. I find that the moment I let a
    woman make friends with me she becomes jealous, exacting,

suspicious and a damned nuisance. I find that the moment I let myself become friends with a woman, I become selfish and tyrannical. So here I am, a confirmed old bachelor, and likely to remain so. After all, Pickering . . .

I'm an ordinary man;
Who desires nothing more
Than just the ordinary chance
To live exactly as he likes
And do precisely what he wants.
An average man am I
Of no eccentric whim;
Who likes to live his life
Free of strife,
Doing whatever he thinks is best for him.
Just an ordinary man.

(A) But let a woman in your life
And your serenity is through!
She'll redecorate your home
From the cellar to the dome;
Then get on to the enthralling
Fun of overhauling
You.

(A2) Oh, let a woman in your life
And you are up against the wall!
Make a plan and you will find
She has something else in mind;
And so rather than do either
You do something else that neither
Likes at all.

(B) You want to talk of Keats or Milton;
She only wants to talk of love.
You go to see a play or ballet,
And spend it searching for her glove.

(A) Oh, let a woman in your life
And you invite eternal strife!
Let them buy their wedding bands
For those anxious little hands;
I'd be equally as willing
For a dentist to be drilling
Than to ever let a woman in my life!
(With sudden amiability)
I'm a very gentle man;
Even-tempered and good-natured,
Whom you never hear complain;
Who has the milk of human kindness
By the quart in ev'ry vein.
A patient man am I
Down to my fingertips;
The sort who never could,
Ever would,
Let an insulting remark escape his lips.
(Violently)
But let a woman in your life
And patience hasn't got a chance.
She will beg you for advice;
Your reply will be concise.

My Fair Lady

And she'll listen very nicely
Then go out and do precisely
What she wants!

You were a man of grace and polish
Who never spoke above a hush.
Now all at once you're using language
That would make a sailor blush.

Oh, let a woman in your life
And you are plunging in a knife!
Let the others of my sex
Tie the knot—around their necks;
I'd prefer a new edition
Of the Spanish Inquisition
Than to ever let a woman in my life!
(The storm over, he "cheeps" sweetly to the bird)
I'm a quiet living man
Who prefers to spend his evenings
In the silence of his room;
Who likes an atmosphere as restful
As an undiscovered tomb.
A pensive man am I
Of philosophic joys;
Who likes to meditate,
Contemplate,
Free from humanity's mad, inhuman noise.
Just a quiet living man.
(With abrupt rage)
But let a woman in your life
And your sabbatical is through!
In a line that never ends
Come an army of her friends;
Come to jabber and to chatter
And to tell her what the matter
Is with you.

She'll have a booming, boist'rous fam'ly
Who will descend on you en masse.
She'll have a large Wagnerian mother
With a voice that shatters glass!

Oh, let a woman in your life . . .
*He turns on one of the machines at the accelerated speed so that
the voice coming over the speaker becomes a piercing female
babble. He runs to the next machine)*
Let a woman in your life . . .
(He turns it on the same way and dashes to the next)
Let a woman in your life . . .
*(He turns on the third; the third being the master control, he
slowly turns the volume up until the chattering is unbearable.
PICKERING covers his ears, his face knotted in pain. Having
illustrated his point, HIGGINS suddenly turns all the machines
off and makes himself comfortable in a chair)*
I shall never let a woman in my life!

A unusual "musical scene," a situation song that has more to
do with the drama than with lyric expression, is the first musical
number of Act Two of *My Fair Lady*. Though this "scene" is
divided clearly into two parts, it is a single entity.

The first "You did it!" is between Higgins and Colonel
Pickering, the second includes Higgins, a chorus of servants, a
footman, and interjections from his housekeeper, Mrs. Pearce.
There is a unifying theme—Higgins's triumph in passing Eliza

off successfully as a "lady" at the embassy ball. It accentuates Higgins's egocentricity, which is fed by Colonel Pickering
and the chorus. By default, it ignores Eliza who is physically present. The triumph is all Higgins's, who here feigns
modesty.

The second part of the number is descriptive of the Hungarian speech expert Zoltan Karpathy and how very much he
was fooled into believing Eliza was not even English. All of this
is a romp at Eliza's expense. It becomes cumulative and builds
up to her inevitable revolt.

This "musical scene" also provides the resolution to the
situation on which the curtain is rung down at the end of Act
One. What we do not know until this point in Act Two is what
actually happened. Despite the fact that the music and lyrics
take on the shape of drama here and are freer than usual, they
are by no means shapeless. Pickering's principal sections in
"You Did It!" are always in the same form. The first two times
the stanzas are exact repetitions; the last time is somewhat
altered.

"YOU DID IT!"

PICKERING
Tonight, old man, you did it!
You did it! You did it!
You said that you would do it,
And indeed you did.
I thought that you would rue it;
I doubted you'd do it.
But now I must admit it
That succeed you did.
You should get a medal
Or be even made a knight.
HIGGINS
It was nothing. Really nothing.
PICKERING
All alone you hurdled
Ev'ry obstacle in sight.
HIGGINS
Now, wait! Now, wait!
Give credit where it's due.
A lot of the glory goes to you.
*(ELIZA flinches violently but they take no notice of her. She
recovers herself and stands stonily as before)*
PICKERING
But you're the one who did it,
Who did it, who did it!
As sturdy as Gibraltar,
Not a second did you falter.
There's no doubt about it,
You did it!
I must have aged a year tonight.
At times I thought I'd die of fright.
Never was there a momentary lull.
HIGGINS
Shortly after we came in
I saw at once we'd eas'ly win;
And after that I found it deadly dull.
PICKERING
You should have heard the ooh's and ah's;
Ev'ry one wond'ring who she was.

HIGGINS

You'd think they'd never seen a lady before.

PICKERING

And when the Prince of Transylvania

Asked to meet her,

And gave his arm to lead her to the floor . . . !

I said to him: You did it!

You did it! You did it!

They thought she was ecstatic

And so damned aristocratic,

And they never knew

That you

Did it!

HIGGINS

Thank Heavens for Zoltan Karpathy. If it weren't for him I would have died of boredom. He was there, all right. And up to his old tricks.

MRS. PEARCE

Karpathy? That dreadful Hungarian? Was he there?

HIGGINS

Yes.

(The SERVANTS *gather around him, hanging on every word*)

(*In his best dramatic manner*)

That blackguard who uses the science of speech

More to blackmail and swindle than teach;

He made it the devilish business of his

"To find out who this Miss Doolittle is."

Ev'ry time we looked around

There he was, that hairy hound

From Budapest.

Never leaving us alone,

Never have I ever known

A ruder pest.

Fin'lly I decided it was foolish

Not to let him have his chance with her.

So I stepped aside and let him dance with her.

Oozing charm from ev'ry pore,

He oiled his way around the floor.

Ev'ry trick that he could play,

He used to strip her mask away.

And when at last the dance was done

He glowed as if he knew he'd won!

And with a voice too eager,

And a smile too broad,

He announced to the hostess

That she was a fraud!

MRS. PEARCE

No!

HIGGINS

Yavol!

Her English is too good, he said,

Which clearly indicates that she is foreign.

Whereas others are instructed in their native language

English people aren.

And although she may have studied with an expert

Di'lectician and grammarian,

I can tell that she was born Hungarian!

Not only Hungarian, but of royal blood, she is a princess!

(The SERVANTS *can no longer contain their admiration*)

SERVANTS

Congratulations, Professor Higgins,

For your glorious victory!

Congratulations, Professor Higgins!

You'll be mentioned in history!

FOOTMAN

This evening, sir, you did it!

You did it! You did it!

You said that you would do it!

And indeed you did.

This evening, sir, you did it!

You did it! You did it!

We know that we have said it,

But—you did it and the credit

For it all belongs to you!

THE REST OF THE SERVANTS

Congratulations,

Professor Higgins!

For your glorious

Victory!

Congratulations,

Professor Higgins!

Sing a hail and halleluia

Ev'ry bit of credit

For it all belongs to you!

There are more comedy songs and song scenes in *My Fair Lady* than in any other show. It is interesting to note that these find their inspiration in anger or in egocentricity. In either case the cause is neither happy nor "normal."

Eliza has a song (a song scene) that is a tirade directed at the lovesick Freddy who is never to be taken seriously. Although it is a reproof to Freddy, it is also a reaction to Higgins, who is much more important to Eliza. What Freddy sings at the outset, the trigger to the tirade, is so brief and innocuous that it could in no way be the real cause of Eliza's outburst.

In this song Eliza's words come tumbling out at the speed of light. It is no small tribute to Lerner's craft that they move easily and clearly despite their rapidity. The stanzas beginning with "Never do I ever want . . ." are particularly swift and vituperative. The reader should try speaking them aloud rapidly in order to fully appreciate how extraordinarily well they are written.

"SHOW ME"

FREDDIE

Speak and the world is full of singing,

And I'm winging

Higher than the birds.

Touch and my heart begins to crumble,

The heavens tumble,

Darling, and I'm . . .

ELIZA

Words!

Words! Words! I'm so sick of words!

I get words all day through;

First from him, now from you!

Is that all you blighters can do?

Don't talk of stars

Burning above;

If you're in love,

Show me!

Tell me no dreams

Filled with desire.

If you're on fire,

Show me!

Here we are together in the middle of the night!

Don't talk of spring! Just hold me tight!

Anyone who's ever been in love'll tell you that

This is no time for a chat!

Haven't your lips
Longed for my touch?
Don't say how much,
Show me! Show me!

Don't talk of love lasting through time.
Make me no undying vow.
Show me now!

Sing me no song!
Read me no rhyme!
Don't waste my time,
Show me!

Don't talk of June!
Don't talk of fall!
Don't talk at all!
Show me!

Never do I ever want to hear another word.
There isn't one I haven't heard.
Here we are together in what ought to be a dream;
Say one more word and I'll scream!

Haven't your arms
Hungered for mine?
Please don't "expl'ine,"
Show me! Show me!

Don't wait until wrinkles and lines
Pop out all over my brow,
Show me now!

Not long before the end of *My Fair Lady*, when Higgins has to face the fact that Eliza has left, he cannot begin to comprehend why. He is given two songs, not widely separated from each other in time. Both concern Eliza's having departed. The first is characterized by anger and bewilderment. The second, which is perhaps the best song in the show, is divided between helplessness and anger. The first, "Why Can't a Woman Be More Like a Man?," like the second is a musical scene, which is to say that it is intermixed with spoken dialogue, and the lyrics develop and continue the action of the drama. The first is also clearly related to Higgins's earlier song, "I'm an Ordinary Man." Higgins here demonstrates his inability to comprehend himself. The second is nearly identical; only the point of view is changed as Higgins now *believes* he is concerned with Eliza. To the contrary, he can only consider Eliza's behavior in the light of his own "reasonableness," or so it seems to him. Higgins, now in need, is like a lost child. A section of the song follows.

"WHY CAN'T A WOMAN BE MORE LIKE A MAN?"

HIGGINS
What in all of Heaven could have prompted her to go?
After such a triumph at the ball?
What could have depressed her?
What could have possessed her?
I cannot understand the wretch at all!
PICKERING
Higgins, I have an old school chum at the Home Office. Perhaps he can help. I'll call him. Whitehall seven, two, double four, please.

HIGGINS
Women are irrational, that's all there is to that!
Their heads are full of cotton, hay, and rags!
They're nothing but exasperating, irritating,
Vacillating, calculating, agitating,
Maddening, and infuriating hags!
PICKERING
(*Into the phone*) Brewster Budgin, please . . . Yes, I'll wait!
HIGGINS
Pickering, why can't a woman be more like a man?

The final song in *My Fair Lady*, "I've Grown Accustomed to Her Face," reconciles these two volatile characters and implies that Eliza, who has just reentered the house, will stay on with Higgins. This song, now at the very end of the play, shows Higgins again in two parts. In the first, which is lyrical, he is soft and tender. This is followed invariably by a fantasy, again the fantasy of everyone who feels hurt and vengeful, projecting an attempt to be hard and unforgiving. Always, however, it is the lyrical part that recurs and wins out.

This song scene bridges a scene change, starting in front of Higgins's house and then going inside where Eliza eventually enters. It was planned, contrary to Shaw, that the ending should appear to promise romance. Each member of the audience will have his own feeling about that, but in the musical the curtain descends as Eliza, smiling, starts toward Higgins, his slippers, which he has commanded, in her hands.

This song in its rough interludes also bears a strong relationship to Eliza's early vengeful song, "Just you wait, 'enry 'iggins." The same use of fantasized punishment is at work.

"I'VE GROWN ACCUSTOMED TO HER FACE"

But I'm so used to hear her say:
Good morning every day.
Her joys, her woes,
Her highs, her lows
Are second nature to me now;
Like breathing out and breathing in.
I'm very grateful she's a woman
And so easy to forget;
Rather like a habit
One can always break—and yet
I've grown accustomed to the trace
Of something in the air;
Accustomed to her face.

To sum up, Alan Jay Lerner has always displayed a keen sense of style. He has a fine perception about what does and what does not "sing." He hardly ever resorts to technical slickness in his work, but on choosing a subject for a song his dramatic inventiveness carries him great distances. He is keenly aware of his characters, expresses them precisely, and keeps them interesting throughout. As a final tribute, I would like to repeat that Lerner wrote more comedy songs for *My Fair Lady* than have ever before been contained in any single show. What enabled him to accomplish this so consummately was his recognition of the fact that characters, like Shaw's Higgins, vain and heartless though they appear to be, are essentially comic figures.

Sheldon Harnick
(b. 1924)

For the beholders or listeners to be moved or amused by a work of art, it is not essential that they comprehend any of the single elements that, when combined, achieve its totality. Michelangelo's *David* or Mozart's *Don Giovanni* can be enjoyed without any deep understanding on the observer's part. On the other hand, if the observer is capable of examining the object of art and possesses an appreciation of its components, he can be more deeply impressed with it because understanding, as opposed to mere enjoyment, will vastly increase his pleasure.

Music and lyrics do not actually exist except as listening experiences. If it is *necessary* to examine them visually in order to comprehend them, then in my opinion they have failed. They must have been structured for listening and what they have to say must be clearly accessible as an auditory experience. However, when slow visual examination becomes possible, in the case of the best music and lyrics, more substance than can reach the ear in swift passing is found.

Prominent among the younger lyricists is Sheldon Harnick (born 1924), who has learned and plied his craft over a period of about twenty-five years. What many of his admirers may not know or remember if they ever did know it, is that Harnick has also written much music. This is because a large part of his fame rests on his lyrics for *Fiorello!, The Body Beautiful, Tenderloin, She Loves Me, The Apple Tree, Fiddler on the Roof,* and *The Rothschilds;* all of which had music by Jerry Bock. However, in addition to these and Harnick's collaborations with other composers, he wrote his own music and lyrics to successful songs in *New Faces of 1952,* John Murray Anderson's *Almanac,* and *The Littlest Revue.* His intimate knowledge of music has obviously helped Harnick to create lyrics that are easily coupled with music and that sing comfortably.

Harnick, in line with growing contemporary sophistication, has frequently selected unexpected subject matter that often appears to have been used for the first time. Examples are numerous. In *The Shape of Things* he holds a comedy song together by emphasizing in each of its four stanzas a different geometric form: circle, square, rectangle, and triangle. In "Let's Evolve" he makes an oblique and bouncy love song out of evolution. He creates another humorous love song by embroidering larceny in "Me and Dorothea."

Like E. Y. Harburg and Harold Rome, Harnick has also dealt with socially significant material and treated it in its most palatable and acceptable manner through satire. Examples are to be found in "Unfair," "Politics and Poker," and "Little Tin Box," all from *Fiorello!*

Lyricists all too rarely write songs of or about love without mentioning that much overused word itself. Harnick has done it many times in "Ice Cream," "Dear Friend," and "Tonight at Eight," all from *She Loves Me,* "Worlds Apart" from *Man in the Moon* (Bil Baird's Marionette production), " 'til Tomorrow" from *Fiorello!,* and "Gloria" from *The Body Beautiful.*

He has also been confronted by the problem of suggesting a kind of Jewish ethnic feeling in the songs for *Fiddler on the Roof* and *The Rothschilds,* which he resolved coloristically and subtly, even universally, while eschewing the more obvious and vulgar methods usually employed by facile and tasteless writers. I will attempt to point out some of his specific methods later in this section.

Along with other distinguished lyricists Sheldon Harnick works to find fresh images and rhymes. He is always himself and has not fallen prey to period evocation through the use of obsolete words or stilted expressions associated with our false ideas of earlier times. In lyrics for the Adam and Eve portions of *The Apple Tree*, the language and images are taken from Harnick's world of the twentieth century, and do not fall into the cheap trap of pseudobiblical expressions. In *Fiddler on the Roof* the words in no way retrogress to a turn-of-the-century style, nor do those of *Tenderloin* or *She Loves Me*.

Harnick's many comedy songs quite properly evolve out of characters in situations and do not stoop to employment of ephemeral jokes that would limit their life-span. They are also truly funny.

One more observation. There is an age-old controversy regarding the effects of creative artists' personalities on their work. Wagner and Beethoven were hardly lovable human beings. Nor were they always honest and scrupulous. Many others, like Lewis Carroll, were noted for their personal idiosyncrasies, foibles, and distinctly unpleasant peculiarities. Sometimes, fortunately, their work emerged showing little if any of the disagreeableness one might have expected it to reflect. Occasionally a creative artist possesses a character and nature that is truly guileless and ingenuous. Sheldon Harnick is one of these. His simple honesty and sweetness are to be discerned everywhere in his work. Never is he vituperative. Though he is invariably gentle, he is never dull or innocuous in his lyrics. The humor they contain is not achieved at the expense of others. The pity and sadness and sweetness are never cloying. Harnick's craft is impeccable, his expression is touching and universal.

In selecting entire lyrics for presentation here, I have tried to choose lesser known songs as well as the more, distinguished ones. First, "The Boston Beguine" from Leonard Sillman's *New Faces of 1952*. Harnick wrote both words and music. It was sung hilariously by a then new performer, Alice Ghostley. I recall her costume as gauche and ultraconservative, making her appear middle-aged, awkward, and somewhat pathetic. The merits of the lyric and its humor are obvious; however, I should like to call attention to the second lines of the second, third, and fifth stanzas. Each consistently qualifies and explains its preceding line. Each suggests that the listener is stupid or at least uninformed or more probably that the singer is excessively naïve and the first two stanzas attempt to be exotic and are outrageously obtuse. The song is funny because the very "square" singer is frustrated, trying to create or recall a romance, though she is painfully remote from things as they actually are.

"THE BOSTON BEGUINE"

Tropical nights . .
Orchids in bloom . .
Sultry perfume . .
Intrigues and dangers
With passionate strangers
I've seen it all . .
As I recall . .

I met him in Boston
In the native quarter
He was from Harvard
Just across the border
It was a magical night
With romance everywhere
There was something in the air
There always is . . in Boston.

We went to the Casbah
That's an Irish bar there
The underground hide-out
Of the D.A.R. there.
Something inside of me said
'Watch your heart, mad'moiselle,
And it might be just as well
To watch your purse . . in Boston.'

We danced in a trance
And I dreamed of romance
Till the strings of my heart
Seemed to be knotted
And even the palms seemed to be potted.
The Boston Beguine
Was casting its spell
And I was drunk with love . .
And cheap Muscatel.

We walked to the Common
That's a pretty park there
As I remember
It was pretty dark there
In this exotic locale
By a silver lagoon
Underneath a voodoo moon . .
We fell asleep . . in Boston.

That was the story of my one romance there
Our dream of adventure didn't stand a chance there
How could we hope to enjoy all the pleasures ahead
When the books we should have read
Were all suppressed . . in Boston?
Exotic Boston . . land of the free . . home of the brave . .
Home of the Red Sox . . home of the bean . .
And home . . of the Boston Beguine!

"Merry Little Minuet" from John Murray Anderson's *Almanac* (1953) also has lyrics and music by Harnick. The catastrophic refrain is introduced ironically by the past two lines of the verse, which serves to put the listener off guard by not delivering what is promised. This lyric is an example of Harnick's social satire.

"MERRY LITTLE MINUET"

There are days in my life
When everything is dreary
I grow pessimistic
Sad and world weary.
But when I am tearful and fearfully upset,
I always sing this merry little minuet.

They're rioting in Africa.
They're starving in Spain.
There's hurricanes in Florida,
And Texas needs rain.

The whole world is festering
With unhappy souls.
The French hate the Germans
The Germans hate the Poles.
Italians hate Yugoslavs

South Africans hate the Dutch
And I don't like anybody very much.

In far away Siberia
They freeze by the score.
An avalanche in Switzerland
Just got fifteen more.

But we can be tranquil
And thankful and proud
For man's been endowed
With a mushroom shaped cloud.
And we know for certain
That some lovely day
Someone will set the spark off
And we will all be blown away.

They're rioting in Africa.
There's strife in Iran.
What nature doesn't do to us.
Will be done by our fellow man.

Another song with both words and music by Harnick is "The Shape of Things" from *The Littlest Revue* (1956). This is the song referred to earlier in which each of the four stanzas takes its topic line from a different geometric figure. This device sustains unity. The song is in the style of a folk ballad. The subject is love that comes to an unfortunate end. The spirit is comic, comedy that is a distillation of unhappiness and tragedy and usually is personal.

"THE SHAPE OF THINGS"

Completely round is the perfect pearl
The oyster manufactures.
Completely round is the steering wheel
That leads to compound fractures.
Completely round is the golden fruit
That hangs in the orange tree.
Yes, the circle shape is quite renowned,
And sad to say, it can be found
In the dirty low-down runaround
My true love gave to me,
Yes, my true love gave to me.

Completely square is the velvet box
He said my ring would be in.
Completely square is the envelope
He wrote farewell to me in.
Completely square is the handkerchief
I flourish constantly,
As it dries my eyes of the tears I've shed,
And blows my nose 'til it turns bright red,
For a perfect square is my true love's head
He will not marry me,
No, he will not marry me.

Rectangular is the hotel door
My true love tried to sneak through.
Rectangular is the transom
Over which I had to peek through.
Rectangular is the hotel room
I entered angrily.
Now, rectangular is the wooden box
Where lies my love 'neath the grazing flocks,

They said he died of the chicken pox,
In part I must agree;
One chick too many had he.

Triangular is the piece of pie
I eat to ease my sorrow.
Triangular is the hatchet blade
I plan to hide tomorrow.
Triangular the relationship
That now has ceased to be.
And the self-same shape is a garment thin,
That fastens on with a safety pin
To a prize I had no wish to win;
It's a lasting memory
That my true love gave to me.

A little-known and amusing song from *Smiling the Boy Fell Dead* (1961) had music by David Baker and was called "Environment—Heredity." Here the concept is original. It involves the scion of an upright family who, rather cheerfully, has turned out to be the black sheep. Again, the humor is derived from the outrageous attitude and the proposition that one plus one does not here equal two.

I would point out the form Harnick indulges in (after the style of Ira Gershwin) in creating several variants that necessarily corrupt the words to create the rhymes: "malfeasant" matching " 'dezent' " (decent) and "criminal" matching " 'hyminal.' "

"ENVIRONMENT—HEREDITY"

I've heard theories that say
It depends on how you're brung up
Whether later on in life
You'll be idolized or strung up
In other words, if a man is a cad
You can blame his being bad
On environment.

My father grew up helter skelter
His childhood was ragged and rough
Of clothing and vittles and shelter
He never had nearly enough

He might have grown up a malfeasant
A scoundrel who gambled and drank
But he grew up honest and 'dezent'
Although his environment stank

He married my virtuous mother
A lady as noble as he;
In time she gave birth to none other
Than good old unscrupulous me

They raised me with love and devotion
Environment simply divine
Between them they haven't a notion
How I could grow up such a swine

Environment, environment
The tree will grow as the twig is bent
A theory, I've heard of it
But I don't believe a word of it.

Now, I've heard theories that say
In regard to vice or virtue

It's heredity alone
That will either help or hurt you
In other words, if a man is a cad
You can blame his being bad
On heredity.

My father's so meek that it's criminal
Incredibly gentle and mild
To hear him hum hymns from a 'hyminal'
You'd never believe I'm his child

No matter how far you may go back
Our family tree does us proud
I can't very well be a throwback
There isn't a bum in the crowd.

Great grandpa was bashful and sober
Great grandma was pure as a shrine
Thank God for one crazy October
Or that was the end of the line

With virtues galore to inherit
It took perseverance and spunk
To keep from inheriting merit
And be such a flourishing skunk

Environment, heredity
A man can be what he wants to be
Be firm, be calm, be sensible
And you, too,
Can be
Reprehensible.

"Me and Dorothea," also from *Smiling the Boy Fell Dead,* could be classified as a kind of romantic song with a major difference: the singer is a thief and he voices his plans for his larcenous activities to his confederate Dorothea. The singing character is a rogue, but it must be pointed out again that it is within this kind of unpleasant situation that comedy can be produced. Many of the lines, even singly, are outrageously funny. There is also playful humor in the well-structured rhymes.

"ME AND DOROTHEA"

There's business
And there's pleasure
Pursuit of love
Pursuit of treasure
Mixing them is sheer stupidity
Yet here am I
About to try
Combining cupid and cupidity

Oh, me and Dorothea
What a tip top team we'll be
Why, I'd almost return every stolen bond
For such a delicious adorable blonde
As she is.

Oh, me and Dorothea
A delightful thought occurs
I meditate merrily more and more
On how many figures I've juggled before
But none like hers.

I ask myself when I look at us
Can two such people combine
Would we be pablum and wine
For here am I
No more a youth
And she's so young
I want the truth
Is she worthy of a passion such as mine?

I dote on Dorothea
What a lucky girl is she
There's a lot in store for
Dorothea and me.

What a precious, priceless partner
She will be to me in time
Very soon I will be start'ner
On a life of crime
How sublime!
Her curriculum I've planned
At first petty larceny,
Nothing grand.

Her course of study
Is just beginning
She'll need some practice
At simple sinning

We'll go to London
The home of Dickens
The fog is perfect
For easy pickin's

Then on to Paris
But we're not staying
I want to teach her the finesse
Of picking up a stylish dress
Without the troublesome necess-
Ity of paying.

Before we're finished
And headed homeward
Italian trinkets
Will lure us Romeward
For relaxation she'll steal an apple
While I remove the ceiling
From the Sistine Chapel.

We'll honeymoon
At the best hotels
Her father's money can buy
Those blissful hours will fly
We'll steal a kiss
And then a towel
Another kiss
Another towel
And we'll pilfer from each other
On the sly!

I'm hers for just the taking
What a lucky girl is she
There's a lot in store for
Dorothea and—

I'll teach her everything!
Dorothea and—
We'll be a millionaire!
Dorothea and me!

The simple, brief, amusing "Gloria" from *The Body Beautiful* (1958), music by Jerry Bock, tells its own little tale. However, within these fourteen lines it is possible to overlook such subtle treasure troves as: "the only girl I love/Named Gloria" and "You're a cup of tea with cream/Or lemon in."

These suggest that the singer is not so positively in love with Gloria.

"GLORIA"

Gloria, darlin' Gloria
You're the only girl I love
Named Gloria
First I'll marry you
Then I'll carry you
To a sweet little suite
In the Waldorf Astoria

Gloria, you're so feminine
You're a cup of tea with cream
Or lemon in
Darlin' Gloria, dainty Gloria,
Dontcha know that I wanna see
More, more and moria
Gloria, you're my girl.

The score (music and lyrics) of *Fiorello!* (1959) constituted Harnick and Bock's first wholly successful triumph. The songs provide abundant contrasts to one another. Many of them are amusing, and many others expressive of romantic feeling. "Marie's Law" is a duet sung in legal terms.

"MARIE'S LAW"

MARIE
My law shall state
To whom it may concern
MORRIS
Your law shall state
To whom it may concern
MARIE
When a lady loves a gentleman
He must love her in return
MORRIS
Loves a gentleman he must love her in re—
MARIE
In re . . my law
Ad hoc . . to wit, to woo
MORRIS
In re . . your law
Ad hoc . . to wit, to woo
MARIE
When a lady feels affectionate
Then the man must follow through
MORRIS
Feels affectionate then the man must follow—
MARIE
Here's another law we women'll
Do our best to legislate
It shall be completely criminal

For a man to break a date
Each offender shall be rapidly
Thrown in jail where he belongs
Thus we'll right our bill of wrongs!

My law is what
The world is waiting for
MORRIS
Your law is what
The world is waiting for
MARIE
Every unrequited lover will be grateful when it
Meets the full approval of the House and Senate
Such enthusiasm as you never saw
Will greet my lovely law.

In re . . my law
It should be understood
MORRIS
In re . . your law
It should be understood
MARIE
With the help of women everywhere
We shall outlaw bach'lorhood
MORRIS
Women everywhere you shall outlaw bach'lorhood
MARIE
What's more . . in lieu
MORRIS
Marie, before you're through
I've got some things
I'd like to say, if you
Have got to outlaw anything
You should outlaw in-laws, too.
MARIE
I'm concerned with what the man must do.
Every girl shall have a honeymoon
Which shall last at least a year
During which aforesaid honeymoon
Every care shall disappear
Ipso facto, let the government
Get the bride and groom alone
After that they're on their own.

Whereas
MORRIS
Whereat
MARIE
Hereby
MORRIS
Hereof
MARIE
Therein
MORRIS
They're out and furthermore
MARIE
By law
MORRIS
Your law
MARIE
Is what
MORRIS
Is what

MARIE
The world
MORRIS
The world is waiting for
MARIE
We are going to rid the country
Of contempt of courtship
MORRIS
Legally replacing it
With davenportship
BOTH
Such enthusiasm as you never saw
Will greet (my/your) lovely law.

"Politics and Poker," also from *Fiorello!*, is a remarkable comedy song, one that is complex for the writer as well as the six performers. A terse dialogue section occurs several times. Each line graphically portrays quite realistically verbal exchanges during a poker game. Each section also contains longer and more serious lines involved with choosing a political candidate. A refrain occurring four times combines the two disparate topics.

"POLITICS AND POKER"

DEALER King bets
2 Cost you five. Tony, up to you.
3 I'm in
4 So am I
5 Likewise
DEALER Me too.
BEN Gentlemen, here we are and one thing is clear
We gotta pick a candidate for Congress this year.
DEALER Big ace
2 Ace bets
3 You'll pay—through the nose
4 I'm in.
5 So am I.
DEALER Likewise.
2 Here goes.
DEALER *(Spoken)*
Possible straight . . Possible flush . . Nothing . . .
BEN Gentlemen, how about some names we can use?
Some qualified Republican who's willing to lose?
2 How's about we should make Jack Riley the guy?
3 Which Riley are you thinkin' of ? Jack B., or Jack Y.?
BEN I say neither one.
I never even met 'em.
4 I say,
When you got a pair of Jacks,
Bet 'em!
ALL
Politics and poker
Politics and poker
Shuffle up the cards
And find the joker.
Neither game's for children,
Either game is rough.
Decisions, decisions, like:
Who to pick,
How to play,
What to bet,

When to call a bluff.
BEN *(Spoken)*
All right, fellas, politics or poker? Which is more important?
DEALER Pair o' treys
2 Bet 'em
3 Little treys,
Good as gold.
4 I'll stay.
5 Raise you five.
DEALER I'll call.
2 I fold.
3 *(Spoken)*
Raise you back.
4 *(Spoken)*
I think you're bluffing.
3 Put your money where your mouth is.
BEN Gentlemen, knock it off and let's get this done.
KIBITZER Try Michael Panyaschenkovitch, I'm certain he'd run.
BEN Mike is out. I'm afraid he just wouldn't sell.
Nobody likes a candidate whose name they can't spell.
DEALER How about Dave Zimmerman?
BEN Davie's too bright.
2 What about Walt Gustafson?
BEN Walt died last night.
3 How about Frank Monohan?
4 What about George Gale?
BEN Frank ain't a citizen
And George is in jail.
5 We could run Al Wallenstein.
BEN He's only twenty three.
DEALER How about Ed Peterson?
2 You idiot, that's me!
ALL
Politics and Poker
Politics and Poker
Playing for a pot
That's mediocre.
Politics and Poker,
Running neck and neck.
If politics seems more predictable
That's because usually you can stack the deck!

REPRISE ALL
Politics and Poker
Politics and Poker
Makes the average guy
A heavy smoker
Bless the nominee
And give him our regards
And watch while he learns that in
Poker and Politics
Brother, you gotta have
That slippery, haphazardous commodity
You gotta have the cards!

In "Little Tin Box," from *Fiorello!*, three witnesses are questioned about the size of their bank accounts and expenditures in view of their small salaries. Each is questioned and each responds in a chorus. It's a comedy song with uncomfortable overtones due to the applicability of the lyrics today, nearly thirty years after La Guardia.

"LITTLE TIN BOX"

DEL
Mr. 'X,' may we ask you a question?
It's amazing is it not
That the city pays you slightly less
Than fifty bucks a week
Yet youve purchased a private yacht!
BEN
I am positive Your Honor must be joking
Any working man can do what I have done
For a month or two I simply gave up smoking
And I put my extra pennies one by one
Into
A little tin box
A little tin box
That a little tin key unlocks
There is nothing unorthodox
About a little tin box
MEN
About a little tin box
About a little tin box
In a little tin box
A little tin box
That a little tin key unlocks
BEN
There is honor and purity
ALL
Lots of security
In a little tin box.
DAVID (Spoken)
Next witness . . .
MIKE
Mr. 'Y,' we've been told you don't feel well
And we know you've lost your voice
But we wondered how you managed on the salary you make
To acquire a new Rolls Royce.
BEN
You're implying I'm a crook and I say no sir!
There is nothing in my past I care to hide
I've been taking empty bottles to the grocer
And each nickel that I got was put aside
MEN
That he got was put aside
BEN
Into
A little tin box
A little tin box
That a little tin key unlocks
There is nothing unorthodox
About a little tin box
MEN
About a little tin box
About a little tin box
MEN
In a little tin box
A little tin box
There's a cushion for life's rude shocks
BEN
There is faith hope and charity
ALL
Hard-won prosperity
In a little tin box.

DAVID (Spoken)
Next witness . . take the stand . .
JULIAN
Mr. 'Z,' you're a junior official
And your income's rather low
Yet you've kept a dozen women
In the very best hotels
Would you kindly explain how so?
BEN
I can see Your Honor doesn't pull his punches
And it looks a trifle fishy I'll admit
But for one whole week I went without my lunches
And it mounted up, Your Honor, bit by bit
MEN
Up Your Honor bit by bit.
It's just
A little tin box
A little tin box
That a little tin key unlocks
There is nothing unorthodox
About a little tin box
About a little tin box
In
A little tin box
A little tin box
All a-glitter with blue chip stocks
BEN
There is something delectable
ALL
Almost respectable
In a little tin box
In a little tin box!

"Artificial Flowers" is, on the surface, a sentimental ballad in the turn-of-the-century style—written for *Tenderloin*. Harnick achieves his period-sense by the combining of words and phrases that have, for the most part, been long ago abandoned. These include: "final reward," "but nine years of age," "ladies of fashion," "dear little fingers," "still clutching," "amidst all the blossoms," "gardens and bowers."

He creates two "jokes" that tip off the listener to the time intention of the lyric. Otherwise, this lyric might seem to be seriously sentimental. In describing poor Annie's making artificial flowers, one stanza concludes: " 'Til cutting and folding, her health slipped away/And wiring and waxing, she waned." A second stanza ending intrudes: "Instead of a halo she'll wear round her head/A garland of genuine flowers." This ballad perpetuates the old "Moth and the Flame" style with one important difference: the former today depends on the performer's "camp" to make it amusing whereas in "Artificial Flowers" the humor is written in and requires only a simple noninterpretive performance.

"ARTIFICIAL FLOWERS"

Alone in the world was poor little Ann,
As sweet a young child as you'd find.
Her parents had gone to their final reward
Leaving their darling behind.
This poor little child was but nine years of age
When Mother and Dad went away.
But bravely she worked at the one thing she knew
To earn her few pennies each day.

She made
Artificial flowers,
Artificial flowers,
Flowers for ladies of fashion to wear,
Artificial flowers,
Artificial flowers,
Fashioned from Annie's despair.

With paper and shears, with wire and wax,
She fashioned each tulip and mum.
As snow drifted in to her tenement room,
Her dear little fingers grew numb.
With paper and shears, with wire and wax,
She labored and never complained.
'Til cutting and folding, her health slipped away,
And wiring and waxing, she waned.

Making
Artificial flowers, etc.

They found little Ann, all covered with ice,
Still clutching her poor frozen shears,
Amidst all the blossoms she fashioned by hand
And watered with all her young tears.
There must be a heav'n where Annie can play
In heavenly gardens and bowers.
Instead of a halo she'll wear round her head
A garland of genuine flowers.

No more
Artificial flowers,
Artificial flowers,
Flowers for ladies of fashion to wear,
Artificial flowers,
Artificial flowers,
Fashioned from Annie's despair.

From *She Loves Me,* "Will He Like Me" is a worry love ballad that every young person can empathize with. It requires no introduction.

"WILL HE LIKE ME"

Will he like me when we meet?
Will the shy and quiet girl he's going to see
Be the girl that he's imagined me to be?
Will he like me?

Will he like the girl he sees?
If he doesn't, will he know enough to know
That there's more to me than I may always show?
Will he like me?

Will he know that there's a world of love
Waiting to warm him?
How I'm hoping that his eyes and ears
Won't misinform him!

Will he like me .. who can say?
How I wish that we could meet another day.
It's absurd for me to worry so this way.
I'll try not to.
Will he like me?
He's just got to!

When I am in my room alone,
And I write,
Thoughts come easily.
Words come fluently then.
That's how it is when I'm alone.
But tonight
There's no hiding behind my paper and pen.

Will he know that there's a world of love
Waiting to warm him?
How I'm hoping that his eyes and ears
Won't misinform him.

Will he like me .. I don't know.
All I know is that I'm tempted not to go.
It's insanity for me to worry so.
I'll try not to.
Will he like me?
He's just got to.
Will he like me?
Will he like me?

Also from *She Loves Me,* "Ice-Cream" is a romantic monologue that includes most unromantic descriptions. It is breathless, full of desire, anxiety, and finally a sense of fulfillment. I find this lyric unique.

"ICE-CREAM"

AMALIA *(Spoken)*
Dear Friend:
(Sung)
I am so sorry about last night.
It was a nightmare in every way,
But together, you and I
Will laugh at last night some day . . .

Ice-cream,
He brought me ice-cream,
Vanilla ice-cream,
Imagine that!

Ice-cream,
And for the first time,
We were together
Without a spat.

Friendly,
He was so friendly.
That isn't like him
I'm simply stunned.

Will wonders never cease?
Will wonders never cease?
It's been a most peculiar day.
Will wonders never cease?
Will wonders never cease?
(Spoken)
Where was I? Oh ..
(Sung—rapidly as possible)
I am so sorry about last night it was a nightmare in every way
But together you and I will laugh at last night some day ..
(Tempo I)
I sat there waiting in that cafe
And never guessing that you were fat—

That you were near—
You were outside looking bald—
(*Spoken*)
Oh, my!
Dear Friend:
(*Sung*)
I am so sorry about last night . . .

Last night
I was so nasty
Well, he deserved it!
But even so . .
That George
Is not like this George.
This is a new George
That I don't know!

Somehow
It all reminds me
Of Dr. Jekyll
And Mr. Hyde.

For right before my eyes
A man that I despise
Has turned into a man I like.

It's almost like a dream,
And strange as it may seem,
He came to offer me
Vanilla ice-cream!

Next I will include a song from *Fiddler on the Roof,* written after the show opened (using melodies from "Tradition"), and meant to function as a "title song." It was recorded a few times. To me this lyric has the quality of a poem in *A Child's Garden of Verses* by Robert Louis Stevenson. Its charm is to be found in its simple naïveté.

"FIDDLER ON THE ROOF"

Away above my head,
I see the strangest sight,
A fiddler on the roof
Who's up there day and night.

He fiddles when it rains,
He fiddles when it snows.
I've never seen him rest,
Yet on and on he goes.

What does it mean, this fiddler on the roof,
Who fiddles every night and fiddles every noon?
Why should he pick so curious a place
To play his little fiddler's tune?

An unexpected breeze
Could blow him to the ground.
Yet after every storm
I see he's still around.

Whatever each day brings,
This odd, outlandish man,
He plays his simple tune
As sweetly as he can.

What does it mean, this fiddler on the roof,
Who fiddles every night and fiddles every noon?
Why should he pick so curious a place
To play his little fiddler's tune?

A fiddler on the roof,
A most unlikely sight.
It might not mean a thing,
But then again it might.

What we think of as Jewish inflections are present here and there in the lyrics of *Fiddler.* There are bona fide Hebrew words like "L'Chaim," or "To Life," which is translated within the lyric, but no vulgarisms, and no broad tasteless "delicatessen" jokes are ever employed. These inflections include: "Like a Solomon the wise" (the inclusion of "a"); "And maybe have a seat by the Eastern wall" ("maybe"—the uncertainty); "May you come to be/In Yisroel a shining name." Aside from the inclusion of "Yisroel" (Israel), the transposition of the phrase that more simply says "May your name shine in Israel" *sounds* like a translation. Also, the tentative quality of "may you come to be" implies the insecurity of superstition: if you were to be *too* certain about it, you might put a hex on it—somewhat like carrying an umbrella in the hope of discouraging rain.

"When did she get to be a beauty?/When did he grow to be so tall?" "Get to be" and "grow to be" for "become," though having a prosodic function, are also associated at least in my own mind with the awkwardness of an expression in an adopted language, that of Jew, German, or Slav speaking English. The same observation applies to:

With our daughters getting married
And this trouble in the town,
You're upset, you're worn out,
Go inside, go lie down.
Maybe it's indigestion.

"If I Were a Rich Man" is by now very well known, a sad comedy song in which the singing character, Tevye, displays his pathetic naïveté, especially in his description of his three staircases.

"IF I WERE A RICH MAN"

If I were a rich man
Daidle deedle daidle
Digguh digguh deedle daidle dum,
All day long I'd biddy biddy bum,
If I were a wealthy man.

Wouldn't have to work hard,
Daidle deedle daidle
Digguh digguh deedle daidle dum,
If I were a biddy biddy rich
Digguh digguh deedle daidle man.

I'd build a big, tall house with rooms by the dozen
Right in the middle of the town,
A fine tin roof and real wooden floors below.
There would be one long staircase just going up,
And one even longer coming down,
And one more leading nowhere just for show.

I'd fill my yard with chicks and turkeys and geese
And ducks for the town to see and hear,
Squawking just as noisily as they can.
And each loud quack and cluck and gobble and honk

Will land like a trumpet on the ear,
As if to say, here lives a wealthy man.
(Sighs)

If I were a rich man,
Daidle deedle daidle
Digguh digguh deedle daidle dum,
All day long I'd biddy biddy bum,
If I were a wealthy man.

Wouldn't have to work hard,
Daidle deedle daidle
Digguh digguh deedle daidle dum,
If I were a biddy biddy rich
Digguh digguh deedle daidle man.

I see my wife, my Golde, looking like a rich man's wife,
With a proper double chin,
Supervising meals to her heart's delight.
I see her putting on airs and strutting like a peacock,
Oi! what a happy mood she's in,
Screaming at the servants day and night.

The most important men in town
Will come to fawn on me.
They will ask me to advise them
Like a Solomon the Wise,
"If you please, Reb Tevye. Pardon me, Reb Tevye,"
Posing problems that would cross a rabbi's eyes.
(HE chants.)
Boi-boi-boi-boi-boi-boi-boi-boi . .

And it won't make one bit of diff'rence
If I answer right or wrong.
When you're rich they think you really know!

If I were rich
I'd have the time that I lack
To sit in the synagogue and pray,
And maybe have a seat by the eastern wall,
And I'd discuss the Holy Books
With the learned men
Seven hours every day.
That would be the sweetest thing of all.
(Sighs)

If I were a rich man,
Daidle deedle daidle
Digguh digguh deedle daidle dum,
All day long I'd biddy biddy bum,
If I were a wealthy man.

Wouldn't have to work hard,
Daidle deedle daidle
Digguh digguh deedle daidle dum,
Lord, who made the lion and the lamb,
You decreed I should be what I am,
Would it spoil
Some vast eternal plan—
If I were a wealthy man?

One of the three grooms-to-be, Motel, a poor tailor, is aglow with the idea of his being loved and he equates this marvel with some of God's greatest miracles.

"MIRACLE OF MIRACLES"

Wonder of wonders, miracle of miracles,
God took a Daniel once again,
Stood by his side, and, miracle of miracles,
Walked him through the lion's den.

Wonder of wonders, miracle of miracles,
I was afraid that God would frown.
But, like He did so long ago in Jericho,
God just made a wall fall down.

When Moses softened Pharaoh's heart,
That was a miracle.
When God made the waters of the Red Sea part,
That was a miracle, too.

But of all God's miracles large and small,
The most miraculous one of all
Is that out of a worthless lump of clay
God has made a man today.

Wonder of wonders, miracle of miracles,
God took a tailor by the hand,
Turned him around, and, miracle of miracles,
Led him to the Promised Land.

When David slew Goliath, yes!
That was a miracle.
When God gave us manna in the wilderness,
That was a miracle, too.

But of all God's miracles, large and small,
The most miraculous one of all
Is the one I thought could never be—
God has given you to me.

"Do You Love Me?" also from *Fiddler on the Roof,* is a dialogue between the hero, Tevye, and his wife of twenty-five years, Golde. After their quarter-of-a-century marriage, Tevye wants an answer to his now burning question "Do you love me?" His matter-of-fact wife is somewhat befuddled and embarrassed. The awkwardness of the situation is what makes the song most touching.

"DO YOU LOVE ME?"

TEVYE
Do you love me?
GOLDE
Do I what?
TEVYE
Do you love me?
GOLDE
Do I love you?
With our daughters getting married
And this trouble in the town,
You're upset, you're worn out,
Go inside, go lie down.
Maybe it's indigestion.
TEVYE
Golde, I'm asking you a question—
Do you love me?
GOLDE
You're a fool.

TEVYE
I know—
But do you love me?
GOLDE
Do I love you?
For twenty-five years I've washed your clothes,
Cooked your meals, cleaned your house,
Given you children, milked the cow.
After twenty-five years, why talk about
Love right now?
TEVYE
Golde, the first time I met you
Was on our wedding day.
I was scared.
GOLDE
I was shy.
TEVYE
I was nervous.
GOLDE
So was I.
TEVYE
But my father and my mother
Said we'd learn to love each other.
And now I'm asking, Golde,
Do you love me?
GOLDE
I'm your wife.
TEVYE
I know—
But do you love me?
GOLDE
Do I love him?
For twenty-five years I've lived with him,
Fought with him, starved with him.
Twenty-five years my bed is his.
If that's not love, what is?
TEVYE
Then you love me?
GOLDE
I suppose I do.
TEVYE
And I suppose I love you, too.
BOTH
It doesn't change a thing,
But even so,
After twenty-five years,
It's nice to know.

In "Forbidden Fruit," from *The Apple Tree*, the Snake sings to Eve in the Garden of Eden. He is, of course, persuading Eve to eat the apple. In one sense this song functions in somewhat the same way as "There's a Boat That's Leaving Soon for New York" in *Porgy and Bess*. In the latter song the lascivious Sporting Life is persuading Bess not unlike the way the Snake here is enticing Eve to do what is forbidden.

"FORBIDDEN FRUIT"

SNAKE
Listen, closely. Let me fill you in
About the rich, ripe, round, red,
Rosy apples they call forbidden fruit.

What I'm about to say is
Confidential so promise you'll be mute
Because if every creature in the garden knows
They'll come 'round like hungry buffalos
And in no time there'll be none of those
Precious apples left for you and me.

Now, in the average apple
You're accustomed to skin, seeds, flesh and core.
But you will find that these are
Special apples that give you something more.
Why, every seed contains some information
You need to speed your education
The seeds indeed of all creation
Are here
Why be foolish, my dear?
Come with me
To that tree.

With every sweet and juicy
Luscious bite of this *not* forbidden fruit
You'll see your mind expand and
Your perceptions grow more and more acute
And you can teach him plumbing and philosophy
New techniques for glazing pottery
Wood-craft, first-aid, home economy!
Madam, Adam will be overjoyed!

When he becomes aware of
Your attainments, he'll beam with loving pride.
And he will say, "O, Eve, you're
Indispensable! Please, don't leave my side!"
And with your nifty, new-found education
He'll relish every conversation
Why you'll be Adam's inspiration
This way.
Just an apple a day!
Wait and see
Come with me
To that tree!
Now!

"Go to Sleep, Whatever You Are," also from *The Apple Tree*, is sung by Eve to her newborn child, a "thing" that puzzles her. Harnick's imagination here is at work on a high plane in conceiving a mother's reaction to her firstborn child, an enigma, but one that mysteriously and seriocomically engenders a feeling of warmth. It is a simple song filled with fresh, touching, maternal mystery.

"GO TO SLEEP, WHATEVER YOU ARE"

EVE
Go to sleep,
Whatever you are.
Lay your head
On my breast.

Close your eyes
And open your paws
You need plenty
Of rest.

Doesn't faze me
If you grow up to be

Pony or poodle
Or sheep.

You're my own,
Whatever you are,
Sleep . . . sleep . . .
Sleep . . .

"What Makes Me Love Him," from *The Apple Tree*, offers a parallel to the Kern-Wodehouse "Bill." I point this out not to fault it but to remind us of what we have all known for some time, namely, that there is nothing basically new. What matters is that, although the basic idea has been used before, it is here again renewed, achieving its own success on its own terms. It illustrates once again the fact that it is not the idea that matters as much as what is done with it. Shakespeare's plots did not originate with the Bard but were well known and exploited long before his time. The plots of the Greek tragedies were all well known when they were undertaken again and immortalized by Aeschylus, Sophocles, and Euripides. Only writers unfamiliar with the past, unfamiliar with history, can presume that what they create is new. Such a notion is foolhardy, self-deluding, and catastrophic.

"WHAT MAKES ME LOVE HIM"

EVE
What makes me love him?
It's not his singing
I've heard his singing.
It sours the milk.
And yet it's gotten to the point
Where I prefer that kind of milk.

What makes me love him?
It's not his learning.
He's learned so slowly
His whole life long.
And tho' he really knows a multitude of things
They're mostly wrong.

He is a good man
But I would love him
If he abused me
Or used me ill

And tho' he's handsome
I know inside me
Were he a plain man
I'd love him still.

What makes me love him?
It's quite beyond me!
It must be something
I can't define
Unless, it's merely that he's masculine
And that he's mine.

I should like to close this section with an especially lovely lyric from *Fiddler on the Roof,* "Far from the Home I Love." The song is sung by Hodel to her father Tevye at a deserted railway station while awaiting the train that will take her to Siberia. There she will marry her student friend Perchik. He has been deported to Siberia because of his political activity.

The following lyric ends on what is called variously a "hook," or "turnaround." These expressions denote an unexpected twist in meaning that, when employed successfully, gives the song a sudden fresh lift. Here Harnick has been able to accomplish this lift in an ingenious way, namely by reordering the words in the title line from "Far from the Home I Love" to "There with My Love, I'm Home."

The scene, situation, and song are all unique. Hodel is leaving her father and her home and will surely never return again. Father and daughter are parting forever. Though there is no joy in this parting, there is, with the last line, an additional and forward-looking feeling of satisfaction and anticipation. She will make a new home with her love, one now understandably more important to her than the one she is abandoning.

"FAR FROM THE HOME I LOVE"

How can I hope to make you understand
Why I do what I do,
Why I must travel to a distant land
Far from the home I love?

Once I was happily content to be
As I was, where I was,
Close to the people who are close to me
Here in the home I love.

Who could see that a man would come
Who would change the shape of my dreams?
Helpless, now, I stand with him
Watching older dreams grow dim.

Oh, what a melancholy choice this is,
Wanting home, wanting him,
Closing my heart to every hope but his,
Leaving the home I love.

There where my heart has settled long ago
I must go, I must go.
Who could imagine I'd be wand'ring so
Far from the home I love?
Yet, there with my love, I'm home.

Sheldon Harnick's development and achievements are distinguished and special. He is one of those who stand at the crossroads, at a peak position in the now passing but once new musical theatre. He celebrates an ending, a high and joyous one, and hopefully, simultaneously, he is one of those who will go ahead in whatever new direction he can help to discover. It is at once his privilege and his responsibility.

Tom Jones
(b. 1928)

The career of Tom Jones (librettist and lyricist) has been tied up exclusively with that of his fellow Texan Harvey Schmidt, composer. Although they had success with *110 in the Shade* (1963), the two-character *I Do! I Do!* (1966), starring Mary Martin and Robert Preston, and *Celebration* (1969), their most distinguished achievement was with their very first show, *The Fantasticks*, which opened Off Broadway in 1960 and as of today—1975—is still running!

The Fantasticks began as one of three one-act plays presented at Barnard College in 1959. Due to the interest of producer Lore Noto, the collaborators expanded it into a full evening's production and it opened the following year in the tiny Off Broadway Sullivan Street Playhouse where it has run ever since.

The Fantasticks is one of the freshest musical shows in many decades. Performed by a cast of eight, with a two-piece musical ensemble, it has a memorable score, charming lyrics, and deals with universal themes of youth and love in original ways. The libretto was suggested by *Les Romanesques,* a play by Edmond Rostand.

Most of the spoken segments of the libretto are in verse. Occasionally they rhyme but more often they do not. The libretto seldom has the *sound* of verse but it nevertheless has a poetic feeling. It also allows the performers to slip in and out of songs without the more usual hard dividing line between speech and song. This is one of *The Fantasticks'* unique features.

The modesty of *The Fantasticks* helps to point up its immense richness. I should like to quote seven songs from the show. These lyrics are innocent, young, fresh, and skillfully executed.

The first "Try to Remember" opens the show. It is begun by El Gallo, the narrator, who is also an important participant in the proceedings. Although I have indicated the complete rhymes, the other rhyming features should be pointed out. These include consonantal rhymes in which this first song abounds. We have callow fellow (which has been rhymed with mellow and yellow); follow and willow (which rhymes with pillow and billow).

There are a number of other features. Remember, which is rhymed with September (this pair is used three times in the first stanza) evolves phonetically to tender *(n* replacing *m* in the scheme of things).

In stanza 1 a sequence of g sounds is heard: grass, green, grain. In stanza 2 we hear three internal rhymes: wept, except, kept and also so (3 times) and no. Also remember and ember, in addition to the triple end rhymes willow, pillow, and billow.

In the third (final) stanza we hear in the second line three internal rhymes: although, know, and snow, which relate to the two end rhymes follow and hollow. Again, there is an evolution *back* to mellow. In other words, in stanza 1 when we heard mellow, yellow, and fellow, change vowel to follow, and change again in stanza 2 to willow, pillow, and billow. In stanza 3 we moved on to follow and hollow and *returned* to mellow.

I should like also to call attention to what I believe is an incredibly beautiful line—"Without a hurt the heart is hollow" with its sequence of three *h* sounds that parallel the three *g* sounds in stanza 1.

"TRY TO REMEMBER"

EL GALLO
Try to remember(1) the kind of September(1)
When life was slow(2) and oh(2) so(2) mellow(3 and 2).
Try to remember(1) the kind of September(1)
When grass was green and grain was yellow(3).
Try to remember(1) the kind of September(1)
When you were a tender and callow fellow(3).
Try to remember, and if you remember,
Then follow.

LUISA
Follow, follow, follow, follow.

EL G
Try to remember when life was so(2) tender
That no(2) one wept(4) except(4) the willow(5).
Try to remember when life was so(2) tender
That dreams were kept(4) beside your pillow(5).
Try to remember(1) when life was so(2) tender
That love was an ember(1) about to billow(5).
Try to remember, and if you remember,
Then follow.

LUISA
Follow, follow, follow, follow.

MATT
Follow, follow, follow, follow.

FATHERS
Follow, follow, follow, follow.

EL G
Deep in December(1) it's nice to remember(1),
Although(2) you know(2) the snow(2) will follow(2)(6).
Deep in December, it's nice to remember:
Without a hurt the heart is hollow(6).
Deep in December(1), it's nice to remember(1)
The fire of September(1) that made us mellow(3).
Deep in December, our hearts should remember,
And follow.

The young heroine has a song of aspiration—an enthusiastic daydream called "Much More."

The song is propelled by rhythm and organically changing harmony. Melodically, it moves on single tones almost like recitatives, but never becomes monotonous.

The rhymes are numerous and are indicated. The images of the lyric are packed with youth and enthusiasm.

"MUCH MORE"

I'd like to swim in a clear blue stream
Where the water is icy cold(1);
Then go to town(2) in a gold(1)en gown(2),
And have my fortune told(1).
Just once.
Just once.
Just once before I'm old(1).

I'd like to be—not evil,
But a little worldly wise(3).
To be the kind(4) of girl designed(4)
To be kissed upon the eyes(3).
I'd like to dance till two o'clock,
Or sometimes dance(5) till dawn(6),
Or if the band(7) could stand(7) it,

Just go on and on and on(6)!
Just once.
Just once.
Before the chance(5) is gone(6)!

I'd like to waste a week or two(8),
And never do(8) a chore(9).
To wear(10) my hair(10) unfastened
So it billows to the floor(9).
To do the things I've dreamed about
But never done before(9)!
Perhaps I'm bad(11) or wild, or mad(11),
With lots of grief in store(9),
But I want much more(9) than keeping house!
Much more!
Much more!
Much more!

A duet, "Metaphor," between the young lovers, follows. Here the rhymes are few but the images are truly inventive and characteristic of youth and innocence.

In a sly way this duet lampoons a number of classic love songs.

"METAPHOR"

MATT
I love you!
(SHE *swoons*.)
MATT *(Singing vigorously.)*
If I were in the desert deep in sand, and
The sun was burning like a hot pomegranate:
Walking through a nightmare in the heart of
A summer day, until my mind was parch-ed!
Then you are water!
Cool clear water!
A refreshing glass of water!
LUISA
What, dear?
MATT
Water!
(SHE *swoons*.)
MATT *(Sings)*
Love! You are love!
Better far than a metaphor
Can ever ever be.
Love! You are love!
My mystery—of love!

If the world was like an iceberg,
And everything was frozen,
And tears turned into icicles in the eye!
And snow came pouring—sleet and ice—
Came stabbing like a knife!
Then you are heat!
A fire alive with heat!
A flame that thaws the iceberg with its heat!
LUISA
Repeat.
MATT
You are heat!
(SHE *swoons; then revives immediately to join him in song.*)
Love! You are love! (I am love!)

Better far than a metaphor
Can ever ever be.
Love! You are love! (I am love!)
My mystery—(his mystery) of love!

You are Polaris, the one trustworthy star!
You are! (I am!) You are! (I am!)
You are September, a special mystery
To me! (To he!) To me! (To he!)
You are Sunlight! Moonlight!
Mountains! Valleys!
The microscopic inside of a leaf!
My joy! My grief!
My star! My leaf!
Oh—
BOTH
Love! You are love! (I am love!)
Better far than a metaphor
Can ever ever be!
Love! You are love! (I am love!)
My mystery—(his mystery)
Of love!

In the lyric passage "A perfect time to be in love" (not sung) the spoken lyrics are new in today's theatre. Perfect rhymes—there is only one single set in the fourth line—give way to vowel and consonantal rhymes, onomatopoeia and fresh images.

In the first five lines there are seven *w* sounds. In the first six lines there are seven $\overline{ee}$ sounds: leaves (twice), green (twice), see (twice), breathing. In the third and fourth lines there are six long $\overline{i}$ sounds: vines, entwine, like, try, eyes, wise. Beginning in the eighth line there is a long succession of *s* sounds: soundless, sound, shadows (twice), celebrate, sensation, secret, place (twice), special, once (twice), sunlit, spot, beside, someone's, sweeter, stinging, taste, September. In the sixteenth and eighteenth lines there is a parade of *h* sounds: hand (twice), held, honey. This long stanza abounds in rich assonances of all kinds. There is one central image theme—transference of sensation: "see it with your ears" and "hear it with the inside of your hand." This lyric is an original!

"A PERFECT TIME TO BE IN LOVE"

It begins with a forest where the woodchucks woo
And leaves wax green,
And vines entwine like lovers; try to see it:
Not with your eyes(1), for they are wise(1);
But see it with your ears:
The cool green breathing of the leaves.
And hear it with the inside of your hand:
The soundless sound of shadows flicking light.
Celebrate sensation.
Recall that secret place;
You've been there, you remember:
That special place where once—
Just once—in your crowded sunlit lifetime,
You hid away in shadows from the tyranny of time.
That spot beside the clover
Where someone's hand held your hand,
And love was sweeter than the berries,
Or the honey,

Or the stinging taste of mint.
It is September,
Before a rainfall—
A perfect time to be in love.

"Soon It's Gonna Rain" is a lovely ballad with the singularly original idea that rain is desirable since it will bring the two lovers closer together. Like the other songs in *The Fantasticks*, this one is swept along by a feeling of joyous anticipation and enthusiasm.

Again the rhymes are sparse and are therefore the smallest feature of these remarkable lyrics.

The very first line with its two key words—wind and whisper—beginning with *w* suggest the appropriate sound.

The shifting verbs in the first three lines involve the senses: hear, see, and smell, accentuating the experiencing of rain. The recurrent *l* sounds naturally liquefy: leaves, smell, velvet, and falling.

The chorus is in AABA form. The first two sections raise the question of "What are we gonna do?" when it rains. The release (B) answers the question. In the final A, having found the solution, the boy embraces the fact of rain with joy.

In the B section the shifting verbs (action) are again the feature: find, build, bind, duck.

The final A has two perfect rhymes and two imperfect ones (all and walls). Possibly because "walls" is the song's final word and because it is set up inevitably, its imperfection does not seem to matter.

Feeling is the big part of the song.

"SOON IT'S GONNA RAIN"

Hear how the wind begins to whisper.
See how the leaves go streaming by(1).
Smell how the velvet rain is falling,
Out where the fields are warm and dry(1).
Now is the time to run inside and stay(2).
Now is the time to find a hideaway(2)—
Where we can stay(2).

Soon it's gonna rain;
I can see it.
Soon it's gonna rain;
I can tell.
Soon it's gonna rain;
What are we gonna do(3)?

Soon it's gonna rain;
I can feel it.
Soon it's gonna rain;
I can tell.
Soon it's gonna rain;
What'll we do(3) with you(3)?

We'll find four limbs of a tree.
We'll build four walls and a floor.
We'll bind it over with leaves.
Then duck inside to stay.

Then we'll let it rain;
We'll not feel it.
Then we'll let it rain(4);

Tom Jones and Harvey Schmidt (*first row*) with the entire cast of *The Fantasticks*.

Rain pell-mell.
And we'll not complain(4)
If it never stops at all.
We'll live and love
Within our own four walls.

Matt's (the hero's) song "I Can See It" is preceded by what amounts to a verse, but it is not sung. This "verse" is full of rhymes, which are indicated.

The song itself—although it contains some perfect rhymes (also indicated)—is chiefly concerned with the creation of assonances, related imperfect rhymes, and aural images.

The first two lines are concerned with *s* sounds: see, shining, somewhere.

The third has perfect and imperfect rhymes that bite: bright, lights, invite.

The key words ending stanzas 2, 4, 5, 6, and the final 9 rhyme. They have *earn* sounds. They resonate like a Lorelei's song. (I've never *heard* one, but these recurrent sounds have the quality I would imagine such a song to have.)

The $\overline{ee}$ sounds are rhymed in stanzas 3 and 7, but they also dominate stanzas 4, 5, 8, 9!

This is not nearly all. The long *i* sounds of stanza 1 recur—perfectly and imperfectly rhymed—permeating stanza 8: shining, sights, lights, inside (twice), lie, in addition to screeching $\overline{ee}$ sounds.

Also in stanzas 5, 6, and 7 the *s* sounds are prevalent: see (3 times), shining somewhere (twice), lights, once, those, sirens singing (twice), listen, close, knows, visions, just, say.

In stanza 7 the long *a* sounds also sing together: maybe (twice), waiting, say, take. Also "make" begins each of the four lines in stanza 8.

"I Can See It" is a remarkable "sound-piece." It is also a song of enthusiastic anticipation begging to enjoy the unknown: fearless youth yearning to experience regardless of the consequences.

"I CAN SEE IT"

There's a song he must sing;
It's a well-known song(1)
But the tune is bitter
And it doesn't take long(1) to learn(2).

MATT
I can learn(2)!
EL G
That pretty little world that beams(3) so bright(4).
That pretty little world that seems(3) delight(4)ful
can burn(2)!
MATT
Let me learn!
Let me learn!
(*And as the tempo picks up,* MATT *sings of his vision.*)
(1) For I can see it!
Shining somewhere(15)!
Bright(4) lights somewhere invite(4) me to come there(5)
And learn(2)!
And I'm ready!
(2) I can hear(6) it!
Sirens singing!
Inside my ear(6) I hear(6) them all singing:

Come learn(2)!
(3) Who knows—maybe(7)—
All the visions that I see(7)
May be waiting just for me(7)
(4) To say—take me there, and
Make me see it!
Make me feel it!
I know it's so, I know that it really
May be!
Let me learn(2)!
I can see it!
EL G
He can see it!
MATT
Shining somewhere(5).
Those lights not only glitter, but once there(5)—
They burn(2)!
MATT
I can hear it!
EL G
He can hear it.
MATT
Sirens singing!
EL G
Sirens singing.
Don't listen close or maybe you'll never
return(2)!
BOTH
Who knows—maybe(7)—
All the visions he (7) can see(7)—
May be waiting just for me(7)
To say—take me there—and
MATT
Make me see those shining sights(8) inside of me!
EL G
Make him see it!
MATT
Make me feel those lights(8) inside don't lie to me!
EL G
Make him feel it!
MATT
I know it's so, I know that it really
May be.
This is what I've always waited(9) for!
This is what my life's created(9) for!
BOTH
Let me (him) learn(2)!

Jones and Schmidt wrote a lovely lilting waltz song "They Were You" in *The Fantasticks.*

In addition to the indicated rhymes there are more subtle colorings. The long *a* sound is heard again and again in stanzas 1 and 2: May, stage, holiday, way, rainbows, away, fade.

Long *i* sounds are heard throughout: I (often), shining, lights (twice), my, find, wildest, multiplied, by.

Resonating *n*'s also abound: when (7 times), moon, young, month, hung, shining, never, knew, dance, done, went, find, rainbows, near, wonderful, things, fancy, thing. Twenty-three in three stanzas!

All this assonance, in addition to rhymes, constitutes an innocent waltz about love.

"THEY WERE YOU"

MATT
When the moon was young(1),
When the month was May(2),
When the stage was hung(1) for my holiday(2),
I saw shining lights, but I never knew(3)—
They were you(3)
They were you(3)
They were you(3).
LUISA
When the dance was done,
When I went my way,(2)
When I tried to find rainbows far away,
All the lovely lights seemed to fade from view(3)—
They were you(3)

They were you(3)
They were you(3).
BOTH
Without you near me(4),
I can't see(4).
When you're near me(4).
Wonderful things come to be(4).
Every se(4)cret prayer,
Every fancy free(4)
Every thing I dared for both you and me(4),
All my wildest dreams multipled by two(3),
They were you(3)
They were you(3)
They were you(3).

Especially in *The Fantasticks,* Tom Jones made incredible music out of words. Seldom anywhere will one find more.

Courtesy ASCAP

Stephen Sondheim (b. 1930)

The youngest and most promising of our creative theatre contributors is Stephen Sondheim. He has been thoroughly schooled as a composer and was watched over and guided as a lyricist by no less a master than Oscar Hammerstein II. While this grounding was of inestimable importance, Sondheim's many theatre collaborations have provided him with such a wide and significant variety of experiences that no one in our creative theatre world can have equaled him in this respect alone. His talents are unique, and his opportunities for development have already, at forty-four, been endless. He continues to work and to grow and is blessed with a full command of his resources as well as an insatiable eagerness to press onward in a steady stream of new and experimental directions. What makes this forward thrust really significant is that he is knowledgeable both in composing and writing techniques and his theatre experiences already qualify him as a veteran. His experiments are outgrowths of his history and not, as in too many other cases, born out of a vacuous desire to be different. He has at least as secure an idea as anyone living as to what does and does not work in the theatre, and his continual dissatisfaction with his latest accomplishments, plus his recognition of the nearly two-decade stagnation of musical theatre continue to goad him on to explore new paths, to reach out for new discoveries.

It is my conviction that Sondheim has never been strictly in search of a hit, yet has always borne in mind the creator's need to communicate with his audience. Eventually the hit, on a universal and timeless level, must result. But, in Sondheim's case, the goal is self-satisfaction rather than success.

Aside from Sondheim's artistic upbringing, there is no creative person who has been more persistently exposed to collab-

oration with most of the leading talents of our time. At first he served as lyricist to Leonard Bernstein in *West Side Story,* with Arthur Laurents as writer and Jerome Robbins as director. He next created lyrics for Jule Styne's music for *Gypsy,* starring Ethel Merman, with book by Arthur Laurents and direction by Jerome Robbins. He then wrote both music and lyrics for *A Funny Thing Happened on the Way to the Forum,* adapted from a comedy of Plautus by Burt Shevelove and Larry Gelbart, staged by George Abbott, starring Zero Mostel. He again collaborated as composer and lyricist with Arthur Laurents on an original production, *Anyone Can Whistle,* followed by a job as lyricist only, with Richard Rodgers for *Do I Hear a Waltz?,* book by Arthur Laurents, directed by John Dexter.

Sondheim then began a new phase in his career with Harold Prince as producer-director. To date they have brought out *Company, Follies,* and the current *A Little Night Music,* all experimental and largely successful, especially the last. He has provided some lyrics for a new version of Leonard Bernstein's *Candide,* and has also provided music and lyrics for a version of Aristophanes' *The Frogs*! A very great deal of work, invaluable experience, and success for a man of forty-four.

In what follows we are here chiefly concerned with lyrics.

Of the many riches in *West Side Story,* I would like to consider first "Something's Coming." Sung by the hero, Tony, it is a song of high expectation, anticipation of the unknown but certain to be pleasurable. As the something is totally unknown, Sondheim needed to invent out of pure imagination specific lyrical pictures if they were to interest and involve the listener. Examine the following words with only that *one* idea in mind and observe how much Sondheim was able to invent. Also note two other things: the musical phrases are short and terse, telegraphic in style, and this song, which closed a short scene, had to travel *somewhere* dramatically with rapidity and terseness. This was amply fulfilled within the lyrics' final two lines, and not altogether obviously:

Down the block, on a beach . . .
Maybe tonight. . . .

The "on the beach" is pure gold because of its irrelevance: it serves to blur the obvious.

"SOMETHING'S COMING"

Could be! . . .
Who knows? . . .
There's something due any day;
I will know right away
Soon as it shows.
It may come cannonballin' down through the sky,
Gleam in its eye,
Bright as a rose!
Who knows? . . .
It's only just out of reach,
Down the block, on a beach,
Under a tree.
I got a feeling there's a miracle due,
Gonna come true,
Coming to me!

Could it be? Yes, it could.
Something's coming, something good,
If I can wait!
Something's coming, I don't know what it is
But it is
Gonna be great!

With a click, with a shock,
Phone'll jingle, door'll knock,
Open the latch!
Something's coming, don't know when, but it's soon—
Catch the moon,
One-handed catch!

Around the corner,
Or whistling down the river,
Come on—deliver
To me!

Will it be? Yes, it will.
Maybe just by holding still
It'll be there!
Come on, something, come on in, don't be shy,
Meet a guy,
Pull up a chair!

The air is humming,
And something great is coming!
Who knows?
It's only just out of reach,
Down the block, on a beach . . .
Maybe tonight . . .

West Side Story is filled with songs containing the identical problem for the lyricist. In the very next song, "Maria," there is wonderment: a boy has met a girl and they have fallen des-

perately in love with each other. All he knows about her is her name. Where does a lyricist go with so little to work with? The musical problem is far less stringent. The composer has to express something breathlessly akin to passion, but for the lyricist the problem is one of inventing a succession of terse words that convey a definite literal meaning. Sondheim chose simply to embellish the sound of the girl's name, Maria, and he found a wealth of images to keep it alive and invest it with meaning.

"MARIA"

The most beautiful sound I ever heard.
Maria, Maria, Maria, Maria . . .
All the beautiful sounds of the world in a single word:
Maria, Maria, Maria, Maria . . .
Maria, Maria . . .
Maria!
I've just met a girl named Maria,
And suddenly that name
Will never be the same
To me.

Maria!
I've just kissed a girl named Maria,
And suddenly I've found
How wonderful a sound
Can be!

Maria!
Say it loud and there's music playing—
Say it soft and it's almost like praying—
Maria . . .
I'll never stop saying
Maria!
The most beautiful sound I ever heard—
Maria.

The next song, "Tonight," charges the lyricist again with the identical problem. The lyrical embellishment hinges on "It all began tonight." This germ is sufficient not only for a song but for an entire musicalized scene, parallel to Shakespeare's balcony scene in *Romeo and Juliet*. Nor in the end is it merely a love scene song, for it advances the plot by cementing the relationship between hero and heroine, providing information about each, and pointing ahead—normally a mundane, nonpoetic task—to their meeting the next day.

"America," which follows, is also a lyric of many high qualities. First of all it is bouncy, due to the regularly alternating 6/8 and 3/4 rhythms. The argument of the song is constructed along the lines of thesis and antithesis. The lyrics state and refute in a satirical way:

ROSALIE I'll drive a Buick through San Juan—
ANITA If there's a road you can drive on.
and
ROSALIE I'll give them new washing machine—
ANITA What have they got there to keep clean?

Sondheim has managed to achieve a style suggestive of "broken English" through a slight fragmentation while never resorting to dialect.

The lyrics disparage Puerto Rico and Puerto Ricans, but always remain innocent of bigotry since they typify the well-known joking that takes place among the people of a single ethnic group about themselves.

The other songs that complete the score have their own merits and they abound in contrasts: the musical scene "One Hand, One Heart" containing a priestless marriage, a touching exchange of vows, and youthful humor; the sharp funny "Officer Krupke," the moving "Somewhere," and more.

In *Gypsy,* about Gypsy Rose Lee's mother Rose and Gypsy's childhood and subsequent career, there is a song early in the production entitled "Some People," which describes Rose's gutsy pushy character and does so while giving the audience a sympathetic understanding of her; what makes her hard, perhaps somewhat ruthless, and what makes her tick. The language here is markedly different from that of *West Side Story,* just as the characters are from a different time and world. In "Some People" there is a tale of burning ambition. The lyrics as well as the music smell of the large theatre as opposed to records or nightclubs. This style and quality are part of a tradition that characterizes material made for singing actors as opposed to acting singers.

"SOME PEOPLE"

Some people can get a thrill
Knitting sweaters and sitting still—
That's okay for some people who don't know they're alive;

Some people can thrive and bloom,
Living life in a living room—
That's perfect for some people of one hundred and five!

But I
At least gotta try,
When I think of all the sights that I gotta see yet,
All the places I gotta play,
All the things that I gotta be yet—
Come on, Poppa, whaddaya say?

Some people can be content
Playing bingo and paying rent—
That's peachy for some people,
For some humdrum people
To be,
But some people ain't me!

I had a dream,
A wonderful dream, Poppa,
All about June and the Orpheum Circuit—
Give me a chance and I know I can work it!
I had a dream
Just as real as can be, Poppa—
There I was in Mr. Orpheum's office
And he was saying to me,
"Rose!
Get yourself some new orchestrations,
New routines and red velvet curtains,
Get a feathered hat for the Baby,
Photographs in front of the theatre,
Get an agent—and in jig time
You'll be being booked in the big time!"
Oh, what a dream,
A wonderful dream, Poppa,
And all that I need

Is eighty-eight bucks, Poppa!
That's what he said, Poppa,
Only eighty-eight bucks, Poppa . . .

POP
You ain't gettin' eighty-eight cents from me, Rose!
(*He goes*)
ROSE (*Shouting after him*)
Then I'll get it someplace else—but
I'll get it and get my kids out! (ROSE *sings*)
Good-bye
To blueberry pie!
Good riddance to all the socials I had to go to,
All the lodges I had to play,
All the Shriners I said hello to—
Hey, L.A., I'm coming your way!
Some people sit on their butts,
Got the dream—yeah, but not the guts!
That's living for some people,
For some humdrum people,
I suppose!
Well, they can stay and rot—
But not
Rose!

One senses that the lyrics throughout *Gypsy* belong to an earlier period than those of *West Side Story, not* because the earlier scenes are set at a time prior to *West Side Story* but because Jule Styne's music has an earlier orientation than Leonard Bernstein's. Sondheim's style sensitively reflects that of the music to which it is attached.

Two songs occur back to back near the end of Act 1. Rose has at last secured a contract booking her daughter's act on the highly prized Orpheum Circuit. She is stunned and happy, and sings "Mr. Goldstone, I Love You." This is followed by Louise's simple sad one, "Little Lamb." Both explain themselves.

"MR. GOLDSTONE, I LOVE YOU"

ROSE
Have an egg roll, Mr. Goldstone,
Have a napkin, have a chopstick, have a chair!
Have a sparerib, Mr. Goldstone—
Any sparerib that I can spare, I'd be glad to share!
Have a dish, have a fork,
Have a fish, have a pork,
Put your feet up, feel at home.
Have a smoke, have a coke,
Would you like to hear a joke?
I'll have June recite a poem!
Have a lichee, Mr. Goldstone,
Tell me any little thing that I can do.
Ginger-peachy, Mr. Goldstone,
Have a kumquat—have two!
Everybody give a cheer—
Santa Claus is sittin' here—
Mr. Goldstone, I love you!

Have a goldstone, Mr. Egg Roll,
Tell me any little thing that I can do.
Have some fried rice, Mr. Soy Sauce,
Have a cookie, have a few!

What's the matter, Mr. G.?
Have another pot of tea!
Mr. Goldstone, I love you!

There are good stones and bad stones
And curbstones and Goldstones
And touchstones and such stones as them!
There are big stones and small stones
And grindstones and gallstones,
But Goldstone is a gem.

There are milestones, there are millstones,
There's a cherry, there's a yellow, there's a blue!
But we don't want any old stone,
Only Goldstone will do!

ALL (Singing)
Moonstone, sunstone—we all scream for one stone!
Mervyn Goldstone, we love you!
Goldstone!

"LITTLE LAMB"

(*The lights black out in the larger bedroom and fade in slowly on the small room, where a forgotten* LOUISE *sits with the lamb*)

LOUISE (Singing softly)
Little lamb, little lamb,
My birthday is here at last.
Little lamb, little lamb,
A birthday goes by so fast.
Little bear, little bear,
You sit on my right, right there.
Little hen, little hen,
What game shall we play, and when?
Little cat, little cat,
Ah, why do you look so blue?
Did somebody paint you like that,
Or is it your birthday, too?
Little fish, little fish,
Do you think I'll get my wish?
Little lamb, little lamb,
I wonder how old I am.
I wonder how old I am . . .

June, Momma's older daughter whom she has been grooming for the stage, has run away. Rose is at first stunned and then, unable to accept defeat, she is resolved to start again by preparing the younger daughter, Louise (Gypsy), for a career. With this new impetus she becomes almost hysterical as she sings "Everything's Coming Up Roses," an emotional triumph that ends the scene.

This song is an excellent example of a musical number's furthering the plot and adding color and intensity to the character. The lyrics begin ephemerally with a "dream" that is to become a hard song. The growth and development are enormous. Technically these are simple words. The rhyme scheme is simple: a couplet rhyme, then the next line rhymes four lines later. The first of these next three lines is the title that, throughout, never rhymes. As the song progresses toward the last section, expressing total resolution and accomplishment, the lyric gathers momentum by resorting to brief telegraphic lines with more frequent, less separated rhymes. This combination of music and lyrics represents dramatic musical theatre at a gutsy high point.

"EVERYTHING'S COMING UP ROSES"

I had a dream,
A dream about you, Baby!
It's gonna come true, Baby!
They think that we're through,
But,
Baby,
You'll be swell, you'll be great,
Gonna have the whole world on a plate!
Starting here, starting now,
Honey, everything's coming up roses!
Clear the decks, clear the tracks,
You got nothing to do but relax!
Blow a kiss, take a bow—
Honey, everything's coming up roses!
Now's your inning—
Stand the world on its ear!
Set it spinning,
'N' that'll be just the beginning!
Curtain up, light the lights,
You got nothing to hit but the heights!
You'll be swell,
You'll be great,
I can tell—
Just you wait!
That lucky star I talk about is due!
Honey, everything's coming up roses for me and for you!

You can do it,
All you need is a hand.
We can do it,
Momma is gonna see to it!
Curtain up, light the lights,
We got nothing to hit but the heights!
I can tell,
Wait and see!
There's the bell,
Follow me,
And nothing's gonna stop us till we're through!
Honey, everything's coming up roses and daffodils,
Everything's coming up sunshine and Santa Claus,
Everything's gonna be bright lights and lollipops,
Everything's coming up roses for me and for you!

A theatre expression has grown up called "the eleven o'clock number." This refers to some large-scale, last minute kind of "concerto" for the star: a big attention-getter, something new (not a reprise of something heard earlier), a showoff piece. One of the most successful examples of an eleven o'clock number, "Rose's Turn," occurs in *Gypsy*. Rose has visited the now successful Louise (Gypsy Rose Lee) in her dressing room and has left lonely and embittered. What follows is a large musical scene. After the number Louise enters, mother and daughter are reconciled, and they exit together.

"ROSE'S TURN"

ROSE
"I thought you did it for me, Momma." "I thought you did it for me, Momma . . ." I thought you made a no-talent ox into a star because you like doing things the hard way, Momma. (*Louder*) And you *haven't* got any talent!—not what *I* call

talent, Miss Gypsy Rose Lee! (*The lights now begin to come up, showing the whole stage, bare except for a few stacked flats of scenery used earlier in the big production number.* ROSE *shouts defiantly*) I made you!—and you wanna know why? You wanna know what I did it for?! (*Louder*) Because I was born too soon and started too late, that's why! With what I have in me, I could've been better than ANY OF YOU! What I got in me—what I been holding down inside of me—if I ever let it out, there wouldn't be signs big enough! There wouldn't be lights bright enough! (*Shouting right out to everyone now*) HERE SHE IS, BOYS! HERE SHE IS, WORLD! HERE'S ROSE!! (*She sings*)

CURTAIN UP!!!
LIGHT THE LIGHTS!!!
(*Speaking*)
Play it, boys.
(*Singing*)
You either got it,
or you ain't—
And, boys, I got it!
You like it?
ORCHESTRA
Yeah!
ROSE
Well, I got it!
Some people got it
And make it pay,
Some people can't even
Give it away.
This people's got it
And this people's spreadin' it around.
You either have it
Or you've had it.
(*Speaking*)
Hello, everybody! My name's Rose. What's yours? (*Bumps*)
How d'ya like them egg rolls, Mr. Goldstone?
(*Singing*)
Hold your hats,
And Hallelujah,
Momma's gonna show it to ya!
(*Speaking*)
Ready or not, here comes Momma!
(*Singing*)
Momma's talkin' loud,
Momma's doin' fine,
Momma's gettin' hot,
Momma's goin' strong,
Momma's movin' on,
Momma's all alone,
Momma doesn't care,
Momma's lettin' loose,
Momma's got the stuff,
Momma's lettin' go—
(*Stopping dead as the words hit her*)
Momma—
Momma's—
(*Shaking off the mood*)
Momma's got the stuff,
Momma's got to move,
Momma's got to go—
(*Stopping dead again, trying to recover*)
Momma—
Momma's—

Momma's gotta let go!
(*Stops; after a moment she begins to pace*)
Why did I do it?
What did it get me?
Scrapbooks full of me in the background.
Give 'em love and what does it get you?
What does it get you?
One quick look as each of 'em leaves you.
All your life and what does it get you?
Thanks a lot—and out with the garbage.
They take bows and you're battin' zero.
I had a dream—
I dreamed it for you,
June,
It wasn't for me, Herbie.
And if it wasn't for me
Then where would you be,
Miss Gypsy Rose Lee!
Well, someone tell me, when is it my turn?
Don't I get a dream for myself?
Startin' now it's gonna be my turn!
Gangway, world,
Get offa my runway!
Startin' now I bat a thousand.
This time, boys, I'm takin' the bows and
Everything's coming up Rose—
Everything's coming up Roses—
Everything's coming up Roses
This time for me!
For me—
For me—
For me—
For me—
FOR ME!

In this section I have analyzed the lyrics less and less and have become more involved with their positioning in the play. This, I think, is as it should be, and it is due to progress in the theatre. Lyrics in the best shows have become more integrated. If they are truly successful they more and more serve plot and character.

The cleverness of rhymes that at one point in our history comprised a bright jewel in a particularly theatrical moment gave enormous pleasure to listeners because these were newly discovered features, newly explored facets. Nowadays, a polished lyricist is more concerned with what he has to say and if he is a craftsman, he will say it well. Expressiveness has by now assumed a primary place ahead of smartness often for its own sake.

Sondheim's role as both composer and lyricist in *A Funny Thing Happened on the Way to the Forum* was for him a new one, carrying with it double responsibilities. The opening number of the show, "Comedy Tonight," an amusing and functional piece, was, I am told, written after the show had opened on its pre-Broadway tour. This, I feel, is par for the course. I have long contended that theatre writers should not write their openings until they have completed everything else, since it is not until the total shape of the show is known that writers can be certain of what they will actually need at the beginning. The same need for a more functional opening happened in the case of *Wonderful Town*. "Christopher Street" did not take its place in the show until its sixth week, at the opening in Philadelphia, following New Haven and Boston engagements.

"Comedy Tonight" introduces the principal character who, flanked by three minor characters, sets the style and content of the show. He explains the locale, the time, points out three houses, describes their occupants (most of the show's principals), their situations, and identifies himself. All this is done humorously and in a kind of burlesque style.

It is interesting to note that Sondheim does not sound his first rhyme until the tenth and eleventh lines. After that they occur frequently. The music assumes a position secondary to the lyrics and is interspersed with spoken sections.

"COMEDY TONIGHT"

PROLOGUS
Something familiar,
Something peculiar,
Something for everyone:
A comedy tonight!
Something appealing,
Something appalling,
Something for everyone:
A comedy tonight!
Nothing with kings,
Nothing with crowns.
Bring on the lovers, liars and clowns!
Old situations,
New complications,
Nothing portentous
Or polite;
Tragedy tomorrow,
Comedy tonight!
(During the following, HE brings on the three PROTEANS.)
Something convulsive,
Something repulsive,
Something for everyone:
A comedy tonight!
Something esthetic,
PROTEANS
Something frenetic,
PROLOGUS
Something for everyone:
A comedy tonight!
PROTEANS
Nothing of gods,
Nothing of Fate.
PROLOGUS
Weighty affairs will just have to wait.
PROTEANS
Nothing that's formal,
PROLOGUS
Nothing that's normal,
PROTEANS
No recitations to recite!
ALL
Open up the curtain!
(The curtain parts halfway, then closes as if by accident, causing confusion. After a moment, it reopens completely, revealing a street in Rome. Stage center stands the house of SENEX; on either side, the houses of LYCUS and ERRONIUS. SENEX's house is hidden behind another curtain.)

Comedy tonight!
PROLOGUS (Speaks.)
It all takes place on a street in Rome, around and about these three houses. (Indicates ERRONIUS's house.) First, the house of Erronius, a befuddled old man abroad now in search of his children, stolen in infancy by pirates. (Sings.)

Something for everyone:
A comedy tonight!
(The PROTEANS appear in the upper window of the house and pantomime.)
Something erratic,
Something dramatic,
Something for everyone:
A comedy tonight!
Frenzy and frolic,
Strictly symbolic,
Something for everyone:
A comedy tonight!
(Speaks, indicating LYCUS's house.) Second, the house of Lycus, a buyer and seller of the flesh of beautiful women. That's for those of you who have absolutely no interest in pirates. (Sings.)

Something for everyone:
A comedy tonight!
(PROTEANS dance in front of the house; one of them disappears into the floor. PROLOGUS reacts, then continues, speaking.)
Raise the curtain!
(Inner curtain drops into floor.)
And finally, the house of Senex, who lives here with his wife and son. Also in this house lives Pseudolus, slave to the son. Pseudolus is probably my favorite character in the piece. A role of enormous variety and nuance, and played by an actor of such . . . let me put it this way . . . I play the part. (Sings.)
Anything you ask for:
Comedy tonight!
(PROTEANS reenter.)
And these are the Proteans, only three, yet they do the work of thirty. They are difficult to recognize in the many parts they play. Watch them closely.
(PROTEANS appear in and out of SENEX's house in assorted costumes.)
A proud Roman.
A patrician Roman.
A pretty Roman.
A Roman slave.
A Roman soldier.
(PROTEAN appears with crude wooden ladder.)
A Roman ladder.
(PROTEAN enters, juggling.)
Tremendous skill!
(HE juggles badly. PROTEAN enters.)
Incredible versatility!
(HE fumbles in changing wigs. PROTEAN enters with gong.)
And, above all, dignity!
(HE strikes gong, his skirt falls.)
And now, the entire company!
(THE COMPANY enters from SENEX's house.)
ALL (Sing.)
Something familiar,
Something peculiar,
Something for everybody:
Comedy tonight!

STAGE RIGHT
Something that's gaudy,
STAGE LEFT
Something that's bawdy,
PROLOGUS
Something for everybawdy:
ALL
Comedy tonight!
MILES
Nothing that's grim,
DOMINA
Nothing that's Greek!
PROLOGUS *(Indicating* GYMNASIA.)
She plays Medea later this week.
ALL
Stunning surprises,
Cunning disguises,
Hundreds of actors out of sight!
ERRONIUS
Pantaloons and tunics!
SENEX
Courtesans and eunuchs!
DOMINA
Funerals and chases!
LYCUS
Baritones and basses!
PHILIA Panderers!
HERO Philanderers!
HYSTERIUM Cupidity!
MILES Timidity!
LYCUS Mistakes!
ERRONIUS Fakes!
PHILIA Rhymes!
DOMINA Mimes!
PROLOGUS Tumblers!
Grumblers!
Fumblers!
Bumblers!
ALL No royal curse,
No Trojan horse,
And a happy ending, of course!
Goodness and badness,
Man in his madness:
This time it all turns out all right!
Tragedy tomorrow!
Comedy tonight!
(ALL *exit, except* PROLOGUS. HE *addresses the heavens.*)
PROLOGUS. Oh, Thespis, we place ourselves in your hands.
(To audience.) The play begins. *(Exits.)*

Hero and Philia are the two young lovers in *A Funny Thing Happened on the Way to the Forum.* Sondheim has written an original love song for them that turns out actually to be comedic. Philia has just told Hero that she cannot do anything right.

"I'M LOVELY"

I'm lovely,
All I am is lovely,
Lovely is the one thing I can do.
Winsome,

What I am is winsome,
Radiant as in some
Dream come true.
Oh,
Isn't it a shame?
I can neither sew
Nor cook nor read nor write my name.
But I'm happy
Merely being lovely,
For it's one thing I can give to you.
HERO Philia . . .
PHILIA Yes?
HERO Say my name.
PHILIA Just say your name?
HERO Yes.
PHILIA Very well. *(A blank look.)* I have forgotten it.
HERO *(Disappointed.)* It's Hero.
PHILIA Forgive me, Hero. I have no memory for names.
HERO You don't need one. You don't need anything. *(Sings.)*
You're lovely,
Absolutely lovely,
Who'd believe the loveliness of you?
Winsome,
Sweet and warm and winsome,
Radiant as in some
Dream come true.
Now
Venus would seem tame,
Helen and her thou-
Sand ships would have to die of shame.
BOTH And I'm happy,
Happy that you're (I'm) lovely,
For there's one thing loveliness can do:
It's a gift for me to share with you!

Later there is a witty duet between father (Senex) and son (Hero). Senex has been led to believe that Philia (Hero's girl) is the new maid in the house and he is pursuing her. Hero becomes apprehensive. The two of them sing.

"IMPOSSIBLE"

SENEX *(Sings, to audience)*
Why did he look at her that way?
HERO *(Sings, to audience.)*
Why did he look at her that way?
BOTH Must be my imagination . . .
SENEX She's a lovely, blooming flower,
He's just a sprout—impossible!
HERO She's a lovely blooming flower,
He's all worn out—impossible!
SENEX Just a fledgling in the nest . . .
HERO Just a man who needs a rest . . .
SENEX He's a beamish boy at best . . .
HERO Poor old fellow . . .
SENEX He's a child and love's a test
He's too young to pass—impassable!
HERO He has asthma, gout, a wife,
Lumbago and gas—irascible!
SENEX Romping in the nursery . . .
HERO He looks tired . . .

SENEX   *(To* HERO, *warmly.)*
Son, sit on your father's knee.
HERO   *(To* SENEX, *warmly.)*
Father, you can lean on me.
BOTH   *(To audience.)*
Him?
*Im*possible!
HERO   But why did she wave at him that way?
SENEX   Why did she wave at him that way?
BOTH   Could there be an explanation?
HERO   Women often want a father,
She may want mine—it's possible!
SENEX   He's a handsome lad of twenty,
I'm thirty-nine—it's possible!
HERO   Older men know so much more . . .
SENEX   In a way, I'm forty-four . . .
HERO   Next to him, I'll seem a bore . . .
SENEX   All right, fifty!
HERO   Then again, he *is* my father,
I ought to trust—impossible!
SENEX   Then again, with love at my age,
Sometimes it's just—impossible!
HERO   With a girl, I'm ill-at-ease . . .
SENEX   I don't feel well . . .
HERO   *(To* SENEX, *helplessly.)*
Sir, about those birds and bees . . .
SENEX   *(To* HERO, *helplessly.)*
Son, a glass of water, please . . .
BOTH   *(To audience.)*
The situation's fraught,
Fraughter than I thought,
With horrible,
Impossible
Possibilities!

In *Company* (1970), with book by George Furth, directed and produced by Harold Prince, Sondheim made enormous forward strides in every way. Musically and lyrically he seemed to have dug deeper toward defining and expressing a more personal style. The show became a fresh note in musical theatre experience.

The story concerns a single young man Robert, who tries to identify himself; five couples, all devoted to him in their own ways; and three separate girls outside his social circle. Each of the girls represents a particular type.

The chorus of the title song sets up a proposition (as in geometry) for the entire show: one, in this case, to be disproved. However, it represents the status quo. It is a statement that the unfolding of the show will take care of. The triple interior rhymes of the two parallel opening lines are a kind of tour de force, and then the double interior rhymes of the next three lines, with their alternating end rhymes, further demonstrate the lyricist's resources. After one more rhyming couplet, the entire business of rhyming is discarded in favor of simple statements.

"COMPANY"

ROBERT
Phone rings, door chimes, in comes company!
No strings, good times, room hums, company!
Late nights, quick bites, party games,

Deep talks, long walks, telephone calls,
Thoughts shared, souls bared, private names,
All those photos up on the walls
"With love,"
With love filling the days,
With love seventy ways,
"To Bobby, with love"
From all
Those
Good and crazy people, my friends,
Those
Good and crazy people, my married friends!
And that's what it's all about, isn't it?
That's what it's really about,
Really about!

A singularly original and bitter song slithers in a little later. We have been shown a scene between one of the couples, Harry and Sarah, in essence a not unfamiliar scene. Robert, our hero, watches as Sarah and Harry indulge in a humorous exhibition of karate. At a point when Sarah has overcome her husband, Joanne enters. The other three freeze and she sings "The Little Things You Do Together," which simultaneously comments on what we have seen and tells us in comedic-sardonic terms her own view of marriage. The song is interrupted twice by dialogue and Joanne is joined in the second section by the show's other couples. The production is so fluid because of its basic concept, Prince's direction, and Boris Aronson's more or less abstract set that the appearance and disappearance of people not basically a part of a scene does not seem questionable.

In the 8 lyric lines of the first section there are nine assonances or rhymes and all of them are internal. They are do, do, do, pursue, accrue, misconstrue. There are no end rhymes. In the second assonance (repetition) there are two sets of three interior rhymes: share, swear, wear; and enjoy, annoy, destroy. Incidentally, these rhymes themselves *almost* reveal the whole content and certainly the spirit of the song.

"THE LITTLE THINGS YOU DO TOGETHER"

JOANNE
It's the little things you do together,
Do together,
Do together,
That make perfect relationships.
The hobbies you pursue together,
Savings you accrue together,
Looks you misconstrue together
That make marriage a joy.
Mm-hm . . .

It's the little things you share together,
Swear together,
Wear together,
That make perfect relationships.
The concerts you enjoy together,
Neighbors you annoy together,
Children you destroy together,
That keep marriage intact.

It's not so hard to be married
When two maneuver as one,
It's not so hard to be married
And, Jesus Christ, is it fun.

It's sharing little winks together,
Drinks together,
Kinks together,
That makes marriage a joy.

It's the bargains that you shop together,
Cigarettes you stop together,
Clothing that you swap together,
That make perfect relationships.

Uh-huh . . .
Mm-hm . . .
ALL
It's not talk of God and the decade ahead that
Allows you to get through the worst.
It's "I do" and "You don't" and "Nobody said that"
And "Who brought the subject up first?"
It's the little things, the little things, the little
    things . . .
It's the little things, the little things, the little
    things . . .
The little ways you try together,
Cry together,
Lie together,
That make perfect relationships,
Becoming a cliché together,
Growing old and gray together.
JOANNE
Withering away together,
ALL
That makes marriage a joy.
MEN
It's not so hard to be married,
WOMEN
It's much the simplest of crimes.
MEN
It's not so hard to be married,
JOANNE
I've done it three or four times.
JENNY
It's people that you hate together,
PAUL and AMY
Bait together,
PETER and SUSAN
Date together,
ALL
That make marriage a joy.
DAVID
It's things like using force together,
LARRY
Shouting till you're hoarse together,
JOANNE
Getting a divorce together,
ALL
That make perfect relationships.
Uh-huh . . .
Kiss, kiss . . .
Mm-hm.

Lack of space forbids my quoting even nearly all the songs in
Company, but I must not bypass "Sorry-Grateful" without a
word. First the concept itself seems perfectly natural until you
realize that it has probably never before been verbalized, cer-

tainly not in a show. Just as the title itself is concerned with
bringing opposites together, so also is the body of the song. One
inner section must be quoted here if only to present a sample of
this oppositeness and its strong emotional impact.

"SORRY-GRATEFUL"

You're always sorry,
You're always grateful,
You hold her, thinking, "I'm not alone."
You're still alone.
You don't live for her,
You do live with her,
You're scared she's starting to drift away
And scared she'll stay.

This last line suggests a brilliant comedy song occurring
much later in *Company*. An airline stewardess, April, following
a love scene (Robert says several times during it, "If only I
could remember her name"), goes to bed with Robert. The
night has passed. The alarm clock rings. Both are exhausted.
She begins getting into her clothes.

"BARCELONA"

ROBERT   Where you going?
APRIL   Barcelona.
ROBERT   . . . oh . . .
APRIL   Don't get up.
ROBERT   Do you have to?
APRIL   Yes, I have to.
ROBERT   . . . oh . . .
APRIL   Don't get up.
(Pauses)
Now you're angry.
ROBERT   No, I'm not.
APRIL   Yes, you are.
ROBERT   No, I'm not.
Put your things down.
APRIL   See, you're angry.
ROBERT   No, I'm not.
APRIL   Yes, you are.
ROBERT   No, I'm not.
Put your wings down
And stay.
APRIL   I'm leaving.
ROBERT   Why?
APRIL   To go to—
ROBERT   Stay—
APRIL   I have to—
APRIL and ROBERT   Fly—
ROBERT   I know—
APRIL and ROBERT   To Barcelona.

ROBERT   Look,
You're a very special girl,
Not just overnight.
No, you're a very special girl,
And not because you're bright—
Not *just* because you're bright.
(Yawning)
You're just a very special girl,
June!
APRIL   April . . .
ROBERT   April . . .
(There is a pause)

APRIL   Thank you.
ROBERT   Whatcha thinking?
APRIL   Barcelona.
ROBERT   . . . oh . . .
APRIL   Flight Eighteen.
ROBERT   Stay a minute.
APRIL   I would like to.
ROBERT   . . . so? . . .
APRIL   Don't be mean.
ROBERT   Stay a minute.
APRIL   No, I can't.
ROBERT   Yes, you can.
APRIL   No, I can't.
ROBERT   Where you going?
APRIL   Barcelona.
ROBERT   So you said—
APRIL   And Madrid.
ROBERT   *Bon voyage.*
APRIL   On a Boeing.
ROBERT   Goodnight.
APRIL   You're angry.
ROBERT   No.
APRIL   I've got to—
ROBERT   Right.
APRIL   Report to—
ROBERT   Go.
APRIL   That's not to
Say
That if I had my way . . .
Oh well, I guess okay.
ROBERT   What?
APRIL   I'll stay.
ROBERT   But . . .
(As she snuggles down)
Oh, God!

The husbands have a cynical song entitled "Have I Got a Girl for You?" After each has described a delectable prize, the song ends with "Whaddaya wanna get married for?"

In musical theatre this song is unique. What makes it effective is its universally recognizable laugh at ourselves and our sincerest friends.

This song is followed by Robert's "Someone Is Waiting," which underscores his loneliness and clearly demonstrates his confusions as to whom or what it is that he wants. This is summed up succinctly in the song's third section. I would also like to call attention to the sibilants that occur, surely not by accident, at least once in every line.

"HAVE I GOT A GIRL FOR YOU?"

My niece from Ohio . . .
It'll just be the four of us . . .
You'll loooooooooooooove her!
(The wives exit and the husbands now sing "Have I Got a Girl for You?")
LARRY
Have I got a girl for you? Wait till you meet her!
Have I got a girl for you, boy? Hoo, boy!
Dumb!—and with a weakness for Sazerac slings—
You give her even the fruit and she swings.
The kind of girl you can't send through the mails—
Call me tomorrow, I want the details.

PETER
Have I got a chick for you? Wait till you meet her!
Have I got a chick for you, boy? Hoo, boy!
Smart!—She's into all those exotic mystiques:
The Kamasutra and Chinese techniques—
I hear she knows more than seventy-five . . .
Call me tomorrow if you're still alive.
HUSBANDS   *(In canon)*
Have I got a girl for you? Wait till you meet her!
Have I got a girl for you, boy? Hoo, boy!
Boy, to be in your shoes what I wouldn't give.
I mean the freedom to go out and live . . .
And as for settling down and all that . . .
Marriage may be where it's been, but it's not where it's at!

Whaddaya like, you like coming home to a kiss?
Somebody with a smile at the door?
Whaddaya like, you like indescribable bliss?
Then whaddaya wanna get married for?
Whaddaya like, you like an excursion to Rome,
Suddenly taking off to explore?
Whaddaya like, you like having meals cooked at home?
Then whaddaya wanna get married for?
Whaddaya wanna get married for?
Whaddaya wanna get married for?
Whaddaya wanna get married for?
(The husbands exit, leaving ROBERT alone.)

"SOMEONE IS WAITING"

ROBERT
Someone is waiting,
Cool as Sarah,
Easy and loving as Susan—
Jenny.
Someone is waiting,
Warm as Susan,
Frantic and touching as Amy—
Joanne.

Would I know her even if I met her?
Have I missed her? Did I let her go?
A Susan sort of Sarah,
A Jennyish Joanne,
Wait for me, I'm ready now,
I'll find you if I can!

Someone will hold me,
Soft as Jenny,
Skinny and blue-eyed as Amy—
Susan.
Someone will wake me,
Sweet as Amy,
Tender and foolish as Sarah—
Joanne. . . .

Another of Sondheim's remarkably fresh songs is sung by a secondary character, Marta. It has no preparation, but occurs at the very start of a scene, Marta seated on one end of a park bench, Robert on the other. I would like to quote the entire scene since the other two girls who figure in Robert's life are obliquely "embraced" by, if not included in, the song. "Another Hundred People" is universal. Although the narrative lyrics tell a complete tale, the intermittent dialogue specifies and develops personal aspects of the song.

A very strong feature of both the sentiments and the lyrics that express them is the cold, abrasive nonromantic descriptive language, thought in most songs to be nonlyrical. As employed here by Sondheim, they are the very essence of the song. I refer to words like "got off," used four times in the first stanza. Then there are unloving and quite accurate words: crowded, guarded, rusty, dusty, battered, postered, and crude in the second, third, and fourth sections, plus realistic expressions of frustration such as " 'Cause I looked in vain" and "my service will explain . . ."

This is an extraordinarily accurate and evocative picture of New York in the 1970s (not the 1930s or any other time) from the point of view of a young person who sees it without history or prejudice.

"ANOTHER HUNDRED PEOPLE"

MARTA
Another hundred people just got off of the train
And came up through the ground
While another hundred people just got off of the bus
And are looking around
At another hundred people who got off of the plane
And are looking at us
Who got off of the train
And the plane and the bus
Maybe yesterday.

It's a city of strangers—
Some come to work, some to play—
A city of strangers—
Some come to stare, some to stay,
And every day
The ones who stay
Can find each other in the crowded streets and the guarded
    parks,
By the rusty fountains and the dusty trees with the battered
    barks,
And they walk together past the postered walls with the crude
    remarks,
And they meet at parties through the friends of friends who
    they never know.
Will you pick me up or do I meet you there or shall we let it go?
Did you get my message? 'Cause I looked in vain.
Can we see each other Tuesday if it doesn't rain?
Look, I'll call you in the morning or my service will explain . . .

And another hundred people just got off of the train.

(APRIL, in an airline stewardess' uniform, enters and sits next to ROBERT. MARTA, although she is not included, listens to the scene)

APRIL   I didn't come right to New York. I went to Northwestern University for two years, but it was a pitiful mistake. I was on probation the whole two years. I was getting ready to go back to Shaker Heights when I decided where I really wanted to live more than any other place was—Radio City. I thought it was a wonderful little city near New York. So I came here. I'm very dumb.

ROBERT   You're not dumb, April.

APRIL   To me I am. Even the reason I stayed in New York was because I just cannot get interested in myself—I'm so boring.

ROBERT   I find you very interesting.

APRIL   Well, I'm just not. I used to think I was so odd. But my roommate is the same way. He's also very dumb.

ROBERT   Oh, you never mentioned him. Is he—your lover?

APRIL   Oh, no. We just share this great big apartment on West End Avenue. We have our own rooms and everything. I'd show it to you but we've never had company. He's the sweetest thing, actually. I think he likes the arrangement. I don't know, though—we never discuss it. He was born in New York, so nothing really interests him. I don't have anything more to say. (She exits)

MARTA   (Sings)
And they find each other in the crowded streets and the guarded parks,
By the rusty fountains and the dusty trees with the battered barks,
And they walk together past the postered walls with the crude remarks,
And they meet at parties through the friends of friends who they never know.
Will you pick me up or do I meet you there or shall we let it go?
Did you get my message? 'Cause I looked in vain.
Can we see each other Tuesday if it doesn't rain?
Look, I'll call you in the morning or my service will explain . . .
And another hundred people just got off of the train.

(Now KATHY enters and sits next to ROBERT on the bench)

KATHY   See, Bobby, some people have to know when to come to New York, and some people have to know when to leave. I always thought I'd just naturally come here and spend the rest of my life here. I wanted to have two terrific affairs and then get married. I always knew I was meant to be a wife.

ROBERT   You should have asked me.

KATHY   Wanna marry me?

ROBERT   I did. I honestly did . . . in the beginning. But I . . . I don't know. I never thought that you ever would.

KATHY   I would. I never understood why you'd never ask me.

ROBERT   (Puts his arm around her) You wanted to marry me? And I wanted to marry you. Well then, how the hell did we ever end up such good friends?

KATHY   Bobby, I'm moving to Vermont.

ROBERT   Vermont? Why Vermont?

KATHY   That's where he lives. I'm getting married.

ROBERT   (A pause; takes his arm away) What?

KATHY   Some people still get married, you know.

ROBERT   Do you love him?

KATHY   I'll be a good wife. I just don't want to run around this city any more like I'm having a life. (She pauses) As I said before, some people have to know when to come to New York and some people have to know when to leave.

(And she's gone. MARTA continues singing)

MARTA   Another hundred people just got off of the train
And came up through the ground
While another hundred people just got off of the bus
And are looking around
At another hundred people who got off of the plane
And are looking at us
Who got off of the train
And the plane and the bus
Maybe yesterday.

It's a city of strangers—
Some come to work, some to play—

A city of strangers—
Some come to stare, some to stay,
And every day
Some go away.
(She looks off in the direction in which KATHY *has gone)*
Or they find each other in the crowded streets and the guarded
    parks,
By the rusty fountains and the dusty trees with the battered
    barks,
And they walk together past the postered walls with the crude
    remarks,
And they meet at parties through the friends of friends who
    they never know.
Will you pick me up or do I meet you there or shall we let it go?
Did you get my message? 'Cause I looked in vain.
Can we see each other Tuesday if it doesn't rain?
Look, I'll call you in the morning or my service will explain . . .

And another hundred people just got off of the train.
And another hundred people just got off of the train.
And another hundred people just got off of the train.
And another hundred people just got off of the train.

Late in the second act Joanne sings a grim satiric song, "The Ladies Who Lunch." From the singing character's point of view, it is nasty and hateful. I think it amuses the audience because none of us is very far away from the lady herself, especially when we are unfulfilled. What Sondheim accomplishes in the lyrics both expressively and technically will be obvious to the reader.

"THE LADIES WHO LUNCH"

Here's to the ladies who lunch—
Everybody laugh—
Lounging in their caftans and planning a brunch
On their own behalf.
Off to the gym,
Then to a fitting,
Claiming they're fat,
And looking grim
'Cause they've been sitting,
Choosing a hat—
(She stands)
Does anyone still wear a hat?
I'll drink to that.

Here's to the girls who stay smart—
Aren't they a gas?
Rushing to their classes in optical art,
Wishing it would pass.
Another long exhausting day,
Another thousand dollars,
A matinée, a Pinter play,
Perhaps a piece of Mahler's—
I'll drink to that.
And one for Mahler.

Here's to the girls who play wife—
Aren't they too much?
Keeping house but clutching a copy of *Life*
Just to keep in touch.
The ones who follow the rules,

And meet themselves at the schools,
Too busy to know that they're fools—
Aren't they a gem?
I'll drink to them.
Let's *all* drink to them.

And here's to the girls who just watch—
Aren't they the best?
When they get depressed, it's a bottle of Scotch
Plus a little jest.
Another chance to disapprove,
Another brilliant zinger,
Another reason not to move,
Another vodka stinger—
Aaaahh—I'll drink to that.

So here's to the girls on the go—
Everybody tries.
Look into their eyes and you'll see what they know:
Everybody dies.
A toast to that invincible bunch—
The dinosaurs surviving the crunch—
Let's hear it for the ladies who lunch—
Everybody rise! Rise!
Rise! Rise! Rise! Rise! Rise! Rise!

The closing song of *Company,* sung by Robert, is an affirmation. It is a cry. It must be pointed out—one of the questions that *Company* asks—that the "somebody" of this lyric is never specified and that high above this desire to be tied to a "somebody" is "Being Alive." Perhaps this is the only possible resolution, not in itself very attractive, certainly nonromantic, but probably sufficient, accentuating the last words of "Barcelona," when Robert finally got what he thought he wanted, "Oh, God!" The strong expressiveness of these lyrics transcends the technical means used to produce them which explain themselves.

"BEING ALIVE"

Somebody hold me too close,
Somebody hurt me too deep,
Somebody sit in my chair
And ruin my sleep and make me aware
Of being alive, being alive.

Somebody need me too much,
Somebody know me too well,
Somebody pull me up short
And put me through hell and give me support
For being alive.
Make me alive.
Make me confused, mock me with praise,
Let me be used, vary my days.
But alone is alone, not alive.

Somebody crowd me with love,
Somebody force me to care,
Somebody let me come through.
I'll always be there, as frightened as you,
To help us survive
Being alive, being alive, being alive.

Follies is a curious show, a commendable exercise in pastiche, a serious attempt to discover something new in something old. It is an experiment working toward the future, deserving of admiration and always interesting. Sondheim's superb craftsmanship operates as usual, and I should like to quote the final lyric, heavily larded (intentionally, of course) with clichés, evocative of the past and ending on an abrupt note of bitterness. The sparseness of the rhymes after the verse, often separated by great spaces, accentuates the feeling of acidity.

"LIVE, LAUGH, LOVE"

CHORUS
Here he comes,
Mister Whiz.
Sound the drums,
Here he is.

Raconteur,
Bon vivant.
Tell us, sir,
What we want
To know.
The modus operandi
A dandy should use
When he is feeling low.
(Behind him, a line of CHORUS BOYS *and* CHORUS GIRLS *appears.*
*BEN *joins the line, leading the number like a suave song-and-
dance man)*
MEN
When the winds are blowing,
CHORUS
Yes?
BEN
That's the time to smile.
CHORUS
Oh?
BEN
Learn how to laugh,
Learn how to love,
Learn how to live,
That's my style.
When the rent is owing,
CHORUS
Yes?
BEN
What's the use of tears?
CHORUS
Oh?
BEN
I'd rather laugh,
I'd rather love,
I'd rather live
In arrears.

Some fellows sweat
To get to be millionaires,
Some have a sport
They're devotees of.
Some like to be the champs
At saving postage stamps,
Me, I like to live,
Me, I like to laugh,
Me, I like to love.

Some like to sink
And think in their easy chairs
Of all the things
They've risen above.
Some like to be profound
By reading Proust and Pound.
Me, I like to live,
Me, I like to laugh,
Me, I like to love.

Success is swell
And success is sweet,
But every height has a drop.
The less achievement,
The less defeat.
What's the point of shovin'
Your way to the top?
Live 'n' laugh 'n' love 'n'
You're never a flop.
So when the walls are crumbling,
CHORUS
Yes?
BEN
Don't give up up the ship.
CHORUS
No.
BEN
Learn how to laugh,
Learn how to love,
Learn how to live,
That's my tip.
When I hear the rumbling,
CHORUS
Yes?
BEN
Do I lose my grip?
BEN *and* CHORUS
No!
BEN
I have to laugh,
I have to love,
I have to live.
That's my trip.

Some get a boot
From shooting off cablegrams
Or buzzing bells
To summon the staff.
Some climbers get their kicks
From social politics.
Me, I like to love,
Me, I like to . . .
(He forgets his lyric, calls for it from the conductor, recovers his
poise)
Some break their asses
Passing their bar exams,
Lay out their lives
Like lines on a graph . . .
One day they're diplomats—
Well, bully and congrats!
Me, I like to love,
Me, I . . .

(BEN *suddenly goes blank. He can't remember what comes next. He tries to keep on dancing, stutters out a phrase or two, calls for help to the conductor, who shouts the lyrics to him.*
It's no good. His desperation grows. Behind him, as if nothing at all were wrong, the chorus line of boys and girls goes right on dancing. Making one final effort, BEN *half-sings*)
Me, I like—me, I love—me.

A Little Night Music (1972), with a book by Hugh Wheeler based on Ingmar Bergman's film *Smiles of a Summer Night,* staged and produced by Harold Prince and designed by Boris Aronson, in my opinion represents one large rounded complete piece of American musical theatre, so important and so filled with freshness that it is next to impossible to select lyrics for quotation here. In fact, it is necessary that I be arbitrary.

The music is all in 3/4 time (a bit in 6/8 with a feeling of 3/4), yet it never reminds one of any of the "waltz kings." For me *A Little Night Music* is a joyous lilt. Now and again there are explosions of anger or frustration, but never sadness. Those bitter moments always amuse. The show provides a unique experience that may require some time for full appreciation, but meanwhile it succeeds in communicating enough to the general audience to have become a recognized success. I feel personally that it is an unqualified and timeless triumph.

The first song I should like to quote, "Now," is sung by Fredrik, the husband married to a much younger wife who after many months is still a virgin. Fredrik, a lawyer, is clearly characterized by his use of clear logic, frequent employment of three-syllable words, and his two alternate plans of attack, "A" and "B," against his wife's continuing virginity. The rhymes are consistent and playful.

"NOW"

FREDRIK
Now, as the sweet imbecilities
Tumble so lavishly
Onto her lap . . .

Now, there are two possibilities:
A, I could ravish her,
B, I could nap.

Say it's the ravishment, then we see
The option
That follows, of course:

A, the deployment of charm, or B,
The adoption
Of physical force . . .

Now B might arouse her,
But if I assume
I trip on my trouser
Leg crossing the room . . .

Her hair getting tangled,
Her stays getting snapped,
My nerves will be jangled,
My energy sapped . . .

Removing her clothing
Would take me all day
And her subsequent loathing
Would turn me away—

Which eliminates B
And which leaves us with A . . .

Now, in so far as approaching it,
What would be festive
But have its effect?

Now, there are two ways of broaching it:
A, the suggestive
And B, the direct . . .

Say that I settle on B, to wit,
A charmingly
Lecherous mood . . .

A, I could put on my nightshirt or sit
Disarmingly,
B, in the nude . . .

That might be effective,
My body's all right,
But not in perspective
And not in the light . . .

I'm bound to be chilly
And feel a buffoon,
But nightshirts are silly
In mid-afternoon . . .

Which leaves the suggestive,
But how to proceed?
Although she gets restive,
Perhaps I could read . . .

In view of her penchant
For something romantic,
De Sade is too trenchant
And Dickens too frantic,
And Stendhal would ruin
The plan of attack,
As there isn't much blue in
The Red and the Black . . .

De Maupassant's candor
Would cause her dismay.
The Brontës are grander
But not very gay.
Her taste is much blander,
I'm sorry to say,
But is Hans Christian Ander-
Sen ever risqué?
Which eliminates A . . .

Now, with my mental facilities
Partially muddied
And ready to snap . . .

Now, though there are possibilities
Still to be studied,
I might as well nap . . .

Bow though I must
To adjust
My original plan . . .

How shall I sleep
Half as deep
As I usually can? . . .

When now I still want and/or love you,
Now as always,
Now,
Anne?

Fredrik's son by an earlier marriage, Henrik, a frustrated theology student and amateur cellist, reveals his pathetic character and situation (he is secretly in love with his young mother-in-law, Anne). This song of frustration can only be comprehended as amusing.

"LATER"

HENRIK
Later . . .
When is later? . . .
All you ever hear is, "Later, Henrik! Henrik, later. . . ."
"Yes, we know, Henrik,
Oh, Henrik—
Everyone agrees, Henrik—
Please, Henrik!"
You have a thought you're fairly bursting with,
A personal discovery or problem, and it's
"What's your rush, Henrik?
Shush, Henrik—
Goodness, how you gush, Henrik—
Hush, Henrik!"
You murmur,
"I only . . .
It's just that . . .
For God's sake!"
"Later, Henrik . . ."

"Henrik" . . .
Who is "Henrik"? . . .
Oh, that lawyer's son, the one who mumbles—
Short and boring.
Yes, he's hardly worth ignoring
And who cares if he's all dammed—
—I beg your pardon—
Up inside?

As I've often stated,
It's intolerable
Being tolerated.
"Reassure Henrik,
Poor Henrik.
Henrik, you'll endure
Being pure, Henrik."
Though I've been born, I've never been!
How can I wait around for later?
I'll be ninety on my deathbed
And the late, or rather later,
Henrik Egerman!
Doesn't anything begin?

The two preceding songs are extraordinarily combined with a *third* one sung by the young bride Anne, "Soon." Desirée, referred to in this ingenious trio, is a glamorous actress, the heroine of the show. One extraordinary aspect of this trio is that in the putting together of the three songs, nearly all of the lyrics of each are comprehensible. Most important is the fact that the personal characteristics of each of the people clearly emerge, and each of them promises a course of action. The song is also very humorous.

"SOON"

ANNE
Soon, I promise.
Soon I won't shy away,
Dear old—
Soon. I want to.
Soon, whatever you say.
Even now,
When you're close and we touch,
And you're kissing my brow
I don't mind it too much.
And you'll have to admit
I'm endearing,
I help keep things humming,
I'm not domineering,
What's one small shortcoming?
And think of how I adore you,
Think of how much you love me.
If I were perfect for you,
Wouldn't you tire of me?
Soon,
All too soon?
Dear old—
(The sound of HENRIK'S cello, ANNE goes into the other room and stops him.)
ANNE
Soon—

HENRIK
"Later". . .

ANNE
I promise.

HENRIK
When is "later"?

ANNE	HENRIK	FREDRIK
Soon	"Later, Henrik, later."	
I won't shy	All you ever hear is,	
Away,	"Yes, we know, Henrik, oh Henrik,	
Dear, old . . .	Everyone agrees, Henrik, please, Henrik!"	
Soon.		
I want to.	HENRIK	FREDRIK
	"Later". . .	Now,
	When is "later"?	As the sweet imbecilities
	All you ever	Trip on my trouser leg,
Soon,		
	Hear is	
Whatever you		
say.	"Later, Henrik,	
		Stendhal eliminates
	Later."	A,
	As I've often	
	Stated:	
	When?	But when?
Even	Maybe	Maybe
Now,		
When you're	Soon, soon	Later.
close		
And we touch,	I'll be ninety	

And you're
kissing
My brow,
I don't mind it

Too much,

And you'll have
to
Admit
I'm endearing
—I help
Keep things

Humming, I'm

Not domineer-
ing,
What's one
small
Shortcoming?
And
Think of how
I adore you,
Think of how
Much you love
me.
If I were per-
fect
For you,
Wouldn't you
tire
Of me
Later?

We will,
Later.

We will . . .
Soon.

Soon.

Soon.

And
Dead.

I don't mind it

Too much,

Since I have to
Admit
I find peering

Through life's

Gray windows
Impatiently
Not very cheer-
ing.
Do I fear
death?
Let it
Come to me
Now,

Now,

Now,

Now.

Come to me
Soon. If I'm
Dead,
I can
Wait.

How can I
Live until
Later?

Later . . .

Later . . .

When I'm kiss-
ing
Your brow
And I'm strok-
ing your head,

You'll come
into my bed.
And you have
to
Admit
I've been
hearing
All those trem-
ulous cries
Patiently,

Not interfering
With those trem-
ulous thighs.

Come to me
Soon,

Soon,

Soon,

Soon.

Come to me
Soon,

Straight to me,
never mind
How.

Darling,
Now—
I still want and/
or
Love
You,

Now, as
Always,

Now,
Desirée.

Later Fredrik visits his onetime amour, Desirée, in search of understanding, not to mention sex. Both characters explain their own actions during the twenty years since their affair quite frankly. Fredrik begins a duet, "You Must Meet My Wife," a hilarious musical scene. Each singer retains his own character: he is somewhat obtuse, she is realistic, and makes legitimate fun of every attribute he lavishes on his wife. What Sondheim achieves that is so very difficult (in addition to the unrelenting humor) is that most of this number consists of two- or three-syllable exchanges from one to the other. To do this and to keep the music, the drama, the humor, and the credibility going is an enormous achievement.

"YOU MUST MEET MY WIFE"

FREDRIK   She lightens my sadness,
She livens my days,
She bursts with a kind of madness
My well-ordered ways.
My happiest mistake,
The ache of my life:
You must meet my wife.

She bubbles with pleasure,
She glows with surprise,
Disrupts my accustomed leisure
And ruffles my ties.
I don't know even now
Quite how it began.
You must meet my wife, my Anne.

One thousand whims to which I give in,
Since her smallest tear turns me ashen.
I never dreamed that I could live in
So completely demented,
Contented
A fashion.

So sunlike, so winning,
So unlike a wife.
I do think that I'm beginning
To show signs of life.
Don't ask me how at my age
One still can grow—
If you met my wife,
You'd know.

DESIRÉE   Dear Fredrik. I'm just longing to meet her. Sometime.
FREDRIK   She sparkles.
DESIRÉE   How pleasant.
FREDRIK   She twinkles.
DESIRÉE   How nice.
FREDRIK   Her youth is a sort of present—
DESIRÉE   Whatever the price.
FREDRIK   The incandescent—what?—the—
DESIRÉE   (Proffering a cigarette) Light?
FREDRIK   (Lighting it)—Of my life!
You must meet my wife.
DESIRÉE   Yes, I must, I really must. Now—
FREDRIK   She flutters.
DESIRÉE   How charming.
FREDRIK   She twitters.
DESIRÉE   My word!
FREDRIK   She floats.
DESIRÉE   Isn't that alarming?
What is she, a bird?
FREDRIK   She makes me feel I'm—what?—
DESIRÉE   A very old man?
FREDRIK   Yes—no!
DESIRÉE   No.

FREDRIK   But—

DESIRÉE   I must meet your Gertrude.

FREDRIK   My Anne.

DESIRÉE   Sorry—Anne.

FREDRIK   She loves my voice, my walk, my moustache,
          The cigar, in fact, that I'm smoking.
          She'll watch me puff until it's just ash,
          Then she'll save the cigar butt.

DESIRÉE   Bizarre, but
          You're joking.

FREDRIK   She dotes on—

DESIRÉE   Your dimple.

FREDRIK   My snoring.

DESIRÉE   How dear.

FREDRIK   The point is, she's really simple.

DESIRÉE   Yes, that much seems clear.

FREDRIK   She gives me funny names.

DESIRÉE   Like—?

FREDRIK   "Old Dry-As-Dust."

DESIRÉE   Wouldn't she just?

FREDRIK   You must meet my wife.

DESIRÉE   If I must—yes, I must.

FREDRIK   A sea of whims that I submerge in,
          Yet so lovable in repentance.
          Unfortunately still a virgin,
          But you can't force a flower—

DESIRÉE   Don't finish that sentence!
          She's monstrous!

FREDRIK   She's frightened.

DESIRÉE   Unfeeling!

FREDRIK   Unversed.
          She'd strike you as unenlightened.

DESIRÉE   No, I'd strike her first.

FREDRIK   Her reticence, her apprehension—

DESIRÉE   Her crust!

FREDRIK   No!

DESIRÉE   Yes!

FREDRIK   No!

DESIRÉE   Fredrik . . .

FREDRIK   You must meet my wife.

DESIRÉE   Let me get my hat and my knife.

FREDRIK   What was that?

DESIRÉE   I must meet your wife.

FREDRIK   Yes, you must.   DESIRÉE   Yes, I must.

Desirée's old mother, Mme. Armfeldt, usually singing from a queenly position in a wheelchair, has a sharp witty song of recollection of the good old days when there was an art to being a successful mistress and to being properly compensated. The haughty tone of this song, so antithetical to the subject matter, makes it incredibly funny. Several of the rhymes are so unusual that I should like to call attention to them in advance.

There are four rhymes in two brief lines, two of them nearly hidden: "Liaisons today?" "Hardly pay their shoddy way."

Then, other fun rhymes: "I acquired some position/Plus a tiny Titian. . . ."; "indiscriminate/Women, it"; "Where's craft?"/"I acquired a chateau/Extravagantly o-/Verstaffed."

There is a fiendishly clever use of *I* assonances, plus some rhymes in one sequence:

Untidy—take my daughter, *I*
Taught her, *I*

Tried my best to point the way.
I even named her Desirée.

"LIAISONS"

MME. ARMFELDT

At the villa of the Baron de Signac,
Where I spent a somewhat infamous year,
At the villa of the Baron de Signac
I had ladies in attendance,
Fire-opal pendants. . . .

Liaisons! What's happened to them,
Liaisons today?
Disgraceful! What's become of them?
Some of them
Hardly pay their shoddy way.

What once was a rare champagne
Is now just an amiable hock,
What once was a villa, at least,
Is "digs" . . .
What once was a gown with train
Is now just a simple little frock,
What once was a sumptuous feast
Is figs.
No, not even figs—raisins.
Ah, liaisons!

Now let me see . . . Where was I? . . . oh, yes . . . .
At the palace of the Duke of Ferrara,
Who was prematurely deaf but a dear,
At the palace of the Duke of Ferrara
I acquired some position
Plus a tiny Titian . . . .

Liaisons! What's happened to them,
Liaisons today?
To see them—indiscriminate
Women, it
Pains me more than I can say,
The lack of taste that they display.

Where is style?
Where is skill?
Where is forethought?
Where's discretion of the heart,
Where's passion in the art,
Where's craft?
With a smile
And a will
But with more thought,
I acquired a chateau
Extravagantly o-
Verstaffed.

Too many people muddle sex with mere desire,
And when emotion intervenes,
The nets descend.
It should on no account perplex, or worse, inspire.
It's but a pleasurable means
To a measurable end.
Why does no one comprehend?
Let us hope this lunacy is just a trend.

Where was I? . . . oh, yes. . . .
In the castle of the King of the Belgians
We would visit through a false chiffonier,
In the castle of the King of the Belgians
Who, when things got rather touchy,
Deeded me a duchy. . . .

Liaisons! What's happened to them,
Liaisons today?
Untidy—take my daughter, I
Taught her, I
Tried my best to point the way.
I even named her Desirée.

In a world where the kings are employers,
Where the amateur prevails and delicacy fails to pay,
In a world where the princes are lawyers,
What can anyone expect except to recollect
Liai. . . .
(She falls asleep.)

Desirée's lover, Carl-Magnus, a handsome young soldier,
demanding, and by her own account stupid, has another kind
of character song. It is a soliloquy in which he is obviously
disturbed. He has found Desirée in the middle of the night with
Fredrik wearing Carl-Magnus's dressing gown. Fredrik has
explained that as Desirée's lawyer he had come to have her sign
papers and that his being without clothes is due to his having
slipped into a hip bath. Carl-Magnus has previously accepted
both preposterous explanations but is now disturbed and
reexamining them.

Aside from Sondheim's ingenious parody, the humor of the
song derives from Carl-Magnus's disturbed state of mind. The
lyrics also characterize him as thick-witted, overly male, unaware of his wife's (Charlotte) real feelings, and vain.

"IN PRAISE OF WOMEN"

CARL-MAGNUS   She wouldn't . . .
Therefore they didn't . . .
So then it wasn't . . .
Not unless it . . .
Would she?

She doesn't . . .
God knows she needn't . . .
Therefore it's not.

He'd never . . .
Therefore they haven't . . .
Which makes the question absolutely . . .
Could she?

She daren't . . .
Therefore I mustn't . . .
What utter rot!

Fidelity is more than mere display,
It's what a man expects from life.
Fidelity like mine to Desirée
And Charlotte, my devoted wife.

The papers . . .
He mentioned papers,
Some legal papers which I didn't see there.
Where are they,

The goddamn papers
She had to sign?

What nonsense . . .
He brought some papers,
They were important,
So he had to be there.
I'll kill him . . .
Why should I bother?
The woman's mine!

Besides, no matter what one might infer,
One must have faith to some degree.
The least that I can do is trust in her
The way that Charlotte trusts in me.

Capable, pliable . . .
Women, women . . .
Undemanding and reliable,
Knowing their place.
Insufferable, yes, but gentle,
Their weaknesses are incidental.
A functional but ornamental
Race.
Durable, sensible . . .
Women, women . . .
Very nearly indispensable,
Creatures of grace.
God knows the foolishness about them,
But if one had to live without them
The world would surely be a poorer,
If purer,
Place.

The hip bath . . .
About that hip bath . . .
How can you slip and
Trip into a hip bath?

The papers . . .
Where were those papers?
Of course he might have
Taken back the papers. . . .
She wouldn't . . .
Therefore they didn't . . .
The woman's mine!

It is difficult to bring this latest of Stephen Sondheim's accomplishments to an end here. It would be simpler to include
"The Sun Won't Set," the charming roundelay "A Weekend in
the Country," the duet "It Would Have Been Wonderful," the
trio "Perpetual Anticipation," Desirée's sensitive "Send in the
Clowns," and others, but there must be some limit and I have
chosen the song of the maid Petra," The Miller's Son," for last.
It resembles a folk song and is fantastically compelling. Allow
me to point out a few of its many lyric features that might go
unnoticed. The whole idea is fun-loving and the words,
repeated three times— "There are mouths to be kissed/Before
mouths to be fed"—explain the maid's point of view.

Here Sondheim plays with like sounds—sometimes vowels,
sometimes consonants, and, along with the song's meanings, he
develops a freedom of verbal play that I cannot recall anywhere
else. Take the alliterations: "marry the miller's," "piece of
property," "wink and a wiggle," "giggle on the grass," "A pinch
and a diddle, In the middle of what passes by."

It's a very short road
From the *pinch* and the *punch*
To the *paunch* and the *pouch*
And the *pension*.

This last verse is a fantastic picture of the movement from youth to age, then old age (in four short lines), but despite the seriousness, the fun-with-words goes on unabated. As if these lines had not accomplished enough on their own, two of them contain words that rhyme in the ensuing verse:

It's a very short road
To the ten-thousandth *lunch*
And the belch and the *grouch*
And the sigh.

The ballad or storytelling element is kept alive first with "I shall marry the miller's son" changed to "Or I shall marry the businessman" and then to "Or I shall marry the Prince of Wales" ending with "And I shall marry the miller's son."

There is a formidable series of rhymes in the last section:

From the fling that's for fun(1)
To the thigh(2) pressing un(1)-
Der the ta(3)ble.
It's a very short day(3)
Till you're stuck with just one(1)
Or it has to be done(1)
On the sly(2).

And, not to be missed, is the fact that these four *un* rhymes also rhyme with the very last line (eleven lines later): "And I shall marry the miller's son."

"THE MILLER'S SON"

PETRA
I shall marry the miller's son,
Pin my hat on a nice piece of property.
Friday nights, for a bit of fun,
We'll go dancing.
Meanwhile. . . .
It's a wink and a wiggle
And a giggle on the grass
And I'll trip the Light Fandango,
A pinch and a diddle
In the middle of what passes by.
It's a very short road
From the pinch and the punch
To the paunch and the pouch
And the pension.
It's a very short road
To the ten-thousandth lunch
And the belch and the grouch
And the sigh.
In the meanwhile,
There are mouths to be kissed
Before mouths to be fed,
And a lot in between
In the meanwhile.
And a girl ought to celebrate
What passes by.
Or I shall marry the businessman,
Five fat babies and lots of security.
Friday nights, if we think we can,
We'll go dancing.
Meanwhile. . . .
It's a push and a fumble
And a tumble in the sheets
And I'll foot the Highland Fancy,
A dip in the butter
And a flutter with what meets my eye.
It's a very short fetch
From the push and the whoop
To the squint and the stoop
And the mumble.
It's not much of a stretch
To the cribs and the croup
And the bosoms that droop
And go dry.
In the meanwhile,
There are mouths to be kissed
Before mouths to be fed,
And there's many a tryst
And there's many a bed
To be sampled and seen
In the meanwhile.
And a girl has to celebrate
What passes by.

Or I shall marry the Prince of Wales.
Pearls and servants and dressing for festivals.
Friday nights, with him all in tails,
We'll have dancing.
Meanwhile. . . .
It's a rip in the bustle
And a rustle in the hay
And I'll pitch the Quick Fantastic,
With flings of confetti
And my petticoats away up high.
It's a very short way
From the fling that's for fun
To the thigh pressing un-
Der the table.
It's a very short day
Till you're stuck with just one
Or it has to be done
On the sly.
In the meanwhile,
There are mouths to be kissed
Before mouths to be fed,
And there's many a tryst
And there's many a bed,
There's a lot I'll have missed
But I'll not have been dead
When I die!
And a person should celebrate everything
Passing by.

And I shall marry the miller's son.

I need say no more, but I cannot refrain from repeating briefly that in my opinion Stephen Sondheim through talent, preparation, and now consummate skill is the young hope of the American musical theatre. We can be grateful for what he has already achieved. What lies ahead should be truly wonderful because it will come of what he wants to give and not what he hopes to get!

Leonard Sillman: New Faces

From the early part of this century, revues large and small helped to develop composers and lyricists. The reasons are clear. There was no score as such, only a series of disconnected songs that could be incorporated, transposed, sung by a different character, or deleted at will. Trying out new writers presented no hazards: if they worked, all well and good; if not, little was lost.

In the big revues the girls, the parade of stars, and the scenery and costumes provided whatever guidelines there were. One show after another tried to outdo its predecessors and competitors. The whole idea eventually wore itself out. The smaller revue substituted literate ideas and satire for what had formally been considered indispensable: girls, stars, and production opulence. When new writers developed, it was often a case of serendipity at work. And indeed many of the most important writers *did* serve apprenticeships in one or the other kind of revue.

What made Leonard Sillman's *New Faces* different was the fact that Sillman was actually looking for songs, sketches, lyrics, and performers among the young and as yet unknown. This was the reverse attitude of the large revues and an exaggerated vision of the smaller shows' credos.

Sillman, starting in 1934, produced seven of these revues through 1968. The casts included a host of fairly unknown people: James Shelton, Henry Fonda, Imogene Coca, Charles Walters, Van Johnson, Hildegarde Halliday, Eartha Kitt, Alice Ghostley, Ronny Graham, Inga Svenson, Carol Lawrence, Madeline Kahn, and Maggie Smith. The writers included Neil Simon; the composers and lyricists included Nancy Hamilton, Morgan Lewis, James Shelton, June Carroll, Arthur Siegel, Robert Sour, E. Y. Harburg, Irvin Graham, Will Irwin,

Sheldon Harnick, Ronny Graham, Murray Grand, Harold Karr, Matt Dubey, Dean Fuller, Marshall Barer, Jack Holmes, William Roy, Clark Gesner, Alonzo Levister, Paul Nassau, Hal Hackady, David Shire, Michael Brown, and many, many more.

Leonard Sillman deserves great credit for his enterprise and judgment. Time makes us applaud both.

Of the many songs in the seven productions I should like to quote the lyrics from "You're My Relaxation" (1934) (music by Charles Schwab, lyrics by Robert Sour), "Guess Who I Saw Today?" (1952) (music by Murray Grand, lyrics by Elisse Boyd), "Boston Beguine" (1952) (music and lyrics by Sheldon Harnick) (see chapter on Harnick), "Lizzie Borden" (1952) (music and lyrics by Michael Brown), "I'm in Love with Miss Logan" (1952) (music and lyrics by Ronny Graham), "Penny Candy" (1952) (music by Arthur Siegel, lyrics by June Carroll), and "April in Fairbanks" (1956) (music and lyrics by Murray Grand).

"YOU'RE MY RELAXATION"

REFRAIN
You're My Relaxation,
You're my soothing touch.
Worry you erase away
So please don't turn your face away;
I like you so much

You're my daily tonic,
Ginger ale and rye.
I would be indebted if
You would be my sedative;
Please keep standing by.

When you hold my hand I
Can understand why
I get a thrill.
When on panic I have bordered
The doctor ordered
A little pill like you,
There's so much you can do.

You're My Relaxation,
You're my food and drink.
I'll follow, dear, where you may lead,
For you're exactly what I need.
I love you—I think.

"GUESS WHO I SAW TODAY?"

VERSE

You're so late getting home from the office,
Did you miss your train?
Were you caught in the rain?
No, don't bother to explain.
Can I fix you a quick martini?
As a matter of fact I'll have one with you,
For to tell you the truth
I've had quite a day too!

REFRAIN

Guess who I saw today, my dear!
I went in town to shop around for something new
And thought I'd stop and have a bite when I was through.
I looked around for someplace near and it occurred to me
    where I had parked the car
I'd seen a most attractive French cafe and bar.
It really wasn't very far.
The waiter showed me to a dark, secluded corner
And when my eyes became accustomed to the gloom,
I saw two people at the bar
Who were so much in love
That even I could spot it clear across the room.
Guess who I saw today, my dear!
I've never been so shocked before;
I headed blindly for the door,
They didn't see me passing through
Guess who I saw today! I saw you!

"LIZZIE BORDEN"

VERSE ONE

One hot day in old Fall River,
Mister Andrew Borden died,
And they booked his daughter Lizzie
On a charge of homicide.
Some folks say, "She didn't do it."
Others say, "Of course, she did."
But they all agree Miss Lizzie B.
Was quite a problem kid.

CHORUS ONE

'Cause you can't chop your poppa up in Massachusetts,
Not even if it's planned as a surprise.
No, you can't chop your poppa up in Massachusetts;
You know how neighbors love to criticize.

VERSE TWO

Now, she got him on the sofa,
Where he'd gone to take a snooze,
And I hope he went to heaven,
'Cause he wasn't wearing shoes.
Lizzie kind of rearranged him
With a hatchet, so they say.
And then she got her mother in
That same old-fashioned way.

CHORUS TWO

But you can't chop your momma up in Massachusetts,
Not even if you're tired of her cuisine.
No, you can't chop your momma up in Massachusetts;
If you do, you know there's bound to be a scene.

VERSE THREE

Oh, they really kept her hopping
On that August afternoon,
With both down and upstairs chopping
While she hummed a ragtime tune.
And her maw, when Lizzie whacked her,
Looked an awful lot like paw,
Like somebody in a tractor
Had been backing over maw.

CHORUS THREE

Oh, you can't chop your poppa up in Massachusetts,
And then blame all the damage on the mice.
No, you can't chop your momma up in Massachusetts;
That kind of thing just isn't very nice.

VERSE FOUR

Now, it wasn't done for pleasure
And it wasn't done for spite,
And it wasn't done because the
Lady wasn't very bright.
She had always done the slightest thing
That mom and poppa bid.
They said, "Lizzie, cut it out,"
And that's exactly what she did.

CHORUS FOUR

But you can't chop your poppa up in Massachusetts,
And then get dressed to go out for a walk.
No you can't chop your poppa up in Massachusetts;
Massachusetts is a far cry from New York.

"I'M IN LOVE WITH MISS LOGAN"

VERSE

What's the matter with me?
What's the matter with me?
School is let out and it's way after three;
But I'm sittin' here with my chin on my knee,
Say, what is the matter with me?
I should be at home, and I wanna go home,
But I knew darn well I'm not gonna go home!
So I just sit here with my chin on my knee;
What the heck is the matter with me?
What if the gang saw me sittin' like this?
They'd think I was waitin' for some girl.
So what if they saw me? they couldn't hee-haw me,
'Cause I'm not waitin' for any girl!

Then what am I waitin' here for?
And why am I watchin' the door?

REFRAIN
I'm in love, I'm in love, I'm in love with Miss Logan
I'm in love, I'm in love, I'm in love with Miss Logan
Tho' I still hate arithmetic,
I'll pass arithmetic,
Long as Miss Logan is teachin' arithmetic!
I'm in love with Miss Logan
And I wish, I wish I was not!

"PENNY CANDY"

VERSE
Life has been kind to me,
I've riches enough to buy
Whatever catches my eye,
But nothing catches my eye!
My appetite has faded, alas!
The lady's jaded!
When I was a little girl, poor and plain,
All I asked of life was in this refrain:

CHORUS 1
Penny candy,
Candy for a penny;
I wish I could still get a kick
From a penny peppermint stick
Or an indigestible gummy hat
That stuck to my teeth and made me fat.
Penny candy,
Candy for a penny.
I wish I could bounce a red ball
On the brick of a tenement wall,
And never ask for more at all, at all.
Candy! Candy!
The candy store I could never pass
Without pressing my nose against the glass.
Candy! Candy!
And oh, how I'd sigh! Alack, alas!
For a doll made of sweet chewing wax!
Penny candy,
Candy for a penny,
I ask for more than a penny now;
I've grown very wise, you see,
But I wish that a sweet
Were still fun to eat.
Now a penny's a memory.

CHORUS 2
Penny candy,
Candy for a penny;
I wish I could still get a kick
From a penny peppermint stick

Or a black and shiny licorice drop
And a lemon yellow lollypop.
Penny candy,
Candy for a penny.
I wish I could bounce etc.

"APRIL IN FAIRBANKS"

VERSE
Autumn in New York
And April in Paris
Are no longer chic.
Winters in Mallorca
And summers in Capri
Are gone, so to speak.
The people who have the wherewithal
Have found a new place to have a ball.
They've deserted the Champs-Elysees,
The Piazza d'Spagna
Is no longer gay.
They say their thanks for Fairbanks,
Alaska.

CHORUS 1
April in Fairbanks,
There's nothing more appealing.
You feel your blood congealing
In April in Fairbanks.
Bright Arctic moonlight illuminates the ice-floes
And ev'rybody's breath shows
In Fairbanks.
You've never known the charm of Spring until you hear a
    walrus sighing.
The air is perfumed with the smell of blubber frying.
April in Fairbanks;
You'll suddenly discover
A Polar Bear's your lover
In Fairbanks.

CHORUS 2
Heavenly weather
Will turn your skin to leather
And lock your jaws together
In April in Fairbanks.
North Polar breezes will sing you a cadenza
And bring you influenza
In Fairbanks.
I'll leave the Riviera to the fools who want a fancy palace.
Give me an igloo and the Aurora Borealis.
April in Fairbanks;
I simply can't believe it.
I know I'll never leave it alive this April.

Courtesy ASCAP

three

THE KURT WEILL COLLABORATIONS

In the last decades of the nineteenth century the success of Gilbert and Sullivan created a new idea in the history of musical theatre, that of the composer and lyricist as an inseparable team, two names functioning as a single entity. But it was not until fifty years ago that this particular kind of wedding became general practice. The duo designations also announced, not creative writers, but performers. These included Harrigan and Hart, McIntyre and Heath, Gallagher and Shean, Weber and Fields, and many others.

Although Johann Strauss's *Die Fledermaus,* written only three years prior to Gilbert and Sullivan's first collaboration, *Trial by Jury,* was based on a French farce by Meilhac and Halévy, and rendered into German by Haffner and Genée, Strauss's best-known work has come to posterity as the work of the composer alone.

Likewise, two decades earlier in Paris, Jacques Offenbach began a formidable career as an operetta composer. The names of his numberless librettists are to be found in encyclopedias, but *La Périchole, La Belle Hélène, Orphée aux Enfers,* and the nearly ninety others achieved their particular immortality as the work mainly of their composer. Nor was Offenbach the exception. We remember *Aïda* as Verdi's, *Carmen* as Bizet's, *Madama Butterfly* as Puccini's, *Robin Hood* as De Koven's, *Mlle. Modiste* as Herbert's, and so on. These and many other stage works requiring collaboration are remembered principally as the work of the composer, occurred approximately during the fifty years between Gilbert and Sullivan and Rodgers and Hart. The latter were inseparable until Hart's death and the new team became Rodgers and Hammerstein. The Gershwin brothers merged as a single name. Porter, Loesser, Rome, and often Sondheim took care of both departments. Much of Lerner has been with Loewe, Dietz most often with Schwartz, all of Jones with Schmidt, and much of Harnick with Bock. And so the dual designation of a show's musical authorship was largely reestablished. However, Harburg and Dorothy Fields worked with many different composers and as a result the dual label was never fully established. On the other hand, Kern and Weill had so many collaborators that they, as composers, again took solo bows.

Kurt Weill began his career as a composer of serious music when he was about twenty-four. For about four years he wrote only operas, and these tended increasingly to express his taste for American popular music. *Mahagonny,* one of these operas, and a children's opera *Der Jasager* had texts by Bertolt Brecht, who also collaborated with Weill on the fantastically successful *Die Dreigroschenoper (The Threepenny Opera)* (1928).

Due to the rise of Adolf Hitler, the Weills (Mrs. Weill is Lotte Lenya) left Germany in 1933 and came to the United States in 1935 via Paris and London. Here he began a new career for which he was (through practice) eminently prepared.

In addition to the style of Weill's music, which is instantly recognizable in everything that he wrote, three other major facts emerge and all of them set him apart from all other writers in our theatre.

The first is that Weill orchestrated all his own scores, a fact that indicates that a prodigious amount of work *had* to have been done before rehearsals began.

Secondly, he began as an opera composer and although he added many hit songs to our repertoire, he remained fundamentally an opera composer. His Broadway shows reflect this propensity, and three years before his untimely death in 1950 he actually wrote another true opera, *Street Scene.* His idiom was his own, but it reflected his passionate interest in the popular music of America.

Lastly, nearly all his American compositions (1936-1949) were created with *different* lyricists, an unusual practice in the theatre.

For this reason I should like to reproduce here a few lyrics from several shows. Those marked with an asterisk have been covered in earlier chapters devoted to the works of specific lyricists. A list of Weill's American stage works, together with their lyricists, follows.

Johnny Johnson (1936) Paul Green
The Eternal Road (1937) was written earlier with Franz

Werfel, but not produced here until after *Johnny Johnson*
Knickerbocker Holiday (1938) Maxwell Anderson
Lady in the Dark (1941) Ira Gershwin *
One Touch of Venus (1943) Ogden Nash
The Firebrand of Florence (1945) Ira Gershwin
Street Scene (1947) Langston Hughes
Love Life (1948) Alan Jay Lerner *
Down in the Valley (1948) Arnold Sondgaard
Lost in the Stars (1949) Maxwell Anderson

After Weill's death, *The Threepenny Opera* was produced most successfully Off-Broadway (1954) in an adaptation of Brecht's book and lyrics by Marc Blitzstein.

Of these varied lyricists, Gershwin and Lerner had become fixtures in the Broadway theatre. Paul Green was a playwright, Maxwell Anderson, a writer of poetic plays, Ogden Nash, author of light and humorous verse, Arnold Sondgaard, a playwright, and Langston Hughes, playwright and poet.

The few lyrics quoted need no comment, but I thought it fitting that those not principally regarded as lyricists be represented here as Weill collaborators.

"LISTEN TO MY SONG" ("JOHNNY'S SONG")

Johnny Johnson (1936)
Lyrics by Paul Green

When man was first created
I'm sure his maker meant
He'd be of good intent,
Kind heart and love,
Forgiving wrong,
And though through ages fated
To climb our wandering way,
At last we'll find the day
When joy shall be our song.
I hear from ev'ry doubting Thomas
The world's a mighty cruel place,
The broken heart, the broken promise,
The evil of the human race,
But you and I don't think so,
We know there's something still
Of good beyond such ill
Of right beyond wrong.
And we'll never lose our faith and hope and trust in all mankind.
We'll work and strive while we're alive, that better way to find.
As up and down I wander my weary way and long,
I meet all kinds of folks who listen to my song.

"SEPTEMBER SONG"

Knickerbocker Holiday (1938)
Lyrics by Maxwell Anderson

VERSE ONE
When I was a young man courting the girls,
I played me a waiting game:
If a maid refused me with tossing curls,
I'd let the old earth take a couple of whirls,

While I plied her with tears in lieu of pearls
And as time came around she came my way,
As time came around she came.

REFRAIN
Oh, it's a long, long while
From May to December,
But the days grow short
When you reach September.
When the autumn weather turns the leaves to flame,
One hasn't got time for the waiting game.
Oh, the days dwindle down to a precious few,
September,
November!
And these few precious days
I'll spend with you,
These precious days
I'll spend with you.

VERSE TWO
When you meet with the young men early in spring,
They court you in song and rhyme,
They woo you with words and a clover ring,
But if you examine the goods they bring,
They have little to offer but the songs they sing
And a plentiful waste of time of day,
A plentiful waste of time.

REFRAIN REPEATED

"SPEAK LOW"

One Touch of Venus (1943)
Lyrics by Ogden Nash

Speak low when you speak, love.
Our summer day withers away too soon, too soon.
Speak low when you speak, love,
Our moment is swift, like ships adrift, we're swept apart too soon.
Speak low darling, speak low
Love is a spark lost in the dark too soon, too soon,
I feel wherever I go that tomorrow is near, tomorrow is here
And always too soon.
Time is so old and love so brief,
Love is pure gold and time a thief.
We're late darling, we're late
The curtain descends, ev'rything ends too soon, too soon
I wait darling, I wait
Will you speak low to me, speak love to me and soon.

"LONELY HOUSE"

Street Scene (1947)
Lyrics by Langston Hughes

At night when ev'rything is quiet
This old house seems to breathe a sigh.
Sometimes I hear a neighbor snoring,
Sometimes I hear a baby cry.
Sometimes I hear a staircase creaking,
Sometimes a distant telephone.
Then the quiet settles down again. . . .
The house and I are all alone.

Lonely house, lonely me!
Funny—with so many neighbors,
How lonely it can be!
Oh lonely street!
Lonely town!
Funny—you can be so lonely with all these folks around.
I guess there must be something
I don't comprehend—
Sparrows have companions,
Even stray dogs find a friend.
The night for me is not romantic.
Unhook the stars and take them down.
I'm lonely in this lonely house—
In this lonely town.

"WHAT GOOD WOULD THE MOON BE?"

Street Scene (1947)
Lyrics by Langston Hughes

I've looked in the windows at diamonds,
They're beautiful but they're cold.
I've seen Broadway stars in fur coats
That cost a fortune so I'm told.
I guess I'd look nice in diamonds, and sables might add to my
    charms,
But if someone I don't care for would buy them
I'd rather have two loving arms!

What good would the moon be
Unless the right one shared its beams?
What good would dreams-come-true be
If love wasn't in those dreams?
And a primrose path
What would be the fun
Of walking down a path like that without the right one?
What good would the night be
Unless the right lips whisper low:
Kiss me, oh darling, kiss me,
While ev'ning stars still glow?
No, it won't be a primrose path for me,
No, it won't be diamonds or gold,
But maybe there will be
Someone who'll love me,
Someone who'll love just me
To have and to hold!

"LOST IN THE STARS"

Lost in the Stars (1949)
Lyrics by Maxwell Anderson

Before Lord God made the sea and the land,
He held all the stars in the palm of His hand,

And they ran through his fingers like grains of sand,
And one little star fell alone.
Then the Lord God hunted through the wide night air
For the little dark star on the wind down there
And he stated and promised he'd take special care
So it wouldn't get lost again.
Now a man don't mind if the stars grow dim
And the clouds blow over and darken him,
So long as the Lord God's watching over them,
Keeping track how it all goes on.
But I've been walking through the night and the day
Till my eyes get weary and my head turns gray,
And sometimes it seems maybe God's gone away,
Forgetting the promise that we heard him say
And we're lost out here in the stars,
Little stars, big stars, blowing through the night,
And we're lost out here in the stars,
Little stars, big stars, blowing through the night,
And we're lost out here in the stars.

"THOUSANDS OF MILES"

Lost in the Stars (1949)
Lyrics by Maxwell Anderson

How many miles to the heart of a child?
Thousands of miles, thousands of miles.
When he lay on your breast,
He looked up and smiled across tens of thousands, thousands
    of miles.
Each lives alone in a world of dark,
Crossing the skies in a lonely arc.
Save when love leaks out like a leaping spark over thousands,
    thousands of miles.
Not miles, or walls, or length of days,
Nor the cold doubt of midnight can hold us apart,
For swifter than wings of the morning,
The pathways of the heart.

How many miles to the heart of a son?
Thousands of miles, thousands of miles.
Farther off than the rails or the roadways run across tens of
    thousands, thousands of miles.
The lines on the map stretch far and thin,
To the streets and days that close him in,
But then as of old he turns 'round to grin over thousands,
    thousands of miles.
Not miles, or walls, or length of days,
Nor the cold doubt of midnight can hold us apart,
For swifter than wings of the morning,
The pathways of the heart over tens of thousands of miles!

four

A BOUQUET OF LYRICS
FROM SUCCESSFUL MUSICAL SHOWS

The lyricists quoted extensively in Chapter 2 took lyric writing from its earlier clumsier state and brought it into clear focus. They brought lyric writing in the American musical theatre through lifetimes of practice, talent, and ever increasing technical knowledge to the point where it became a high art.

Much of the music and lyrics of these writers formed the backbone of popular song literature and eventually was transformed to the category of standard. The ingenuity of these writers also established models for those others who have followed so successfully in recent times.

In this chapter, due to space limitations, I have chosen a single show as representative of the work of each lyricist, most of them currently participating in the big leagues on Broadway, television, and films. I have selected only one or two lyrics from each show, and it is my feeling that these properly represent the best achievements of each of the lyricists. There is a considerable variety of style and purpose among them. This will be evident. All are successful and their contributions represent a large part of our contemporary musical theatre.

"LOOK FOR THE SILVER LINING"

Sally (1920)
Lyrics by Bud De Sylva
Music by Jerome Kern

(HE) VERSE 1

Please don't be offended if I preach to you awhile,
Tears are out of place in eyes that were meant to smile.
There's a way to make your very biggest troubles small,
Here's the happy secret of it all.

CHORUS
Look for the silver lining
Whene'er a cloud appears in the blue.
Remember somewhere the sun is shining
And so the right thing to do is make it shine for you.
A heart full of joy and gladness
Will always banish sadness and strife

So always look for the silver lining
And try to find the sunny side of life.

(SHE) VERSE 2
As I wash my dishes, I'll be following your plan,
Till I see the brightness in ev'ry pot and pan.
I am sure your point of view will ease the daily grind,
So I'll keep repeating in my mind.

CHORUS REPEATED

"I'M JUST WILD ABOUT HARRY"

Shuffle Along (1921)
Lyrics and Music by Noble Sissle * and Eubie Blake

VERSE ONE
There's just one fellow for me in this world
Harry's his name
That's what I claim
Why for ev'ry fellow there must be a girl
I've found my mate
By kindness of fate.

REFRAIN
I'm just wild about Harry and Harry's wild about me.
The heav'nly blisses of his kisses fill me with ecstasy
He's sweet just like choc'late candy, and just like honey from
  the bee
Oh, I'm just wild about Harry
And he's just wild about, cannot do without,
He's just wild about me.

VERSE TWO
There are some fellows who like all the girls,
I mean the vamps,
With cruel lamps,
But my Harry says I'm the girl of all girls,

* Sissle (with Blake) provided lyrics for two other editions of *Shuffle Along* in 1933 and 1952.

I'm his ideal,
How happy I feel.

REFRAIN REPEATED

"BYE BYE BLACKBIRD"

Bye Bye Blackbird (1926)
Lyrics by Mort Dixon
Music by Ray Henderson

VERSE ONE
Blackbird
Blackbird singing the blues all day
Right outside of my door
Blackbird
Blackbird
Why do you sit and say
"There's no sunshine in store"
All thru the winter you hung around
Now I begin to feel homeward bound
Blackbird
Blackbird gotta be on my way
Where there's sunshine galore

CHORUS
Pack up all my care and woe here I go singing low
Bye Bye Blackbird
Where somebody waits for me sugar's sweet so is she
Bye Bye Blackbird
No one here can love and understand me
Oh what hard luck stories they all hand me
Make my bed and light the light
I'll arrive late tonight
Blackbird Bye Bye

VERSE TWO
Bluebird
Bluebird calling me far away
I've been longing for you
Bluebird
Bluebird
What do I hear you say
"Skies are turning to blue"
I'm like a flower that's fading here
Where ev'ry hour is one long tear
Bluebird
Bluebird this is my lucky day
Now my dreams will come true

CHORUS REPEATED

"THE BIRTH OF THE BLUES"

George White's Scandals (1926)
Lyrics by B. G. De Sylva and Lew Brown
Music by Ray Henderson

VERSE
Oh! They say some people long ago
Were searching for a diff'rent tune,
One that they could croon
As only they can.
They only had the rhythm
So

They started swaying to and fro.
They didn't know just what to use,
That is how the blues really began:

REFRAIN
They heard the breeze in the trees
Singing weird melodies
And they made that
The start of the blues.
And from a jail came the wail
Of a downhearted frail,
And they played that
As part of the blues.
From a whippoorwill
Out on a hill,
They took a new note,
Pushed it through a horn
'Til it was worn
Into a blue note!
And then they nursed it, rehearsed it,
And gave out the news
That the Southland gave birth to the blues!

"HALLELUJAH!"

Hit the Deck (1927)
Lyrics by Leo Robin and Clifford Grey
Music by Vincent Youmans

VERSE
I'm recallin' times when I was small, in light and free jubilee
   days.
Old folks prayin' ev'rybody swayin',
Loudly, I chanted my praise.
How I sang about the Judgement morn,
And of Gabriel tootin' his horn.
In that sunny land of milk and honey,
I had no complaints,
While I thought of Saints
So I say to all who feel forlorn:

REFRAIN
Sing "Hallelujah! Hallelujah!" and you'll shoo the blues away;
When cares pursue ya, "Hallelujah"
Gets you through the darkest day.
Satan lies awaitin' and creatin' skies of gray,
But "Hallelujah! Hallelujah!" Helps to shoo the clouds away.

"MAKIN' WHOOPEE"

Whoopee (1928)
Lyrics and Music by Gus Kahn and Walter Donaldson

VERSE
Ev'ry time I hear that march from Lohengrin
I am always on the outside lookin' in.
Maybe that is why I see the funny side
When I see a fallen brother take a bride.
Weddings make a lot of people sad,
But if you're not the groom you're not so bad.

CHORUS 1
Another bride, another June,
Another sunny honeymoon,
Another season another reason

For makin' whoopee!
A lot of shoes, a lot of rice,
The groom is nervous, he answers twice,
It's really killing that he's so willing
To make whoopee.
Picture a little lovenest
Down where the roses cling,
Picture the same sweet lovenest,
Think what a year can bring.
He's washing dishes and baby clothes,
He's so ambitious he even sews.
But don't forget, folks, that's what you get, folks
For makin' whoopee!

CHORUS 2
Another year or maybe less,
What's this I hear? Well, can't you guess?
She feels neglected and he's suspected
Of makin' whoopee!
She sits alone most ev'ry night,
He doesn't phone her, he doesn't write.
He says he's "busy," but she says "Is he?"
He's makin' whoopee.
He doesn't make much money,
Only five thousand per,
Some judge who thinks he's funny
Says "You'll pay six to her."
He says "Now, judge, suppose I fail,"
The judge says "Budge right into jail.
You'd better keep her. I think it's cheaper
Than makin' whoopee!"

"LOVE ME OR LEAVE ME"

Whoopee (1928)
Lyrics and Music by Gus Kahn and Walter Donaldson

Love me or leave me, and let me be lonely;
You won't believe me, and I love you only;
I'd rather be lonely, than happy with somebody else.
You might find the night-time, the right time for kissing;
But night-time is my time for just reminiscing,
Regretting, instead of forgetting with somebody else.
There'll be no one unless that someone is you;
I intend to be independently blue.
I want your love, but I don't want to borrow,
To have it today, and to give back tomorrow;
For my love is your love, there's no love for nobody else!

"MORE THAN YOU KNOW"

Hit the Deck (1929)
Lyrics by William Rose and Edward Eliscu
Music by Vincent Youmans

VERSE
Whether you are here or yonder,
Whether you are false or true,

Whether you remain or wander
I'm growing fonder of you.
Even though your friends forsake you,
Even though you don't succeed,
Wouldn't I be glad to take you,
Give you the break you need.

REFRAIN
More than you know, more than you know,
Girl o' my heart, I love you so.
Lately I find you're on my mind,
More than you know.
Whether you're right, whether you're wrong,
Girl o' my heart, I'll string along.
You need me so
More than you'll ever know.
Loving you the way that I do
There's nothing I can do about it,
Loving may be all you can give but honey,
I can't live without it.
Oh, how I'd cry,
Oh, how I'd cry,
If you got tired and said "goodbye,"
More than I'd show
More than you'd ever know.

"BODY AND SOUL"

Three's a Crowd (1930)
Lyrics by Edward Heyman, Robert Sour, and Frank Eyton
Music by Johnny Green

VERSE
Life's dreary for me
Days seem to be long as years
I look for the sun, but I see none through my tears.
Your heart must be like a stone
To leave me here all alone
When you could make my life worth living
By simply taking what I'm set on giving.

REFRAIN
My heart is sad and lonely,
For you I sigh, for you, dear, only.
Why haven't you seen it?
I'm all for you, Body and Soul!
I spend my days in longing
And wond'ring why it's me you're wronging
I tell you I mean it,
I'm all for you, Body and Soul!
I can't believe it,
It's hard to conceive it
That you'd turn away romance.
Are you pretending, it looks like the ending
Unless I could have one more chance to prove, dear,
My life a wreck you're making,
You know I'm yours for just the taking;
I'd gladly surrender myself to you,
Body and Soul!

"TIME ON MY HANDS"

Smiles (1930)
Lyrics by Harold Adamson and Mack Gordon
Music by Vincent Youmans

VERSE
When the day fades away into twilight,
The moon is my light of love;
In the night, I am quite a romancer;
I find an answer above.
To bring me consolation,
You're my inspiration,
This is my imagination.

REFRAIN
Time on my hands,
You in my arms,
Nothing but love in view;
Then if you fall,
Once and for all,
I'll see my dreams come true.
Moments to spare for someone you care for;
One love affair for two.
With time on my hands
And you in my arms
And love in my heart all for you.

"THROUGH THE YEARS"

Through the Years (1931)
Lyrics by Edward Heyman
Music by Vincent Youmans

Through the years,
I'll take my place, beside you,
Smiling through the years.
Through your tears,
I'll keep my place beside you;
Smiling through your tears.
I'll be near, no matter when or where,
Remember, what is mine, I'll always share.
Through the night,
I'll be a star to guide you;
Shining bright,
Though clouds may come and hide you.
Through the years till love is gone and time first disappears,
I'll come to you, smiling through the years.

"BUCKLE DOWN WINSOCKI"

Best Foot Forward (1941)
Lyrics and Music by Hugh Martin and Ralph Blane

OLD GRAD
If you shout hooray for the Pennsylvania Dutchmen
They will cover the ground for a number one down or a touch
Every one is agreed that you have to concede to the Dutchmen
Shout hooray for the Pennsylvania Dutch.
GREENIE
If you shout hooray for the Pennsylvania Dutchmen
Every team that they play will be carried away with a crutch.
When they're out on the field if they're wearing the shield of the
  Dutchmen
Shout hooray for the Pennsylvania Dutch.

CHORUS AND GREENIE
Buckle down Winsocki buckle down
You can win Winsocki if you knuckle down
If you don't give in take it on the chin
You are bound to win if you will only buckle down

Make 'em tell Winsocki, make 'em yell
You can win Winsocki if you give 'em hell
If you don't give in take it on the chin
You are bound to win if you will only buckle down

If you fight you'll chuckle at defeat
If you'll fight your luck'll not retreat
Knuckle down Winsocki knuckle down
You can win Winsocki if you buckle down

If you mow them down if you go to town
You can wear the crown if you will only buckle down
You can win Winsocki if you knuckle down
If you break their necks if you make them wrecks

You can break the hex, so buckle down
Make 'em only buckle down
If you fight you'll chuckle at defeat
If you fight your luck'll not retreat

Knuckle down Winsocki knuckle down
You can win Winsocki if you buckle down
If you mow them down if you to go town
You can wear the crown if you will only buckle down.

They will cover the ground for a number one down or a touch
Everyone is agreed that you have to concede to the Dutchmen
Shout Hooray for the Pennsylvania Dutch

If you shout hooray for the Pennsylvania Dutchmen
Every team that they play will be carried away with a crutch
When they're out on the field if they're wearing the shield of the
  Dutchmen

"SHADY LADY BIRD"

Best Foot Forward
Lyrics and Music by Hugh Martin and Ralph Blane

VERSE
Lady bird, lady bird,
Fly away home.
Your heart's on fire,
You better go home.

Lady bird, lady bird,
Sure as you're born,
Leave the boy blue.
Come blow your horn.

CHORUS
I'm gonna be a shady lady bird.
I've got an awful lot to learn.
But if you tell me that my heart's on fire,
I'm gonna let it burn.

I'm gonna be a shockin' mockin' bird.
I'm gonna mingle with the best.

I'm gonna try to find my heart's desire.
I'm gonna rob the nest.

Just like little Miss Muffet
Eating her whey and curds;
When I act a bit tough it
Frightens away the birds.

I'm gonna be a slummin' hummin' bird
I'm gonna pass along the word.
I'm gonna have my fun and never tire.
And if my technique seems absurd;
That's because I've never been a shady lady bird.

I'm gonna be a shady lady bird
I'm gonna bag myself a moose
I'm gonna be the latest Disney dream
A goose that's on the loose.
I'm gonna be a fightin' nightingale
I'm gonna make the others blink
I'm gonna lead my horses to the stream
I'm gonna make 'em drink.

That's because I've never been a shady lady bird.

Just like the little ole woman
Living inside the shoe
I'll be a much better woman
Knowing just what to do.

I'm gonna be a wicked chicadee
I'm gonna sit upon the fence
I'm gonna build myself a lovely dream
And if I don't use common sense

That's because I've never been a shady lady bird.

2ND CHORUS
I'm gonna be a regal eagle bird
I'm gonna build my nest up high
I'm gonna catch my prey and soar away
I'm gonna hit the sky.

I'm gonna be an indignet cygnet bird
I'm gonna be a baby swan
I'm gonna scout around to find a neck
That I can nestle on.

Just like little Jack Spratt's wife
Living up on the fat
I'm gonna live a nine cat's life
What do you think of that.

I'm gonna be a shady lady bird.
I hope the payment is deferred.
And if I fly back safely to my perch
And find the worst has not occurred.

That's because I've never been a shady lady bird.

"I STILL GET JEALOUS"

High Button Shoes (1947)
Lyrics by Sammy Cahn
Music by Jule Styne

VERSE PAPA
Time has treated our love kindly
For I still adore you blindly

There can never be
Another love for me.

CHORUS
I still get jealous when they look at you
I may not show it but I do
PAPA
It's more than I can bear
When they start to stare
Guess they think you're too good to be true.

I still get jealous when we kiss goodnight
Unless you hold me extra tight

And dear, I know a secret
You didn't think I knew
I still get jealous 'cause it pleases you!
MAMA
Our flame should have died gently
Still it's burning, not just ment'lly
There can never be
Another love for me.

CHORUS MAMA
I still get jealous when they look at you
PAPA
Remember the time you winked at a
guy and I got a punch in the eye
MAMA
I may not show it but I do
PAPA
(Why can't you flirt with guys that are small
Instead of the guys that are tall)
MAMA
It's more than I can bear (PAPA: Inside)
When they start to stare (PAPA: My pride!),
Guess they think you're too good to be true.
PAPA
A man that married the homelier kind
married for peace of mind
MAMA
Jealous when we kiss goodnight
PAPA
Your kisses are sweet and I like 'em a lot
They're worth all the trouble I've got
MAMA
Unless you hold me extra tight.
PAPA
Because I'm jealous as can be
I wish that you would flirt with me.
BOTH
And dear I know a secret
You didn't know I knew
I still get jealous 'cause it pleases you.

"NEXT TO TEXAS I LOVE YOU"

High Button Shoes (1947)
Lyrics by Sammy Cahn
Music by Jule Styne

VERSE
When I fell in love with you
I had to split my heart in two

Tho' my love for you is great
It's half and half with the Lone Star State.

When a Texan takes a bride,
He still has Texas deep inside
You may as well know the worst,
What I'm trying to say,
Is that Texas comes first.

CHORUS
Your eyes are like the prairie flowers
When they're refreshed by sudden showers
Next to Texas I love you.

Your smile is like the sun ablazin'
Above a herd of longhorns grazin'
Next to Texas I, darling, love you.

My heart is so full of love for you it's bustin'
I sure was afeared but you appeared—
And just in time

To all the folks I've been declarin'
There's someone else for whom I'm carin'
If they gossip'd it's because they knew
Next to Texas I love you.

"DIAMONDS ARE A GIRL'S BEST FRIEND"

Gentlemen Prefer Blondes (1949)
Lyrics by Leo Robin
Music by Jule Styne

VERSE 1
The French are glad to die for love,
They delight in fighting duels,
But I prefer a man who lives,
And gives expensive jewels;

REFRAIN 1
A kiss on the hand may be quite Continental
But diamonds are a girl's best friend,
A kiss may be grand
But it won't pay the rental on your humble flat
Or help you at the Automat.
Men grow cold as girls grow old
And we all lose our charms in the end.
But square-cut or pear-shape,
These rocks don't lose their shape,
Diamonds are a girl's best friend.

VERSE 2
A well conducted rendezvous
Makes a maiden's heart beat quicker,
But when the rendezvous is through,
These stones still keep their flicker;

REFRAIN 2
There may come a time when a lass needs a lawyer,
But diamonds are a girl's best friend,
There may come a time
When a hard boiled employer thinks you're awful nice,
But get that "ice" or else no dice.
He's your guy when stocks are high,
But beware when they start to descend.

It's then that those louses
Go back to their spouses,
Diamonds are a girl's best friend.

"LAZY AFTERNOON"

The Golden Apple (1954)
Lyrics by John LaTouche
Music by Jerome Moross

HELEN, *vocalizing languidly*
It's a lazy afternoon
And the beetle bugs are zoomin
And the tulip trees are bloomin
And there's not another human
In view But us two

It's a lazy afternoon
And the farmer leaves his reapin
In the meadows cows are sleepin
And the speckled trout stop leapin
Upstream As we dream

A fat pink cloud hangs over the hill
Unfolding like a rose
If you hold my hand and sit real still
You can hear the grass as it grows

It's a lazy afternoon
And my rockin chair will fit yer
And my cake was never richer
And I've made a tasty pitcher
Of tea
So spend this lazy afternoon with me.

A fat pink cloud hangs over the hill
Unfolding like a rose
If you hold my hand and sit real still
You can hear the grass as it grows

It's a lazy afternoon
And I know a place that's quiet
Cept for daisies running riot
And there's no one passing by it
To see
Come spend this lazy afternoon with me.

"A NEW TOWN IS A BLUE TOWN"

The Pajama Game (1954)
Lyrics and Music by Richard Adler and Jerry Ross *

A new town is a blue town,
A "Who do you know" and "show me what you can do" town.
There's no red carpet at your feet,
If you're not tough they'll try to beat you down,
In a new, blue town.
The old town,
It's not like the old town.
You don't take long to find that you're in a cold town,
But you know you can lick it,
Didn't buy a round-trip ticket

* Adler and Ross also contributed songs to John Murray Anderson's *Almanac* (1953) and *Damn Yankees* (1955). After Ross's death, Adler wrote *Kwamina*, songs (shows) for TV and commercials.

Courtesy Museum of the City of New York

Pajama Game

To this
Cold, cold, new blue town.
Well nobody asked me to come here
And nobody asked me to stay.
Made up my own mind
And I know that I'll find my own way.
Since that first day
When I said, "Hi town!"
They've darn well tried to make me say, "Good-bye town!"
But I won't leave until I make it my town,
They'll see,
This one-horse, two-bit, hick of a new town
Ain't gonna lick me.

"SMALL TALK"

The Pajama Game (1954)
Lyrics and Music by Richard Adler and Jerry Ross

SID
I don't wanna talk Small Talk
Now that I'm alone with you.
I don't wanna talk Small Talk,
We've got bigger things to do.
Let's not talk of the weather,
Or the fashions for the fall.
Why don't you stop all this Small Talk?
I've got something better for your lips to do,
And that takes no talk at all.
BABE
I gotta buy me a dressy dress,
The one I have is such a mess!
SID
Small talk!
BABE
Who will you vote for next election?
How do you like the stamp collection?
SID
Small talk!
Read in a book the other day
That halibut spawn in early May,
And horses whinny and donkeys bray
And furthermore
The pygmy tribes in Africa may
Have a war.
BABE
No?
SID
Yes!
I don't
Wanna talk small talk.
BABE
What do you think they charge for ham now?
SID
Now that I'm alone with you.
BABE
Got so a buck ain't worth a damn now.
SID
I don't want to talk small talk.
BABE
Read that the winters are gettin' milder.
SID
We've got bigger things to do.

BABE
And that the teenage kids are wilder.
SID
Let's not talk of the weather.
BABE
One of these days I'll paint the kitchen,
SID
Or the fashions for the fall.
BABE
Get Pop to put a new light switch in.
SID
Why don't you stop all this Small Talk?
BABE
Like I was sayin'
SID
I've got something better
BABE
What I mean is
SID
For your lips
BABE
I was only
SID
To do, and that takes no talk at all.

"WHY NOT KATIE"

Plain and Fancy (1955)
Lyrics by Arnold Horwitt *
Music by Albert Hague

EZRA
Comes a time in his life
When a man should take a wife;
If I have to take a wife,
So why not Katie?

Milking cows Katie knows,
Katie mends and Katie sews,
And a farm with Katie goes,
So why not Katie?

It could be if I wait
Comes along a perfect mate
But for this a man could wait
Until he's eighty.

So in meeting when I stand
With my hand in Katie's hand,
And a wedding dinner making in the pot,
When they ask, "Do you take Katie?"
I will answer like a shot:
"Do I take Katie—?
Why not?"
SAMUEL LAPP
She's a nice girl, Katie always was.
EZRA
When her father says, 'Shut up' to her,
She always does.
ABNER MOSES
You could marry Bertha Broder,

* Horwitt contributed lyrics and/or sketches to *Call Me Mister* (1944), *Inside USA* (1948), and *Make Mine Manhattan* (1948).

SMALL TALK

Words and Music by **RICHARD ADLER** and **JERRY ROSS**

FREDERICK BRISSON, ROBERT E. GRIFFITH & HAROLD S. PRINCE *present*

JOHN RAITT JANIS PAIGE
EDDIE FOY JR.

IN A NEW MUSICAL COMEDY

(Based on the novel "7½ Cents" by RICHARD BISSELL)

Book by
GEORGE ABBOTT and **RICHARD BISSELL**

Music and Lyrics by

with CAROL HANEY · RETA SHAW · RALPH DUNN
STANLEY PRAGER · JACK WALDRON

Production Directed by
GEORGE ABBOTT and **JEROME ROBBINS**

Scenery and Costumes by
LEMUEL AYERS

Choreography by　Musical Direction by　Orchestrations by
BOB FOSSE　HAL HASTINGS　DON WALKER

From The Score

HEY THERE
STEAM HEAT
HERNANDO'S HIDEAWAY
SMALL TALK

PRICE **$1.00** IN U.S.A.

FRANK MUSIC CORP.

Sole Selling Agents: KEYS MUSIC, INC. · 146 West 54th Street, New York 19, N. Y.

Like a dream she cooks.
JACOB YODER
Like an ox she's healthy.
EZRA
Like an ox she looks!
ABNER ZOOK
Kate's a bissel skinny where she should be fat.
EZRA
When the kids start coming, she won't be so flat.
ABNER MOSES
With the hand of Anna Gruber comes a lot of cash.
EZRA
With the face of Anna Gruber comes a big moustache.
IKE PILERSHEIM
Once you promised Ilsa Brett
When she grew up, you she'd get.
EZRA
But she ain't stopped growing yet,
So I'll take Katie!
JACOB YODER
Once I kissed Dora Land!
I found schmutzing Dora grand!
EZRA
So did half of Bird-in-Hand!
So I'll kiss Katie.

It could be if I wait,
Comes along a perfect mate,
ALL
But for this a man could wait
Until he's eighty.
EZRA
So tomorrow when I stand
With my hand in Katie's hand
And in meeting house they put me on the spot,
In a clear and honest voice,
Since I ain't got no other choice,
I'll answer: "Katie—"
AMISHMEN
Sweet and lovely Katie—!
EZRA
Hard-working Katie!
Why not?

"THIS IS ALL VERY NEW TO ME"

Plain and Fancy (1955)
Lyrics by Arnold Horwitt
Music by Albert Hague

HILDA
All at once the room is reeling,
Bells are pealing,
Butterflies are fluttering inside.
All at once I get to feeling
Just like a new-born bride.

This is all very new to me,
This is all very fine,
This so sunny-like,
Sort of funny-like,
Milk-and-honey-like feeling of mine.

This is all very new to me
And I'm knocking on wood.
What to do? What to say?
How to make it go on this way?
Wish that I understood,
TRIO
Do you seem to float in space?
HILDA
With the silliest look on my face
And a light in my eye.
TRIO
Do you feel all out of breath?
HILDA
Upside down, scared to death!
TRIO
Are you wondering why?
HILDA
It's as simple as pie!

"AROUND THE WORLD IN EIGHTY DAYS"

Around the World in Eighty Days (film) (1956)
Lyrics by Harold Adamson
Music by Victor Young

Around the world I've searched for you
I've wandered on when hope was gone to keep a rendezvous.
I knew somewhere, some time, somehow
You'd beckon me and I would see the smile you're smiling now.
It might have been in County Down,
Or in New York, or Gay Paree, or even London Town.
No more will I go all around the world
For I have found my world in you.

"MY LOVE"

Candide (1956)
Lyrics by John LaTouche and Richard Wilbur
Music by Leonard Bernstein
Book by Lillian Hellman, based on Voltaire's Candide

Poets have said
Love is undying, my love;
Don't be misled;
They were all lying, my love.

Love's on the wing,
But now while he hovers,
Let us be lovers.
One soon recovers, my love.

Soon the fever's fled,
For love's transient blessing.
Just a week in bed,
And we'll be convalescing.

Why talk of morals
When springtime is flying?
Why end in quarrels,
Reproaches and sighing,
Crying for love?

For love undying, my love,
Is not worth trying, my love.

Never, my love,
Mention forever, my love.

Let it be lively,
Let it be lovely,
And light as a song,
But don't let it last too long!

"GLITTER AND BE GAY"

Candide (1956)
Lyrics by Richard Wilbur
Music by Leonard Bernstein
Book by Lillian Hellman, based on Voltaire's *Candide*

Glitter and be gay,
That's the part I play.
Here am I, unhappy chance.
Forced to bend my soul
To a sordid role,
Victimized by bitter, bitter circumstance.

Alas for me, had I remained
Beside my lady mother,
My virtue had remained unstained
Until my maiden hand was gained
By some Grand Duke or other.

Ah, 'twas not to be;
Harsh necessity
Brought me to this gilded cage.
Born to higher things,
Here I droop my wings,
Singing of a sorrow nothing can assuage.

And yet, of course, I rather like to revel, ha, ha!
I have no strong objection to champagne, ha, ha!
My wardrobe is expensive as the devil, ha, ha!
Perhaps it is ignoble to complain . . .

Enough, enough
Of being basely tearful!
I'll show my noble stuff
By being bright and cheerful!

Ha, ha ha ha . . .
(Reciting, to music)
Pearls and ruby rings. . . .
Ah, how can worldly things
Take the place of honor lost?
Can they compensate
For my fallen state,
Purchased as they were at such an awful cost?

Bracelets . . . lavalieres . . .
Can they dry my tears?
Can they blind my eyes to shame?
Can the brightest brooch
Shield me from reproach?
Can the purest diamond purify my name?

And yet, of course, these trinkets are endearing, ha ha!
I'm oh, so glad my sapphire is a star, ha ha!
I rather like a twenty-carat earring, ha ha!
If I'm not pure, at least my jewels are!

Enough, enough!
I'll *take* their diamond necklace

And show my noble stuff
By being gay and reckless!

Ha ha ha ha ha . . .

Observe how bravely I conceal
The dreadful, dreadful shame I feel.
Ha ha ha ha ha, ha . . .
(Puts on a giant diamond necklace)
Ha!

"GOODNIGHT, MY SOMEONE"

The Music Man (1947)
Lyrics, Music, and Book by Meredith Willson *

Goodnight, My Someone. Goodnight, my love.
Sleep tight, my someone, sleep tight, my love.
Our star is shining its brightest light
For goodnight, my love for goodnight.
Sweet dreams be yours, dear, if dreams there be;
Sweet dreams to carry you close to me.
I wish they may and I wish they might.
Now goodnight, my someone, goodnight.
True love can be whispered from heart to heart
When lovers are parted they say
But I must depend on a wish and a star
As long as my heart doesn't know who you are
Sweet dreams be yours, dear, if dreams there be;
Sweet dreams to carry you close to me.
I wish they may and I wish they might.
Now goodnight, my someone, goodnight.
Goodnight, Goodnight.

"TILL THERE WAS YOU"

The Music Man (1957)
Lyrics, Music, and Book by Meredith Willson

There were bells on the hill, but I never heard them ringing,
No, I never heard them at all
Till There Was You.
There were birds in the sky, but I never saw them winging,
No, I never saw them at all
Till There Was You.
And there was music and there were wonderful roses, they tell
me
In sweet fragrant meadows of dawn, and dew,
There was love all around, but I never heard it singing,
No, I never heard it at all
Till There Was You.

"THE FOREST RANGER"

Little Mary Sunshine (1959)
Lyrics, Music, and Book by Rick Besoyan †

Stout-hearted is the Forest Ranger,
He's a scout;

* Willson also wrote *The Unsinkable Molly Brown* (1960), *Here's Love* (1963), and *1491* (1969).
† Besoyan (d. 1970) also wrote *The Student Gypsy* (1963) and *Babes in the Wood* (1964).

GOODNIGHT, MY SOMEONE

By MEREDITH WILLSON

Meredith Willson's

THE MUSIC MAN

Starring
ROBERT PRESTON · SHIRLEY JONES
Co-Starring
BUDDY HACKETT · HERMIONE GINGOLD · PAUL FORD
PRODUCED AND DIRECTED BY MORTON DaCOSTA
MUSIC SUPERVISED BY RAY HEINDORF | TECHNIRAMA® TECHNICOLOR® Ⓦ®
SCREENPLAY BY MARION HARGROVE | PRESENTED BY WARNER BROS.

From The Score
Of The Motion Picture
GOODNIGHT, MY SOMEONE
IT'S YOU
LIDA ROSE
SEVENTY SIX TROMBONES
TILL THERE WAS YOU
BEING IN LOVE

Price .75 Each
In U.S.A.

071003 00
Printed in U. S. A.

FRANK MUSIC CORP. and RINIMER CORPORATION
Sole Selling Agents; FRANK DISTRIBUTING CORP. • 119 West 57th Street, New York, N. Y. 10019

He's thoughtful, friendly, courteous and kind,
He's reverent and grave,
He's healthy and he's brave,
He's clean in soul and body and mind.
(Shouted) Yes, Sir!
He's cheerful, honest, thrifty and obedient;
To love the good and hate the bad is his plan,
So if there's any danger
You can be sure the Forest Ranger
Ever will march on, man to man.

The lonely coyote in the prairie
Isn't very tough to us.
The grizzly bear in his lair, he
Isn't very rough to us.
We've nerves made of steel,
Bodies of iron,
It's our environment,
So please don't estrange
The Forest Ranger,
For he's quite magnificent.

Stout-hearted is the Forest Ranger, etc.

"LOOK FOR A SKY OF BLUE"

Little Mary Sunshine (1959)
Lyrics, Music, and Book by Rick Besoyan

VERSE
Don't be sad and gloomy,
Come and hearken to me,
Please be gay.
There's no time for tear drops,
When there's rain we hear drops,
But they quickly fade away.
Just because we haven't got a penny in our pockets,
And life seems a great morass;
Pray, don't be offended,
Kind thoughts are intended:
You don't see the cheery side; alas:

REFRAIN
Whene'er a cloud appears,
Filled with doubt and fears,
Look for a sky of blue,
Whene'er a cloud of gray
Seems to waft your way,
Look for a sky of blue.
Remember, sometimes the sun is shining,
It may be shining someday for you-oo-oo-oo-oo,
So 'til that happy day
We must learn to say
"Look for a sky of blue."

"YESTERDAY I LOVED YOU"

Once Upon a Mattress (1959)
Lyrics by Marshall Barer
Music by Mary Rodgers

Yesterday I loved you
As never before.
But please don't think me strange—

I've undergone a change
And today I love you even more.
My heart cannot be trusted,
I give you fair warning,
I openly confess:
Tonight I love you less
Than I will tomorrow

Yesterday I loved you as never before.
But that was long ago
And now it's best you know
That today I love you even more.
My heart cannot be trusted,
I give you fair warning,
I tremble at your touch—
Not nearly half so much as l will tomorrow morning.

Yesterday you seemed so lovely to me
As anyone ever could be.
Now I see what tricks my eyes can play!
Yesterday I must have been utterly blind,
Or else I was out of my mind
For I find you so much lovelier today.
My heart cannot be trusted.
I give you fair warning
For yesterday I loved you, as never before.
In a little while,
Just a little while,
You and I will be
One, two, three, four.
But that was long ago,
And now it's best you know
In a little while
I will see you smile
On the face of my son-to-be,
Forever hand in glove
That today I love you even more.
Is the way I have it planned

My heart cannot be trusted.
I give you fair warning
I openly confess
Tonight I love you less
Than I will tomorrow morning.

"MANY MOONS AGO"

Once Upon a Mattress (1959)
Lyrics by Marshall Barer
Music by Mary Rodgers

Many moons ago in a far-off place
Lived a handsome prince with a gloomy face,
For he did not have a bride.
Oh, he sighed "alas"
And he pined alas,
But alas, the prince couldn't find a lass
Who would suit his mother's pride.
For a princess is a delicate thing,
Delicate and dainty as a dragon fly's wing.
You can recognize a lady by her elegant air,
But a genuine princess is exceedingly rare.
On a stormy night, to the castle door,

Came the lass the prince had been waiting for.
"I'm a princess lost," quoth she.
But the queen was cool and remained aloof
And she said: "Perhaps, but she'll need some proof.
I'll prepare a test and see."

"I will test her thus," the old queen said:
"I'll put twenty downy mattresses upon her bed
And between those twenty mattresses I'll place a tiny pea.
If that pea disturbs her slumber, then a true princess is she."

Now, the bed was soft and extremely tall,
But the dainty lass didn't sleep at all,
And she told them so next day.
Said the queen: "My dear, if you felt that pea,
Then we've proof enough of your royalty.
Let the wedding music play."

And the people shouted quietly: "Hooray!"

For a princess is a delicate thing,
Delicate and dainty as a dragon fly's wing.
You can recognize a lady by her elegant air,
But a genuine princess is exceedingly rare.

"MIRA"

Carnival! (1961)
Lyrics and Music by Bob Merrill *

I came on two buses and a train!
Can you imagine that? Can you imagine that?
Two buses and a train!
Would you believe
Would you believe
This is the first time I've traveled?
I came from a town
The kind of town where you live in a house
'Til the house falls down,
But if it stands up, you stay there.
It's funny, but that's their way there.

I came from the town of Mira,
Beyond the bridges of St. Claire.
I guess you never heard of Mira,
It's awf'ly small, but still it's there.
They have the very greenest trees
And skies as bright as flame,
But what I liked best in Mira . . .
Is ev'rybody knew my name!

Can you imagine that? Can you imagine that?
Ev'rybody knew my name.

A room that's strange is never cozy,
A place that's strange is never sweet.
I want to have a chair that knows me,
And walk a street that knows my feet.
I'm very far from Mira now
And there's no turning back.
I have to find a place, I've got to find a place.
Where ev'rything can be the same . . .

* Merrill also wrote the music and lyrics for *New Girl in Town* (1957), *Take Me Along* (1959), *Henry, Sweet Henry* (1967), and the lyrics for *Funny Girl* (1968).

A street that I can know,
And places I can go,
Where ev'rybody knows my name.

Can you imagine that? Can you imagine that?
Ev'rybody knew my name!

"A SWORD AND A ROSE AND A CAPE"

Carnival! (1961)
Lyrics and Music by Bob Merrill

MARCO
. . . Roamed the land with naught to protect him but a sword
. . . and a rose . . . and a cape!

In me you see the relic
Of a long-lamented age
When masculine behaviour
Wrote a grand romantic page
With every man a lover
Like a hero on a stage
With a sword
And a rose
And a cape

Where are the great romantics
Who would languish for a rose
Who fought a duel with one hand
While the other hand wrote prose
Who scaled milady's balcony and swung upon her drape
With a sword and a rose and a cape
They have flown, have flown like ashes
Ah, they reappear in flashes
ROUSTABOUTS
But they find themselves
Contrary to the mode
MARCO
These aristocrats and highbrows
Meet with such astonished eyebrows
ROUSTABOUTS
They inevitably wither and corrode
MARCO
Where are the flaming Frenchmen
And the seething Viennese
In Spain today they'll hug a horse
And let a mistress freeze
And now the male Italian
Just gets passionate for cheese
Ah, the sword and the rose and the cape
And so, if when I look at you
I flutter like a moth
ROUSTABOUTS
Ah ah ah ah ah ah ah
MARCO
It's just that I am of the breed
And woven from the cloth
ROUSTABOUTS
Ah ah ah ah ah ah ah
MARCO
Of men who lived to fight a duel
Or plight a lover's troth

ROUSTABOUTS
Men who would twine her hair
And peel milady's grape
Leap from her balcony in glorious escape
MARCO *(Spoken)*
Perpetrate a rape?
ROUSTABOUTS *(Sung)*
With a sword
And a rose
And a cape.

"MY HOMETOWN"

What Makes Sammy Run? (1964)
Lyrics and Music by Ervin Drake

This should have been my hometown.
At last I'm in my hometown.
It's not the place of my birth
But where on earth
Is there such a town?

The kind of people you find
I find are strictly my kind
This place gets under my skin,
From here on in
This is my hometown!

Why bother to travel farther?
What move could improve
When here I stand
In my own Promised Land!

I'm gonna haunt every street,
There's not a soul I won't meet,
Their style is sweet and sincere,
Hits me right here
So I'm settlin' down
In what I'm proud to call my hometown!

For some guys
The dream is Paris,
But I found a shrine
Where Hollywood Boulevard crosses Vine.

I'm gonna haunt every street,
There's not a soul I won't meet;
Their style is sweet and sincere,
Hits me right here
So I'm settlin' down
In what I'm proud to call my hometown!

"YOU'RE NO GOOD"

What Makes Sammy Run? (1964)
Lyrics and Music by Ervin Drake

Of all the things that you are,
You've one darling trait
That I simply can't hate.

SAMMY *(Suspiciously)*
I still can send for your car
If this little toast
Is a rap at your host.
Spill it quick . . .
LAURETTE
Mister Glick . . .

You're no good!
And it does my black heart good to see
You're just like me;
You're no good!
SAMMY
You're my twin!
Underneath your sterling silver skin
You're solid tin;
You're no good!
LAURETTE
You're no lamb!
You'd attack poor "Jack the Ripper"
You were weaned on pure witches' brew.
SAMMY
You know, ma'am,
Though Delilah was a clipper,
Next to you she was an ingenue!
LAURETTE
If I could
I would never change a speckle of my sweet, sweet,
Cobra's little hood.
SAMMY
You're a trap, a lure,
And a counterfeit for amour.
SAMMY *and* LAURETTE
You're no good!
LAURETTE
You're my breed!
Underneath your boutonniere's a weed!
We're common seed;
You're no good!
SAMMY
You're my style!
Your expensive silk and satin smile
Is lined with lisle;
You're no good!
LAURETTE
You're no rose!
I would cast you as a heavy,
You could play, say, Simon Legree.
SAMMY
You'd foreclose
On the homestead and the Chevy
Of that saintly soul, sweet Mother Machree!
LAURETTE
In a wood
I would turn up ev'ry rock till I discovered where
My darling stood!
SAMMY
You're for me, I'm sure,
Lady, my heart's a connoisseur . . .
LAURETTE *and* SAMMY
You're no good! . . . You're no good!

SAMMY *(As the song concludes)* Listen, Laurette, I'll get rid—
LAURETTE   It's *still* Miss Harrington! Careful, Sammy. I hit harder than your brother.
SAMMY
Hear me good!
I'm the wolf you won't escape,
You little . . .
(Mouths epithet as orchestra blasts out)
. . . Red Riding-Hood!
You're so smart, so sure:
Next to me you're an amachoor!
You're—no—good!
You're no good!!

"CAN'T YOU SEE IT?"

Golden Boy (1964)
Lyrics by Lee Adams *
Music by Charles Strouse

Can't you see it?
It's clear as it can be!
It makes a sunny beam of light
That seems to follow me.

Can't you hear it?
Sopranos everywhere!
A chorus of the choicest voices
Trilling in the air.

It makes the soot
Underfoot
Flash like diamonds,
And every cop
Dances by
Like Fred Astaire!

Can't you see it?
It's splashed across the sky.
If you can see it,
You're as happy as I.

Can't you feel it?
It's pleasanter than spring.
It's like the humble peasant felt
The day they made him king.

It makes those fumes
From the bus
Smell delicious,
And every bum
On a bench
Sings just like Bing!

Can't you see it?
It makes the buildings fly.
If you can see it,
You're as happy as I!

* Adams (with Strouse) also wrote *Bye Bye Birdie* (1960), *All American* (1962), *It's a Bird . . . It's a Plane . . . It's Superman* (1966), and *Applause* (1970).

"WHERE IS THE TRIBE FOR ME?"

Bajour (1964)
Lyrics and Music by Walter Marks

Where? Where? Where is the tribe for me?
Where living in some primitive stage is that unstudied breed
Who've somehow managed coming of age unhelped by Margaret Mead?
Where? Where? Where is my ethnic group?
Where are the savage Preadamites who live unseen unknown?
Waiting to show me puberty rites, that I can call my own!

You're not an etymologist until you get the word!
You're not an ornithologist until you get the bird!
Like some unfrocked theologist
I haven't got a prayer,
I'm not an anthropologist until I write a diatribe on why a tribe is there!

But drat! Where can they be at!
Where's their natural habitat?
Where they still roam free—anthropologically,
Tell me where? Where is the tribe for sometimes I—
I see myself searching searching thru the jungle, dark and deep,
On a safari searching for my tribe!
Thru the wild birds AWK! AWK!
And the poison darts PHT-TT
And the jungle cats R-R-R
And the (SLAP) tse-tse flies
Food gone water gone
All our guides have run away and the drums! the drums!
Searching for my tribe!
Thru the boa-constrictors SS-SS!
And the gorillas AH-I-AH
And the quick sand SHLURP-SHLURP
And the AWK! AWK! PHT-TT! R-R-R! (SLAP) TSE-TSE FLIES
Onward thru the area! Burning with malaria
Alone on my safari and there's no one to be sorry if I rot with dry rot

But wait! Wait! Look there! Look there!
Thru the giant bushwood trees
Grass huts cooking fires! Can it be my tribe?
Now they're coming, strangely painted savages!
And at last I've found them!
Here is the tribe for me!
No more laughing Hyenas HEE-HEE-HEE
No more stampeding elephants ONK! ONK!
No more drums BOB-A-LU-AI-AY!
No more SS-SS! AH-I-AH! SHLURP! SHLURP! AWK! AWK! PHT-TT! R-R-R! (SLAP) TSE-TSE FLIES!
Yes, here is my tribe!

And now they come to greet me crying Bwanna! Bwanna. . . .
Yes, I Bwanna!
I bwanna tribe—and they take me to their chief!
I enter a large hut! and I hear the strange music of
No it can't be! It's It's
Albert, you beat me to it again!
Albert tell me, tell me please!

Where? Where? Where is the tribe for me?
One that has not heard of NYU—D.A.R. or L.B.J.

People that bear no allegiance to CIO or CIA
Oh please! I'm on my bended knees! Where are these
    Aborigines
Who were meant to be my PHD? Tell me where? Where the
    tribe for me?

"TOO CHARMING"

Ben Franklin in Paris (1964)
Lyrics by Sidney Michaels
Music by Mark Sandrich, Jr.

You've always been too gallant to resist,
Too gracious to conceive;
You've always been too dashing to forget
And Too Charming to believe.

You must remember your persuasive powers I know,
You're still exhilarating, scintillating, generating, palpitating,
The answer is no!
You've always been too ardent to restrain,
Too noble to defeat;
Our loving was too tender to reproach,
And Too Charming to repeat.

I know you well, Ben, Lafayette and Moses combined,
You're still rejuvenating, fascinating, captivating, devastating,
And I won't change my mind!

You've always been too gallant to resist,
Too gracious to conceive;
You've always been too dashing to forget,
And Too Charming to believe.

"I INVENTED MYSELF"

Ben Franklin in Paris (1964)
Lyrics by Sidney Michaels
Music by Mark Sandrich, Jr.

VERSE
One dark night, a rainy one,
Accounts for some lightning and thunder,
I was puttering in my laboratory,
For an idea, a new a brainy one
(Spoken)
Now what did the world really need?
What contraption for use and for free?
Well, I made a working model the following day.
I called it "THE PUBLIC ME!"

CHORUS
The left hand's a poker for stirring up trouble,
The right hand's a pipe for blowing a bubble;
The neck is made of curtain rods, it certainly never bends,
I invented myself out of odds and ends.

The foot is a ramrod for ramming a door down,
One foot is a rock for holding the floor down;
The fingers they are feathers fit to tickle the other sex,
I invented myself out of bits and specks.

But the damn thing works, the damn thing works,
Tho' it's not plumb true or level;
Tho' it don't quite fit
Tho' it ain't well knit,
The damn thing works like the devil.

The liver's a barrel of brandy in one sense,
The lungs are two bags of hot air and nonsense;
I made the skin it's wrapped in from the hide of a grizzly bear,
I invented myself out of thin blue air!

"IT'S SIMPLE"

Baker Street (1965)
Lyrics and Music by Marian Grudeff and Raymond Jessel

HOLMES
Come, come, your profession isn't hard to perceive—
Your manner, your bearing—
The very clothes you're wearing—
—that handkerchief tucked in your sleeve—
A military custom, I believe?

Of course you're an officer—
—Sandhurst, am I right?
And you're too young for a major
And so I should gauge you're
A captain.
GREGG
Well, I'll be—
HOLMES
Quite.
GREGG
Sir, I'm amazed!
HOLMES
You show surprise?
And yet the facts are there before your very eyes.
And it's so simple,
Sublimely simple,
If you learn not just to see but to observe.
Put your brain to work, not just the optic nerve.
If you put your mind to use
You will find the most abstruse
Becomes so simple.
WATSON
Oh yes, so simple
Just as simple as a simple thing can be.
HOLMES
And it's hardly very hard
To see he's in the palace guard.
WATSON
Oh no, it's simple as A B C.
GREGG
Now wait a minute! How did you know that I was in the palace
    guard?
HOLMES
My dear Captain
The line of your sunburn—straight across your brow.
No cap with a visor
Makes that mark, and I, sir,
Ask what type of headgear could possibly do that?
—a brimless bearskin hat!

Now who wears a busby?
You answer that and then
All other suppositions you discard—

Just guardsmen—and then only when
On duty in the palace yard!

GREGG
Well, I'll be bound!
HOLMES
Does it astound?
What other possible solution could be found?
It's all so simple,
Absurdly simple.
Why do people always fail to realize
That it's not enough to merely use their eyes?
They keep going 'round half-blind
Never using what's behind!
WATSON
You see it's simple
GREGG
Oh yes, it's simple
WATSON AND GREGG
However difficult it might at first appear
HOLMES
And it isn't hard to place
There's a woman in the case—
WATSON AND GREGG
Oh no it's simple
So very simple
It's as simple—

"I SHALL MISS YOU"

Baker Street (1965)

Lyrics and Music by Marian Grudeff and Raymond Jessel

MORIARTY
I shall miss you, Holmes,
For in truth we are fellow connoisseurs
And it grieves me, Holmes,
To eclipse such an intellect as yours.

I've enjoyed each thrust and parry
And riposte.
Yes, your genius was indeed a match for mine—
Almost.

I shall miss you, sir
I regret your reversion into dust.
Life is hard, dear Holmes,
And one does what one must.

Your demise ensures
The unobstructed birth
Of an empire that will
Circumscribe the earth!

The Jubilee gifts are a mere beginning. Two million pounds for
the purchase of power. Through drugs, through lust, through
secret cravings in the minds of men. And how they shall love
me for my tolerance of their weaknesses! That is why I shall
rise to my zenith—whilst you are blown to dust. (Triggers
time bomb, which begins to tick.)

Ah! You can't know how profoundly
I shall miss you, Holmes,
'Though your death is essential to my schemes.
You must die, dear Holmes,
Yet as strange as it seems

I shall mourn
As I have never mourned before
When the stately Holmes of England
Is no more.

"TO EACH HIS DULCINEA"

Man of La Mancha (1965)
Lyrics by Joe Darion *
Music by Mitch Leigh

To each his Dulcinea,
That he alone can name . . .
To each a secret hiding place
Where he can find the haunting face
To light his secret flame.

For with his Dulcinea
Beside him so to stand,
A man can do quite anything,
Outfly the bird upon the wing,
Hold moonlight in his hand.

Yet if you build your life on dreams
It's prudent to recall,
A man with moonlight in his hand
Has nothing there at all.

There is no Dulcinea,
She's made of flame and air,
And yet how lovely life would seem
If every man could weave a dream
To keep him from despair.

To each his Dulcinea
Though she's naught but flame and air!

"A LITTLE GOSSIP"

Man of La Mancha (1965)
Lyrics by Joe Darion

A little gossip . . . a little chat . . .
A little idle talk . . . of this and that . . .
I'll tell him all the troubles I have had
And since he doesn't hear, at least he won't feel bad.

When I first got home my wife Teresa beat me,
But the blows fell very lightly on my back.
She kept missing every other stroke and crying from the heart
That while I was gone she'd gone and lost the knack!
(Spoken)
Of course I hit her back, Your Grace, but she's a lot harder than
I am, and you know what they say—"Whether the stone hits
the pitcher or the pitcher hits the stone, it's going to be bad
for the pitcher." So I've got bruises from here to—
(He sings)
A little gossip . . . a little chat . . .
A little idle talk . . . of this and that . . .
If no one listens, then it's just as well,
At least I won't get caught in any lies I tell!

* Darion also wrote lyrics for Shinbone Alley (1957) and Illya Darling (1967).

Oh, I haven't fought a windmill in a fortnight,
And the humble joys get duller every day.
Why, when I'm asleep a dragon with his fiery tongue a-waggin'
Whispers, "Sancho, won't you please come out and play?"

"SO WHAT?"

Cabaret (1966)
Lyrics by Fred Ebb *
Music by John Kander

You say fifty marks,
I say one hundred marks;
A difference of fifty marks,
Why should that stand in our way?
As long as the room's to let,
The fifty that I will get
Is fifty more than I had yesterday, ja?
When you're as old as I—
Is anyone as old as I?
What difference does it make?
An offer comes, you take.

For the sun will rise and the moon will set,
And you learn how to settle for what you get.
It'll all go on if we're here or not,
So who cares? So what?
So who cares? So what?

When I was a girl my summers were spent by the sea, so what?
And I had a maid doing all of the housework, not me, so what?
Now I scrub up the floors and I wash down the walls,
And I empty the chamber pot.
If it ended that way then it ended that way, and I shrug and I
    say, so what?

For the sun will rise and the moon will set,
And you learn how to settle for what you get.
It'll all go on if we're here or not,
So who cares, so what?
So who cares, so what?

When I had a man, my figure was boyish and flat, so what?
Through all of our years he was so disappointed in that, so
    what?
Now I have what he missed and my bosom is full,
But he lies in a churchyard plot.
If it wasn't to be that he ever would see the abundance of me,
So what?

For the sun will rise and the moon will set,
And you learn how to settle for what you get.
It'll go on if we're here or not,
So who cares, so what?
So who cares, so what?

So once I was rich, and now all my fortune is gone, so what?
And love disappeared and only the memory lives on, so what?
If I've lived through all that, and I've lived through all that,

* Ebb also wrote *Smiling, The Boy Fell Dead* (1961) with David Baker,
Morning Sun (1963) with Paul Klein, *The Happy Time* (1968) with John
Kander, *Zorba* (1968) with John Kander, *70, Girls, 70* (1971), and
Chicago (1975).

Fifty marks doesn't mean a lot.
If I like that you're here, and I like that you're here,
Happy New Year, my dear, so what?

For the sun will rise and the moon will set,
And you learn how to settle for what you get.
It'll all go on if we're here or not,
So who cares . . . so what?
So who cares . . . so what?
It all goes on,
So who cares? Who cares? Who cares? So what?

"MARRIED"

Cabaret (1966)
Lyrics by Fred Ebb
Music by John Kander

SCHULTZ
How the world can change,
It can change like that
Due to one little word—
Married.

See a palace rise
From a two-room flat
Due to one little word—
Married.

And the old despair
That was often there
Suddenly ceases to be.
For you wake one day,
Look around and say,
Somebody wonderful
Married me.
(The lights come up in FRAULEIN SCHNEIDER'S *bedroom.
    Through the wall, we see* FRAULEIN SCHNEIDER *sitting
    thoughtfully on the edge of her bed)*
FRAULEIN SCHNEIDER
How the world can change,
It can change like that
Due to one little word—
SCHULTZ AND FRAULEIN SCHNEIDER
Married.
FRAULEIN SCHNEIDER
See a palace rise
From a two-room flat
Due to one little word—
SCHULTZ AND FRAULEIN SCHNEIDER
Married.
FRAULEIN SCHNEIDER
And the old despair
That was often there
Suddenly ceases to be.
SCHULTZ AND FRAULEIN SCHNEIDER
For you wake one day,
Look around and say,
SCHULTZ
Somebody wonderful,
FRAULEIN SCHNEIDER
Somebody wonderful
SCHULTZ AND FRAULEIN SCHNEIDER
Married me.

"OPEN A NEW WINDOW"

Mame (1966)

Lyrics and Music by Jerry Herman *

MAME AND ALL
Open a new window,
Open a new door,
Travel a new highway
That's never been tried before,
Before you find you're a dull fellow
Punching the same clock,
Walking the same tightrope,
As everyone on the block—
The fellow you ought to be is three dimensional,
Soaking up life
Down to your toes,
Whenever they say you're slightly unconventional,
Just put your thumb up to your nose,
And show 'em how to
Dance to a new rhythm,
Whistle a new song,
Toast with a new vintage,
The fizz doesn't fizz too long—
There's only one way to make the bubbles stay;
Simply travel a new highway,
Dance to a new rhythm,
Open a new window every day!

"GOOCH'S SONG"

Mame (1964)

Lyrics and Music by Jerry Herman

AGNES   I'll try. (Singing)
With my wings resolutely spread, Mrs. Burnside,
And my old inhibitions shed, Mrs. Burnside,
I did each little thing you said, Mrs. Burnside,
I lived! I lived! I lived!

I altered the drape of
A drop of my bodice,
And softened the shape of my brow;
I followed directions
And made some connections,
But what do I do now?

Who'd think this Miss Prim would
Have opened a window
As far as her whim would allow?
And who would suppose it
Was so hard to close it?
Oh, what do I do now?

I polished and powdered and puffed myself—
If life is a banquet, I stuffed myself!

I had my misgivings,
But went on a field trip
To find out what living's about;
My thanks for the training,
Now, I'm not complaining,

* Herman also wrote the music and lyrics for *I Feel Wonderful* (1954), *Nightcap* (1958), *Parade* (1960), *Milk and Honey* (1961), *Hello, Dolly!* (1964), *Dear World* (1969), and *Mack and Mabel* (1974).

But you left something out . . .
Instead of wand'ring on with my lone remorse
I have come back home to complete the course!
Oh, what do I do . . .

Mrs. Burnside,
I traveled to hell in my new veneer,
And look what I got as a souvenir!

But still I'll defend you
As guide and instructor,
Would I recommend you . . . and how!
Although I was leery,
I thrived on your theory
That life can be a wow:
You said, "There's nothing wrong with a harmless smooch,"
So I'm gonna call him "Burnside Gooch,"
But what do I do now?

"SNOOPY"

You're a Good Man, Charlie Brown (1967)

Lyrics, Music, and Adaptation by Clark Gesner

SNOOPY
They like me,
I think they're swell.
Isn't it remarkable
How things work out so well?
Pleasant day, pretty sky,
Life goes on, here I lie.
Not bad, not bad at all.
Cozy home, board and bed,
Sturdy roof beneath my head.
Not bad, not bad at all.

Faithful friends always near me,
Bring me bones, scratch my ear.
Little birds come to cheer me,
Every day
Sitting here
On my stomach
With their sharp little claws
Which are usually cold
And occasionally painful,
And sometimes there are so many
That I can hardly stand it . . .

Rats!
I feel ev'ry now and then that I gotta bite someone.
I know ev'ry now and then what I wanna be,
A fierce jungle animal crouched on the limb of a tree.
I'd stay very very still till I see a victim come.
I'd wait, knowing very well ev'ry second counts,
And then, like the fierce jungle creature I am,
I would pounce.
I'd pounce.
I'd pounce.
I'd . . .
You know, I never quite realized it was so far down to the
    ground from here. Hm.
Let me see, where was I?
Oh, that's right. The pretty sky.
Not bad, not bad at all.
I wonder if it will snow tonight.

"HAPPINESS"

You're a Good Man, Charlie Brown (1967)
Lyrics, Music, and Adaptation by Clark Gesner

CHARLIE BROWN   Happiness is finding a pencil.
SNOOPY   Sleeping in moonlight.
LINUS   Telling the time.
SCHROEDER   Happiness is learning to whistle.
LINUS   Tying your shoe
For the very first time
PATTY   Happiness is playing the drum
In your own school band.
CHARLIE BROWN   And happiness is walking hand in hand.
Happiness is two kinds of ice cream.
LUCY   Knowing a secret.
SCHROEDER   Climbing a tree.
CHARLIE BROWN   Happiness is five different crayons.
SCHROEDER   Catching a firefly.
LINUS   Setting him free.
CHARLIE BROWN   Happiness is being alone every now and
   then.
ALL   And happiness is coming home again.
CHARLIE BROWN   Happiness is morning and evening,
Daytime and nighttime too.
For happiness is anyone and anything at all
That's loved by you.
LINUS   Happiness is having a sister.
LUCY   Sharing a sandwich.
LUCY AND LINUS   Getting along.
ALL   Happiness is singing together
When day is through,
And happiness is those who sing with you.

Happiness is morning and evening,
Daytime and nighttime too.
CHARLIE BROWN   For happiness is anyone and anything at all
That's loved by you.

"WALK AWAY"

How Now, Dow Jones (1967)
Lyrics by Carolyn Leigh *
Music by Elmer Bernstein

The clocks don't stop when they ought to stop
They tick relentlessly on
Tonight the world is your pastry shop
Too soon the goodies are gone

How in the world did your hopes get
Out of hand there?
Time you got up off the ropes, pet
Don't just stand there

Walk away, walk away
Can't you tell that it's reveille blowing
Time to turn the boy loose
There are no more excuses to stay

* Leigh also wrote *Peter Pan* (1954) with Mark Charlap, *Wildcat* (1960) with Cy Coleman, and *Little Me* (1962).

Walk away, walk away
It's a great little dream you were growing
But the dreams of the night
Can't outdistance the light of day

Nothing lost, nothing owing
It was bright, it was gay, it was glowing
It was mindless and heedless
And words that are needless to say

Only where was it going?
Only one little slip and it's showing
You walked into his arms
And let come willy-nilly what may
Now come through, little girl
Let's see you, little girl
Walk away

"OPENING"

How Now, Dow Jones (1967)
Lyrics by Carolyn Leigh
Music by Elmer Bernstein

The market is a ticker
A slender piece of tape
That notifies the public of its economic shape
Which if it weren't legal would be statutory rape
That's perpetrated daily
From ten to ha' past three
A simple little business,
It's A B C

"A" is for Analyst.

These are highly skilled professionals who spend their whole lives studying the market. Sir, do you think the market is going up or down?
ANALYST
We have every confidence that if there is no decline, the market
   will go higher.
CYNTHIA & TOURISTS
From here to Saud Araby
If Johnson blows his nose
Run and hock the baby
That's how the money goes, oh yeeaaah!
CYNTHIA
The market has a logic
Whose wonders never cease
It's basically predictable
And free of all caprice

It hits the floor in time of war
And lower when there's peace
And all the smart investors
Rely on L S D
A simple little business
It's A B C

"B" is for Broker.
BROKER
You're thinking of buying US Steel? Great idea!
You're thinking of selling US Steel? Great idea!
CYNTHIA
He thinks it's a great idea whether you buy or whether you sell.
   How come? "C" is for Commissions.

COMMISSIONS MAN
Three per cent . . . two per cent . . . five per cent . . .
TOURISTS
They deal below the table
And steal beneath your nose
Watch your bloomers, Mabel
That's how the money goes, oh yeeaah!
CYNTHIA
The market is a hot tip
Your neighbor will supply
In which you keep investing till
Its price has hit the sky
So when you go to sell it
There is no one left to buy
It's plunge ahead with Edsel
And sell A T & T
A simple little business
It's A B C

"D" is for Dow Jones. You've all heard about the Dow Jones averages. When the Dow Jones is up, it's good. Down, not so good.
(Intervening dialogue)
CYNTHIA
And honestly, isn't Wall Street wonderful?
TOURISTS
Yes!
CYNTHIA & TOURISTS
They're down on steel and carbon
And high on the U F O's
Up your I.G. Farben
That's how the money goes

And money makes the world go round
To that we all agree
Which brings us back to business
A simple little business

It's A B C 2 3 4 5

"FOR ONCE IN YOUR LIFE"

Golden Rainbow (1968)
Lyrics and Music by Walter Marks

Lady forget rhyme or reason for once in your life,
Don't do what's right,
Do what's pleasin' for once in your life.
Just forget your intellectual alibiing
Spread your wings and I suspect you will soon be flying
Do something silly and senseless for once in your life,
What if your heart is defenseless for once in your life.
Let's forget the wrong or right of it,
Come tonight let's make a night of it,
Take a chance for once in your life.

Do something you never would do for once in your life,
Something you wish you could do for once in your life.
Kick your heels and dance the night away,
Come what may. (miss,) 'Cause tonight you've got the right of
                    way (sir,)
It may be wrong,
But what of it for once in your life,
It may turn out that you love it for once in your life.

Take your point of view and give it up,
Start out fresh tonight and live it up,
Take a chance for once in your life.

"I'M ME! I'M NOT AFRAID"

Your Own Thing (1968)
Lyrics and Music by Hal Hester and Danny Apolinar

DANNY
I don't have to show anyone
I want to be one of them;
'Cause deep inside is the feeling of pride,
The me from which the mighty oaks stem.
MICHAEL
This is a man, look at his hair,
Not your idea of a he-man.
DANNY
Think what you will, what do I care?
I just want to be a free man,
To be me, man.
JOHN
This is a man, look at his clothes,
Not your idea of a tough man.
DANNY
Think what you will, this is no pose.
Don't have to pretend I'm a rough man,
I'm enough, man.
MICHAEL
This is a man, look at his eyes,
They're expressive.
DANNY
I can feel.
JOHN
This is a man, look at his heart,
It's impressive.
DANNY
I am real.
ALL
Why does everybody have to be afraid to be a human being?
Why does everybody have to be afraid of other people seeing?
DANNY
Everybody has emotion buried deep inside.
When they feel one truthful emotion,
They feel that's what they've got to hide.
JOHN
Me—I'm not afraid to cry,
Me—I'm not afraid to die,
I'm not afraid to weep when I'm sad,
I'm not afraid to laugh when I'm glad,
I'm not afraid to know when I'm bad,
I'm not afraid of love.
MICHAEL
Me—I'm not afraid to live,
Me—I'm not afraid to give,
I'm not afraid when the nights are too long,
I'm not afraid to admit when I'm wrong,
I'm not afraid to sing a new song,
DANNY
I'm not afraid to love.
Me—I'm not afraid to be,
Me—I'm not afraid to see,
I'm not afraid to give all my love,

I'm not afraid of heaven above,
I am the new man, a true man, more human and free,
But most of all, I'm not afraid of me.
ALL
Our generation can't live in the past.
I know that tomorrow won't last.
That's the reason our hearts beat much faster.
DANNY
I'm not the starry-eyed boy next door,
I'm not the life of the party,
I've got to be what I've got to be.
I'm me!
I'm not the prince in a fairy tale,
I'm not as strong as an oak tree,
I like the feeling of feeling free.
I'm me!

My generation can't live in the past
I know that tomorrow won't last.
That's the reason my heart beats much faster.
ALL
I can do anything I want to do.
I can make every dream I dream come true.
There may be things that I'll never
Completely see.
But look at me! Look! You can see that I'm real!
I'm alive! I'm me.

"THE MIDDLE YEARS"

Your Own Thing (1968)

Lyrics and Music by Hal Hester and Danny Apolinar

OLIVIA
He's twenty, I'm thirty. Does it matter?
When I'm forty, he'll be thirty. Does it matter?
Rules, labels, slots, categories
Lead the way to lonely purgatories.
What does it matter?

I finally made it! I shook myself free!
No more wondering what became of me.
I know where I'm going, no crocodile tears
Solved the riddle, I'm in my middle years.
The nights now are shorter tho' somewhat less gay.
No more time to waste, I live each day.
And I happen to like it, so give a few cheers,
Tune my fiddle, I'm in my middle years.
It's sublime to live and love in my security.
Old man time can't blame it on my immaturity.
Look and see!

I've got a few wrinkles. I wear them with pride.
I've worked hard for them, I've nothing to hide.
No more nights on the town.
No more playing around.
I've won my medal an' done all my pedalin',
Ready for settlin' down.
Hi diddle diddle! Here's to my middle years.

"THE DAY I MET YOUR FATHER"

The Education of H*y*m*a*n K*a*p*l*a*n

Lyrics and Music by Paul Nassau and Oscar Brand *

The day I met your father, the seventeenth of May,
How could I forget it, it was my wedding day.
Our parents had arranged it,
So they looked on with pride,
They thought I was happy
Because, like them, I cried.

Can you imagine how I felt?
All I knew about him was his name.
Can you imagine how I felt?
And I'm sure he felt the same.

But after we'd been married
For just a little while,
Suddenly came laughter
Where there was just a smile.
I loved him so, and the love that came to me
Will come to you, you'll see.

The first time I met your papa, I thought I'd die. I thought my
    parents was making a mistake. But later on I was happy they
    made me marry him.

When two friends wed it's very nice.
They already know each other well.
But when two strangers meet
Just think how much more they have to tell.
The day I met your father
We talked through half the night.
Soon we saw each other
In such a different light
We fell in love, and the happy life we knew
Will some day come for you.

"JULIUS CAESAR"

The Education of H*y*m*a*n K*a*p*l*a*n

Lyrics and Music by Paul Nassau and Oscar Brand

I see the whole scene in a tent
With Julius Caesar in bed
He's trying to sleep but he can't
The thoughts run around in his head
Tomorrow they want to make me king of Rome
Should I do it, or should I stay in bed at home?
PARKHILL *(spoken)*
Mr. Kaplan, these lines are from Macbeth.
KAPLAN *(spoken)*
The lines are from Macbeth and Julius Caesar is talking.
(sung)

Tomorrow and tomorrow and tomorrow
It creeps so slow, what a pity the pace
And when you're choosing wrong, comes only sorrow
With too many syllables and not enough space
And lots of fools can't see what's better just

* Brand and Nassau also wrote the lyrics and music for *A Joyful Noise*
(1966) and Brand wrote the lyrics and music for *How to Steal an
Election* (1968).

Because their lights get covered up from dust.
PARKHILL (*spoken*)
Dusty death doesn't mean that . . .
KAPLAN (*sung*)
So Caesar gets so weary from the worry
Which way to turn—what way do I choose
Go out, go out, short candle, you should hurry
Which way do I win, which way do I lose?
A person's got to pick what's right for her or
Things will get much worser than they were.
PARKHILL (*spoken*)
"I'm afraid I'm a little confused."
KAPLAN (*spoken*)
"It's perfectly clear. I'll explain."
  (*sung*)
  Life is like a walking shadow
  A player who's so poor he's losing games
  His time is running out like someone else I know
  Don't worry, I'm not mentioning no names.

  Ohhhhhh
  When you're choosing wrong, life is a nothing
  A mixup like a bowl of chop suey
  A story told by crazy people
  Full of foolish sounds and phooey.
PARKHILL (*spoken*)
"That's fury!"
KAPLAN (*spoken*)
"Of course."
  (*sung*)
  So, instead of Caesar staying in his bed
  He says, tomorrow and tomorrow and tomorrow
  Gets up, goes to work and drops down dead!

"KNOWING WHEN TO LEAVE"

Promises, Promises (1968)
Lyrics by Hal David
Music by Burt Bacharach

Go while the going is good
Knowing when to leave
May be the smartest thing
That anyone can learn.
Go—
I'm afraid my heart
Isn't that smart

Fly while you still have your wings.
Knowing when to leave
Won't ever let you reach
The point of no return.
Fly—foolish as it seems
I still have my dreams

So I keep hoping, day after day,
As I wait for the man I need

Night after night
As I wish for a love that can be
Though I'm sure that
No one can tell
Where their wishes and hopes will lead
Somehow I feel
There is happiness just waiting there for me.

When someone walks in your life
You just better be sure he's right
'Cause if he's wrong
There are heartaches and tears you must pay.
Keep both of your eyes on the door
Never let it get out of sight
Just be prepared
When the time has come for you to run away.
Sail when the wind starts to blow.
But like a fool I don't know when to leave . . .

"PROMISES, PROMISES"

Promises, Promises (1968)
Lyrics by Hal David
Music by Burt Bacharach

Promises, promises,
I'm all through with promises, promises now.
I don't know how
I got the nerve to walk out.
If I shout
Remember I feel free.
Now I can look at myself and be proud
I'm laughing out loud.
Oh, promises, promises,
This is where those promises, promises end.
I won't pretend
That what was wrong can be right.
Every night I'll sleep now.
No more lies.
Things that I promised myself fell apart
But I found my heart.
Promises, their kind of promises
Can just destroy your life.
Oh, promises, those kind of promises
Take all the joy from life.
Oh, promises, promises, my kind of promises
Can lead to joy and hope and love,
Yes, love.

"MOMMA, LOOK SHARP"

1776 (1969)
Lyrics and Music by Sherman Edwards

Momma, hey, Momma,
Come lookin' for me.
I'm here in the meadow
By the red maple tree.
Momma, hey, Momma,
Look sharp—here I be.
Hey, Hey—
Momma, look sharp!

Them so'jurs, they fired,
Oh, Ma, did we run,
But then we turned round
An' the battle begun.
Then I went under—
Oh, Ma, am I done?
Hey, Hey—
Momma, look sharp!

My eyes are wide open,
My face to the sky.
Is that you I'm hearin'
In the tall grass nearby?
Momma, come find me
Before I do die.
Hey, Hey—
Momma, look sharp!
COURIER, MCNAIR, AND LEATHER APRON
I'll close y'r eyes, my Billy,
Them eyes that cannot see,
An' I'll bury ya, my Billy,
Beneath the maple tree.
COURIER
An' never ag'in
Will y'whisper t'me,
"Hey, Hey—"
Oh, Momma, look sharp!

"MOLASSES TO RUM"

1776 (1969)
Lyrics and Music by Sherman Edwards

Molasses to
Rum to
Slaves!
Oh, what a beautiful waltz!

You dance with us,
We dance with you, in
Molasses and
Rum and
Slaves!
(Afro-rhythm.)
Who sail the ships out of Boston,
Laden with Bibles and Rum?
Who drinks a toast
To the Ivory Coast,
"Hail, Africa! The slavers have come."
New England, with Bibles and Rum!

Then,
It's off with the Rum and the Bibles
Take on the Slaves, clink! clink!
Then,
Hail and farewell!
To the smell of the African
Coast!

Molasses to
Rum to
Slaves!
'Tisn't morals, 'tis money that saves!
Shall we dance to the sound
Of the profitable pound, in
Molasses and
Rum and
Slaves!

Who sail the ships out of Guinea,
Laden with Bibles and Slaves?
'Tis Boston can boast
To the West Indies coast:

"Jamaica! We brung what y'craves!
Antigua! Barbados!
We brung Bibles
And Slaves!"
(He speaks. Afro-rhythm continues.)
Gentlemen! You mustn't think our northern friends merely see
   our slaves as figures on a ledger. Oh, no, sir! They see them as
   figures on the block! Notice the faces at the auctions, gen-
   tlemen—white faces on the African wharves—New England
   faces, seafaring faces: "Put them in the ships, cram them in
   the ships, stuff them in the ships!" Hurry, gentlemen, let the
   auction begin!
(He sings.)
Ya-ha . . .
Ya-ha . . . ha-ma-ha-cundahhh!
Gentlemen, do y' hear?
That's the cry of the auctioneer!

Ya-ha . . .
Ya-ha . . . ha-ma-ha-cundahhh!
Slaves, gentlemen! Black gold, livin' gold—gold!
From:
Annn-go-laah!
Guinea-Guinea-Guinea!
Blackbirds for sale!

Aaa-shan-tiiii!
Ibo! Ibo! Ibo! Ibo!

Blackbirds for sale!
Handle them!
Fondle them!
But don't finger them!
They're prime, they're prime!

Ya-ha . . .
Ya-ha . . . ha-ma-ha-cundahhh!
(Music stops.)
BARTLETT, pleading:
For the love of God, Mr. Rutledge, please!
(Music resumes.)
RUTLEDGE
Molasses to
Rum to
Slaves!

Who sail the ships back to Boston,
Laden with gold, see it gleam?
Whose fortunes are made
In the triangle trade?
Hail, Slavery, the New England
Dream!

Mr. Adams, I give you a toast!
Hail, Boston!
Hail, Charleston!
Who stinketh the most?!

"CAPRICIOUS AND FICKLE"

Promenade (1969)
Lyrics by Maria Irene Fornes
Music by Al Carmines

Capricious as I am, and fickle,
In spite of my renowned restlessness;

In spite of my noted changeability,
My versatility, my spirit of adventure,
One day because of your winning ways,
I gave you all I had.
But you in your typical fashion,
Conceited, flippant and complacent,
Just threw it all away,
Just threw it all away.
You heel!
You cad!
You treated me the way I treated others.
You scoundrel!
How dare you bring shame,
Bring shame to my life.
Shame, shame.
One day, because of your amorous claims,
I learned that pleasure does not need fabrication;
That true love catches you by surprise,
That true love catches you by surprise.
But you confirmed egotist, you were just playing games.
You insisted on reenacting a moment from your past;
Either a moment that you lived or a moment, a moment that
   you imagined.

You heel!
You are just playing games,
You are just playing games.
Shame, shame.
I am conceited, flippant and deceitful,
And I am flighty, frivolous and vain;
And you scoundrel, you treated me the way I treated others.
Just who do you think you are?
In spite of my reputation as a lady without heart,
I gave my heart to you,
I gave my heart to you, you heel!
And here I am, I've lost my heart, my heart to you,
Unaccustomed as I am to asking a man for his favor,
I'm asking you,
I'm asking you.
Come, come, come, come, come, come,
Come, I'm helpless without you.

"WELCOME TO THE THEATER"

Applause (1970)
Lyrics by Lee Adams
Music by Charles Strouse

Welcome to the theater,
To the magic, to the fun!
(She sings)
Where painted trees and flowers grow,
And laughter rings fortissimo,
And treachery's sweetly done!

Now you've entered the asylum,
This profession unique,
Actors are children
Playing hide-and-ego-seek . . .

So welcome, Miss Eve Harrington,
To this business we call show,

You're on your way
To wealth and fame,
Unsheath your claws,
Enjoy the game!
You'll be a bitch
But they'll know your name
From New York to Kokomo . . .

Welcome to the theater,
My dear, you'll love it so!

Welcome to the dirty concrete hallways,
Welcome to the friendly roaches, too,
Welcome to the pinches from the stagehands,
It's the only quiet thing they do . . .
Welcome to the Philadelphia critics,
Welcome, Librium and Nembutal,
Welcome to a life of laryngitis,
Welcome to dark toilets in the hall . . .
Welcome to the flop
You thought would run for years,
Welcome to the world
Of tears and cheers and fears . . .

Welcome to the theater,
With some luck you'll be a pro,
You'll work and slave
And scratch and bite,
You'll learn to kill
With sheer delight,
You'll only come
Alive at night
When you're in a show!
Welcome to the theater,
You fool, you'll love it so.

"WHISPERS ON THE WIND"

Whispers on the Wind (1970)
Lyrics and Book by John B. Kuntz
Music by Lor Crane

NARRATOR
Whispers, whispers,
Whispers on the wind,
Fading on the summer's air,
Were they ever really there?
Whispers, whispers on the wind.
1ST WOMAN
Will she love you?
2ND MAN
Will he return?
1ST MAN
How many children?
2ND WOMAN
What do you earn?
NARRATOR
What's for dinner?
1ST MAN
My, how they've grown.
ALL
Living together,
Dying alone.

Whispers, whispers,
Whispers on the wind,
Fading on the summer's air,
Were they ever really there . . .?

"MIDWESTERN SUMMER"

Whispers on the Wind (1970)
Lyrics and Book by John B. Kuntz
Music by Lor Crane

NARRATOR
Midwestern summer,
Spiderweb fine
And tigerswallow free,
FIRST WOMAN
Up with the dawn
Cause there's so much
To do and to see.
FIRST MAN
Midwestern summer,
Hollyhock hot
And dandelion dry.
ALL
Dust from the field
Leaves a film
On the blue of the sky.
FIRST MAN
The kids down the block
Pound on the screen door,
Ask, "Can you come out to play?"
ALL
Saturday,
FIRST MAN
And
Midwestern summer,
Dinner is done, chase a firefly spark.
Mother will soon
Call you in cause it's gettin' so dark.
It's gettin' so dark.
ALL
Midwestern summer,
Blackberry green
And honeysuckle slow.
Sun sittin' still
On a breeze that
Refuses to blow.

Midwestern summer,
Milkyway sweet,
And watermelon cool.
Open your eyes
You can see
The whole length of the pool.

They're building a house
Workman deserted.
No one to chase us away,
Not today,
It's
FIRST WOMAN
Midwestern summer,

SECOND WOMAN
Field-sparrow fast.
SECOND MAN
And tissue paper thin.
FIRST WOMAN
Hide and go seek
ALL
'Til it's late
And it's time to go in.
FIRST MAN
How I hate to go in.
OTHERS
But you gotta go in.
FIRST MAN
I don't wanta go in.
OTHERS
But you gotta go . . .
FIRST WOMAN
In.

"NEW-FANGLED PREACHER-MAN"

Purlie (1970)
Lyrics by Peter Udell
Music by Gary Geld

Ain't gonna promise no pie in the sky,
Life ever after right after you die.
I got a diff'rent banner to wave.
How 'bout some happiness this side of the grave?

The Lord lives up in heaven,
The devil lives in hell,
And you and me, we live the best we can.
Move over, Billy Sunday,
Move over, Billy Graham.
Make way for a new-fangled preacher-man.
Make way for a new-fangled preacher-man.

Ain't gonna promise no chariot ride,
No glorious life on that great other side.
I got a diff'rent message to spread.
How 'bout some glory days before we are dead?

The Lord lives up in heaven,
The devil lives in hell,
And you and me, we live the best we can.
Move over, Billy Sunday,
Move over, Billy Graham.
Make way for a new-fangled preacher-man.
Make way for a new-fangled preacher-man.

Ain't gonna tell you the Lord loves you best,
He's gonna prove it when you're laid to rest.
I got a different trumpet to play.
How 'bout some lovin' 'fore they put us away?

The Lord lives up in heaven,
The devil lives in hell,
And you and me, we live the best we can.
Move over, Billy Sunday,
Move over, Billy Graham.
Make way for a new-fangled preacher-man.
(Spoken) Wait, I say! And we'll see who's gonna dominize this
    valley! Ol' Cap'n or me!
(Sung) Make way for a new-fangled preacher-man.

"PURLIE"

Purlie (1970)
Lyrics by Peter Udell
Music by Gary Geld

I love to sit and hear him dream.
He tells it like a story.
He talks about a better time:
Happy days and glory.
No more scratchin' for a livin'
Like a chicken, peckin'.
He's got the whole world figured out
And even more . . . I reckon. . . .

The moon don't rise
To light the sky.
The moon comes up to shine on Purlie,
Purlie,
My Purlie.

The spring don't spring
To charm the bees.
The flowers flower just for Purlie,
Purlie,
My Purlie.

I ain't ever seen a man
Do the things that that man can.
He can still the ev'nin' breezes,
Stare the sun down till it freezes.

I just can't wait
To greet each day,
To blink my eyes and say to Purlie,
Purlie,
Purlie,
You just thrill me through and through.
Purlie, you're too good to be true.
Purlie, I'm in love with you,
Purlie, wow!
My Purlie.

"MY MOST IMPORTANT MOMENTS GO BY"

The Last Sweet Days of Isaac (1970)
Lyrics by Gretchen Cryer
Music by Nancy Ford

INGRID
My most important moments go by
And I don't even know it 'til they're gone
I hear the hurdy-gurdy of a time that is past
A time that didn't last.
ISAAC
I know what you mean.
INGRID
I open up a cedar chest of handkerchiefs and lace
Years folded in their place
I press them to my face
And the old perfume reminds me
Of a time that is past
A time that didn't last
When I took today

And I folded it away
for tomorrow.
ISAAC
My dear . . .
INGRID
And I cry yes
That was important
Yes, that day was important
I know it now, I didn't know it then
I'm living yes in retrospect
In images so indirect
The moment is gone
And never can I touch it again
I fold away the handkerchiefs and lace
I fold the years and put them in place
I hear the hurdy-gurdy fading far down the street
I wonder did we meet
Did we ever really meet

My most important moments go by
And I don't even know it 'til they're gone
And time's an old calliope
Its music drifts away from me
And haunts me from the past
The music didn't last
I didn't know it then
But never will I hear it again.

I'm not living, Isaac. In the moment, I mean, well, look, let's
    face it. I ride up and down this elevator a thousand times a
    year and until this very moment I've never realized *really*
    what it means to be in this elevator. I mean, the walls, the
    ceiling, the floor, this little space, smell, touch, the ins, the
    outs, the ups, the downs, everything! The essence! You know
    what I mean?
ISAAC
My dear. My dear. I know what you mean.
INGRID
That's pretty sad.
ISAAC
Yes, it is.
INGRID *(Sung)*
I didn't know it then
I know it now
I must try to touch the moment while I have it
Somehow

"THE LAST SWEET DAYS OF ISAAC"

The Last Sweet Days of Isaac (1970)
Lyrics by Gretchen Cryer
Music by Nancy Ford

This is my thirty-third year
The year that I am to die
The days are pressing in on me
I feel their wild immediacy
And in the air expectancy
Fulfillment of prophecy
The last days of Isaac
O the Last Sweet Days of Isaac

Etched in burning sunlight
On the inside of my eye

Will I burst into oblivion
Burn in Armageddon
Will my flaming ashes light the sky?

O where will I be
Where will I be
Where will I be when darkness
Descends on me?

"ALL FOR THE BEST"

Godspell (1971)
Lyrics and Music by Stephen Schwartz *

JESUS
When you feel sad or under a curse,
Your life is bad, your prospects are worse,
Your wife is sighing, crying,
And your olive tree is dying,
Temples are graying and teeth are decaying and creditors
  weighing your purse;
Your mood and your robe are both a deep blue
You'd bet that Job had nothing on you.
Don't forget that when you get to heaven you'll be blest.
Yes, it's all for the best.

JUDAS
Some men are born to live at ease, doing what they please,
  richer than the bees in honey;
Never growing old, never feeling cold, pulling pots of gold
  from thin air.
The best in ev'ry town, best at shaking down, best at making
  mountains of money.
They can't take it with them, but what do they care?
They get the center of the meat, cushions on the seat, houses on
  the street where it's sunny,
Summers at the sea, winters warm and free, all of this and we
  get the rest.
But who is the land for, the sun and the sand for?
You guessed—it's all for the best.

OTHERS
Yes, it's all for the best.

JESUS   (Spoken)
You must never be distressed

OTHERS
Yes, it's all for the best.

JESUS   (Spoken)   All your wrongs will be redressed.

OTHERS   Yes, it's all for the best.

JUDAS   (Spoken)   Someone's got to be oppressed!

ALL   Yes, it's all for the best.

"SAVE THE PEOPLE"

Godspell (1971)
Lyrics and Music by Stephen Schwartz

When wilt Thou save the people?
O, God of mercy, when?
The people, Lord, the people,

* Schwartz also wrote the lyrics and music for *Pippin* (1972) and *The
Magic Show* (1974).

Not thrones and crowns, but men!
Flow'rs of Thy heart
O, God are they.
Let them not pass like weeds away.
Their heritage a sunless day,
God save the people.
Shall crime breed crime forever,
Strength aiding still the strong?
Is it Thy will, O Father,
That man shall toil for wrong?
"No" say Thy mountains,
"No" say Thy skies.
Man's clouded sun shall brightly rise.
And songs be heard instead of sighs.
God save the people.
(Repeat)

"QUESTIONS"

Don't Bother Me, I Can't Cope (1972)
Lyrics and Music by Micki Grant

Questions
Questions
Knocking on the doors of my mind
Questions
Questions
And somewhere there are answers I must find

So many voices preaching
So many hands keep reaching
Which sound do I listen to
Which hand do I shake

Questions
Questions

With ev'ry day I'm finding
Another road is winding
There's a fork in ev'ry road
Which one do I take

Questions
Questions
Knocking on the doors of my mind

Questions
Questions
And somewhere there are answers I must find

So many times I've wondered
Where will my name be numbered
Will I stand among the crowd
Or will I stand alone

Questions
Questions

Yes I can hear you preaching
I study all your teaching
Still I know that I must find
Some answers of my own

Questions, etc.

"FIGHTING FOR PHARAOH"

Don't Bother Me, I Can't Cope (1972)
Lyrics and Music by Micki Grant

History's pages say Man through the ages
Has never run short of war
For he's always found something worth fighting
And killing and dying for

Fighting for Pharaoh
Fighting for Caesar
Fighting for Good King Arthur
Fighting for glory
Fighting for Power
State or religion
Fighting for jurisdiction and territory
Dying for freedom
Dying for slav'ry
Dying for cotton and for oil and gold
Dying for country
Dying for honor
Dying for God
And peace and banners on a pole
Before we lose our humanity
Let's stop this insanity
And turn our children's history books around
Let's do a little living in peace
Not dying but living in peace
If ev'ry man in ev'ry land
Reached out his hand in understanding
We could do a little living
Do a little living
Do a little living in peace

"FREDDY, MY LOVE"

Grease (1972)
Lyrics, Music, and Book by Jim Jacobs and Warren Casey

Freddy, my love, I miss you more than words can say.
Freddy, my love, please keep in touch while you're away.
Hearing from you can make the day so much better,
Getting a souvenir or maybe a letter.
I really flipped over the gray cashmere sweater.
Freddy, my love
(Freddy, my love, Freddy, my love, Freddy, my lo-oove)

Freddy, you know, your absence makes me feel so blue.
That's okay, though, your presents make me think of you.
My ma will have a heart attack when she catches
Those pedal pushers with the black leather patches.
Oh, how I wish I had a jacket that matches.
Freddy, my love
(Freddy, my love, Freddy, my love, Freddy, my lo-oove)

Don't keep your letters from me,
I thrill to every line.
Your spelling's kinda crummy
But honey, so is mine.
I treasure every giftie,
The ring is really nifty.
You say it cost you fifty
So you're thrifty,

I don't mind!
(Woe-ohh-ohh-oh)

Freddy, you'll see, you'll hold me in your arms someday
And I will be wearing your lacy lonjeray.
Thinking about it, my heart's pounding already
Knowing when you come home we're bound to go steady
And throw your service pay around like confetti
Freddy, my love
(Freddy, my love, Freddy, my love, Freddy, my lo-oove)

"BEAUTY SCHOOL DROPOUT"

Grease (1972)
Lyrics, Music, and Book by Jim Jacobs and Warren Casey

Your story's sad to tell:
A teenage ne'er do-well,
Most mixed-up non-delinquent on the block,
Your future's so unclear now.
What's left of your career now?
Can't even get a trade-in on your smock.

Beauty school dropout,
No graduation day for you.
Beauty school dropout,
Missed your midterms and flunked shampoo.
Well, at least you could have taken time
To wash and clean your clothes·up
After spending all that dough to have
The doctor fix your nose up.
Baby, get movin'
Why keep your feeble hopes alive?
What are you provin'?
You got the dream but not the drive.
If you go for your diploma you could join a steno pool
Turn in your teasing comb and go back to high school.

Beauty school dropout,
Hangin' around the corner store.
Beauty school dropout,
It's about time you knew the score.
Well, they couldn't teach you anything,
You think you're such a looker,
But no customer would go to you
Unless she was a hooker.
Baby, don't sweat it,
You're not cut out to hold a job.
Better forget it,
Who wants their hair done by a slob?
Now your bangs are curled, your lashes twirled,
But still the world is cruel.
Wipe off that angel face and go back to high school.

Baby, ya blew it.
You put your good advice to shame.
How could you do it?
Betcha Dear Abby'd say the same.
Guess there's no way to get through to you,
No matter who may try.
Might as well go back to that malt shop in the sky.

"SIDEWALK TREE"

Raisin (1973)
Lyrics by Robert Brittan
Music by Judd Woldin

Sidewalk tree hanging low . . .
Won't forget you when I go.
I'll remember flying high in space . . .
And when mama'd scold me,
You'd be there to hold me . . .
Giving me the room to cry . . .
A hiding place.

Sidewalk tree, no more time.
No more swinging, no more climb.
They all tell me I've been thinking small.
Other trees are growing . . .
That's where I'll be going . . .
Where I'll have a chance to grow,
To show them all.

Gonna have the good things Daddy never had . . .
Even though I'm happy living with the bad.

Sidewalk tree what an end.
Gain a fortune, lose a friend.
Bright tomorrow, but not for me to share.
Rather be right here next year than anywhere.

"MEASURE THE VALLEYS"

Raisin (1973)
Lyrics by Robert Brittan
Music by Judd Woldin

When a breeze gets to losin' ground . . .
Better ask all the trees around.
When the wind's gettin' slow . . .
Look at where it's had to go,
Measure the valleys, measure the hills.

When a stream's nearly dry as bone . . .
Better count ev'ry turn, ev'ry stone.
When it's all runnin' thin . . .
Take a look at where it's been.
Measure the valleys, measure the hills.

When you know how a dream can fade . . .
How a man comes to be so afraid.
When you know where he's been . . .
Take a look at him again,
Measure the valleys, measure the hills.
Measure the valleys, measure the hills.

"MY DAUGHTER THE COUNTESS"

Fashion (1974)
Lyrics by Steve Brown
Music by Don Pippin

MRS. TIFFANY   When you're living for your daughter's sake
People always say you've made a big mistake

Ev'ry mother knows how wrong they were
But if I err
It's for her!

My daughter the countess-to-be
Owes all to her mother—that's me
Like mother like daughter—mais oui
And soon I can say:
My daughter her grace
Her mother's own face
Her mother's own chin
Her mother's her twin!
Here comes the bride—who's at her side?
Here comes the bride—me at her side!
Me and the bride none can divide
It's what mothers all dream about
The diff'rence is this:
Other mothers say "Oh what I'd give to see"
Seraphina's mother's gonna live to see
My daughter the countess-to-be
Her mother the duchess—you'll see
Like daughter like mother—mais oui
And soon I can say . . .

Hello Paree
Are you ready for me?
Well ready or not here I come
When you get to Paree
Look up the countess and me
And you can see what's underneath the duchess's thumb
For example look at that chair
And tell me from where
For example look at these shoes
Can you guess who's?

Ev'rything about me was Marie Antoinette's
From her bathtub to her boudoir to her bed
I've got a ruby from her crown
I've got her guillotining gown
Ev'rything but her head
Ev'rything I'm wearing was Marie Antoinette's
From my stockings to my earrings to my fur
I could even wear her wig
If her head were twice as big
But other than that—I'm her!

For my daughter the countess
Ennobles whate'er she touches
My daughter the countess
Won't rest till her ma's a duchess
Other mothers say "Oh what I'd give to see"
Seraphina's mother's gonna live to see
My daughter her grace
Acres of lace
Mountains of curls
Bushels of pearls
Here comes the bride—me at her side
Make way for the countess
Bow down to the countess
My daughter the countess
Make way for the countess plus me

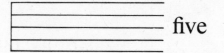 five

NEW LYRICISTS

The following lyrics—one or two each by as yet unproduced lyricists—are drawn from writers in my Broadcast Music, Inc., Musical Theatre Workshops in New York, Los Angeles, and Toronto. They are not the only new talents at work but due to my intimate acquaintance with and admiration for their work, I have presented them here.

Nearly all of these lyrics were created for theater projects based on existing plays, novels, legends, history, motion pictures and so on. Some of their works are on the verge of production.

Their styles are varied.

I am proud to include small examples of this work-in-progress. None of these writers is an amateur. All of them are aware of the art of lyric writing. All are talented.

The following lyrics are presented in alphabetical order according to the lyricists' names.

"A WOMAN LOVED"

In This Corner
Lyrics and Music by Renée Bondy

You see.
You see that young girl standing there
With shining eyes and sun streaked hair.
Her body long, her firm limbs strong
And running without care.
You see, oh yes, you see.

Well let's not speak of her,
No let's not speak of her,
Of that young creature standing at life's door.
I am no longer young,
My songs have all been sung.
And just to dwell on youth can age me even more.

You think.
You think how easy life would be for you
If you were without care.
Without a wife, a home and child
And debts strewn everywhere.
You think, oh yes, you think.

Well don't remind me of
The price of married love
Or how you might have lived if you'd been free.
My life is often gray
Devoid of laugh or play
And I find little comfort in what life could be.

You watch.
You watch that woman of the world
With her success and her career.
Her clothes, her talk, her steadfast walk,
All feminists would cheer.
You watch, oh yes, you watch.

Well don't compare my life
Of motherhood and wife
With that of women whose lives I don't share.
I am a clinging vine,
All yours and little mine.
Though sometimes thoughts of freedom tempt me to despair.

No please don't bother me
With dreams that cannot be,
With youth and beauty, freedom and success.
But then you could, if you just would,
Enfold me in your arms and all my tears repress.

In your arms. I will become that bright young girl, that woman free,
That sun streaked hair.
I will become your every dream and fantasy so fair.
I will become . . . a woman loved.

226

"OWED TO MIDDLE AGE"

In This Corner
Lyrics and Music by Renée Bondy

Excuse me, though this may seem a trifle boring,
It's time my soul did some out pouring,
I have a problem with my age.

I'm forty, and though I'm told I'm in my prime years,
I seem to just be marking time, dears
With tired notions as my gauge.

When I was young and eager
Life really wasn't simple,
Yet I would cry for joy now
If I could find a pimple.
Just a symbol that I'm

Growing, not merely dried up like a raisin,
With no more rainbows left for chasin'.
I'll have my Scotch on Epsom salts.

Masters & Johnson meant well
With books on bedroom action,
Sex once a week is real swell,
But I end up in traction.
Please have no doubt that it's

Sad when, your conversation with a pal can
Concern his latest root canal, and
His current battle with the gout.

I think of grass as green stuff
And bread as what gets toasted,
And thoughts of Frank Sinatra,
Still keep my bloomers roasted.
Till he takes his toupee

Off, oh, I've got premenopausal jitters,
My eighteen hour girdle titters,
Because it knows it's working overtime.
What firm and bouncy girl said middle age was so sublime?

"MISSING MAN"

The New York Adventure*
Lyrics by Ruth Bourne
Music by Jeff Silverman

Missing . . .
One missing man . . .
Out there, somewhere,
One wanted man . . .
'Round some corner
There he'll be,
Up a mountain . . .
By a sea . . .
Wand'ring . . . wishing . . .
Missing . . . missing . . . me . . .

REPRISE
Eyes, blue . . .
Or brown, or grey . . .

*Based on *Mrs. 'Arris Goes to Paris* by Paul Gallico.

Last seen—who knows?—
Just yesterday . . .
In some doorway
There he'll stand,
Looking my way . . .
Looking grand . . .
Smiling . . . whistling . . . list'ning . . .
Holding . . . out his . . . hand . . .

"GO TO NEW YORK!"

The New York Adventure
Lyrics by Ruth Bourne

MRS. 'ARRIS (VERSE)
Where do you go when you want a vacation from 'ome?
Where do you fly when the beer in your life's lost its foam?
When the old daily appalls you,
Where is the city that calls you—?
There on the 'Udson, all shining with promise and chrome . . .

CHORUS
It's a city I've seen in the cinema,
Where the gents soup-and-fish it after dark,
And the ladies I see in the cinema
All ride 'acknies 'round the park . . .
How they tap-dance along Broadway Boulevard,
How they sing in a pub called the "Stork"!
Oh, whatever you seek,
Drop the world for a week
And go to New York!

2ND CHORUS
There's an auto for every last resident,
There's the building where Chryslers are made,
Lincoln Center, the 'ome of the President,
Every Friday a parade!
'Ow they smile as they greet new arrivals there,
'Ow they lay out their best knife and fork—
So whoever you are,
Hitch your hopes to a star
And go to New—
LITTLE 'ENRY   Go to New—
ADA BUTTERFIELD   Go—go to New York!

"HER MOUTH MAKES ROSES"

Getting Up Nights
Lyrics and Music by Charles Burr

Her mouth makes roses.
Her hair makes halos.
Her brow makes monuments to thought.
Her eyes make starlight
Seen through a soft spring snow
And the glow they show
Can't be taught.

The palms of her hands,
Uncurled,
Make warm brown nests.
And no other woman in the world
Understands

The way her breasts
Make breasts.

She's not a child
But has childhood in her.
I know it's wild,
But if I could win her
One day . . .

There'd be
Acres of children
Who'd look quite a bit
Like me . . .
Until they smiled . . .
And then you'd see . . .
The way her mouth
Makes roses
Makes roses
Makes roses.

"PERSEPHONE"

Persephone

Lyrics and Music by Charles Burr

(Buck is alone in the frost-patterned greenhouse very late at
    night writing his book. He stops to write a note to Persephone
    and it turns into this lyric, the show's terminal song.)

The bloom is off the asphodel,
Persephone, Persephone,
Forget me not and fare thee well,
Persephone, Persephone.
While ice and snow disguise the sod
And winter walks where once you trod
My sneeze recalls your goldenrod,
Persephone.

The frost designs a shrine for you,
Persephone, Persephone,
Where columbine combine with rue,
Persephone, Persephone.
While you your street and subway roam,
The ivy leagues beneath the loam,
With roses wild to have you home,
Persephone.

I dedicate my book to you,
Persephone, Persephone.
Revere, adore, and look to you,
Persephone, Persephone.
And here in my florescent lair,
Bemused by myth and maidenhair,
I cultivate you everywhere,
Persephone.

All this, sub rosa, you know well,
Persephone, Persephone.
From old Homeric parallel,
Persephone, Persephone.
The story told of your rebirth
Means man can only know his worth
When love and joy regain the earth,
Persephone. . . .

"JANICE AND JARVIS AND ME" *

Lyrics by Bill Edwards
Music by Tom Whitney

What is a we?
In my case it's three
There's brother and me and the bride
And we'll always be side by side.

We'll make a team
And that's not a dream
Not one or the other, we need one another
Like coffee needs sugar and cream.

It's Janice and Jarvis and Me
A trio that's known as a we
Like birds of a feather, we're always together
At breakfast and dinner and tea.

It's Janice and Jarvis and Me
At the Louvre or on Zuider Zee
We'll travel together in all kinds of weather
On land, in the air or by sea

We'll first have a wedding
And sing happy tunes
And then we'll be heading
To many gay honeymoons

Just Janice and Jarvis and Me
I say with unqualified glee
They don't know like I know, where they go then I go
That's something that they've yet to see

I haven't the slightest doubt
That they will be glad to find out
That their married life's going to be
One big Janice and Jarvis and Me.

"A COZY BORDELLO"

Nineveh!

Lyrics by Richard Engquist
Music by Doug Katsaros

Duet for a Babylonian prostitute and a traveling salesman, one
    of her frequent customers

SALESMAN
There's a cosy bordello in Babylon town
With a fence 'round the yard where the garden hangs down;
Where a pent-up young fellow finds instant release
Without curbing his drives or disturbing the peace.
You can sate any hunger and quench any thirst,
For the girls are all bully and fully rehearsed
To be sure that the customer always comes first . . .
In that cozy bordello!
PROSTITUTE
It's a sleazy hotel overlooking the dumps,
Where we cater to satyrs and salesmen and chumps;

* Written as an exercise for *The Member of the Wedding* by Carson
McCullers.

Where the blinds never open, the doors never shut,
And the girls take their lumps while the cops take their cut.
Oh, the sheets are all damp and the lamps are all red.
There's a sob in my throat and a throb in my head
From the cramps in my legs and the tramps in my bed . . .
In this cosy bordello!

SALESMAN
It's a nice little haven . . .

PROSTITUTE
With mice in the wall.

SALESMAN
With a cot for your pleasure . . .

PROSTITUTE
A pot down the hall.

SALESMAN
You can pick from the best Babylonian chicks . . .

PROSTITUTE
Though the tricks are all phoney, alas! not the pricks.

SALESMAN
You can meet any need . . .

PROSTITUTE
If the need isn't chaste.

SALESMAN
It's a Garden of Eden to suit every taste . . .

PROSTITUTE
Where the girls go to seed, and the seed goes to waste . . .

BOTH
I suppose we could yell Auld Lang Syne . . .
In this cozy bordello of mine!

"SOMEWHERE IN THE WORLD"

Nineveh!
Lyrics by Richard Engquist
Music by Doug Katsaros

Somewhere in the world
A bird is flying free;
Looking all around
For the place he's meant to be.

Searching high and low;
Always on the go,
Always on the wing . . .
Looking for his nest and the rest that home can bring.

Somewhere in the world
A bird has lost his way;
Looking all around
For the place he's meant to stay.

Searching high and low.
Longing for the moment when
Somewhere in the world he'll find his little world again.

"MY PARTICULAR PRINCE"*

Lyrics and Music by Jack Feldman

My particular prince
Will ride into town on a horse.

* From a musicalization of Hugh Wheeler's *Look: We've Come Through.*

And the thunder will roll like drums,
And all his subjects will bow when he comes,
And there'll be music, of course, to welcome
My particular prince,
Who travels the subway to work.
His arrival has been delayed
Because his bills aren't all fully paid.
You see, he's only a clerk.

And I can see him clearly:
Young and ripe, and full of wild adventures, or an
Older type, with graying hair and dentures.
Most decidedly of undecided means,
Born in Paraguay or Pakistan or Queens.

My particular prince
Was raised on a farm in the West.
Very rural, reserved and shy,
He never got much beyond junior high;
He was severely oppressed. (Such hardship!)

My particular prince
Descends from a long line of wealth.
He's society's favorite host,
And every winter he lives on the coast
Because it's good for his health.

I picture him so clearly:
Laced with scars, obtuse or intellectual.
A man from Mars, divorced or homosexual.
I'm totally resigned to what he'll be,
Just as long as he resigns himself to me.

My particular prince
Will ride into town on a horse.
And they won't have to sound the alarms,
And you won't need a glimpse of his charms.
You will know he's the one
By the way that I run
Into his arms!

"NEW BEGINNINGS"*

Lyrics and Music by Jack Feldman

Here's to new beginnings,
To the future and good things to come.
Eyes straight ahead beyond the horizon,
All memories dead, all feelings numb.

Be a brand new person.
Grab a dustrag and polish the chrome.
Don't waste your time retrieving the pieces.
Put in a dime and see who's home.

And if I think of you, believe me,
It'll only be the good things.
See, I really am romantic at heart.
I'll miss those long walks on the weekends for a start.
And reading over your shoulder,
Buying cards for your birthday,
Watching you growing older through the years,

* From a musicalization of Hugh Wheeler's *Look: We've Come Through.*

And fixing your breakfast,
And wearing your bathrobe,
And naming our babies, and

Here's to new beginnings,
Celebrations and painting the town.
We had some fun, but listen, it's over.
What's done is done; the curtain's down.

Find a brand new hobby.
Knitting sweaters just might be a kick.
Go to a fête and be the odd number,
Or better yet, pick up a trick.

And you'll forgive me if I start to
Reminisce about the bad things,
But I really am a cynic inside.
I sure loved burying your sheep dog when he died.
And playing wife for your mother,
Sleeping two on the sofa,
Getting set for another round of tears,
And buying your liquor,
And doing your laundry,
And meeting your girl friends, and

Here's to new beginnings.
And so what if I hope against hope?
Living is tough, but quitting is tougher.
Enough's enough. It's time to cope.

So if I don't jump off a building
Chalk it up to being stupid,
But there's still some thing I'd like to get done.
For instance, visiting New Jersey might be fun.
And think of cashing in every token,
Moving out to Long Island,
Leaving all of these broken souvenirs,
And buying a Chevy,
And owning a mortgage,
And giving up lousy careers.
Goddammit!

Here's to new beginnings,
And here's to you, kid,
And here's to me!

"AT A TIME LIKE THIS"

Neighbors*
Lyrics by Victor Fisch
Music by Vivian Millman

At a time like this
When I think of her name
If I could I would use dirty words
Phrases that fit
Like you're full of—that
Which is dropped on earth by birds.

At a time like this
There's a part of a man

* Based on *Spofford* by Herman Shumlin.

I could call her—but then I'd sin
I know she's sick
But I'd shout, "You're a—word
That describes being stuck by a pin."

When I think of how she hurt my daughter
If she'd ever walk in this shop
She'd be sorry from the minute I caught her.
The slaughter would never stop.

At a time like this
When my temp'rature climbs
'Cause I'm mad at that snotty hog
She may be rich
But I'd call that snob
A son of a female dog.

Goodness knows if I could
I would love to enjoy
Words that Webster would never miss
Like, "You snake in the grass—
I'll kick your—donkey,"
At a time like this.

"AT WHAT AGE"

Neighbors*
Lyrics by Victor Fisch
Music by Vivian Millman

For a man who's sixty-four
Nature should have shut the door
On frivolities like sex.
But instead of ending such desire
She has only banked the fire
And my muscles continue to flex.

I take one look
If she's a feast
A woman still
Brings out the beast.
At what age will I fail to hear the call?

I'm slower now
And much more tame
But comes the thrill
It's still the same.
At what age will I fail to care at all?

A woman has a softness only she has
A quality aside from her physique
And something in that mystifying softness
Activates my masculine mystique.

A kiss or two
A glass of wine
She's in my arms
I'm feeling fine.
At what age will it be past history?

The way I feel today
That feeling's here to stay.
At what age will it end?

Never, for me!

"I CAN SEE MY FATHER"

Three Cheers for Whatsizname
Lyrics by Ellen Fitzhugh
Music by Johnson Delgarten

I can see my father, ridin' bareback into town . . .
Heavin' sacks of flour 'cross the horse's rump.
Climbin' up a dogwood tree and hangin' upside down,
And haulin' back a bucket from the backyard pump . . .

And I wonder how it happened,
I could come from him.
I'm an indoor child, raised on chocolate shakes,
Makin' telephone calls . . .
Durin' station breaks.

I can see my father, with a Bible in his hand,
Sayin' God will help him, but he can't say how.
Believin' in an after-life he doesn't understand,
And givin' his here-after all his here-and-now . . .

And we couldn't be more different,
I live day to day—
For the fun I find in the hours I keep,
And the end of my life . . .
Means a good night's sleep.

How can it be
That he is my father . . . ?

I don't feel any kinship—
I don't feel any ties.

What do I see
When I see my father . . . ?

A tired way of walkin' . . .
And half-closed eyes.

I can see my father, waitin' up for me at night.
He looks at me and knows I've had a cryin' spree.
He asks me if that ugly boy and I have had a fight.
And he tells me that there's no boy good enough for me.

And he makes me mad, my father,
Loving me like that . . .
When I never do what he wants me to . . .
And I'll never understand . . .
What he loves me for.

Should I go see my father . . . just once more?

"YOU GOT WHAT YOU DESERVED"

Three Cheers for Whatzisname
Lyrics by Ellen Fitzhugh
Music by Johnson Delgarten

I'm not afraid of the questions I see in your mother's accusing
  eyes.
I'm not afraid when the newspapers say that you had an untimely demise.

When all of your friends showed up,
I showed appropriate grief;

Now I feel so alone—My God, it's such a relief,

And you got what you deserved.
(Well, I couldn't help it, could I?)
The car just suddenly swerved,
And you got what you deserved.

Me and the kids gotta start right away, buildin' up all that you
  tore down.
Learnin' again how to laugh and play, now that you're safely
  underground.

And we're gettin' sweet pea blooms
Where you let everything die;

And we got fifteen grand to remember you by,

And you got what you deserved.
(Well, I couldn't help it, could I?)
The car just suddenly swerved,
And you got what you deserved.

You always said you had it worse than me, and maybe this one
  time, it's true.
But, boy, is it hard, keepin' everything straight, with the ex-
  plainin' I have to do—

Like when the detective came,
At first he filled me with fright,

But he's not a bad guy. We're havin' dinner tonight.

And you got what you deserved.
(Well, I couldn't help it, could I?)
'Cause when the thoroughfare curved,
Well, you made me so unnerved,
That you got what you deserved.

"MAIA'S ELEGY"

Second Edition*
Lyrics and Book by Faith Flagg
Music by Tom Whitney

I strung you some words on a cobweb,
I carved you a verse in the sand,
But the waves in their play
Swept the meaning away
And the words fell apart in my hand.
Shadows of sweetness, echoes of dreams—
Nothing is ever as real as it seems.

I painted your portrait with sunlight
And dust from a butterfly's wing,
But the wind in its rage
Brushed your face from the page
And left me as lonely as spring.
Lingering traces of May in July—
Nothing is ever too perfect to die.

I wanted to go to the ocean
To hide from the world for a while,
But the sky and the sea
Would be brooding at me,
And the waves, all reflecting your smile.
Touches of sadness are yesterday's clues.
Nothing is ever too lovely to lose.

* Based on Karel Čapek's *R.U.R.*

"TEACH ME!—SERVE HIM!"

Gone!*

Lyrics and Book by Faith Flagg
Music by John Sparks

STUDENTS
Teach me a katydid,
Spell me a spiderweb,
Paint me a chickadee's tune!
Where is a gamma ray?
Why is a cloud?
Draw me the tides of the moon!
JESUS FREAKS
Serve Him, show Him,
Need Him, know Him,
Purge your soul of sin!
Seek Him, find Him,
Trust Him, mind Him,
Let His Light shine in!
STUDENTS
Bathe me in waterfalls,
Light me with fireflies,
Feed me the secret of grain!
How does a sycamore?
Who can I be?
Sing me the cycle of rain!
JESUS FREAKS
Bless Him, reach Him,
Praise Him, preach Him,
Satan shall not win!
Touch Him, hear Him,
Love Him, fear Him,
Let His Rule begin!

"ENDSONG" †

Lyrics and Music by Carey Gold

Come to me openly;
Here's where we lose love.
Honestly, I can see
Nothing but the blues, love.

Feeling's gone; why go on
Carefully pretending?
Tired and late,
Let's not wait
For the fateful ending.

Free, we had a time,
And the climb was long.
Still, we'll wander through;
Wonder who went wrong.

What are we separately?
Half a heart and hollow.
Back inside, open wide—
So much pride to swallow.

True, you always tried,
Justified the game.
I try in my way,
Every day the same.

Age has ways of making days
Melt and fuse and simmer.
We can still love until
Memories grow dimmer.

Here we're nearly through,
Starting to end.
I cry silently—
Cry with me, friend.

"SOMETIMES, IN THE MIDDLE OF THE NIGHT" *

Lyrics and Music by Carey Gold

Sometimes, in the middle of the night, I wake up frightened.
Sometimes, in the middle of the night, I wake up alone.
Sweet secret fantasies are dying, I can see them.
They disappeared, and I was just about to free them.

Sometimes, in the middle of the night, I wake up smiling.
Sometimes, in the middle of the night, I wake up and dream.
Salt breezes sting my eyes and sing into my pillow.
Mood music bends and weeps and flutters like a willow.

Out, get up, start the day.
Can't let it slip away.
Try to play the part and do my share.
Try to make the start—it's waiting there.
Someday. Someday.

Sometimes, in the middle of my life, I wake up wond'ring.
Sometimes, in the middle of my life, I wake and ask why:
So many dreams are passing by as I lay sleeping.
So many memories of promises worth keeping.

Sometimes, in the middle of my life,
I think, "Could it be?"
Sometimes, in the middle of my life,
I wonder, "Is that me?"

"THE DARK SIDE OF MY LOVE"

Dance on a Country Grave *

Lyrics, Music, and Book by Kelly Hamilton

If I turn away,
And whistle in the wind,
And try not to look at you tenderly,
It's just so you'll be
Unable to see
The Dark Side of My Love.

When you take my hand,
I know it's only chance;

* Based on Philip Wylie's *The Disappearance.*
† *Lady Macbeth in the Park* by Susan Slade.

* *Lady Macbeth in the Park* by Susan Slade.
† Based on *The Return of the Native* by Thomas Hardy.

But I'll hold it a moment, most willingly.
Then, I must let it go,
So you'll never know
The Dark Side of My Love.

Then, I'll chase the wind,
And follow the changing moon,
And never look back over my shoulder;

Hoping this foolish dream
That seems to grow each day
Will learn to fade away, as it grows older.

So, walk your chosen road,
And I'll walk mine alone;
And if we meet again, pretend I'm anyone but me.

For, as close as we have been,
We were never meant to be
Closer than the far side of the sea.

And so, I shall learn
To love in other ways.
I'll watch from afar, most unfailingly.
And never let your smile
Light up, the slightest while,
The Dark Side of My Love . . .
The Dark Side of My Love . . .
And you won't know my love,
My love.

"THIRTEEN COLONIES"

Saga

Lyrics, Music, and Book by Kelly Hamilton

Thirteen Colonies
Sat by the sea,
And decided that they should be free.
Thirteen reasons
For one revolution;
Thirteen daughters of England,
Stitching up a patchwork banner to wave.
And all the red rockets
Were shot to the Heavens;
And all the white stars
Came falling through,
To land on a field of blue, my love,
For you, my love,
For you.

"VIRGINIA CITY"

Saga

Lyrics, Music, and Book by Kelly Hamilton

I'll build a city in Nevada,
For you, my love;
Where all the silver in the foothills
Shines through, my love.
Between the green Sierra pines,
The Truckee River is a-falling free . . .
And pebbles are washed,
Amd rushed to the sea;
Leaving silver and gold

For you . . . and me.
(PROSPECTORS *and* MINERS *gather round, and sing philosophically*)
MINERS
In Virginia City,
The silver runs deep, and the gals ain't pretty.
In Virginia City,
The Colt 45 sings a mighty mean ditty.
In Virginia City,
The red-eye's a dollar a shot, and shitty!
But I'm gonna make
Virginia City my home!

In Virginia City,
It's a five-card stud so-cie-itty.
In Virginia City,
There's a rule of poker pro-prie-itty:
In Virginia City,
The winner is hung by a town committee!
But I'm gonna make
Viriginia City my home!

Now, I don't mind bunkin' with a bevy of fleas;
Walkin' the streets,
And sinkin' in mud to my knees.
Don't mind if the coffee
And the hominy's gritty,
In Virginia City . . .

Cause I'm down in the mines all morning,
And down at the mint all day.
A bowl of cream will feed the kitty,
But silver feeds Virginia City!

And in Virginia City,
They cuss, and they curse, and the jokes ain't witty.
In Virginia City,
There ain't much shame, and there ain't much pity.
In Virginia City,
There ain't no ass, and there ain't no titty!
But I'm gonna make
Virginia City my home.

In Virginia City, I'm a-settlin'
In Virginia City, I'm a-settlin'
In Virginia City, I'm a-settlin' Ma'm,
Hot damn!
In Virginia City,
In Virginia City,
In Virginia City, yes I am!
(JULIA BULETTE *appears, and sizes up the situation*)
JULIA BULETTE
I've got a feeling
Something is needed here.
Such a sad and lonely town
With only lonely men
Needs me!
MINERS
Yes, Ma'm!!
JULIA
Well, come on, you weavers of legend,
Make me bold and fancy-dancin' now;
Dress me fine, and call me Madame!!
And I'll be Queen of the Comstock,

Brave, legendary Julia Bulette
Will set
The West on sweet, sweet fire!
MINERS
When Julia Bulette came into town,
Everybody settled down!
She brought a bevy of cat-house ladies,
And dressed 'em all in silk and satin.
And built a row of *clap*-board cottages,
And lit 'em with bright, red lanterns!
(*Young, pretty* PROSTITUTES *now appear, and sing as they strut by*)

PROSTITUTES
Saturday night, 'round a quarter past ten,
That's where you'll find Virginia City men.
Everybody's going down 'round "Sportin' Row"!
MINERS
Julia Bulette, light yer bright, red light—
Virginia City ladies are walkin' tonight—
And everybody's going down, going down
'Round "Sportin' Row"!!
(MATRONS *appear. They are shocked and disapproving*)
MATRONS
(*Pointing at the goings-on in horror*)
Can *that* extravaganza be
What all the fussing's for?
That so-called "Big Bonanza" be-
Hind that bolted door
Is just the village *whore!!!*
(JULIA *and* PROSTITUTES *are now leading the men of the town in a wild, abandoned dance*)

JULIA
Come on, you high-hoofin' men,
Step it light, light, light!
Hold 'em tight, tight, tight!
The fiddler is a-tunin' up,
And I got a feeling
We'll be Virginia Reeling
In Virginia City tonight!!!

ENSEMBLE
Now,
In Virginia City,
The silver's all mine, and the gals are pretty!
In Virginia City,
The ragtime piano plays a mighty fine ditty!
And in Virginia City
Plenty o' ass and *plenty* o' titty!!
And I'm gonna make Virginia City my home . . .

In Virginia city, I'm a-settlin'
In Virginia City, I'm a-settlin'
In Virginia City, I'm a-settling, Ma'm—

In Virginia City
In Virginia City
In Virginia City,
Yes, I am!!!

"THE LANGUAGE BARRIER"

The Language Barrier
Lyrics and Book by Bill Jacobson

THE YOUNG
Youth is like a tooth
That aches when it's well

Youth is like a thunderbolt
Caged in a shell
THE OLD
Age is like a page
No one wants to read

An autumn crop unharvested
Allowed to go to seed
THE YOUNG
Youth is like the truth
Our elders would deny

Security, an old man's tune
To which the young must die
THE OLD
Age is like a sage
Whose wisdom is obscured

Experience, a blinding wound
And anarchy the "cure"
THE YOUNG
Age is for the toothless
Whose bite still can kill
THE OLD
Youth is for the ruthless
Whose truth is in a pill
THE YOUNG
Age is full of self-deceit
That strangles like a vine
THE OLD
Youth calls lies what cannot fit
Upon a picket sign
THE YOUNG (*Impatiently*)
Jesus! Why is it so hard
To make them set us free
To teach them not to cling so long
To things that must not be?
THE OLD (*wearily*)
Dear Lord! Why won't they listen
Why won't they pay us mind
And let us help reveal the things
They break their hearts to find?
THE YOUNG
Life is like a tender bud
On a slender reed
THE OLD
Breaking through the cobblestones,
Life's a stubborn weed!

Life is not for babes
Life's a grownup's game
THE YOUNG
Life has changed the targets
You never change your aim!
BOTH
Oh, God . . . Dear Lord . . .

Let us find a
Way to bridge the gap

To cross the language barrier
To still avoid the trap

Mother . . . Daughter. . .
Father . . . Son . . .
Let them see *our* light!
Let them see *our* light!
BOTH
(sudden change of tone)
Hippies!
Looters!
  Pigs!
    Polluters!
Unwashed!
  Brain-washed!
    Racists!
Junkies!
Drop-outs!
  Cop-outs!
Perverts!
  Flunkies!
Holy Father.
  Mother-*f*---
(Tympani crash. Lights out.)
(fading)
Goodbye, light . . .
Welcome, night . . .

"SAM'S SOLILOQUY, OR FAREWELL TO THE PROTESTANT ETHIC"

The Language Barrier
Lyrics and Book by Bill Jacobson

Hey, Sam Carter,
Don't be a bleedin' martyr
Get up and do what has to be done
Let the devil take the hindmost
'Cause he collects that kind most
And you get out and have some bleedin' fun

Hey, Sam Carter,
You'll be an added starter
Move your arse until your race is run
Turn the flame a little higher
'Cause the fat is in the fire
And it's better that you're burned than underdone

Don't sit there broodin'
And lookin' clammy
Don't grind your choppers
In silence, Sammy,
It's time you face your cravin's like a man
So give a lusty cheer that's sonic
Give your career a high colonic
And don't wait around for fate to hit the fan!

Yay, Sam Carter,
Unsnap your bleedin' garter
Go out and jump the bloomin' gun
Tell the boss to go to Hades
And get crackin' with the ladies

And remember, till your span is spun
You're entitled
—Yes, you're bloody well entitled—
You're entitled to some bleedin'
Yes, you're bloody well indeed en-
Titled to some bleedin' fun!

"WALKING THE BOARDS"

Boardwalk
Lyrics by Robert Joseph
Music by Donald Siegal

People are walking the boards
People are walking the boards
People are strutting their stuff
People are strutting their beautiful stuff
What a way to strut
Gets you in the gut
They go swimming a while
Then they go reading the mails
Then they go washing their hair
Then they go cleaning their nails
They're healthy
They love it
And they take great care of it
Showcase for thousands
Hot time for millions
Boardwalk

Women are walking in mink
Women are walking in mink
Women are sweating in mink
Women are sweating and dying in mink
What a way to die
Watch the days go by
They go walking in heels
Then they get stuck in the cracks
Then they go take their shoes off
Then they sit down to relax
They're steaming
They're cooking
And no, they're not good-looking
Ladies with blue hair
What do you do here?
Boardwalk

CHORUS
Live!
When you are alone at night
Remember you got an appetite
Time to begin relishing in YOU
Live!
One season to play the game
By August you'll never be the same
Time to begin relishing in . . .
(the SNAP of cameras)

Take notice: that ice cream cake is growing orange mold
SNAP
Take notice: that ring on sale is not 10 carat gold
SNAP
Take notice: that beauty queen really needs a shave

SNAP
Take notice: a little girl is drowning in that wave

CHORUS   Cheese!

People are selling themselves
People are selling themselves
People are eating it up
People are eating it, all of it up
Lay the rouge on thick
Let the lipstick stick
They go walking in wigs
Then they check into motels
Then they administer love
Quality merchandise sells
They push it
They shove it
And though they do not love it
Many will learn here
Mattresses burn here
Boardwalk

CHORUS
Live!
When you are alone at night
Remember you got an appetite
Time to begin relishing in YOU
Live!
One season to play the game
By August you'll never be the same
Time to begin relishing in . . .

People are walking the boards
People are walking the boards
People are strutting their stuff
People are strutting their stuff
They go swimming a while
Then they go reading the mails
Then they go washing their hair
Then they go cleaning their nails
They're healthy
They love it
And they take great care of it
Making their fun plans
Nurturing suntans
Checking their watches
Groping their crotches
Here anything goes
Kingdom of Bingoes
Bored
Bored
Boardwalk!

"MAN ON A SUBWAY TRAIN"

Boardwalk
Lyrics by Robert Joseph
Music by Donald Siegal

You get up in the morning
You leave the house by eight
You think that walking to the subway you will meet: her

By the time you buy the token
It's a quarter after eight
And you search the double A train until you see: her
But she's surrounded by ten people who are hiding her from
    view
So you open up your copy of the Collected Works of Balzac
Which you happen to be reading just in case she's an
    intellectual
And there is your basis for starting a conversation
By the time you've started reading
It's already 34th Street
You look up
It's too late
She's gone. . . .
They always get off at 34th Street
They never make it up to 59
And they look like they might be interested
But there's no way to show that they might be interested
'Cause she's a woman
A face in a crowd
And you're a man on a subway train
Finally one morning she gets on at West 4th Street
She's attractive but not garish
She just happens to be holding the Collected Works of Balzac
She sits next to you and smiles, as if to say,
"Good morning, hi, I am a woman
And I like the way you looked at me
So why don't you smile back?"
That I do, until I notice
We already passed 34th Street
She's still there, smiling back, that's a sign
A miracle still holding the Collected Works of Balzac
And I think it might all be worth it
We're already past 42nd Street
She's still here, next to me, book in hand, smiling back
They usually get off at 34th Street
They never make it up to 59
And they look like they might be interested
But there's no way to show that they might be interested
'Cause she's a woman
A face in a crowd
And you're a man on a subway train
At last! It all has happened, as I hoped it always would
And we both squeeze out through the crowd at 59th Street
Stop!
Hello, I couldn't help but notice you are reading Balzac, too
And she smiles again at me, and says, "Oui, monsieur?"
So I shuffle my feet
And give a laugh
And make some dumb-dumb American wisecrack
How she far surpasses Brigitte Bardot
But she simply can't speak English
It's already quarter to, and grasping her edition of the un-
    translated Works of Balzac
She smiles at me one last time
And leaps off into the morning
And the Central Park South skyline
And I realize how wrong I was to have taken high school
    Spanish
Nananananananananana (etc.)
And they look like they might be interested
But there's no way for anybody in the whole wide world to even
    show

That they might be interested
'Cause she's a woman
A face in a crowd
And you're a man on a subway train
You're a man on a subway train

"THE ILLUSION OF LOVE"

Lyrics and Music by Maurice Keller

You visit now and then,
And you leave with part of me.
You'll come back again,
Clever author of duplicity.
Your kind of love could be hateful,
But strange as it seems, I'm grateful.
This tawdry affair is not what I planned,
But you must understand . . .

The illusion of love
Is better than nothing;
I know, because I've had less.
The illusion of love
Is the shadowy something
On which I build happiness.

So thanks for the kiss,
And thanks for the lies;
I wouldn't venture
To minimize
The value that you give—
A person has to live
(You do have to live).

The illusion of love
May conjure emotion
That otherwise wouldn't be there.
My delusion of love
Can change false devotion
To something that looks like you care.

So hail to deception!
Hail to the fake!
What I can get
Is what I will take!
And what I take I will use;
If it can't be for real, then I choose
A little of
The illusion of love.

"THE ORIENT EXPRESS"

All the World—A Production
Lyrics and Music by Maurice Keller

JANE
Old spy movies with their desperate expedients
Require certain absolutely minimal ingredients—
Not the least of which, old pal,
Is a well selected locale. (Example . . .)

You have hastily decamped from the land of the hamburger
   and frito,
With a passport curiously stamped: "Persona incognito."
Your pockets well filled with many a pre-devalued dollar.
   (Remember?)

And you're wearing the trenchcoat with the mandatory
   turned-up collar.
(Then you're ready—providing . . .)
You're in Paris, and it's starting to rain
As you get aboard a certain train. . . .

When you ride the Orient Express,
A conveyance fraught with history,
You cultivate an air of mystery,
And remember, the walls have ears.

When you ride the Orient Express
Down from Paris to Istanbul, you
Should know a spy will try to fool you,
And you learn that the walls have ears.

Romanoff princes looking quite decadent,
Islamic pilgrims, presumably Mecca-bent—
All on the train.

Secretive people regarding the sinister
Heidelberg scar on the face of a minister,
All (Minister?) on the train.

Matters may suddenly get very gory. Like
Pistols and poison and things Peter Lorre-like
Here on the train.

Is that invisible ink he is using? He
Ought to quit changing his face—it's confusing me
Here on the train.

When you ride the Orient Express,
There's a Prussian who stares through a monocle
Till you think that your head must be conical.
And of course, "All der valls haff ears!"

Those who ride the Orient Express
Have a look of intriguing suspicion. And
Without that you don't gain admission, and
You will not know the walls have ears.

Who is the one who shot the ambassador?
Should I reveal I saw in first class a door
Gone from the train?

Which is the thief who stole the tiara? They
Must catch him soon or he'll be too faraway
Gone from the train.

Plans for the fortifications are missing. Some-
One who was guarding is eagerly kissing some-
One on the train.

Every compartment is brewing skulduggery,
Crooked conniving and all kinds of thuggery
Fun on the train.

When you ride the Orient Express,
There's a sense of doom and treachery,
And quite a lot of room for lechery . . .
What a pity the walls have ears.

When I rode the Orient Express,
In the end the trip was jolly good,
Because I disembarked in Hollywood
Where that train has stood for years,
And where the walls do indeed have ears!

"LAWYERS"

Lyrics and Music by Edward Kleban *

*Based on any number of Daumiers and sung by a
Puerto Rican couple*

Lawyers are nice, they're a helava bunch
Finding the right one's like playing a huh-huh-hunch
Some of them steal from you, hand you a line
But I'm very glad I've got . . .

Mine	I'm very glad I've got
I'm very glad I've got	Mine
Mine	I'm very glad I've got
I'm very glad I've got	Mine

"Mmmorris Rappaport . . .   Mine
Esquire!
Se Habla Espanol"

Lawyers are good when you've something to hide
Lawyers are bad on the opposite si-hi-hide
Lawyers are best when there's something to sign
So I'm very glad I've got . . .

Mine	I'm very glad I've got
Doctor turns out to be	Mine
Quack	Doctor, he turns out to be
Storekeeper won't take it	Quack
Back	Storekeeper, he won't take it . . .
Just mention that you have a	Just mention that you have a . . .
Lawyer	. . . mention that you have a . . .
Watch ev'ryone take a new	Watch ev'ryone take a new . . .
Tack!	Watch ev'ryone take new
Watch ev'ryone take new	Watch
Tack!!	Watch ev'ryone take new
Take a new watch?	Watch
	What's a new tack?
La-la-la	La-la-la

Lawyers are swell, they're a beautiful group
'Spec-ially when you find that you're in the sou-hou-houp
Chances without one are none-out-of-nine
So I'm very glad I've got mine

A-*bo*-ga-*do* . . . a-*bo*-ga-*do*-ga . . .

Eight weeks he keeps me	Eight weeks he keeps me
Waiting	Eight weeks he keeps me
I never shout or	I never shout or
Curse	I never shout or
Going alone to	Going alone to
Courthouse	Going alone to
Strikes me as even . . .	Strikes me as even . . . *(Clap)*
La-la, la-la, la-la	La-la, la-la, la-la

Half of the money	Half of the money
He takes	Half of the money
It's like we're going	It's like we're going
Dutch	It's like we're going
Fifty per-cent of	Fifty per-cent of

Nothing	Fifty per-cent of
Wouldn't amount to . . . *(Clap)*	Wouldn't amount to . . . *(Clap)*
La-la, la-la, la-la	La-la, la-la, la-la
La-la, la-la, la-la, la-la-la . . .	La-la, la-la, la-la, la-la-la . . .

Laywers are nice, they're a helava bunch
Findin the right one's like playing a huh-huh-hunch
Some of them steal from you, hand you a line
But I'm very glad I've got . . .

Mine	I'm very glad I've got
I'm very glad I've got	Mine
Mine	I'm very glad I've got
I'm very glad I've got	Mine
"Mmmorris Rappaport . . .	Mine
Esquire!	
Se Habla Espanol"	Mine

Some of them steal from you, hand you a line
But I'm very glad I've got . . .
I'm very glad I've got . . .
I'm very glad I've . . . got . . .
. . . "Esquire!" . . .
Miiiiiiiiiine!

"GAUGUIN'S SHOE"

Lyrics and Music by Edward Kleban

Were I in Gauguin's shoes
What would I have to lose?
I would embrace the Muse
And even thank her (He means the Muse)
And I would choose
What ever Gauguin chose (He chose)
And walk around in only Gauguin's clothes (His clothes)
And I would go wherever Gauguin goes (Gauguin goes)
He was a banker (A-ti--pi-ty-tap, A-tip-pi-ty-tap)

And as he sat in his cage
Listening to the takeover bids (102, 103)
He just flew into a rage
And suddenly left his wife and his kids (Ding-Dong!)
For trouble in Tahiti
Wasn't he a sweetie?

Had I but Gauguin's dash (His dash)
Had I his cute moustache (moustache)
Why I'd convert to cash (to cash)
And have a ball (and have a ball)
If I were (if I were)
Banker . . .
Painter . . .
Gauguin . . . . (Comma!)
Paul

Fabulous feet
Indescribably sweet
In distress in da street
Goin' hippitty-hoppitty
Hansel and Gretel
Jumped over the shtetel
But oh those sillies!

* Edward Kleban has written the lyrics for *A Chorus Line.*

Taggin' along
A gagg-ling throng
Of cuties in booties and such
Fetish is fine
God knows I have mine
But this is a little too much

Heeling and toeing
And none of them knowing
That my heart is going
A-clippitty-cloppitty
Tappers 'n' squeakers
Or flappers in sneakers
I get the willies!
Needless to say
Another day
And somebody loses his grip . . . Me!
A-tippitty-tap
A-tippitty-tap
A-tappitty-tip!
You're asking

Do we love feet?
Yes we do
We cannot tell a lie
Absence of feet
Makes us blue
And meaning no malice
We become callous

Is it podiatry?
Buy a shoe, buy a tree?
Is it psychiatry?
Flippitty-floppitty
Every piggilly
Flippin' my wiggilly
What a thrill 'ees
Kickin' his heels
The mind . . . it reels
My senses have gone into heat
Caught in a grab in a gabble of fabulous
Caught in a grab in a gabble of fabulous

Feet! (My goodness)
Always a treat (My goodness)
Take the repeat (My goodness . . . Where?)
Were I in

Gauguin's shoes
What would I have to lose?
I would embrace the Muse
And even thank her

Whatever Gauguin chose
In only Gauguin's clothes
Wherever Gauguin goes
He was a banker

And as he sat in his socks
Thinkin' about the mess he was in
He said to hell with the stocks
And suddenly thought of Anthony Quinn (Ding-Dong, Ding-Dong!)
And started to grin (Ding-Dong, Ding-Dong!)

Had I but Gauguin's dash (His dash)
Had I but Gauguin's pash (His pash)
Had I but Gauguin's stash (His stash)
I'd have a ball (I'd have a ball)
If I were (If I were)
Banker (Banker)
Painter (Painter)
Gauguin (Gauguin)
Fabulous feet (Fabulous feet)
Paul (. . . Pawwawawawawawawl)
Caught in a grab in a gabble of fabulous feet (Ditto)
Paul! (Paul!)

"BLANCHE'S SONG" *

Lyrics by Elena Kondracki

Night, maybe you, maybe you will be my friend
Hide me in your darkness
Help me to pretend
that things are not the way they seem
Maybe you will let me dream
of gentle men with tender ways
of living endless pastel days
with someone kind
Maybe you will let me dream
Sir Galahad is waiting there
all gallant and all debonair
for me alone.

And I will wear a jewelled crown
a soft and floating silver gown
and be a queen so proud and sure
so sweet, so clean, so good, so pure.

Night, maybe you, maybe you will be my friend
Hide me in your darkness
Help me to pretend
that things are not the way they seem
Maybe you will let me dream
of garden walks with flowered trees
of living in unending ease
with someone kind
Maybe you will let me dream
that birds are singing everywhere
of a child's sweet laughter in the air
for me alone.

And I will wear a gingham dress
and know a lover's sweet caress
and be a woman proud and sure
whose love's a thing that will endure.

Night, maybe you, maybe you will be my friend.

* Based on Tennessee Williams's *A Streetcar Named Desire*.

"WHERE IS THE WEAVER?" *

Lyrics by Elena Kondracki
Music by Katrina Knerr

It's really quite strange when feelings change
and loss rearranges your dreams
when there's no one to guide you
and you haven't a chart
when there's no place to hide
and you're coming apart
only love sews together the seams.

Where is the weaver?
Where is the thread?
Where is the man who should be here instead?

I never found lies when I looked in your eyes
you can really disguise what you feel
Your arms were my haven
Your laughter my song
I was your slave and I know I was wrong
My God, love's not a thing you should steal!

Where is the weaver?
Where is the thread?
Where is the man who should be here instead?

I'll have to pretend 'til I find a friend
who will help me by mending the seams
that my heart's not in pieces
the material's fine
there're no wrinkles or creases
I don't want to resign
Only love sews together your dreams.

Where is the weaver?
Where is the thread?
Where is the man who should be here instead?

"THE ANCIENT FISH OF THE SEA" †

Lyrics and Music by Jack Labow

Before the sea was salty,
And before the sky was blue,
He was skimming along,
Swimming along,
He's older than me or you.

He helped to paint the Red Sea red;
Taught Moby Dick to dive.
He even knew the Dead Sea
When the Dead Sea was alive.

As old as old can be,
The Ancient Fish of the Sea!

But every single minute
He was learning something new.
He was yearning to know,
Burning to know,
He's wiser than me or you.

He knows why Noah's Ark did not
Take fish. And I suppose
He knows so much by now
He doesn't know how much he knows.

As wise as wise can be,
The Ancient Fish of the Sea!

He's exceedingly impressive;
He's excessively profound.
He's a landmark; he's a legend.
He's the only one—
Of whatever it is he is—around!

But if you try to see him,
That's a tricky thing to do,
'Cause he's down in the depths,
He's over the hill,
He's farther than me or you.

The journey takes a day, and night,
And day, and night, and day.
But if you need an answer,
Then you must go all the way.

Go all the way to see
The Ancient Fish of the Sea.
The Ancient Fish,
The Ancient Fish of the Sea.

"BRIGHTEN UP THE DARK" *

Lyrics and Music by Jack Labow

The sea around us is darker than night.
You have a feeling now that nothing is right.
Positive thinking's gonna shed a little light.
Come on and smile,
And brighten up the dark around you.

No way of knowing which way you should turn,
It's only natural to show your concern.
But here's a trick that you'll be very glad to learn:
You only smile,
And brighten up the dark a little.

It doesn't take a lightning bolt. No!
It doesn't use a single volt. No!
To give the gloom a cheerful jolt. No!
The power you need is inside you.

You're in deep water, and that's why you're blue;
You're too far down to let the sunshine come through.
But you can be on top if you know what to do—
You have to smile,
And brighten up the dark. Just do it.

When things look dismal, it's easy to cry,
And hope that help will come from some other guy.
But you can make it, all you have to do is try.
If you will smile,
And brighten up the dark, it's easy.

When you feel gloomy and way under par,
It's time to look around and see where you are.

* Based on *The Ginger Man* by J. P. Donleavy.
† From *Felicia Flounder*, a musical show for children.

* From *Felicia Flounder*, a Musical Show for Children.

No matter where it is, at least you got this far.
So you should smile,
And brighten up the dark. Just try it.

It doesn't take a lightning bolt. No!
It doesn't use a single volt. No!
To give the gloom a cheerful jolt. No!
The power you need is inside you.

Whatever happens, wherever you go,
It's up to you to make the happiness flow.
And you can do it, just remember that you know
You have to smile,
And brighten up the dark. You have to
Smile, and brighten up the dark.

"WHAT IS SHE TO HIM?"

Paper Moon *
Lyrics by Nancy Leeds
Music by Bert Draesel

I'd like to crawl in a hole and pull the dirt on top
Every time she looks at him—I want to holler stop—
But why should I care?
Why is it all a nightmare?

What is she to him?
She's such a floosie
He never made a play for anyone that way
But he can't lose me!

What is she to him?
There's so much of her?
The most expensive clothes can't hide a pair of those
He couldn't love her!

He couldn't get to know her
In as short a time as this!
I'd like to have him see
How many other men she'll kiss!
He'll find out . . . I'll see to that
And when he does . . . he'll leave her flat!

What is he to me?
He's pretty special!
We laugh an awful lot—He's really all I've got . . .
That makes him special!
I don't know if he's my father
But it isn't worth the bother or the fuss!
I like it better when there's just the two of us!

"IF I HAD YOU"

The Tempest
Lyrics by Nancy Leeds
Music by Joe Clonick

I knew what I wanted
Played the field a bit
Knew the kind of girl I'd missed. . . .
Even though I hunted
I hated to admit
That she's not likely to exist!

* Based on *Addie Pray.*

I've waited all my life
For someone just like you
Someone who'd smile
And every star would light.
Someone who'd touch my hand
And I would know
Why love makes children sing and flowers grow!

I've waited all my life
To share my days and nights
With someone else
Who needed someone too.
The way you looked at me
It isn't hard to see
How all of this could be . . . if I had you!

I've traveled every place in search of romance
I've looked at every face in search of love!
But seeing you was so astounding
All at once I knew I'd found
That someone I'd been dreaming of!

That magic moment comes
But once to every one
And this is mine . . .
Whatever else I do!
I never knew before
A lonely heart could soar!
I'd ask for nothing more . . . if I had you!

"FENCE PAINTING"

Mark Twain's Tom Sawyer, a Children's Show
Lyrics by Annette Leisten
Music by Sheldon Markham
Book by Richard Stockton

HUCK
Hey, Tom
Whatcher doin'?
TOM
Whuts it look like I'm doin'?
HUCK
Looks like
Yer paintin' the fence
TOM
Well, that's whut I'm doin'
I'm paintin' the fence
HUCK
Too bad!
Fine day fer fishin'
Shame you have to work!
TOM
Whatcher callin' work?
HUCK
Callin' paintin' work!
TOM
T'ain't so!
It suits Tom Sawyer!
How many boys you know git to do it?
You gotta be somebody special to do it!
It ain't every day a boy gits to paint a fence!
(Whistle interlude: TOM *paints industriously)*

HUCK
Hey Tom!
Gittin' tired?
TOM
Why should I be
Tired?
HUCK
Hard work
Paintin' that fence
TOM
I ain't hardly started
Paintin' this fence
HUCK
Well, now
I'll give you half my apple
If you let me paint a bit
TOM
Wouldn't think of it!
HUCK
Here, take all of it!
TOM
That suits Tom Sawyer!

If you promise to be neat
And keerful when you do it
And do it exactly
The way that I do it
It ain't every day
A boy gits to paint a fence
(*Whistle interlude: Boys paint,* SID *enters*)
SID
Hey Huck!
Whatcher doin'?
HUCK
Whuts it look like I'm doin'?
SID
Looks like
Yer paintin' our fence
HUCK
Well that's whut I'm doin'
I'm paintin' yer fence
SID
I swear!
I can't believe it!
Seein' Huck at work!
TOM
Whatcher callin' work?
SID
Callin' paintin' work
HUCK
T'ain't so!
TOM
It suits Tom Sawyer!
TOM AND HUCK
How many boys you know git to do it?
You gotta be somebody special to do it!
It ain't every day a boy gits to paint a fence!
(*Whistle interlude:* SID *is intrigued*)
SID
Hey, Huck
Lemme try it!

HUCK
Hey Tom! Can he try it?
TOM
Heck no!
Sid can't paint a fence!
SID
Can so!
Can so paint a fence!
C'mon now
I'll give you this here doorknob
Says here it's solid brass!
TOM
Yer full of sassafras!
SID
No, honest! Solid brass
HUCK
Sure 'nuff!
TOM
Well that suits Tom Sawyer
If you promise to be neat
And keerful when you do it
And do it exactly
The way that I do it
It ain't every day
A boy gits to paint a fence
(*Whistle interlude:* SID *and* HUCK *paint industriously, as* TOM *enjoys his apple and polishes his doorknob*)
TOM, HUCK AND SID
How many boys you know git to do it?
You gotta be somebody special to do it!
It ain't every day a boy gits to paint
A fence! A fence! A fence!

"FLAMINGO STEW"

Swiss Family Robinson, a Children's Show
Lyrics by Annette Leisten
Music by Sheldon Markham
Book by Jerome Coopersmith

When you live on desert isle
Cooking very strange
Familiar food you haven't got
Menu has to change
When family is hungering
And dinner's overdue
Out of pure necessity
You make flamingo stew

Flamingo, flamingo
Flamingo, flamingo stew

If you haven't got a cooking pot
You use a turtle shell
If you haven't got a spoon, so what
An oar will stir as well
If you can't find a flamingo
What you have will have to do
Just mix it up with love
And you have got flamingo stew

Flamingo, flamingo
Flamingo, flamingo stew

Throw in some oysters from the sea
Or plantains from the ground
Or nuts from some exotic tree
You chance to see around
Then add some crab or porcupine
Or even kangaroo
Anything and everything
Will make flamingo stew

Flamingo, flamingo
Flamingo, flamingo stew

Sometimes the gravy's very thick
Sometimes it's sort of thin
Anything they carry home
Mama throws right in
The recipe is simple
If it ran, or swam, or flew
It's gonna be delicious
In Mom's flamingo stew

Flamingo, flamingo
Flamingo, flamingo stew

Serve it in a cocoanut
Or clamshell if you wish
The nicest thing about it is
You never wash a dish
It gives you indigestion
Like you never never knew
There's nothing in this
Whole wide world
Like Mom's flamingo stew

Flamingo, flamingo
Flamingo, flamingo stew!

"ROSEMARY'S BABY"

Lyrics and Music by Brooks Morton

A wise old man once told me—
I think he spoke the truth—
"Remember that the future
Lies in the hands of youth."
While musing on the time I count the sands of
I wonder how we'd all fare in the hands of

Rosemary's Baby.
An infant so rare
From his dear little fangs and his dear little claws
To the dear little snakes in his hair.

Rosemary's Baby.
A child set apart.
When he cries, should we burp him or change him?
Or just drive a stake through his heart?

His mother was heard to say (as the child clutched her
    clammily)
"There's been some mistake,
Or else he must take
After his father's family."

Rosemary's Baby
Is something unique.
When he mutters and sings in the night,

You hear flutters and wings in the night,
You see clutters of things in the night
Exotic and new.
And someday, maybe,
Rosemary's Baby
Will grow up and go after you.

"I'M GONNA GET HIM BACK" *

Lyrics and Music by Brooks Morton

VERSE
All I have to do is walk through that doorway
And I'll be free . . . and alone . . .
Isn't it convenient? Things have worked out your way
With your little playmate, all your own.
How very neatly you have everything arranged!
My plans have suddenly changed:

CHORUS
You Europeans play such charming games.
I, also, Madame, have read Henry James.
Now hear this Yankee: "Addio, Hanky-Panky."
I'm gonna get him back!

Your "dolce vita" is nipped in the bud.
Your "gem collection" is losing one stud.
Shall I be clearer? You bet your bottom lira,
I'm gonna get him back!

You think that my husband adores yah—
Well, I'm here to tell you, "You're through."
Ferrara had Lucretia Borgia
And Venice, dear lady, has you.

One final outburst I can't quite control:
The years, Contessa, have taken their toll.
You're no Love Goddess. That well-preserved facade is
Starting to crinkle and crack.
Well, go crack on your time.
Right now it's out-the-door time.
You think you own him,
You've never really known him,
Forget you met him,
I'm gonna get him back!

"VOYEUR'S LAMENT

Conversations with Pierre
Lyrics and Music by Alan Menken

Age eight . . . barely pubescent
I only saw the front of the class at the bell
Never could find the fertile crescent
But I knew some other terrain pretty well
Pink undies . . . soiled with dirt
And on Sunday . . . the lace of her undershirt
Thirteen . . . an expert astronomer
But to her I was four eyes next door
Each night without a thing on her
Never thinking I had some more eyes in store
Slow strip . . . purely a tease

* Based on Arthur Laurents's *The Time of the Cuckoo.*

My hands grip . . . I'm always falling from trees
All the girls I knew as a boy
Saddled my mind with a curse
All the girls I couldn't enjoy
Changed my whole life for the worse
Eenie meenie minie moe
Catch a tiger by the toe
If he hollers let him go
My mother says he's a snake
What does it matter?
Who does it hurt?
There's nothing sadder
Than a lying flirt
Baby you can't see me
But that's alright
Don't come nearer
I'm a one way mirror
Reflecting upon your light
Eighteen . . . the sexual peak
I'm becoming a man after all
Had a hot little thing with Monique
Which lasted until she was ripped off the wall
Free love . . . right on the floor
Enough . . . but she keeps on asking for more and more and
        more and more
Every girls who passes me by
Don't know what she do me
Every girl who catches my eye
Probably sees right thru me
A my name is Alice
My husband's name is Al
We come from Adam and Eve
And we sell apples
What does it matter?
Who does it vex?
There's nothing sadder
Than spectator sex
Baby you and I are
One of many such pairs
I'm the man who's standing
On the first floor landing
While you're at the top of the stairs.

"TRENDELL TERRY"

Conversations with Pierre
Lyrics and Music by Alan Menken

I opened up my daily paper and
Turned to the page that should have been sports
Instead I saw a man on the ledge of a building
Somewhere in the garment district
They said his name was Trendell Terry
Who said he was gonna jump
And crush his life upon the pavement
Next to the firepump
It's just a picture in a paper
The ink rubs off, the story fades
They took him back to the institutions
That drove him there in the first place
Indifferent eyes watched him wave his life
Some desperate psychotic loner
Said he couldn't get a job to support his wife

And kids somewhere in Corona
I could have seen the whole thing happen
At Thirteen-Seventy Broadway
But now as I walk by the pictures in color
And I realize I'm looking the wrong way
I sing a song for Trendell Terry
Cause I saw his picture in the paper
Lured off the roof by a bottle of whiskey
Which distracted his attention
The bottle was provided
Courtesy of Exclusive Knitwear
To ease the operations
Of the rescue
This is a song for Trendell Terry
Who somehow felt he wanted to die
Perched before the public eye
Soaked by the pouring rain

"HOW DOES THE BALLAD END?"

Mandrake Moon*
Lyrics by Nathaniel Miller
Music by Frank Hamilton

How does the ballad end?
I won't think about it now.
How does the river bend?
It don't think about as how.

How does the ballad start?
That's what I'd rather know.
Why do lovers part
When there's still so far for them to go?

Some of them start on a river bank,
And some in the tall summer corn,
In some the boy is dark and lank,
Or ruddy and small as a faun.

In some he's a Lord and she is a troll,
But they set their clothes aside.
The pull between them—body and soul,
Could raise an ocean tide

Maybe ballads never die
Like the love they're all about,
And you can always hear their sigh
When you snuff the candles out.

How does the river bend?
It don't think about as how.
How does the ballad end?
I won't think about it now,
Not now

"WHEN FIRST I SAW MY BARB'RA FAIR"

Mandrake Moon
Lyrics by Nathaniel Miller
Music by Frank Hamilton

When first I saw my Barb'ra fair
Eagle high above the world

* Based on *Dark of the Moon* by Berney and Richardson.

The sun was tangled in her hair
On Smokey Crest where she lay curled

My eagle veered like he was blind
I coaxed him down to see her clear
We brushed her cheek; she paid us mind
Her smile was frozen like in fear

Witchin's made of shadow
But lovin's spun with light
Once I was so sad, O
A thing of fear and night
Then I loved a human
A human that loved me
And I became a true man
Cast off from witchery

Our kissin' made my eagle fuss
I set him free to soar above
No words we spoke the two of us
And in soft silence we made love

At first her hair with sun entwined
Lay golden on my heaving heart
But black it was with stars behind
When we could bring ourselves to part

"TELL ME SOMETHING NEW" *

Lyrics and Music by Ethan Mordden

Tell me something new;
I have a wondering thirst to slake.
Scheme a new idea,
Point me a path that I can take.
Paint me a vision of a place to stay in, so I can believe it.
Show me a way at last to make my way in, and also teach me
How to leave it.

Call me a new name.
I'd like that, something foreign and sweet.
Lead me to your house
And bind my hands and feet.
The only thing I ask of life is variety—
Please think of something new and tell that new thing to me.

List me things to do.
Rhyme me the principal parts of speech.
Set me fruit to pick
That no one else in town can reach.
Boil me a medicine to heal the sickly and banish their worry.
I know my feet are apt to stray too quickly, so won't you kindly
Try to hurry?
I should look ahead.
With help, I could pick up the knack.
Make me fear the past,
So I don't dare look back.
Hum me the notes to serenade you one dazzling song!
But make it right away, for I can't stay long!

"COME DOWNTOWN" *

Lyrics and Music by Ethan Mordden

Come downtown;
There's so much here to see.
Try your luck—
You never know how good it can be, 'til you go to town.

Every piece can be had for a fee.
Everyone has a dream—
And every dream has a price.
Pick up something nice.
Come and see . . .

Push yourself along the main street;
Slip from pillar to post.
Try to figure out what you require the most.
You might select a tame caribou
Or a chimpanzee that purrs like a dove,
Or an hour or two of baroque and demoniacal love!

Whatever you seek,
You will find it in town.
Come and learn—
Things of value are never for free.
Come and see . . .
Come and try . . .
But come to buy!

In this ditch,
We put nothing to waste.
If you're rich,
You can afford to have a specialized taste—
Come in haste.

What a crowd!
Will the fun never fade?
Young and old—
Pressing noses in the passing parade;
Haggling for a ring.
Buy a pretty thing . . .

Old age takes a holiday.
Pass in single file!
Wondering what sort of stranger hides behind the smile.
Touching, holding, trading, glaring,
Looking into eyes . . .
Make your move—for beauty never lies!

Check the street—
Never know whom you'll meet!
So sublime!
Let's pretend it will be different this time.
Why not dare?
We're all there—
At the big-town fair!

---

* Based on *Zuleika Dobson* by Max Beerbohm.

* Based on William Shakespeare's *Measure for Measure*.

"ACT ONE"

Act One with Music *
Lyrics by Marvin D. Mossmond

Act One
A beginning
All things must
Have a beginning
The longest journey starts
With but a single step
The step is done
And we've begun
Act One

Act One
An adventure
This life can
Be an adventure
But one must look within
To find out who you are
When that is done
Then we've begun
Act One

If you have hopes
You must study how to change
Who you are
Into the who you must become

If you have dreams
You must try to rearrange
The directions of your life
To one

Act One
The beginning
Things yet unborn
Are beginning
So burn your brightest
Fly so high
That you may learn
To even light the sky

All that comes from
That little step
Act One

"THEY ARE MAKING A MACHINE IN CALIFORNIA"
(that will measure how little I care)

Act One with Music *
Lyrics by Marvin D. Mossmond

Please don't trouble me with stories
Of the frightful plight of people
Who are lazy to the quick!
Of my store of human kindness
I have simply not a modicum to spare
They are making a machine in California
That will measure how little I care

I have not a whit of sufferance
For the crisis and supplications

* Based on Moss Hart's *Act One*.

Of the self-indulgent sick
If the human race has fallen
Why not simply let the bastards languish there?
They are making a machine in California
That will measure how little I care

This machine will weigh the flutter
Of the gentlest butterfly
It will register brute forces
If a spider blinks an eye
It will mark the barest tracings
Of a hummingbird in flight
And its gauges will all tremble
When they feel the weight of light!

It will magnify the measure
Of a molecule in space
It will calculate the thickness
Of a freckle on a face
Or the weight of an expression
In the past or present tense
And it's all to be developed
At government expense!

It will be a great occasion
When the scientists assemble
In their gowns of sterile white
And before that august body
Like a sacrificial lamb I will be led
As in great anticipation
An entire generation
Feels the hush of great discovery in the air
As they measure
How little
I care

"A NICE PLACE TO VISIT"

Ye Gods *
Lyrics by William Okie
Music by Sammy Prager

VERSE
HEBE
Where but in Thebes
Does history have links
To a riddle by the Sphinx?
Where but in Thebes?
MEN
Where's the common meeting ground for hedonist and stoic?
There's no other place around more gamey or heroic.
HERA
Where but in Thebes
Could Oedipus the King
Do his own outrageous thing?
Where but in Thebes?
MEN
If you want to rub elbows with patricians and plebes,
You'll never find another town like little old Thebes!

* Based on *Amphitryon '38* by S.N. Behrman.

FIRST CHORUS

ALL

It's a nice place to visit, but I wouldn't want to live there!
It's a much better place to be from.

HEBE

There's an atmosphere that's wild there; you'd never raise a
child there.
It's a gaudy, bawdy gilded kind of slum!

ALL

It's a fun place to visit—but the morals are peculiar
From the gutter right up to the throne.

HERA

When the citizens are callous to incest in the palace,
Does it show how very civilized we've grown?

ZERO

There's pleasure for sale at popular prices . . .

MEANDER

A smorgasbord assortment of your favorite vices!

MEN

And furthermore
There's garbage galore.
Thebes can really show you what a city's for!

ALL

It's a nice place to look at with its temples and pavilions.
There are those who would say it's exquisite.
That's a mask on the face,
But if you like a merry chase,
It's a real nice place to visit!

SECOND CHORUS

MEN

They've luxuries there too costly for Croesus
And things we never hear of in the Peloponnesus.

ZERO

Like urban blight . . .

MEANDER

And screams in the night . . .

MEN

Little indications things are not quite right!

ALL

It's a nice place to get to, but it's nicer when you're leaving.
Is it heaven or hell—or what is it?
It's a downright disgrace,
But if a guy can take the pace
It's a real nice place . . .

ZERO

A cradle of sin
For wallowing in!

ALL

. . . It's a real nice place to visit!

"HALF AND HALF"

Ye Gods *

Lyrics by William Okie
Music by Sammy Prager

VERSE

When he leaves me, I'm not a person at all.

* Based on *Amphitryon '38* by S. N. Behrman.

I'm the stay-at-home half of a marriage.
I'm simply a decimal
Infinitesimal,
Shallow, divided, and small.

When he leaves me, less than a woman is left,
Only fifty percent of a marriage,
An unfinished article,
More like a particle,
Beaten, bewildered, bereft . . .

1ST CHORUS

Half and half make one simple whole.
A wife is half a heart; a husband's half a soul.
Put them in conjunction,
And things begin to function.
Join them up and what comes up'll
Be one single married couple.

Half and half make most simple things.
If she's an empty lute, then he's the missing strings.
Match them up and tune it;
You'll have a working unit.
Pick your wedding march at random;
Just be sure to step in tandem.

Where can I hide from lonely distraction
Whenever he's gone for a day?
Down deep inside, I'm only a fraction
While he's away.

Life's no laugh when life's incomplete.
How long before I'll hear the clatter of his feet?
I can tell you kiddo,
It's rough to be a widow
With my flag in the middle of the staff
Until I see
The better half of me
In our personal half and half

2ND CHORUS

Half and half make one thing entire:
A husband's half demand; a wife is half desire.
Rub the two together
In dry or soggy weather.
What results will be amazing,
Just one happy bonfire blazing.

Call me a shred, a fragment, a portion,
Whenever he's not very near.
Call me instead a hopeless abortion
Until he's here.

Catch the calf we'll kill when he comes.
We'll spread a marriage feast and beat the welcome drums.
When we're reunited,
Won't my half be excited!
Until then it'll have to stand the gaff,
Just waiting for
The half that I adore
In our personal half and half.

"DISCONTENTED"

Apartment House
Lyrics by Muriel Robinson
Music by Norman Curtis

I used to have a house with a garden in the suburbs
And a stationwagon
My wife used to drive me to the station in the morning
In my stationwagon
And in the evening she would pick me up
And take me home
And I

Kept feeling discontented
Loose ends had me tied in knots
Had the hots for
Don't know what it is

My wife was nicely scented
Good cook at soufflés and such
We still keep in touch
You know how it is

So I moved to the city
A very dramatic, furnished apartment
Not this one
There I baby-sat for a cat
While my new love went on vacation
It turned out that
She went with her husband for a reconciliation
I kept the cat
With whom I have a very open relationship
Meow
Ow

Now I take out the garbage
Watch the TV I've rented
And I'm very
Discontented

"THE VIEW FROM QUEENS"

Apartment House
Lyrics by Muriel Robinson
Music by Norman Curtis

Policemen and firemen, teachers and truckers
A magazine writer I drink with
Salesmen and mailmen, some stray chicken pluckers
A philosophy student I think with
My friends and myself and a few fellow artists
I spent twenty years on the brink with
Have taken our moderated dreams
And made an exodus
The lot of us
To Queens

Refugees all, we crawled out of Manhattan
We were beaten, more dead than alive there
It's middle-class misfits, white, black and Latin
Too much in the middle to thrive there
Not thick-skinned or crazy, rich, crooked or lazy
Didn't have what it takes to survive there
So we took what was left of our means
And brought our shattered nerves

To the calm preserves
Of Queens

When the sky is clear, we can see the towers
When the sky is clear, it's nice to know they're there
But, when the wind is still, every smokestack, and each factory
Makes the air unsatisfactory
It's consoling to watch Manhattan disappear

Not much like country, not even a suburb
Just semi-detached from the city
Connecticut, Jersey and Eastern Long Island
Commuters regard us with pity
While they wait for their trains or sit stalled on the highway
They use us to try to be witty
We just let it pass
Sitting on the grass
In Queens

So let the traffic crawl by
To where the Gypsy Moths fly
Let Hell's Angels get raucus
When the wind's from Secaucus
I shake my head
And make my bed
In Queens

"CALL GIRL"

The Second Coming
Lyrics, Music, and Book by Bob Rodgers

THELMALINDA SUE
(Spoken)
You know it's funny how all of a sudden people can fall into a
new career. I mean, I was just having a drink with my girl
friend Mona when this guy came over and asked her if she
was busy tonight. Of course she was busy! When you look
like Mona, men don't give her time to pee! Anyway, he turns
to me and says, "How about you? There's lots of bread
involved"

(Sung)
My first reaction was—who me?
To think he thought to ask—threw me!
I was very flattered, wouldn't you be?
Let's face it
Me, I look like last year's model Honda
Mona looks more like pre-war Jane Fonda!

My next reaction was—hey you
No thinking person would—pay you
For the opportunity to lay you
While I was
Laughing at myself, before I knew it
Mona tells this guy that I will do it!

(Spoken)
Then this guy goes and phones some other guy, see . . . and he
says he's sending over . . . are you ready for this . . . a CALL
GIRL! He meant me! I couldn't believe my own ears!

(Sung)
Saint Peter blessed me . . . I'm a call girl!
Someone arrest me . . . I'm a call girl!

My amateur standing's been dealt a death blow
As of tonight you can call me a pro!

I'm a call girl
Wait till Hugh Hefner gets wind of my fame
He won't be the same

Center-fall girl
Wearing a tattoo and showing no shame
"Crotch Conners" is the name

(Spoken)
To think after only one year at business college . . . five months
at Tiny Naylors . . . nine weeks on unemployment, I am a
housecalling prostitute! Oh this land's been good to me!

(Sung)
Till now life's been a losing contest
Now I can pay my orthodontist
I'll be so damn famous, I'll be on teevee
Cavett and Carson will fight over me

I'll be all girl
When I am starred in a Hollywood pic
My own porno flick!

I'm a ball girl
All of a sudden I kinda feel sick!
It's happening too quick!

(Spoken)
Why am I rattling on like this for? I'm sick all right! Sick in the
head!

(Sung)
He'll know soon enough I'm all sham
Because every curve that I am
Was purchased in my neighborhood
At Fredericks of Hollywood

Unless he is deaf, dumb and blind
He'll notice I've got no behind
He'll see when his hands take the tour
My bust is a "bust" . . . that's for sure!

Flat girl
Although this "flat girl" is willing to please
There's nothing to squeeze!

Here's your hat, girl
Why take the chance? He won't like what he sees
Not when the man sees . . . these!

I'm sort of sorry now I said I'd go
I'll just drop by to say a fast hello
Who knows things may work out
Supposing they do (well then)
Here comes a new call . . . (move over Mona) . . . girl!

"DON'T TELL ME YOUR NAME!"
The Second Coming
Lyrics, Music, and Book by Bob Rodgers

Don't tell me your name
I don't want to know it
God forbid it might be Rena
Even Lena or Edwina
And that, take my word—would blow it!

Lust is what I feel.
Names will not enhance it
I could never trick with "Cora"
Or stick a chick named "Dora"
No names if you please—can't chance it.

To know too much would encumber
I know me too well so don't scoff
Your social security number
Might even turn me off!

Drop all talk tonight
Or I'll get psychotic
I feel no anticipation
For your views about inflation
I need something more—erotic

Tell me where you're from
But do it by letter!
To find out you're from Toledo
Might just screw up my libido
The stranger you are—the better.

Don't spoil this by being human
For Pete's sake don't let down your hair!
You know why you're here, I'm assumin'
So park it over there

Don't tell me you're ill
I don't want to hear it!
It's goodbye and nice to see ya
If you mention pyorrhea
So take my advice
Clam up and play nice
If it's all the same
Don't tell me your name!

"HOOKED"
Boy Girl Boy Girl
Lyrics and Music by Connie Romer

MYRA
Back in the Stone Age
Cavemen had their own stage
A rock, or a hill.
They'd put on a show
A marvelous tableau
Dramatizing their kill.
I'm sure the audience sat rapt
I'm sure the audience all clapped.
And when they did,
The performers felt a glow . . .
And I know—

They were hooked
They were hooked
Their goose or whatever was cooked
They had chosen the work
That would drive them berserk
Quote unquote.
It's a blessing
It's a curse
Feast or famine
Sometimes worse

But there's no business like it,
As Berlin wrote.
Chekhov and Miller
Fontanne and Phyllis Diller
Brecht and Brahms
The singers of psalms
The kids into rock
And every disc jock
Dancers and mimers
The two-a-day old-timers
Opera stars and dogs who drive cars
The girls in their veils
The guys who eat nails
Loved the life that they chose
The yesses, the maybes, the nos.
Any other life was overlooked
They had a passionate addiction
An incurable affliction
They were hooked
They were hooked
They were hooked

"MY FIRST DRESSING ROOM"

Boy Girl Boy Girl
Lyrics and Music by Connie Romer

BELLA

Look at this crazy cracked mirror
I look like an abstract oil.
Maybe I'll plant some tomatoes
On the floor there's an inch of soil.
I know I should be positive
Not negative, when I speak.
Okay, I will be positive
But thank god, we'll only be here a week.

I love this place
There's so much space
A witch could park her broom.
It's nice and warm
And ants all swarm
Through my first dressing room.
The plumbing leaks
The toilet reeks
I'll douse it with perfume
I love the light
It's khaki, right?
In my first dressing room.
There isn't a closet
Just a nail
And I could faint
When I inhale
Every star went through this
It's an experience
That I wish I could miss.
It's not like home
All glass and chrome
It's garbage time in bloom.
Oh, I won't cry
I just might die
In my first dressing room.
(Speaks)

Let's see your place, David.
DAVID
My place? This *is* my place.
(Sung)
My little friend
I must amend
A state that you presume.
Aren't you aware
That we're to share
Our first dressing room?
This two by four
With broken door
This aromatic tomb
This grubby shrine
Is yours and mine
Our first dressing room.
I'm sorry, dear Bella
BELLA
Billy—
DAVID
Billy. Please don't cry.
But we'll survive it
You and I.
You're starting a career
Write on this dirty wall
"Billy Burton was here!"
And don't explode
We're on the road
That should dispel the gloom
Let's carry on
Let's clean the john!
In our first dressing room.

"ODE TO FREUD"

Beacon Hill*
Lyrics by Lennoy Ruffin
Music by Howlett Smith

CATHERINE
George, last night after Eleanor was asleep, I kept thinking about that book she mentioned, by that man with the queer name . . .
GEORGE
Oh, you mean Freud.
CATHERINE
Yes . . . I thought I should know something about it, but I couldn't find it in her room.
GEORGE
Well . . . after what she said . . . I thought perhaps I should glance at it . . . just to check up of course . . . I think I dropped it back here somewhere . . .
CATHERINE
Is that why you didn't come to bed until two in the morning?
GEORGE
Well . . . frankly yes . . . (singing)
I found the whole thing most illuminating . . .
Though controversial I read the book right through . . .

*Based on *The Late George Apley* by Marquand and Kaufman.

Whereas I feel he does some overstating . . .
Freud has a theory so absolutely new . . .

For instance . . . I was quite surprised to find . . .
The strange way human relationships affect the mind . . .
CATHERINE
(Speaking) What sort of relationships?
GEORGE
Well . . . I don't know how to put it . . .
CATHERINE
(Speaking) Why ever not?
GEORGE
Don't know what word to choose . . .
CATHERINE
(Speaking) Please say what you mean, George.
GEORGE
Then I'll have to resort to a word I never use . . .
It's largely all about sex . . .
CATHERINE
(Speaking) But how can he write a whole book about that?
GEORGE
(Speaking) Well . . . he does seem to pad it a little . . . here
and there . . . *(Singing again)*
Still Doctor Freud did keep me up last night . . .
I must admit his book is just a bit complex . . .
And while perhaps his premise may be right . . .
I'm still perplexed about a certain Mister X . . .
CATHERINE
(Speaking) Whatever do you mean, George . . . what about
him?
GEORGE
It seems when he was only four years old . . .
He shared a moment with his nurse that isn't plain . . .
It colored all his later life I'm told . . .
CATHERINE
(Speaking) But how?
GEORGE
He had the same recurring dream about a train . . .
(Speaking) I remember my own nurse very well and neither of
us
forgot ourselves even for a moment . . . *(Singing again)*

I guess that Freud and Emerson are much the same . . .
They say our dreams can be revealing there's no doubt . . .
And even though the doctor seems to have no shame . . .
He only tries to do with sex the same thing Emerson did
without . . .

Though sex may govern other people's lives . . .
The man is from Vienna where that might be true . . .
But here in Boston where good breeding thrives . . .
We have so many more important things to do . . .
CATHERINE
(Speaking) George . . . I had a strange dream the other night . . .
GEORGE
(Speaking) Perhaps you'd better not tell me about it until
you've looked this over. *(Singing again)*

I find his theory most illuminating . . .
But it simply doesn't apply to me . . . or you.

"A LONG LONG WAY"

Lyrics by Lennoy Ruffin
Music by Howlett Smith

I've come a long . . . long . . . way . . .
I've come through hell for beauty . . .
My lonely search is through . . .
It ended when I looked at you . . .
I've come a long . . . long . . . way . . .

I know beauty . . .
Beauty is the sound of thunder that promises rain . . .
Beauty is an open meadow that ripens with grain . . .
It's the land . . . all round . . . it's the ground where I've lain . . .

You are beauty . . .
Beauty like the blush of morning that colors the hills . . .
Beauty like the mist of evening that softens and stills . . .
All my pain . . .
Words are beauty . . .
Words are music . . . and silence . . . and laughter . . .
And sunlight . . . and shadows . . .

Beauty is the taste of summer that sweetens the tongue . . .
Beauty is the blaze of autumn when visions are young . . .
Everywhere . . . songs are sung . . . beauty's there . . .

I've come a long . . . long . . . way . . .
I've searched the world for beauty . . .
My lonely search is through . . .
My journey ends with you . . .

Come away with me . . .
Stay for all my years . . .
We can make a home . . . the kind of home . . .
I've hungered for . . .

Come and live with me . . .
Give me all your fears . . .
If you'll share my life . . . I'll find my life . . .
Worth so much more . . .

I've come a long . . . long . . . way . . .
I've come a long . . . long . . . way . . .

"FEMME FATALITY"

Hey, People, Listen! *
Lyrics by Alene Smith
Music by Woolf Phillips
Book by Alene Smith and David Smith

The first thing I remember . . .
At the ripe old age of three . . .
Was getting "Susie Simple" . . . a doll as big as me.
It talked and drank and wet its pants and called me "Mama"
too . . .
What bunk . . . it stunk!

But ev'ry day 'til I was ten . . .
I had to be a mother hen . . .
And play with tiny dishes, stoves and sweepers . . .
While Daddy grinned and Mother purred . . .

*Based on *The Male Animal* by James Thurber and Elliott Nugent.

I found this mini-life absurd . . .
A training ground for Lilliput's housekeepers.
Still all the way up to sixteen . . .
I had to be so goddam clean . . .
With Mary Janes and Ruffles 'cross my fanny . . .
Okay to waltz . . . okay to knit . . .
But never sweat and never spit . . .
Oh . . . how I envied Little Orphan Annie.

(Spoken) Can you believe mothers? I mean, how they worry?
    All I wanted was one lousy plastic dump truck and she says
    things like "All my life I wanted a daughter." Well, for God's
    sake . . . she's got one!

So I like boy things . . .
Am I a bad person?
At such a question . . . my Ma pretends she's deaf . . .
I like to fool with engines . . .
But I also like to cook . . .
And my birth certificate says that I'm an "F."
So I like boys things . . .
That makes me a leper?
Should I start blushing at towels embroidered "His?"
I'm pretty good at plumbing . . .
But I sew about the same . . .
And the shape I'm in will testify I'm a Ms.

I don't understand the furor over female versus male . . .
I feel that peace with honor's overdue . . .
If God had meant this argument to reach so grand a scale . . .
He would have made all babies pink or blue.

Do I like boy things? . . .
Should I join a convent?
Or a monastery in another town?
I've intercepted passes . . .
On the playing field or off . . .
And you'll find the seat in my john is always down.

(Spoken) I mean this may seem like a little thing, but it's still
    proof . . . right? All the time . . . I gotta prove . . . I mean . . .
    it's crazy.

Now that I'm legally adult . . .
I'm shocked to find that I insult . . .
Society when I slough off my label . . .
I'm militant and avant-garde . . .
My feathers neatly trimmed and tarred . . .
My family considers me unstable.
But comes the time I feel I should . . .
Succumb to joys of motherhood . . .
A solemn promise that I plan to keep'll
Be to rear a new phenomenon . . . have neither daughter nor a
    son . . .
I swear that I will fin'lly raise a people!

"BABY TALK"

Even at Our Age *
Lyrics by Alene Smith
Music by Genny Boles
Book by Genny Boles and Alene Smith

The joys of pending motherhood are grossly underrated . . .
You'll find that you give less than you receive . . .
In fact, you get so many things that even simply stated . . .
They make a list that you would not believe!

You get nausea in the mornings but that leaves you in a
    while . . .
It's replaced by bladder pressure and a little touch of bile . . .
You get gassy in the evening . . .
And a figure like a house . . .
And congratulations tendered to your chauvinistic spouse.

Nausea . . . pressure . . . gassy . . . fat . . .
Help yourself to this or that . . .
Fa la la and lackaday . . .
The joys of being in a family way.

You get stretch marks on your tummy and your fanny and your
    hips . . .
You get air-conditioned clothing as the vital stitching rips . . .
You get monumental heartburn . . .
And a pair of swollen feet . . .
You're enchanting and seductive as a dinosaur in heat.

Heartburn . . . stretch marks . . . swelling . . . fat . . .
Help yourself to this or that . . .
Fa la la and lackaday . . .
The joys of being in a family way.

You get winded bending over 'cause that belly interferes . . .
And you watch with rapt amazement as your navel
    disappears . . .
You get told that you are glowing . . .
When you'd like to kill yourself . . .
And two boobies like Mount Whitney sitting neatly on a shelf.

Winded . . . boobies . . . belly button . . . fat . . .
Help yourself to this or that . . .
Fa la la and lackaday . . .
The joys of being in a family way.

You get skirts with funny cut-outs and a dozen tacky
    smocks . . .
And your book is tossed akimbo when the kid abruptly
    knocks . . .
You get flashes like infernos . . .
And your legs look like a map . . .
You amuse yourself forlornly waving "bye bye" to your lap.

Tacky . . . flashes . . . varicose . . . fat . . .
Help yourself to this or that . . .
Fa la la and lackaday . . .
The joys of being in a family way.

You get names to call the baby and advice that turns you
    pale . . .

* Based on *Never Too Late* by Sumner Arthur Long.

You take showers 'cause your tub will not accommodate a
whale . . .
You get symptoms that Hippocrates . . .
Could never diagnose . . .
But you sure don't get no lovin' 'cause your hubby can't come
close.

Showers . . . symptoms . . . sexless . . . fat . . .
Help yourself to this or that . . .
Fa la la and lackaday . . .
The joys of being in a family way.

While our figures grow more chubby . . .
Let us drink a toast to hubby . . .
Let's hear it for the guy who pays the bill . . .
That mighty over-sexed one . . .
Sure as hell can have the next one . . .
We will take the bows and he can take the pill.

"NORMA'S AWAKE NOW!" *

Lyrics by Bruce Sussman
Music by Stephen Hoffman

Norma's awake now!
A brand new night is dawning
And here's the heroine hardly yawning.
Cue on battalions of people
To make a big to-do.
This girl's been snoozing
Since March '52.
But Norma's awake now!
And though she seems unsteady,
I warn you, ready or not, she's ready.
So much of Norma is standing by
Waiting to come into play.
There's much more to Norma than I
Can say.
By the way,
I'm Norma.
(She yawns but catches herself and continues)
Look who's awake still.
This princess ain't pretending.
She's heading straight for a happy ending.
On with the wedding, the banquet,
The dainty dinner mints.
Juice-up the preacher
And spruce-up the prince.
I'm raring to play house,
Complete with washer-dryer,
T.V., two maids and a deep fat fryer.
Moments ago I was sound asleep
Living the life of a clam.
Then Lord knows what happened
But here I am
Wide awake,
Up and awake,
Look who's awake
NOW!
(She yawns violently and collapses into a deep sleep)

* Based on Arthur Laurents's *Invitation to a March*.

"GOING HOME ALONE"

Families
Lyrics by Bruce Sussman
Music by Stephen Hoffman

How many cigarettes . . . wasted?
Count all the butts pasted
In the ashtray.
How many tables hopped?
Numbers swopped?
Egos shot and blown?
All of those evenings spent choosing
Whom you're cruising . . .
All of those long walks back home alone.

You smile.
You stare.
Display your savoir faire.
You sweat.
You groan.
You need some more cologne.
The hours go flying. Huh.
And what do you hear? Last call!
You wish you could sneak out.
You frequently freak-out
And get on all fours and just crawl.
You lie.
You boast.
You make an idle toast.
You sit.
You stand.
You're rarely in demand.
They turn all the lights on.
Now why are you so depressed.
Were you too non-committal?
Or maybe too little?
Too skinny? Too fat? Or too dressed?
You're befuddled and beat
But ready to comb
Every alley and street
On the longest way home.
Then the ultimate joke,
At a quarter to five,
Is that hot-dog and coke
In that feculent dive.
So you sit and you brew
In that god-awful place
At a table for two,
Well . . . just in case.
And you don't want to move
'Cause you're dead as a stone . . .
And once more you're going home alone.

How many four o'clocks wasted,
Counting the butts pasted
In the ashtray?
How many tables turned?
Lessons learned?
I sat.
I stood.
I drank as no one should.
I smiled.

I stared.
My savoir must have . . . faired!
Tonight, I'm not going home
Alone!

"REMEMBERING WHEN"

Skyline

Lyrics, Music, and Book by Jeff Sweet

I remember the headbands and the tie-dyed
T-shirts and jeans and the wide-eyed
Enthusiasm that swept us along.
Boycotting Dow and signing petitions,
Fighting C.C.N.Y. for open admissions,
And marching on the Capitol a half-million strong.
Those memories are coming back to me
Of the reckless and contagious energy
And the glory and the gung-ho spirit that we shared then.
Oh, it seems much too soon to be sitting remembering when.

I remember Woodstock, McCarthy and King,
And the student strike that wonderful spring,
And how it seemed like half the world was playing guitars.
Of Chicago and Daley and the convention.
I remember the peace symbol-decorated cars.
But now, oh, the sensations aren't the same.
Suddenly the scene is so very tame.
If only we could find that old fervor once again.
Yes, it seems much too soon to be sitting remembering when.

Where are they now—the crowds and their cheering?
Are they still there, or have I lost my hearing?
Or have they simply turned and walked away?
Where are they now—the hand-lettered signs,
The sit-ins and strikes and long picket lines?
Does anybody care, or is it all passé?
Tell me, was it all just something I dreamed?
Or was it really as good as it seemed?
I miss the commitment that used to be there before.
And, you know, at times I even almost miss the war.

"MY VERY GOOD FRIEND"

Skyline

Lyrics, Music, and Book by Jeff Sweet

"Sorry," she says, "I don't feel like you do."
"I understand," I say.
"It's not that there's anything wrong with you,"
She says in her earnest way.
"We've got something special,
Let's not break it up.
I'd hate to see it end,
For I think of you as my very good friend,"
She says.
"I want you to be my good friend."

"You know there are so many ways you can love,"
She tells me and I nod.
"There's love for your family, love for a friend,
And of course there's love of God."
She holds my hand close
And says to me, "Hey,
Thanks for the flowers you send,

But I think of you as my very good friend,"
She says.
"I want you to be my good friend."

I wonder why I sit and listen to this?
Am I trying to keep my cool?
If I got up right now and just walked away
Would I look like some kind of fool?
"I need you," she says.
"You don't know how it helps
To have someone I can depend
On. Yes, I think of you as my very good friend,"
She says.
"I want you to be my good friend."

The coffee's been drunk and I pick up the check,
Leave a quarter for the tip.
When she's gotten outside, she turns to me
And kisses me on the cheek.
"Be seeing you soon."
She says it so well,
And that's the way things end.
And now I've got another good friend.

"I'LL WAIT, MR. GREENE"

The Captain's Jester

Lyrics and Music by David Warrack

You're undignified and crude, unforgiveably romantic.
When I'm nice to you, you're rude, and your pace of life is
  frantic.
You're not serious 'bout a thing, why you're nothing but a
  child.
All you do is dance and sing, so why do you drive me wild?

I'll wait, Mister Greene, I'll wait as long as necessary.
Fate, Mister Greene, will decide
Whether I'm to be the one, when your wandering is done,
You will turn to, Mister Greene.
I'll be here, Mister Greene, right here where you can always
  find me.
Dear Mister Greene, I won't hide,
Though I'll never come right out saying what my heart's about
Like I yearn to, Mister Greene.

I'm determined to wait 'til you've had your fling, love's not a
  sometime thing, sir.
So much competition makes you lose perspective,
So until you're more selective, I'm in no hurry.

I'll wait, Mister Greene, and someday I am confident
You'll wake, Mister Greene, and you'll know
There is nothing more to find, and then I'll be on your mind
As that one and only kind, Mister Greene.

"PARLEZ-VOUS L'ENGLISH?"

The Captain's Jester

Lyrics and Music by David Warrack

JOHN Parlez-vous l'English? je n'ai pas le fluency
To get across my point en français.
Je desire de learn it. J'aime la sound et yearn it,
Mais every time I try un peu no one est enchanté.
Avez-vous l'answer? I'm not so bad a dancer,

Mais I don't even dare to try and ask en gay Paree.
C'est très embarrassante. Tout la monde knows what I want.
Mais avec l'English tongue I'm getting no one to say oui.

Lessons I have tried, for I cherish savoir-faire,
And nothing's as impressive as that old bilingual air.
But when I try to practice, thinking finally I'm prepared,
They shake their heads, throw up their hands,
And softly whisper merde.

Parlez-vous l'English? S'il vous plaît assist me.
Qu'est ce que c'est que I need to know?
No one understands, even when I use my hands.
Peut-être they lose patience parce que I must talk so slow.
Avez-vous suggestions? I know all the questions,
Mais I don't even dare to try the Riviera trek.
Maintenant la situation is reaching desperation.
C'est necessaire to solve it or I'll be a nervous wreck.

Why am I to blame that I grew up in London West?
Oh sure, they tried to teach me, but I limped through every test.
No doubt about desire, mais je ne comprendrez pas
Non de personne smile at me or try to dites à moi.

Parlez-vous l'English? Je n'ai pas le fluency
To get across my point en français.
Je desire to learn it. J'aime la sound et yearn it,
Mais every time I try un peu no one est enchanté.
Avez-vous a way out? I would gladly pay out
Anything to help stop me from looking like a fool.
C'est très embarrassante. Je ne vu pas why nous canté
All learn Frenglish in school!

"THE PERFECT STATE"

Ramayana

Lyrics and Music by Maury Yeston

KING

As king, I'm king of all of this land
I show you how to live.
All birds and trees and luxuries
Are mine to take and to give.
And since I'm the best example of
The happiest of lives
My duties are to sample love
With my hundred-thirty-five wives.

And that's the way it works, of course the system has its quirks,
But there could never rise a one so great.
And no one interferes with what has grown a thousand years,
We dare not jeopardize the perfect state.
My duties are to sample love
With my hundred-thirty-five wives.
      (Enter the astrologers and counsels)
As counsel to our glorious king
We give the best advice
Which prince to wed, which plague to dread,
Which bride to buy—at what price.
And should we fail, we'll die behind
His royal prison bars.
So first we learn what's on his mind
Then we find it quick in the stars.

And you'll find everything in its place in old Ayoda
Always has been and always will be so

Never see a new face in old Ayoda
They don't come here—we don't go.
(Enter merchants)
We merchants play a prominent role
By selling all our wares.
We lubricate the perfect state
With business ventures and shares.
We keep the army up to strength
With weapons we provide
And to keep the wars a proper length
We supply the enemy side.

And that's the way it works, etc.
(Enter the populace)
The people of this marvelous land
Are happy with their lot
Each common man in Hindustan
Is grateful for what he's got
This perfect system of renown
This blessing we endure.
The king has wisely set it down
On the shoulders of the poor.

With his hundred-thirty-five wives
It's a state of absolute bliss
In our great and perfect state.

"IN THE MIDDLE OF THE EIGHTEENTH CENTURY"

Casanova

Lyrics and Music by Maury Yeston

The pursuit and the capture of dangerous game
Appears but a trifle and frightfully tame
Compared to the wooing of women of fame
In the middle of the eighteenth century.

Be they Austrians, Germans, Italians or Czechs
Our one common problem with these Madams "X"
Is how to make love while they're breaking our necks
In the middle of the eighteenth century.

Dangerous love, war of romance
Strategies planned as we make our advance,
Shiploads of armor in one fleeting glance,
With our hearts all aflutter
Sweet nothings we utter
Our minds in the gutter
Their husbands in France.

With Mathilde, Brunhilde, Helena and Beth
Together in bed one could forfeit one's breath
And be happily dying a gentleman's death
In the middle of the eighteenth century.

Dangerous love, romantic war
Under the staircase, in back of the door
After each battle we want only more,
I can hear our hearts breaking
As love we'll be taking
And afterwards, making
Our peace as we snore.

If you're footloose and easy and age twenty-five
And don't really care whether you will survive
There is no better time to be young and alive
Than in the middle of
Than in the middle of
Than in the middle of the eighteenth
Century.

"I'LL WALK WITH YOU"

Arden *

Lyrics and Music by Chip Young

With you I played the lark, singing all day,
Chasing across the park, gliding away,
All these years we both have known, as we shared our fun,
We would never play alone: we will be as one.

Remember how we threw dandelion puffs?
Caught by the wind they flew over the bluffs;
Far off they drifted on, then fell from view,
Now those winds are blowing strong, tearing me from you!

Don't go away from me! Don't go away!
It hurts to see you leaving, it hurts me more to stay!
The lark would never sing again, the breeze would die today,
And I could not survive here if, alone, you went away!

With you, I'll find the road we both can run,
Fleeing this dark abode, into the sun,
Like tiny fragile puffs, let's trust the winds blow true!
I have made my only choice, I will walk with you!

* Based on *As You Like It* by William Shakespeare.

A NOTE ON
MUSICAL FORM

Though it is not necessary for the reader of this book to have any knowledge of musical form, some basic facts about song form, especially as it is generally practiced in the American musical theatre, might enhance the reader's enjoyment and understanding of the lyrics, which must parallel the music in form.

For nearly a thousand years Western music has been written in measure-bar units. This is to say that a horizontal line divides the musical notes at certain—usually regular—intervals. In the most conventional manner (popular and folk music are, in this sense, conventional) these lines occur according to the stated time signature that occurs at the start of a composition. Thus, a song in 4/4 time employs one bar line after each four beats. Each of these units or the spaces between bars are called *bars*. (In 3/4 time there are three beats to each bar. The lower number—four—indicates that a fourth or quarter note is equal to one beat.)

Non-Oriental and Western music has developed in four-bar, or four-measure, blocks. These four bars are frequently doubled, so that the separate blocks are eight or even sixteen instead of four.

Let us refer to a well-known Irish folk song. The words of "Believe Me, If All Those Endearing Young Charms" by Thomas Moore will be used here as a basic example. Those title words alone (beat out the accents!) comprise four bars. The complete phrase, however, adds up to eight bars.

(Be)/lieve me if/all those en/dear-ing young/charms
  Which I/
gaze on so/fond-ly to/day/——were to/

The above example constitutes a *phrase* that is difficult to define since it has many different connotations. As applied to a song, however, it usually refers to that part of a melody that seems to conclude, even temporarily and is sung in a single breath.

The form of the entire chorus is expressed in four such equal blocks. The first eight bars are called A, or A1. The second eight are more or less a repetition of the first eight and are called A2.

A2 (were to)/change by to/mor-row, and/fleet in my
  /arms, Like/
fairy gifts/fa-ding a/way. /Thou wouldst/

After A has been heard twice—A1 plus A2—there is need of a contrasting section, which has come to be known by several names: the "bridge," "release," or, in my own term, "relief." This section, in order to provide contrast, is often in a different key, or rhythm, in the music, with a different point of view in the lyrics. The melody, or tune, in this section is often antithetical to the basic A tune. This section is referred to in brief as "B."

B (Thou wouldst)/still be a/dored as this/mo-ment thou
  /art, let thy/
/love-li-ness/fade as it/will,/——And a-/

The final section of the song consists of a third A, or A3, which must include an ending.

A3 (And a-)/round the dear/ru-in each/wish of my/heart
  Would en-/
-twine it-self/verd-ant-ly/still.

These four sections, or blocks, add up to a thirty-two bar song (4 times 8). The form in brief is noted as AABA. This structure has evolved over many centuries in many lands. Often it has assumed the shape AB or ABAB. Sometimes it has been reduced to ABA. If a song is very fast as "I'm in Love with a Wonderful Guy" from *South Pacific*) (Rodgers and Hammerstein), the blocks are made twice as long, that is, each section consists of sixteen bars. Though the number of bars has been doubled, the form, or structure, is identical to the usual one quoted above. The song is still AABA.

Although there is no hard rule requiring the use of this structure, it is not only in general practice now but indeed some version of it has been used through past centuries. There are and have been many variations of it, but the eight-bar block is at the root of all Western art music, folk music, and all theatre music. The lyrics, which go hand in hand with the music, of necessity follow the form.

This AABA structure seems not only satisfyingly natural to us but its elements contribute generously to the potential success of a song, since the main musical theme (A) is heard *three* times during the course of a single chorus or refrain. As most choruses are heard three or four times in the score of a show, the A section must inevitably become well known to the listening audience.

CREDITS

Williamson Music, Inc., owners of publication and allied rights. Sole selling agent: Chappell & Co., Inc. International copyright secured. All rights reserved, including the right of public performance for profit. Used by permission of Chappell & Co., Inc.

"Mr. Goldstone" by Stephen Sondheim. Copyright © 1959 by Norbeth Productions, Inc., and Stephen Sondheim. Stratford Music Corp. and Williamson Music, Inc., owners of publication and allied rights. Sole selling agent: Chappell & Co., Inc. International copyright secured. All rights reserved, including the right of public performance for profit. Used by permission of Chappell & Co., Inc.

"Everything's Coming Up Roses" by Stephen Sondheim. Copyright © 1959 by Norbeth Productions, Inc., and Stephen Sondheim. Stratford Music Corp. and Williamson Music, Inc., owners of publication and allied rights. Sole selling agent: Chappell & Co., Inc. International copyright secured. All rights reserved, including the right of public performance for profit. Used by permission of Chappell & Co., Inc.

"Rose's Turn" by Stephen Sondheim and Jule Styne. Copyright © 1960 by Norbeth Productions, Inc., and Stephen Sondheim. Stratford Music Corporation and Williamson Music, Inc., owners of publication and allied rights. Sole selling agent: Chappell & Co., Inc. International copyright secured. All rights reserved, including the right of public performance for profit. Used by permission of Chappell & Co., Inc.

"Comedy Tonight" by Stephen Sondheim. Copyright © 1962 by Stephen Sondheim. Burthen Music Company, Inc., owner of publication and allied rights. Sole selling agent: Chappell & Co., Inc. International copyright secured. All rights reserved, including the right of public performance for profit. Used by permission of Chappell & Co., Inc.

"I'm Lovely" by Stephen Sondheim. Copyright © 1962 by Stephen Sondheim. Burthen Music Company, Inc., owner of publication and allied rights. Sole selling agent: Chappell & Co., Inc. International copyright secured. All rights reserved, including the right of public performance for profit. Used by permission of Chappell & Co., Inc.

"Impossible" by Stephen Sondheim. Copyright © 1962, 1963 by Stephen Sondheim. Burthen Music Company, Inc., owner of publication and allied rights. Sole selling agent: Chappell & Co., Inc. International copyright secured. All rights reserved, including the right of public performance for profit. Used by permission of Chappell & Co., Inc.

"Company" by Stephen Sondheim. Copyright © 1970 by Music of the Times Publishing Corp. (Valando Music Division) and Beautiful Music, Inc. All rights administered by Music of the Times Publishing Corp. All rights reserved.

"The Little Things You Do Together" by Stephen Sondheim. Copyright © 1970 by Music of the Times Publishing Corp. (Valando Music Division) and Beautiful Music, Inc. All rights administered by Music of the Times Publishing Corp. All rights reserved.

"Sorry—Grateful" by Stephen Sondheim. Copyright © 1970 by Music of the Times Publishing Corp. (Valando Music Division) and Beautiful Music, Inc. All rights administered by Music of the Times Publishing Corp. All rights reserved.

"Barcelona" by Stephen Sondheim. Copyright © 1970 by Music of the Times Publishing Corp. (Valando Music Division) and Beautiful Music, Inc. All rights administered by Music of the Times Publishing Corp. All rights reserved.

"Have I Got a Girl for You" by Stephen Sondheim. Copyright © 1970 by Music of the Times Publishing Corp. (Valando Music Division) and Beautiful Music, Inc. All rights administered by Music of the Times Publishing Corp. All rights reserved.

"Someone Is Waiting" by Stephen Sondheim. Copyright © 1970 by Music of the Times Publishing Corp. (Valando Music Division) and Beautiful Music, Inc. All rights administered by Music of the Times

Publishing Corp. All rights reserved.

"Another Hundred People" by Stephen Sondheim. Copyright © 1970 by Music of the Times Publishing Corp. (Valando Music Division) and Beautiful Music, Inc. All rights administered by the Music of the Times Publishing Corp. All rights reserved.

"The Ladies Who Lunch" by Stephen Sondheim. Copyright © 1970 by Music of the Times Publishing Corp. (Valando Music Division) and Beautiful Music, Inc. All rights administered by the Music of the Times Publishing Corp. All rights reserved.

"Being Alive" by Stephen Sondheim. Copyright © 1970 by Music of the Times Publishing Corp. (Valando Music Division) and Beautiful Music, Inc. All rights administered by the Music of the Times Publishing Corp. All rights reserved.

"Live, Laugh, Love" by Stephen Sondheim. Copyright © 1971 by Music of the Times Publishing Corporation (Valando Music Division), Beautiful Music, Inc., and Burthen Music Co., Inc. All rights reserved. Used by permission.

"Now" by Stephen Sondheim. Copyright © 1973 by Beautiful Music, Inc., and Revelation Music Publishing Corp. (ASCAP). International copyright secured. All rights reserved.

"Later" by Stephen Sondheim. Copyright © 1973 by Beautiful Music, Inc., and Revelation Music Publishing Corp. (ASCAP). International copyright secured. All rights reserved.

"You Must Meet My Wife" by Stephen Sondheim. Copyright © 1973 by Beautiful Music, Inc., and Revelation Music Publishing Corp. (ASCAP). International copyright secured. All rights reserved.

"Liaisons" by Stephen Sondheim. Copyright © 1973 by Beautiful Music, Inc., and Revelation Music Publishing Corp. (ASCAP). International copyright secured. All rights reserved.

"In Praise of Women" by Stephen Sondheim. Copyright © 1973 by Beautiful Music, Inc., and Revelation Music Publishing Corp. (ASCAP) International copyright secured. All rights reserved.

"The Miller's Son" by Stephen Sondheim. Copyright © 1973 by Beautiful Music, Inc., and Revelation Music Publishing Corp. (ASCAP). International copyright secured. All rights reserved.

"You're My Relaxation" by Robert Sour and Charles Schwab. Copyright © 1934 by HARMS, Inc. Copyright renewed 1961 by Robert Sour and Grace Schwab. All rights reserved. Used by permission of Warner Brothers Music.

"Guess Who I Saw Today" by Murray Grand and Elisse Boyd. Copyright © 1952 by Anne-Rachel Music Corporation. Used by permission.

"Lizzie Borden" by Michael Brown. Copyright © 1952 by Hill and Range Songs, Inc. Used by permission.

"I'm in Love with Miss Logan" by Ronny Graham. Copyright © 1952 by Anne-Rachel Music Corporation. Used by permission.

"Penny Candy" by June Carroll and Arthur Siegel. Copyright © 1952 by Anne-Rachel Music Corporation. Used by permission.

"April in Fairbanks" by Murray Grand. Copyright © 1956 by Second Music Publishing Co., Inc. Used by permission.

"Johnny's Song" by Paul Green and Kurt Weill. Copyright © 1940 by Chappell & Co., Inc. Copyright renewed. International copyright secured. All rights reserved, including the right of public performance for profit. Used by permission of Chappell & Co., Inc.

"September Song" by Maxwell Anderson and Kurt Weill. Copyright © 1938 by DeSylva, Brown, & Henderson, Inc. Copyright renewed, assigned to Chappell & Co., Inc. International copyright secured. All rights reserved, including the right of public performance for profit. Used by permission of Chappell & Co., Inc.

"Speak Low" by Ogden Nash and Kurt Weill. Copyright © 1943 by Chappell & Co., Inc. Copyright renewed. International copyright secured. All rights reserved, including the right of public performance

Index of Show and Song Titles